TO

T. SANDFORD BEATY,

WHOSE NOBLE AND GENEROUS FRIENDSHIP GLADDENED
THE LIFE OF KATE FIELD,

THIS RECORD IS INSCRIBED

WITH THE UNFORGETTING GRATITUDE OF

LILIAN WHITING

"And she the rest will comprehend, will comprehend"

CONTENTS
5711

Contents

ILLUSTRATIONS

KATE FIELD

A RECORD

I salute the immortal. Great minds never die. Becoming invisible in one form, they become resplendent in another. — VICTOR HUGO.

CHILDHOOD AND CIRCUMSTANCE

" The birds sing like angels, so mystical-fine,
    And the cedars are brushing the archangel's feet;
And time is eternity, love is divine,
    And the world is complete.
May God bless the child, father, mother respond,
O Life, O Beyond,
    Thou art strange, thou art sweet."

1

KATE FIELD

" From wave and star and flower
    Some effluence rare
  Was lent thee, a divine, but transient dower."

"I will paint her as I see her."

CHAPTER I

CHILDHOOD AND CIRCUMSTANCE.   AN INTERESTING HEREDITY.
FAMILY LETTERS.   MR. AND MRS. FIELD'S STAGE LIFE.
DEATH OF JOSEPH M. FIELD.   THE MOTHER AND DAUGHTER.

KATE FIELD'S varied and prismatic life rises
        before one like a romance of destiny.   It was
a life strangely rich in a series of brilliant representations and of unique experiences; and still, if an incantation of prophecy had been invoked over her
cradle, voice and vision might well have proclaimed
to her: " It will be yours to wrestle, not to reign."
She was pre-eminently a woman who impressed the
imagination.   She abounded in spiritual energy.
Delicate in physique, artistic in temperament, exquisite in taste, lofty in all poetic and heroic aspiration,
she had in the utmost degree that intense and finely
wrought nature that leaves in some form or other
its haunting impress.   Kate Field was made

" of spirit, and fire, and dew,"

and her tenacity of endurance was a signal illustration
of the power of the mind over the body.

Mary Katherine Keemle Field was the stately baptismal name that will hardly be recognized as identical with the brief and familiar one by which she was known, and which seemed to express her personality; but this was the name given to the little girl born in St. Louis, Mo., on Oct. 1, 1838, the daughter of Joseph M. and Eliza (Riddle) Field. Behind her lay a most interesting heredity. The Field family came originally from Warwickshire, England, and its earliest known representative was Nathaniel Field, one of the Elizabethan dramatists, who wrote several plays, among which there was one called "Woman as a Weathercock." He was a friend of Shakespeare and an actor in his company. Curiously, the first time that Kate Field visited the church at Stratford-on-Avon she found her foot stepping on a grave-slab bearing the name of Field, one of her far-away ancestors. In some revolutionary change the family became located in Ireland, and we find Kate's grandfather, Matthew Field, a leading Catholic in Dublin, and a man so benevolent and beloved that he was commonly known as "the Saint." The rebellion of 1798 came on and all his property was confiscated. Then he came to America with his family, settled in Baltimore where he became a publisher and brought out the first Catholic almanac in this country. He died in early life, leaving a family of young children, of whom his two sons, Joseph and Matthew, were destined to leave more than an ordinary impress on life. The latter was a poet whose work met with considerable recognition from Poe and other of the literary people of his day. His early death cut short what promised to be a literary career of importance. Joseph M. Field was still more brilliantly gifted, — too richly endowed, indeed, in various lines, for that concentration upon any single line which is the condition of special success. He, also, was a poet; his versatility, one might almost say his fatal versatility, — which his daughter inherited in a marked degree, — was manifested as an actor, a playwright, a journalist, an organizer and theatre-manager, and a delightful raconteur of travel and incident. Nothing more conclusively points to the reality of the immortal life than the vision of these rare and richly endowed natures for whom the utmost span of physical existence here is hopelessly inadequate in its time for development and achievement. Joseph M. Field was one of whom it might truly be said: —

> " His life was gentle, and the elements
> So mixed in him that nature might stand up
> And say to all the world, ' This was a man.' "

He was born in 1810, in Dublin, during the brief sojourn of the family in Ireland, and was but two years of age when his father settled in Baltimore. In his earliest youth he went upon the stage and became a great favorite as an actor. He wrote stories and plays, one of which, called " Family Lies," took the prize of $1000 offered by Dan Marble for the best American comedy. Other plays of his were brought out with success; and in a French drama called " Gabrielle," which Mr. Field translated and adapted to the American stage, Charlotte Cushman played the leading rôle, making of it one of her finest successes. It was somewhere about 1836 that Mr. Field, the young actor, excelling in light comedy, first met Miss Riddle, who was engaged in the same company, and had already won recognition for her impersonation of Julia in "The Hunchback."

Eliza Riddle was one of a family somewhat exceptionally gifted. Her mother, Mary (Lapsley) Riddle, was the daughter of an old Philadelphia family of Quakers, and seems to have been an exotic; for at the age of fifteen she ran away from home to go on the stage. She married an actor, Mr. William Riddle, and with him entered on the dramatic life. Of this marriage there were several children,— Sarah, who became well known to the stage under her married name of Mrs. W. H. Smith; Edward and William, who both shared in the brilliant gifts of their family, but who died in comparatively early life; Eliza, who became the wife of Joseph M. Field; and Cordelia, wonderfully gifted in music, who became Mrs. Milton T. Sanford, the wife of a Newport millionaire. The marriage of Kate Field's maternal grandparents — Mr. W. H. Riddle and Miss Mary Lapsley — must have occurred in the very early years of 1800, and Eliza (Mrs. Field) was born about 1812. In 1823 we find Mrs. Riddle, with her young family about her, playing in and around Cincinnati, sharing the life of the strolling actor of those early years. The stage of those days was no such luxurious temple of the Muses as now meets the exaction of polite life, but was frequently a dark and shabby place, and salaries averaged from eight to fifteen dollars a week. Mrs. Mary Riddle was a strong personality, and to her Edwin Forrest owed the aid which led to his first professional success. Lawrence Barrett, in his biography of Edwin Forrest, speaks of the friendship between him and the Riddles as one which, "beginning under the shadow of a mutual poverty, lasted and grew stronger and more dear under the sun of prosperity. To Mrs. Riddle and her family," continues Mr. Barrett, " Edwin Forrest owed in those dark days much of the hope and encouragement which brighten adversity. Their courtesy and unfailing friendship were the ties which bound him to duty, and kept in his mind the example and precepts of his beloved mother and sister. The Riddles had passed many years of honorable labor in their profession, and reached respectable positions, and out of their scanty earnings made Edwin feel at home in a circle where happy contentment helped to banish from the hearthstone the pangs of public neglect or private sorrows. To the end of his life, in fame and prosperity, the name of this early benefactress of his was a dear one to his ears, and he never ceased to speak fondly of her and of her memory."

Mrs. Mary Riddle died in Boston on Dec. 2, 1840, when her grand-daughter, Kate Field, was but two years of age. Edwin Forrest came to stand by the grave that winter day when the snow lay deep over Mount Auburn, and as the faint sunshine shone upon his head, reverently bared, the tears fell unchecked from his eyes. " My heart is full of memories," he said to a friend.

The beneficence of character which so distinguished the mother was shared by all her children, and particularly by Eliza, whose patience and sweetness of nature were almost ideal. She was also lovely in person, — a slender, graceful figure, with oval face shaded by rich brown hair, with eyes which matched it to a shade, and rose tints adding brilliancy to a finely expressive countenance.

May we pause for a moment in contemplation of this prologue of the drama of Kate Field's life? — of these " meeting streams," as George Eliot well calls them. The coming to America of a Catholic publisher from Dublin; the impetuous impulse of a girl of Quaker parentage to enter on the dramatic life; the years of hardship and privation in her profession and of honorable struggle to rear and educate her family of young children; and then the meeting of the son of the one and the daughter of the other, each with the best traditions of life behind, — not the traditions of ease and luxury, but of high aspiration and untiring energy. Was not this indeed an heredity whose influence on the young life to come was one of the utmost nobleness?

It was somewhere about 1835 when Joseph M. Field and Eliza Riddle met as members of the same dramatic company, playing an engagement in Mobile, he about twenty-five and she some two years younger. A letter from him to the girl who had become the star of his dreams, bearing no date save that of " Tuesday night," runs thus: —

My DEAREST, DEAREST LOVE, — Let me call you so. I am so happy and yet so miserable. You don't *look* so discouragingly on me, but I have become a downright coward. In the morning I shall call. When I gave you that little note, you did not reprove me. Oh, I shall hope! My love, my dear love, do not shut up your heart against me and happiness. I cannot even think what it would be to part with you. They are talking to me of engaging for another year, but I can put my mind on nothing but the hope I hold, — that we may arrange our future together. My love, my soul's love, do not be offended. My own dear Eliza, I love you with a pure and honorable love, whose only object is your happiness, and through yours my own.

You "do not think you will ever marry"! But, my love, if marriage has its cares, what are they but a motive for healthy exertion, a stimulant to employ faculties that otherwise might lapse into inaction. Oh, trust me, Eliza, my sweet friend! Let me walk by your side all through this life, shielding you from the world's rough ways; let your heart and hand lie in mine. God bless you, my love, my love!

And again this ardent lover writes to the maiden of his choice: —

MY DEAR ELIZA, — You will go away, and what will there be to remind you of me? . . . I am not happy in what is termed brilliant society; I am weary of that notoriety and show which is so generally sought by members of our profession. I see the folly of indulging in those dreams and fancies which fill the heads of young men to the exclusion of real happiness. I only long for the companionship of the one I love, — yourself. I want to tell all my thoughts to you; to study and improve myself in your society; to know that we may mingle all our joys and cares. You say you fear you do not love me with sufficient devotion. Oh, my dear Eliza (pray pardon me), but may not future regrets make you aware of the true nature of your feelings? I pray to God, my dear Eliza, that regrets may never be yours, whatever becomes of me. . . . I have reflected deeply upon the responsibilities. I am even now able to lay by means. I will exert myself, and I feel I could do anything for you, and time must better my fortunes. As for those near claims you have upon you, *they shall be to me as my own*. I have given my heart to you, Eliza, as a being pure and gentle, with all the qualities that adorn a home. . . . Oh, if you could but love me, all the world

beside may go ! Might we not be most happy together?
I don't care for the dazzle of the world, nor do you.
Think, my dear, beloved Eliza, with the approbation of our
own hearts, and the esteem of the few whose friendship we
value, could we not be most happy? With youth, health,
and industry, too, believe me, my dear, dear Eliza, love and
competence would bless our union. God bless you !

Your devoted,

JOE.

Love, that most intense spiritual potency, cuts its
own channel, creates its own conditions, and the lofty
tenderness of Joseph Field for the woman of his
dreams was no exception to this law. Eliza Riddle
turned to him with the utmost consecration of devotion, and their marriage being celebrated in St.
Louis, Mo., in October of 1837, together the husband and wife entered on that new world which is the
old. Eliza Riddle was then in the first flush of her
artistic fame. She made constant advances in her
art. Of her Isoline, in " John of Procida," a critic
of the time records that it was " a beautiful piece of
acting; " that her conception of the character was
admirable, and that some of her scenes in the most
impassioned passages were executed with a fine intensity of feeling and a fidelity to the character portrayed which had seldom been equalled and never
surpassed. Previously to her marriage Mrs. Field
had supported Sheridan Knowles, and as Mariana to
his St. Pierre, in his play of " The Wife," she inspired
an enthusiasm seldom known in those days.

Happy months came and went, and the first day of
October, 1838, was marked for the Fields by the arrival of the little daughter on the eve of the Feast of
the Holy Angels, which the Catholic Church, into

which her father was born, celebrates on the second of October. The infant was baptized in the Catholic faith, and received the name of Mary Katherine Keemle, the latter being for Charles Keemle, Mr. Field's nearest friend and business partner in a newspaper that he was about establishing, called " The Reveille." The auspices under which the little maid entered on her terrestrial experiences were full of joyous energy. The union of Mr. and Mrs. Field was indeed a " marriage of true minds." He was full of exhilaration, wit, boundless energy, and versatile genius; a poet, a journalist, an actor, a playwright. She was gentle, loving, with a grace and sweetness peculiarly her own, and with an undercurrent of serene strength of character which her husband safely trusted. The first record that has been preserved of their little daughter is in a letter from Mrs. Field to her husband, apparently written in June of 1839, in which she says:

" Our dear baby has so improved since you left and is so joyous. It's as much as I can do to keep her in my arms. If she had wings, I really think she would fly. . . . O my dear love, I cannot express the happiness I feel in hearing of your success. . . . You tell me not to be too economical. I do not think that I am. We have no engagement for next season, dear Joe, so it behooves us to be careful. God bless you, my dear love."

On June 19, 1840, Mr. Field sailed for Europe as correspondent of the New Orleans " Picayune," and also to study the dramatic art of London and Paris. He took with him many important letters of introduction, among which was one from George P. Morris to Theodore Fay of the American Legation at Berlin; and there opened to the young actor a tide of rich opportunities. Mrs. Field writes to her husband soon after his departure that their little Kate is a " perfect chatterbox," and that " she courtesies and kisses her hand on leaving a room in the most graceful manner." That distinction of presence which was always recognized in Kate Field seemed to manifest itself in her infancy. The psychology of childhood is always fascinating in its speculative data, and, remembering Kate Field's ardent interest in politics from the time she was a girl of eighteen, one smiles to read, in the fond mother's nursery chronicles, that at the age of eighteen months the little maid was shouting "Tippecanoe," as she danced and laughed, catching the name from a popular ditty of the hour that ran : —

" Tippecanoe and Tyler too."

Here was shown that same keen perception that always characterized her.

On Oct. 1, 1841, Mrs. Field writes to her husband : —

" This is Kate's birthday. She sends an hundred kisses to her dear father, and hopes that he will bring her something pretty from Philadelphia. She says of course that father will remember the first of October, that it is his darling little Katy's birthday, that he will bring her something very, very pretty. I was sitting very quietly the other day sewing and thinking of you; presently I received a thrust in my side. I started up; there stood Miss Kate with a *wooden dagger*, shouting at the top of her little voice, ' Die ! Die ! ' waving it above her head. I am wishing you were here to see her little tricks; there is no end to them. When I told her that you had sent her a dozen kisses, she looked at the letter and kissed it inside and out.

'Now,' says she, 'you must give *that* father, that *dear* father, a dozen kisses from his darling little Kate.' This morning she rather puzzled me with her questions. She looked up into my face and gravely asked how we came to be made. I replied that God made us. 'Why am I your child if God made me?' 'He gave you to me, darling, to be a blessing to your father and mother.' 'Well, I'll be good, my darling little mother,' — and so this interesting conversation ended. What do you think of our little Kate?"

Mr. Field's letter in reply reveals the tenderness of the father: —

. . . "Your last letter, reminding me that this would be the birthday of our little pet, and containing her little prattle with regard to it, delighted me extremely. Little things become of great consequence sometimes, and Miss Kate being at the distance of a day's journey has wonderfully improved in consequence, bless her little heart!"

Mr. Field's European visit resulted in a larger outlook for his fortunes, and on his return he and Mrs. Field returned to the St. Charles Theatre in New Orleans at a salary of eighty dollars a week for both, which at that time was considered eminently satisfactory. The autumn of 1843 found Mrs. Field with her mother in Boston, while her husband was still playing in the South. Some business perplexities ensued, and the loving wife writes to him: —

" . . . You have more resources within yourself than most men, and as long as you are blessed with health I am content. To be sure, I should be much happier if we were together for such loneliness comes over me when you are away. I don't know why, but I never look for consideration or sympathy from any one but yourself. You are the

only person in the world with whom I could ever be uncon-
strained. . . . Our little Katy is so wild I do not know
what to do with her. The little witch is perfectly healthy,
and growing more intelligent every day. She was very anxious to know last night if the man in the moon would not
take cold ; and she says papa is not very polite to stay away
so long."

In January of 1843 Mrs. Field again says of their
little daughter in a letter to her husband : I asked
Katy if she had anything to say to papa? She replies
that she will write for herself, but not just what she
wrote in her last letter, for she was certainly sure papa
would not like it so well twice.

Again, in the little girl who was only three months
past her fifth birthday is seen the same dawning independence and self-reliance and a foretaste of the literary discrimination that in later life was so signally her
own. One of her own little letters to her father at this
time, which his fond love preserved, runs thus : —

MY DARLING PAPA, — I send you a lock of your little
Katy's hair. You are to make a bracelet of it, and not give
it away, but keep it for yourself. I shall expect you home
next week and then I shall dance and sing all day. I send
a kiss to my darling papa.

In February of 1843 a son was born to Mr. and
Mrs. Field, the " Little Joe " whose brief life of six
years was a rapture of joy to the young father and
mother.

" Little Joe is a true Field and your very image,"
Mrs. Field writes to the father, who had not yet seen
his little son. " He has Katy's eyes and her delicate
hands and feet," continues Mrs. Field. " Katy is as

independent as ever, and I could not write in all day the funny things the little sprite says."

The beautiful spirit of Eliza Field is reflected in every word she writes. As this: —

MY DEAR LOVE, — I have received the check for $60. It came in good time. I look forward to every letter of yours with the greatest happiness. Little Joe will be five weeks old to-morrow. Oh, my dear husband, it is hard for us to be parted at this time, but your little wife tries to be brave and we will be all the happier when we do meet, and you can take Katy and our darling son in your arms. My dear love, as I write this, your letter with check for $100 comes. How thoughtful you are, and, oh, if you can only keep your health, we shall be so happy with our sweet children. Katy sends a hundred kisses to her darling papa.

This was the sweet atmosphere of refinement and love into which Kate Field was born. Her earliest impressions were those of honorable aspiration, devoted love, and a sweet reasonableness regarding all the vicissitudes of life.

The autumn of 1844 was marked to the Fields by a great sorrow in the death of Mr. Field's brother Matthew, whose gentle and poetic nature endeared him to all whom he met. In those days there was a famous theatrical firm known as Ludlow and Smith, and a daughter of Mr. Ludlow became the wife of Matt Field. The two brothers had been familiarly known to the press as "Straws" and "Phasma," and both had written much verse, some of which is not without genuine poetic quality. Matt Field, as he was always called, was for years in delicate health with bronchial trouble, but his death came with the same startling suddenness that was afterward to be the fate of his brother Joseph, and of Kate, his niece. Leaving his young wife and two little children in St. Louis, he went to New York, hoping that a sea voyage would restore his health. Embarking on Nov. 13, 1844, he died at midnight of the following day and was buried at sea. During his last evening his talk had been full of brightness and repartee. The captain of the steamer came to his stateroom, and sitting just outside the door read to Mr. Field for some time. At last, speaking to him and receiving no reply, he arose and turned to the berth only to find the invalid unconscious, and within an hour his spirit had taken flight. The surviving brother expressed his grief in a poem entitled " A Sigh for Phasma," in which occur such lines as these : —

> " Complainings gentle, musical, and low —
> Thy mystic harp, November — Here around
> Mingle the sad vibrations. The dull words
> Breathe their last dirge for summer, their adieu
> To all they love of beauty, all their wealth
> Of vernal shelter, all their tenant throngs,
> Their hymn of patience, their deep sigh of love."

These lines are a typical illustration of Mr. Field's poetic gift, which was not unlike that of Bryant, save in degree. Mr. Field had, however, another vein of wit and rollicking fun, which was almost equally in evidence, and there were in him, as in his daughter, varying gifts which were at times mutually exclusive.

About this time (1844–45) Mr. Field became associated with Mr. Charles Keemle in the publication of the St. Louis "Reveille." Five years later their office was destroyed in the great fire that swept over St. Louis, even destroying steamboats moored on the river, but the mercurial spirits of Mr. Field rose to new endeavor, and he turned from the very smoke of the ruins to write a comedy which proved successful. He also collected a volume of his sketches with the hope that Messrs. Little, Brown, and Co. of Boston would publish it; but when they declined, as their house was then dealing exclusively in legal works, he applied to a Philadelphia house that offered him $250 for the volume outright, which he accepted. Not the least fortunate characteristic of Mr. Field was his power of instantaneous decision, wasting no energy in hesitation and doubt. Mrs. Field accepted an engagement at the St. Charles Theatre in New Orleans, taking her two little children with her. She writes to her husband: —

My DEAREST HUSBAND, — You would think me childish if I were to tell you how much I love you, how constantly you occupy my thoughts. I have a thousand hopes, — a thousand fears. I fear some accident may have happened to you; that you may be ill, and I not there to nurse you; that you may work too hard and so hurt your health; that you have not those comforts about you that you ought to have. Then, again, I am so happy in your love. I know you love me as dearly as I love you, and 't is so delightful to think that we feel so towards each other. You are my world; my thoughts, feelings, affections, are all centred in you. I love my children very dearly, but not as I love you. They may leave me by-and-by; but if you are spared and love me, I can never feel lonely.

A loving mother's details of her children and life and Katy's studies fill every letter.

The parents were even at this time much occupied with thoughts and plans, for their daughter Kate was a brilliant child already, with a kind of inscrutable

2

individuality of her own, with a passionate love of music, and hardly less devotion to literary pursuits. "Katy is very fond of writing," records her mother in a letter when the little girl was some eight years of age. And again in a letter to her sister (Mrs. Sanford), Mrs. Field writes: —

"Katy is getting along finely with her studies. She is as fond of books and study as her father. She is a good, strange child. I think she will make a fine woman. I hope she will not be spoiled; but it is very difficult in the West to keep girls like Kate away from flattery. I hope she will have the good sense to withstand it. She is very quick, very observing, for one of her age."

The dancing-master from whom Kate had lessons while with her mother in New Orleans wished his pupils to give a dance, and in the winter of 1848–49 Mrs. Field writes to her husband: —

"Katy was so anxious to go that I consented. I had no idea a few days before the ball that the children were to be invited. Katy was dressed simply (in a frock she had last winter), and looked and danced prettily. I think she was the most lady-like of the crowd. She is getting very self-willed, however, and I find it hard to manage her. She says if her father were here she is sure he would not deny her. I may be wrong; I think I am right. Tell me in your next what *you* think of it. Kate values your opinion. The perfect freedom she had last winter was an injury to her. She says 'if I will allow her to go to parties this winter, — that is, children's parties, — she will not ask to go again until she is a young lady.' I fear it would make her a young lady too soon. Katy is rather impatient of control; I do not like to refuse her; I know it gives her a great deal of pleasure. 'I must be cruel only to be kind.'

If you do not *agree* with me, say so. I told Kate I would write to you on this subject. She will be anxious to hear your opinion. I do not blame her; it is perfectly natural at her age to desire pleasure. I do not wish her to be selfish; I fear that more than anything else. 'T is bedtime; good-night, my own dear love; I will go to sleep and dream of you."

The strength of will which sometimes, even in her womanhood, degenerated into mere wilfulness, is shown in the young girl in this transcript. Yet around her was the wise and sweet and unselfish care of this ideal mother; but life's experiences, which must be individual for each and every one, were already beginning for Kate Field. Unconsciously circumstances were educating and moulding her nature. The impetuosity of her temperament caused her father serious thought, and he was anxious again to reunite his family in a home, feeling it peculiarly essential for Kate that she should be in a more quiet and regular life; for even before the age of twelve the little girl was recognized as so exceptional in gifts and temperament as to require the most judicious care.

Jenny Lind was entrancing America with her voice, and Kate's artistic temperament was aglow with enthusiasm. To her mother in Mobile she writes, under date of St. Louis, Feb. 22, 1849: —

DEAR MOTHER, — I received a letter from you a few days ago, and would have answered it before, but have not had time. You said that Jenny was expected in Mobile. If you meet her, tell her to call on me when she comes to St. Louis and take me to hear her sing. She will be here in March and you will not be up here, and I shall not hear

Jenny Lind; it is too bad. How much will Father gain by Jenny Lind's being in Mobile? I am enjoying very good health. Give my best love and a kiss to Father, and tell him to come up soon. Give my love to all my relations.

Your little daughter,

KATE.

There was an explosion of a ferryboat here yesterday, and killed about 25 and wounded about eight. It was a dreadful thing, but you will read it in the papers.

This letter for a girl of eleven is in nowise remarkable; but it indicates the temperament that always believed in its own right of way, and shows how early her habit of being interested in affairs asserted itself. In another letter about this date she writes to her mother: —

"Is the theatre doing a good business now? I hope it is. Has any person written in my album? Is Father well? Are you in good health? I went to a Practising Party last night, and I had a great deal of pleasure. I love to dance so much. I never get tired. I think I am improving in Drawing very much. I think it is a beautiful art, and I love it very much. I am half way through Racine, and I can translate very well, but the difficulty is to speak the language; I can read and write French and understand it nearly always when it is spoken, but the difficulty is for me to speak it. I saw two books at the store that I want. They are 'Bleak House' and 'Dombey and Son,' in the same binding as my 'David Copperfield.' "

Remembering her intense appreciation of Dickens in her after life, and the "Pen Photographs" she wrote of his famous readings in Boston, this childish reference is not without interest. In a letter of somewhat later date she wrote to her mother: —

There could be no more characteristic expression of Poe than this letter, revealing all his childish petulance and suspicion of nature, his intense self-love, always tortured by fancied slights, and his genuine enthusiasm for literature and due care for his poetic reputation.

This letter Kate had always treasured carefully. After her death it was given by the friend to whom all her manuscripts were committed to Mr. Edmund Clarence Stedman, whose friendship was one of the most important influences in her life, and in acknowledgment he wrote to the donor of the letter: —

"You have quite touched my heart and taken my breath away. . . . Well, I have Poe's best daguerreotype and a famous Poe MS., and I need just this letter to go with them to make my Memorial complete."

Poe's reference in this letter to Elizabeth Barrett recalls the fact that after her marriage he sent to Mrs. Browning a volume of his poems dedicated to her, with a letter, in which he celebrates her as the noblest of her sex. Mrs. Browning laughed at this expression, and, narrating Poe's fervors to Mr. Kenyon, she said: "What could I say in reply, indeed, when called 'the noblest of my sex,' except 'Sir, you are the most discerning of yours.'"

The winter of 1850 found Mr. Field's desire to unite his family in a settled home partially fulfilled, in that Mrs. Field and her children were together in St. Louis, although Mr. Field was playing in Mobile. To his daughter, under date of February 4, 1850, he writes: —

5711

MY OWN DEAR DAUGHTER, — I address this letter exclusively to you, partly because I have not yet sent you a letter
" all to yourself" and partly because your dear mother may
have started on her way to me. If she set out before the
receipt of my remittances, you must turn business woman
yourself, look after the money, and keep an account of
sums paid out.

This was quite a commission for a girl of twelve.
Mr. Field continues : —

My dear child, your mother evinces much anxiety with
regard to your fancy for balls and parties. Of course your
desire is natural and unobjectionable when indulged only in
a proper degree, but I should think that opportunities of
enjoyment would present themselves often enough among
our own personal friends — where you would not be withdrawn from the company of your mother — to satisfy you.
Believe me, my dearest child, an early habit of curbing
hasty inclinations is the most valuable of all the elements
of personal character, and will conduce more to your lifelong happiness than anything else which you may acquire.
I want to see you gay and sportive ; so does your mother,
but not to a degree which renders you cross and sullen
under wholesome restriction. You are a dear, good, intelligent, and loving child ; the hopes of our heart rest on you ;
your future progress and happiness are all that we look forward to, and with all a father's affection I tell you that you
have in your mother one of the noblest models that ever
lived. If you would be a true and Christian woman, loved and
admired as a credit to your sex, emulate the kindness and the
single-mindedness of your first friend, your fondest protector.

You have asked me, my dear Katy, so many-*hundred*
questions, I believe, that not having your letter by me (I
am writing in the office) I know not what to say. They
have principally, however, been inquiries as to health and

happiness of relatives and friends, and I am happy to say that, as far as I know, they are all well. Business this winter has been very good, and I trust to open in St. Louis under very favorable circumstances. You must remember me most kindly to the Cutlers, to Mrs. Randolph, and all inquirers. Go on with your lessons, and take in season your youthful " fun," as you call it. Grow up an intelligent, discreet, and benevolent young woman, and your friends will not be confined to this world ; those who have left us for a happier land will hold their hands in blessing and protection over you. God bless you, my dear, dear daughter. Your affectionate father.

The summer of 1851 found Mr. and Mrs. Field reunited in their own home in St. Louis, and their plans for the ensuing season are revealed in a letter of Kate's written to a cousin in New Orleans, under date of Sept. 7, 1851. Her father was then having his own theatre built, and the little girl writes : —

" The theatre is progressing rapidly now, but it will not be finished before spring. We are all perfectly delighted with housekeeping, and mother and father say they will never board again if they can help it. I am not to attend school this winter. I shall practise three hours a day, take care of the parlor, study my French lessons, and father says I must begin drawing soon ; so that I shall have enough to attend to. Father intends leaving the house with some friends, and let me remain here, paying my board, so in all probability I shall be here this winter. I shall be thirteen on the first of next October at one o'clock, so when you sit at dinner on this day you can remember it is my birthday."

Kate had been attending a school in St. Louis known as " Mrs. Smith's Seminary," where for three years she took the prize in composition and penmanship, and her childish " compositions " of that period, still preserved, tied with the blue ribbon that invested literary efforts in those days, incite a smile. On one is inscribed, " Mary Kate Field, aged eleven," and its subject is " Three Scenes in the Life of a Schoolgirl," — a subject indicative of that dramatic turn which always persisted in her writings.

" What shall these three scenes be ? " (questions the youthful writer). " My first recollections of school are very indistinct, as I was very young. The first day I went to school I went alone, as my mother was engaged. I think the entrance into a new school ought to be the first scene. . . . Suppose we take for the second that in which a girl is not perfect in her lessons, and she stammers and hems and haws, and if she is kept in she will say to her companions, ' Did you ever see such a stiff, starched teacher ? ' . . . I shall take for the third scene that in which the industrious girl receives the prize. She is encouraged by this to carry on what she has begun, and often rises to fame and fortune."

The intense personal ambition in Kate Field's nature is also foreshadowed in this last line. When she was four years of age she ran away and entered herself as a pupil of a Miss Shaw, who had a little infant school. At the age of seven she entered the " Seminary" of Mr. and Mrs. Smith, and a year later she wrote to a cousin: " I have just begun to learn how to sing. I have got as far as Chili in geography, and I am at the indicative mood in grammar." Again, under date of Feb. 28, 1849, Katy writes to her aunt : —

" You have requested me to write to you, and it gives me a great deal of pleasure to comply with the request. . . .

I have been reading 'Masterman Ready, or a Shipwreck on the Pacific Coast.' It is a very interesting story, but the worst of it is I cannot get the third volume. A gentleman whom I know has gone to California, and promises to send me two barrels of gold dust; if he should do so, I shall be very rich and shall do great wonders, but I do not believe he will, so I need not make such great calculations about it. I have related to you all the interesting news I can think of."

In all this childish writing her keen observation of details is evident, mingled too with a tendency to reflection that is quaint. "Knowledge is a benignant genius," opens one of her efforts. "She bids us follow and obtain the key to unlock the mysteries of nature." Here may be the dawning of the disposition which in her womanhood led her to interview Dr. Schliemann and, later on, Edison, and strive to pluck out for herself the mysteries in archæology and in inventions.

The idolized son of Mr. and Mrs. Field died in St. Louis of cholera, before his seventh birthday, and the tender mother's care for her only remaining child became thus more ardent. On the New Year following the death of "Little Joe," Mrs. Field writes to her husband : —

"Good-morning, my own dear husband, a Happy New Year to you. How much I should like to see you on this day of all others. This is the first New Year I have passed here since the loss of our own little darling angel boy. Well, I will not be sad. I have so much to be grateful for. Perhaps if I am happy on this day, I may be happy all the year."

Mr. Field's letters to his wife were full of the same exquisite ardor and affection that breathed through hers, and from Mobile he writes to her : —

MY OWN SWEET WIFE, — Your joint letter, yours and Katy's, are just received. Let me first speak to you. I am afraid, my dearest love, that you will have become embarrassed for money before the receipt of my remittance. It was my hope to be able to send you the money by this present time, but business is slack and salary day tomorrow. The Logans here now are not attractive, but Lola Montez opens next Monday for a few nights, and she will excite curiosity. I will then send. I am very busy, playing every night, tragedy and comedy, and, strange to say, everybody seems struck with my serious efforts. I think myself I have improved in self-possession and also in earnestness, — the necessary result. I play " Ingomar " night after next. The company is very good, and all acknowledge it. My dear wife, as to propriety of appearances, your good taste and sense must guide you. Should your health or spirits require it, come, come to me, my dear wife. With the fondest and truest affection, I dwell upon your goodness and devotion and love. God bless you.

To Kate he writes : —

" My dear daughter, when you wish to visit the theatre, your dear mother assenting, you must go. You *must* hear all the musicians. Pursue your studies, my dear child, but recreation, particularly in the guise of music, is little less than instruction itself. You promised to write me a letter in ' the finest of French.' This will do you no harm to try. God bless you, my daughter, and keep you in health and happiness ! "

Kate Field's strong individuality began to express itself in her early childhood in many directions. She was the very incarnation of the artistic intensity of the life and environment into which she was born: she was full of radiant joy, and yet, even in her dawning girlhood, the vein of deep intellectual power and a certain wistful reflection began to make itself felt. A journal, whose first date is of August 2, 1852, thus opens : —

"I have finally resolved in my own mind to commence a journal and write regularly each day. I never tried before except when I was in New Orleans, and then I made such foolish work of it that I have never had the courage since to begin another."

This self-critical habit was always characteristic of her. She had the curious power to view herself objectively, as if the higher self kept continual watch over its lower manifestations. The record of this little maid of thirteen runs on : —

"I arose very late this morning — seven o'clock, I am ashamed to acknowledge, but it was a rainy day. I had hardly finished my breakfast when Monsieur le Docteur Xampi came to give me *une leçon française*, which I knew very well. Then I practised as usual. Went out at eleven and got some pens and paper for mother, and at the same time I got this blank book, which cost me 35 cents, and in which I shall record my thoughts. I have heard a great many say that there is a great probability of Benton being elected. The 'Republican,' speaking of him the other day, says that Colonel Benton is the best abused person they have known for years." . . .

The intense interest in political affairs expressed in her after life seems to reveal its dawning in the young girl. Her love of nature is evinced, too, in the opening line of the next day's record, where she says : —

"Such a beautiful day! I longed all day to be out in the country, and do nothing but play and enjoy myself. I suppose some people would say I am too old to play. I entirely differ with such persons. I do not believe in making an old woman out of a little girl. I, not quite thirteen, consider myself quite a little girl, and intend to act accordingly. Many say to me, 'This is the happiest time of your life.' But business before pleasure. The election is over, and the Democrats are victorious, to the chagrin of the Whigs. Colonel Benton is as popular as ever he was among a certain class of individuals, who are termed the rabble."

Another day records the visitation of several little friends for a concert party, and then a sudden illness of her father. She writes: —

"Reading over some scraps in the evening, I found some verses which father wrote, and I will include them here. He calls the poem 'A Calculation.'

> "'Four hundred million breaths make up
>   The term of human life,
> And millions draw the air of heaven
>   In pain, in loss, in strife.'"

The theatre which her father owned at this time was a prominent factor in her amusements, and she chronicles the visit with a party of her little friends to a box, where the loving mother sent in ice-cream and cake to them.

She continued to copy in her journal verses written by her father; and on a Sunday morning, when she heard Rev. Dr. William Eliot speak on Immortality, she writes of it and of a tenor solo that enchanted her. French, music, and drawing occupied her mornings. Spiritualism, in the modern sense, was just dawning in those days; and the little Katy, who seemed to catch everything that was in the air, chronicles a rudimentary discussion she had with a girl friend, and she adds: —

"Father then said, 'How is it, then, when you receive communication that you do not ask and have not the least idea about or the persons present?' Mary said she 'did not know, but the spirits said so.' Electricity is then intelligent, which no person ever was aware of before."

This speculative idea of electricity being intelligent she evidently expresses in a half sarcastic and half wondering way, as if she caught some foregleam of the marvellous power destined within another half-century to be revealed to man.

Kate's journal runs on: —

"*August* 12. Rose early and read the 'Republican,' which is very interesting, being full of politics. Mother took me to a minister to see if he would take me as a pupil in September, and he will. I do not know what the reason is, but I would not go back to Mrs. Smith's school on any account. My French lesson to-day was on Napoleon Bonaparte.

"*August* 13. Mr. Simpson came early in the morning to see if I could come to his studio so that he could work on my portrait again. I sat for him from ten until one, and it was tiresome work. I wrote a letter to Bessie, and sent in it some pressed flowers and a lock of my hair. Emma Crow came for me to go home with her. We went into the theatre to ask mother, who consented, and at Wayman Crow's house we went up to the third story and played till Mary Eliot came in."

On another day Kate copied this stanza, and comments on it : —

> " ' Many a shaft at random sent
>   Finds mark the archer little meant,
>   And many a word at random spoken
>   May soothe or wound a heart that is broken.'

" How true this little piece of poetry ! I know it by experience."

This extreme sensitiveness of the child only deepened rather than lessened in the woman, and as it was fully equalled by her reticence, only those nearest her in sympathetic intuition ever divined all she felt.

Of a little theatre party of her young friends at her father's theatre she writes : —

" We secured a nice box in the second circle. The first piece was the ' Corsican Brothers,' which is perfectly beautiful. Father personated the two Brothers, and mother the character of Emilie. The spectres were beautifully got up. The evening concluded with the comic ballet of the ' Barber's Troubles,' in which Espinosa caused a great deal of laughter. . . . I am reading ' Uncle Tom's Cabin,' which is creating a furore. I finished it before tea. I do not think that the things that she related in the book ever happened. It is too highly wrought. I cried for half an hour when I came to Eva's death ; and poor Uncle Tom, I was so sorry that Mrs. Stowe made him die where she did."

The period of 1852–53 was an interlude of quiet domestic happiness in that Mr. and Mrs. Field enjoyed the unusual and hitherto unprecedented experience of a settled home. Mr. Field was the actor-manager of his own theatre, his wife playing with him almost constantly, and the open, sunny hospitality of their home makes a picture that tempts one to linger over

it. Their house, near the corner of Sixth Avenue and
Market Street, was only a few steps from the theatre,
which stood on the site now marked by the opera
house in St. Louis. On the façade of the new
structure are the dates of the opening and close of
Mr. Field's theatre. The house in which they lived is
still standing, a two-story dwelling painted brown, and
St. Louis friends point out the windows of the room
occupied by Kate in her early girlhood. The Wayman Crows and the family of Rev. Dr. William Eliot,
who became the Chancellor of Washington University, were the nearest friends of the Fields. The best
society in St. Louis was then, as now, marked by
particular refinement and choice culture, and the gifts
and charm of Mr. and Mrs. Field were appreciated.
It was a very congenial atmosphere to the little
daughter, with her keen intellect, her artistic bent,
and her social instincts. It was even too stimulating for so delicately organized a girl, and all her life
Kate Field suffered from that intense nervous self-
consciousness whose best name is perhaps stage-
fright. This is revealed in the girl of thirteen in a
letter to her Aunt Corda, when she says: —

"Aunt Corda, you do not know how foolish I am. I
may know a piece of music perfectly, and if one asks me to
play I make mistakes throughout the entire piece. I am
trying to conquer it."

In March, 1853, Mr. and Mrs. Field, returning from
New Orleans to St. Louis, were twelve days *en route*,
and as Mr. Field was in haste to open his theatre, the
Variétés, with Lola Montez, the annoyance in this
delay can be imagined. Kate writes to her Aunt
Corda: —

3

"Well, Lola Montez appeared at father's theatre last night for the first time. The theatre was crowded from parquette to doors. She had the most beautiful eye I ever saw. I like her very much, but she performed a dumb girl, so I cannot say what she may do in speaking characters or as a danseuse. She is trying to trouble father as much as possible. Madame Anna Shellon is here, and will commence her engagement as soon as the countess leaves. You must know that father has adopted the *starring system* this season. He has been very successful at Mobile. The theatre there is still open. Father had a silver salver together with four goblets presented to him by the citizens of Mobile."

A little later Kate again writes to her aunt: —

"What do you think of Ole Bull? We do not hear anything of Jenny Lind now; I wonder if she will return to America. Do you think that Sontag is equal to her? I am improving very much in music and French, so my teachers say. I have translated Racine and the first volume of Molière. In Music I have Bertini's Instruction Book, and my pieces are now sonatas by Chopin, which are very hard for me. My teacher does not allow me to play waltzes, polkas, or anything of that description. He has sent to Germany for a grand piano, which will be here early in January. What a loss Mr. Chickering must have sustained by the total destruction of his piano manufactory! Father has been gone six weeks; very nearly half the time of his absence has passed away. I think he intends opening the theatre here by the middle of March. Lola Montez is in Mobile now. Do you like Strakosch? Have you read 'Uncle Tom's Cabin'? I think it is an entirely one-sided affair. She makes the colored individuals perfection. I should like to have such a little negro as Topsy. Would not you? The Pacific Railroad is in operation for fifteen miles and that great work is rapidly going on. How is Mr. Sanford's health? You must give my best love to him. I should like to visit you next summer and then go to the World's Fair in New York."

In January, 1853, Mrs. Field writes to her husband in Mobile: —

ST. LOUIS, Jan. 21, 1853.

MY OWN DEAR, HASTY, IMPULSIVE HUSBAND, — You know I had made up my mind to remain here this winter, that it was for the best. Your letter of the ninth which I received yesterday has so unsettled my thoughts and feelings. One moment I feel I ought not to go and leave Kate — the house — they will all miss me so much, it seems selfish. The next moment I feel that I could not wait until spring, although it is not far off now. This is not right, my own dear husband, or wise, to tempt your little wife in this way. You know how much I love you, how much I long to see you, to be with you. I am so happy and delighted to receive this proof of your affection that it makes me wish I could fly into your arms and kiss you a thousand times for it. Poor Kate looks very sad and unwilling to let me off, although she says, ' if father wishes it, of course go.' Her face has been very long since the arrival of your letter. I wish you would write her a letter addressed to her, for herself alone. I think she feels a little hurt that you have not done so. She said this morning that she did not think her father cared so much about seeing her.

About this time Katy pasted in her journal a printed slip that enjoined its readers " always to speak the truth; keep your own secrets if you have any; if any one speaks ill of you, let your life be such that no one will believe him," et cetera; and she comments thus: —

" I think that if every person follows what is on this little piece of printed paper, we would do well. I intend hereafter to try and keep my own secrets. I got through late in the afternoon. I went to the theatre and staid until the first piece was out, which was Job and his children, written by father. It is a beautiful piece."

She finds a sermon on " Doing Good," and copies it entire in her journal. And, again, this girl of thirteen copies in her journal : —

" When troubles flow upon you, dark and heavy, toil not with the waves, wrestle not with the torrent, — rather seek by occupation to divert the dark waters that threaten to overwhelm you into a thousand channels, which the duties of life always present."

All these extracts indicate the trend of life for the gifted, thoughtful young girl, whose spirit is already unconsciously confronting the experiences that await her in the future years, — " the sorrows that were to be." This gift of prescience was born with her and increased and deepened with years. Her father's imaginative genius, her mother's spirituality, both blended in this gift of their daughter. Mr. Field was an idealist and poet. His supreme aim in life was the elevation of the drama, and for this he strove with every energy; and as a friend who knew him well said, he " ruined his health, broke his heart, and emptied his pocket-book," in this effort, — words that would literally describe the close of his daughter's life regarding the work which had become her own treasured ideal. But we must not anticipate. The poet and the prophet have here no continuing city; but still it is forever good to live with lofty aims, and there is no real failure in life except the failure to keep faith with our ideals. Both Joseph Field and his daughter Kate kept theirs unfalteringly, and no poverty of the purse can make poor when there is no poverty of the spirit.

The summer of 1853 was passed by the Fields in St. Louis. The school year then continued into midsummer, and Kate was diligently at work. In this, her fifteenth year, she was already very much of a young lady, very studious, very much given to holding opinions, and quite in her element as a mentor to a young cousin, whose manners and pursuits she directed with a girlish autocracy that held its hints of the little imperiousness of manner which was always associated with her. She was very independent, and inclined to regard her own way as one from which there could be no appeal. The only child, and cherished with even renewed tenderness after the death of her brother, she was naturally the idol of the household, and Kate's wishes and interests, from her early morning rising to her retiring at night, were the important matters to which all else deferred. She was an early riser, and the series of ideal methods of living which attended her always is seen even in her earliest childhood. At this time she was a devotee of cold baths; a very delicate girl, she subjected herself to a severer regimen than was favorable to good health, but she had always a firmness of purpose, and was absolutely unrelenting with herself in any system she set out to practise. Very slender and graceful, with a wealth of chestnut hair falling in clustering curls, with her fair complexion and luminous blue eyes, she was a figure to haunt the imagination. One is tempted to linger on this threshold of her womanhood,—the eager, impetuous girl, so richly gifted, and who was attracted in so many directions that the concentration on any single one seemed impossible. She had learned to dance almost as soon as she had learned to walk, and she had this constant poetry of motion. She had a pride of personal appearance, too, and each morning, immediately after breakfast, she seated herself, book in hand, for her rich masses of hair to be dressed. Elizabeth, the seamstress, whose specialty was to keep Mrs. Field's stage costumes in order and attend to the family sewing, would appear with comb, brush, and a large round curling-stick in hand at the instant Kate sat down in a low chair. Conning her lesson while the maid toiled for half an hour or more over the long, bright chestnut tresses, rolling each curl around the stick, she sat studying, until at the completion of the task a mass of burnished curls fell from the crown of her head below her shoulders in rich clusters, held back from the broad, fair brow by a round comb. Kate was not without her girlish pleasure in the consciousness of being an attractive figure. She had an innate belief always in her own right of way; but could the ideal atmosphere of wise and tender love that enfolded her then have but continued longer, Kate Field would have had a different and a far happier life. She was then rather the queen rose of the rosebud garden of girls; and when this exquisite dawning of her girl-life ended, as it did with the ensuing year, there was left behind something that never could come again. "The flowing conditions of life,"—how true is this expression of Emerson's. Never a year, never a day, repeats itself. Circumstances are fluid in their character, and now, just before the young girl, a new set of circumstances were already forming; already Destiny stood near to lead the tenderly beloved daughter into ways of sorrow and stern discipline, unrevealed to the sapphire blue eyes that looked out on life so eagerly, yet with a certain wistful appeal, too, as if the spirit had some subtle prophecy of all that waited in the unrevealed future of the eventful years.

The spring of 1856 found Mr. and Mrs. Field players in Mobile, and her father thus writes: —

MOBILE, March 14, 1854.

MY DEAR, DEAR DAUGHTER, — Your mother is very busy with study, and must omit, this time, one of her most delightful employments, and that is to write her affections to you. I am just as busy in my turn, but can scribble faster than "mother." Your last composition did honor to your head and heart, my dear child. Such and kindred sentiments are among the results of a fond mother's anxious care and training. God bless you, and long guard within your heart your present feelings of love and simplicity.

Another letter from her father playfully addresses her as "My Dear Miss Long Clothes," and sends her a check for fifty dollars, trusting her "to use it wisely." And the tender mother, writing from Mobile, says that she has three new rôles to acquire and so has little time to write, and adds: "May God bless you, my own dear child, and keep you in health, goodness, and happiness."

In the autumn of 1854 Kate's wish to visit her Aunt Corda (Mrs. Milton T. Sanford) in Boston, was fulfilled, and in November her father and mother left St. Louis for Mobile to enter on their season there. Misfortune had come upon Mr. Field in the burning

of his theatre, the Variétés, but his cheerful fortitude is shown in the following letter to his young
daughter: —

MY DEAR, DEAR KATY, — I have just succeeded in
making a new arrangement with our association by which
I receive myself $2000 present debt, and put myself on a
much better footing with them for the future, without com-
promising, for a moment, my position with the public or
the profession. I need not say that a weight of care has
been removed from my mind, and the first use I make of
it is to drop a few lines to my dear, dear child, whom I
may apparently seem to have neglected for some weeks
back. God bless you, Katy. If fortune should prove
herself capable of taking a clairvoyant peep through her
bandage this winter, as far as my humble prospects are
concerned, I shall be comparatively free in the spring.
Make yourself a *teacher*, by all means, — that is, store your
mind and heart, my child, with the ability to become such,
— but your temperament will never permit you to undertake
the requisite duties of the position, I fear. Still your aim is
a noble one, — you will endeavor to be *able* to be independent and useful. I shall send you money from Mobile
very soon. We start to-morrow. My best love to Uncle
Milton and Aunt Corda. Again, God bless you.

Your affectionate Father.

Mr. Field had, as this letter reveals, an unerring
insight into his daughter's peculiar trend of temperament. Her imperious will was something very
unlike either of her parents. She was an exotic; and
those skilled in the mysteries of heredity might go
back to some far-away ancestor and find the clue to
the unique quality of Kate's nature. She was self-
willed almost to waywardness, and still her entire
character was of the utmost elevation and nobleness

of quality. Mistakes, errors, she could always make, but anything ignoble was utterly foreign to her, — so foreign, indeed, that she was intolerant toward it, and if she were misjudged and misunderstood she would never condescend to explain, when at times a more lenient attitude might have been better as well as wiser. Her nature was as true as steel, as open as the sunlight, as lofty in purpose and aim as an ideal could be; but so mercurial, so impressionable, so sensitive, that a word, a look, would deflect her mood and cause her to seem capricious because the subtle cause of the change eluded observation. All her life she suffered intensely from this invisible friction of average life on a highly wrought and too self-conscious nature. The wise, sweet influence of her parents is shown in two following letters written to her from Mobile, — that of her mother dated Christmas, 1854, and her father's on New Year's Day, 1855. Mrs. Field writes: —

MOBILE, Dec. 25, 1854.

MY DEAR DARLING, — This is Christmas day. 'T is too late to wish you and those I love with you in Boston a Merry Christmas, but not too late to tell you how much I love you, how constantly I am thinking and wishing to be with you all, and how fervently I pray that the opening year and all that are to come may be years of blessedness and peace ; and that my own darling child may grow wiser, better, more useful and unselfish, every day she lives ; that she may not love this world so well as to forget that there is a higher motive for exertion than the approbation of man ; that the farther she advances in goodness and in knowledge in this world, the sooner she will arrive at perfect bliss in the world everlasting. Holidays are always *sad* days to me when I am away from those I love.

Mr. Field's letter runs thus : —

NEW YEAR, 1855.

MY DEAR, DEAR DAUGHTER, — God bless you on this happy day, which here is a bright one indeed, as far as sunshine goes. This day week I sent you a $10 gold piece to buy a present for Uncle Milton, as your mother instructed you. I hope it may have reached you in time. We are well in health and business improving. In a week I expect to remit you more money.

God bless you, my dear Katy, and grant you many, many happy, peaceful returns of this day. You must arrange with Aunt Corda about school. Love to your Uncle and Aunt.

Your affectionate Father.

Little dreamed the young girl that this was the last New Year's greeting she was to have from the father she idolized. So it was written, and she stood on the threshold of changes which were to entirely transform the apparent course of her life. Events dissolve to give new material for the structure.

> "Ever the Rock of Ages melts
> Into the mineral air
> To be the quarry whence to build
> Thought, and its mansions fair."

The first chapter of the story of her sojourn in this part of life was rapidly ending. The atmosphere of idolizing tenderness with the wise and thoughtful love that had encompassed her was to give place to those sterner experiences of life which are as truly the culture of the spirit and are a part of the needed forces for development.

EARLY YOUTH

" In those young eyes so keenly, bravely bent
  To search the mysteries of the future hour,
    There shines the will to conquer, and the power.
  The radiance of the Beautiful was blent
  E'en with thine earliest dreams."

CHAPTER II

But heard are the Voices,
　　Heard are the Sages,
　　　The Worlds and the Ages.
" Choose well: your choice is
Brief, and yet endless."

GOETHE.

" Sculptors of life are we as we stand
　　With our souls uncarved before us,
　Waiting the hour when, at God's command,
　　Our life-dream passes o'er us.
If we carve it then on that yielding stone
　　With many a sharp incision,
The angel dream shall become our own
　　Our lives shall reflect the vision ! "

EARLY YOUTH. ASPIRATIONS AND STUDIES. INTEREST IN ART
AND LITERATURE. ARDENT DEVOTION TO MUSIC.

IN the winter of 1855 Kate entered Lasell Seminary in Auburndale, near Boston. The change
from the ideal atmosphere of the home in which she
had been reared to that of a boarding-school, however well conducted, was naturally hard to bear. Yet
the sweet influences had wrought their impress in
her, and she endeavored to adapt herself to the
changed circumstances. " I should much prefer
rooming alone," she writes to her mother, " as you
know I have a passion for having no other companions than my own thoughts and books when I am
studying, but I cannot, so I must be satisfied." She
writes to her mother of the annoyances of inter-

ruption in her study, and this sweet counsel comes in reply : —

" I know, my dear child, it is not always pleasant when our minds are engaged with study, or our own thoughts, to answer questions, but nevertheless good breeding and consideration for others often compel us to do what is not always agreeable to our feelings."

There began to come now into Kate's life an influence that had the potency of destiny. Her mother's youngest sister, Cordelia Riddle, one of the most beautiful, gifted, and charming of women, had become the wife of Milton T. Sanford, a man of wealth and influence. Mrs. Sanford (born in 1824) was only fourteen years the senior of her niece, and her youth and the harmony of taste between them in the passionate love of music, drew the aunt and niece together in an absorbing affection which had in it the elements of tragedy. This expression regarding a family relation seems to savor of exaggeration; but however inexplicable the cause, it is still true that between Kate and her Aunt Corda there was a feeling akin to that of a romantic love. The young aunt satisfied the more impassioned side of the girl's nature. Mrs. Sanford was a born artist. She had great beauty and distinction of presence, an exquisite voice, a passionate love of art. She was a very keen and not too charitable critic of life and people. She had the family uprightness and honor, but she lacked the great love, the infinite patience, sweetness, and philosophic tolerance that so characterized Mrs. Field. Of the two sisters, Mrs. Field would win where Mrs. Sanford would dazzle. She had a bewildering fascination about her, and with her youth,

beauty, wealth, artistic gifts, and just sufficient sen-
iority to charm the fancy of a young girl, she became
the most potent influence in Kate's life. A girl of
sixteen has no fixed character. She is one thing or
another in her plastic youth according to circumstances and influences. Mrs. Sanford had no children, and this clever, unique niece became her idol
and delight. Brilliant, responsive, sympathetic, an
artist and the friend of artists, a *persona grata* in an
enchanting world which this young girl had dreamed
of but not seen, Mrs. Sanford's vivid personality was
ineffaceably stamped upon the mind and heart of her
niece. Mrs. Sanford had the dramatic temperament,
and had it not been for her early marriage she would
undoubtedly have made a name on the lyric stage.
When a girl of seventeen Mrs. Sanford discovered
the rare musical genius of Adelaide Phillipps, then a
little child playing juvenile parts on the stage of the
Boston Museum. Corda Riddle gave Adelaide Phillipps her first music lesson, and was from that time her
life-long friend. After Miss Riddle's marriage to
Mr. Sanford, her husband's wealth enabled her to
become a generous patron of art; and in her beautiful villa in Newport, she drew around her a choice
and distinguished circle of friends, among whom
were Charlotte Cushman, Edwin Booth, Mr. and Mrs.
Edwin P. Whipple, Thomas Ball, the sculptor, Charles
Caryll Coleman, Mrs. Julia Ward Howe, Adelaide
Phillipps, and other persons whose names have flown
to world-wide fame. Into this stimulating atmosphere came Kate Field. Auburndale is almost a
Boston suburb, and her aunt was in almost daily communication with her by visit or letter. The artistic
side of her nature responded to all this brilliant art

life: with this she had, as we have seen, a vein of mysticism and fervent, though undefined religious longing which her Aunt Corda could not wholly comprehend, although in the later life of Mrs. Sanford this element in her character revealed itself. But the girl who had copied sermons, at thirteen, into her diary, found irksome the ceremonial religious observances of the school, for she had no sympathy with formal piety. And to her mother she wrote, expressing something of this feeling, to which Mrs. Field replied: —

"It makes me happy to know you are in good spirits, my darling child. You have much to be grateful for, and I trust your education will enlarge your ideas without engendering pride (that sin of the shallow-minded). I could wish to see you free from all prejudice or suspicion, kind and considerate of the feelings of others. When you see faults in those around you, remember how many good qualities they have, and judge charitably. Make it a habit before going to sleep, my darling daughter, to think over your own conduct, — all you have done and thought (for thoughts should be pure as well as actions), and this practice will help you, and lead to happiness not only in this world, but what is far better, prepare you for the world that is to come. You say in your letter, my dear child, 'that you think you will never succeed in becoming unselfish, selfishness has become so *firmly seated* within you.' If you really and truthfully think this, set about the case, do not rest until you have *eradicated* it from your heart. You can never be happy yourself or make those about you so with such feelings in your bosom. I would be wretched, my own darling child, if I thought you would grow up a selfish woman. I know that it is one of the strongest feelings of our nature, and one that requires the greatest struggle on our part to overcome; but we can, with God's help, overcome that, as many other sins. You would be shocked to be called a thief or a liar, and yet in the eye of God, selfishness is a great sin. Think that the pure spirit of your little darling brother is always hovering about you, sorrowing when you do wrong, rejoicing when you are good. With this thought constantly in your mind, it will purify your heart, you cannot be selfish, it will teach you to do to others as you would wish others to do unto you; to be good from principle. We cannot depend upon our impulses; they as often lead us to do wrong as right. I know, my dear child, I do not practise these teachings, but I will struggle and endeavor to do so; and if my life is spared I hope I shall be a better woman, and if I am better I shall be happier. Never say again, my own dear child, if you love your mother and wish to make her happy, 'that you will *never* succeed in becoming *unselfish.*'"

Mrs. Sanford takes her niece to the theatre during this winter, and Kate writes to her father that she thinks Forrest very successful in his characters; and that Adelaide Phillipps has just opened an operatic engagement, adding that it is very sad that the strength of Miss Phillipps is unequal to the tax of her great mind, and " if this be true, a genius will be lost to the world, such an one as we cannot hope to see again." Even then, as a school-girl, Kate discerned truly the noble genius and wonderful power of Adelaide Phillipps whom, as artist and woman, America now holds in reverence as an embodied ideal of lofty character.

Again Kate writes: —

" Have you or has father read ' Hiawatha,' Longfellow's new poem? If you have not, do so and give me your opinion. I have just commenced it. They accuse him of

4

plagiarism from the German, then again others say it is not worth the precious time devoted to the perusal. For myself the singular metre has a peculiar charm, and there seems to be an undercurrent of harmony breathing throughout it. I have read but a few pages, however."

Kate gave herself to musical study with all the ardor of her nature, and in a letter to her mother she says : —

"I am to sing in two more choruses, one from 'Macbeth' and the other from Rossini. I am very well, and have finished the 'Corsican Brothers' with the exception of two pages."

Italian, too, is now added to her studies, and the girl records: "I am quite bewildered with the language, and I shall make rapid progress with it." Writing to her mother in the December of that year, Kate says: —

"Sixteenth of December. This year will have soon passed away, and we shall have entered upon '56. How short is life in this world ! How short in comparison with eternity, and yet it seems to me as though all our labor, all our strivings, were for earthly objects, as fleeting and uncertain as our own mortality. Whenever I think on this, I resolve to try to be a Christian, but my resolutions seem to fail, and I am the same uncharitable, restless spirit. There is always such a tumult going on in my brain that I never can decide what I am, what I will be, what I was created for, or what it is my ambition to be. I suppose I am what is designated as 'rather queer.'"

In this girl only just past her seventeenth birthday there was striving the same feeling that William Watson voiced in his "World-Strangeness."

" Strange the world about me lies,
Never yet familiar grown, —
Still disturbs me with surprise,
Haunts me like a face half known.
. . . . . .

" On from room to room I stray
Yet my Host can ne'er espy,
And I know not to this day
Whether guest or captive I.

" So, between the starry dome
And the flow of plains and seas,
I have never felt at home,
Never wholly been at ease."

Toward the end of that December it would almost
seem as if a premonition of the sorrow that was so
near came upon her, and she writes : —

MY OWN DEAR, DARLING MOTHER, — I am homesick,
very homesick, and how I long to see you and father ! It
seems to me as though the time would never come when I
shall be with you once more. I can only reconcile by
anticipating the pleasure which is in store for me, Providence permitting. I think there is something inspiring in
looking forward to what will be. It urges me to renewed
exertion in whatever I am engaged upon. My poor father,
how often I think of him, confined to his room and suffering !
May his health be speedily restored ! "

Serious thoughts of the future begin to stir in her
mind, and in a letter to her mother she says : —

Yesterday Aunt Corda made me an offer as generous as
it was surprising, yet one which I dread to accept and
would not if I did not know the displeasure my refusal
would cause Uncle Milton. It is to finish this year at
Lasell, and to study music at their expense. Aunt Corda

urged it so earnestly, and I remembered how last summer when at the St. Nicholas I refused to take some bank bills that Uncle Milton threw into my lap, I hurt his feelings so that I dare not refuse again. And yet, dear mother, it gives me great pain to place myself under such great obligation to my aunt and uncle, and I shall not rest till I can repay them. I shall devote all my energies to singing with a view to making it a means of support. My French I could turn to account and might teach beginners, the same with my English. But I prefer the singing if I can make myself capable. I have often thought I would like to practise writing sketches with father, if he would criticise them and tell me if they were in the least meritorious. But I have been away from him so much, and when he was last here he was so ill and so full of cares, that I did not dare to mention such a foolish and trifling occupation. Has he ever told you what he thought of my capacities, — where he thought my little talent lay? I have none, I can excel in nothing, I am good for nothing. Write me very often, dear mother, take good care of your health, and remember that you have a

devoted daughter,   KATEY.

Again under date of Jan. 20, 1856, Kate writes to her mother: —

"The opening opera to-morrow night is ' Il Trovatore.' Ah, woe, ah, woe is me ! I shall be a model for despair if I do not hear ' Linda de Chamounix ' Friday night. Do you remember the two gold dollars that father gave me to see Rachel in Adrienne? I did not need the money then, and I have treasured them ever since, waiting for something to ' turn up.' I think that if I spend $1.50 upon the opera of ' Linda,' it will be a profitable investment. What is your opinion of the matter? . . . Present my remembrances to Mr. and Mrs. Barney Williams. Is it true that they intend visiting Europe? Ask them to remember me if they have an opportunity of collecting autographs or curiosities of any description. I wonder if it will ever be our destiny to journey over the old world. If wishing would accomplish it, such a consummation would soon come to pass."

Already Destiny was on its way, in the guise of a sorrow of which the young girl little dreamed. She attends Thackeray's first lectures in Boston, and then writes: —

" As I expected, I attended Thackeray's lecture Friday night. I shall not yet pass my judgment, as we had a seat near the entrance, and I only heard about half he said. The lecture was by no means an extraordinary composition, simply pleasing, chatty, and conversational. Not at all historic, but this latter he acknowledged he avoided, from the fact that he did not aspire to the position of an historian, but a recorder of the manners and times of the age of the Georges. I thought his lecture a complete satire, and certainly I could not help feeling that he arrived at the most unamiable and uncharitable conclusions concerning the individuals upon whom he dilated, as were possible to any human being. They say the opening one is the most inferior; hereafter I shall hear what I shall hear, and shall then give my impressions. Thackeray was conducted to the hall (which was crowded with the élite and literati of Boston) by James T. Fields. Mr. Thackeray is no orator, merely a pleasant speaker, very easy in his manner. His voice is quite monotonous, though at the same time it does not weary you. It must arise from his being so perfectly natural."

On Jan. 23, 1856, Kate wrote the last letter she was ever to write to her beloved father, — a letter that tells its own story of the eager young life: —

"Something has turned up in reality. Let me tell you the news. Aunt Corda and Uncle Milton are to visit Aunt Charlotte as long as the opera remains in Boston; further-more, we are all going next Friday night to hear Linda, which character La Heusler is to sustain. The greatest curiosity is of course manifested to see her, the American Prima Donna. Tableaux are progressing. I am becoming exceedingly nervous about my part in the performance. It will be hard for me to commit ' Come è bello ' to memory, as I have not yet learned a note of it. Oh, dear me ! what will become of me? We have seen the proof sheet of pro-grammes, which has quite a nice appearance. My name looks quite imposing in print. I think, talk, and dream nothing but tableaux, and this is the case with my three co-laborers."

It was one of these strange sequences recurring in Kate Field's life that on the very night of the amateur tableaux the telegram should come to her bearing the news of the death of her idolized father.

The New Year of 1856 dawned, and several of the pupils of Lasell gave this musical soirée with tab-leaux. A local paper describing the entertainment says : —

"But there was a touching episode connected with the entertainment which was the cause of sudden gloom to one young lady, who had been ' the observed of all observers ' during the evening, and whose charming accomplishments had elicited the admiration of the company there gathered. Miss Kate Field, to whom we allude, had borne the most prominent part in the tableaux, and was the only girl who had favored the company with vocal music, she having sung ' Casta Diva ' and ' She wore a Wreath of Roses,' in a manner which her sweet and vibrant though not powerful voice made irresistibly pleasing. A dispatch was received

in Boston that evening stating that her father, Mr. Joseph
M. Field, the well-known actor, had died during the morning at Mobile. It was deemed prudent not to make the
announcement to the young lady until late in the evening,
but what must have been the private grief that overwhelmed
her joyous spirits on the reception of such news at such a
time, it is easy to imagine. As the sad tidings were whispered about after the close of the entertainment, each heart
seemed touched with melting sympathy for the unfortunate
young lady whose evening's transition from delight to sadness was so sudden."

In Mobile, where Mr. and Mrs. Field had played
for so many seasons, came his sudden death on the
morning of Jan. 28, 1856. The previous day (Sunday) he had driven out with his wife, and although he
was ill, no one dreamed of immediate danger. The
journals of the day were full of tribute to him as a
dramatic artist of rare power, a man of brilliant intellect and noble life, — a high-minded gentleman. The
funeral services were held in the Episcopal church on
St. Emanuel Street in Mobile, and his body was
brought to Boston and buried in the family lot in
Mount Auburn. A leading writer of the day said of
Mr. Field : —

" He was affectionate and faithful in all his family relations, true to all his friendships, and honorable in the dis-
charge of all the duties of life. His pilgrimage has been a
diversified and toilsome one ; yet he bore its burdens cheerfully, and has gone to his final rest with a consciousness of
having acted well his part on earth. No one could know
Mr. Field without being drawn toward him by his genial
nature, and that accomplishment and vivacity of mind which
rendered his society always instructive and agreeable. As

a writer he was distinguished for refinement and wit, and as an actor for that nice conception and correct delineation which rendered his impersonations models in the histrionic profession."

To the loving wife, the devoted daughter, the loss was one whose sadness lay too deep for tears, but there was a spirituality in the nature of both that led them instinctively to lay hold of the realities of the life after death and of the intimate way in which all life in the Seen and the Unseen is related. The generous kindness of heart that so signally characterized Mrs. Field's brother-in-law, Mr. Sanford, is shown in a note dated Jan. 31, 1856, which he wrote to her, saying : —

" Come home to us as soon as may be. You will draw on me for any funds that you require. Kate will soon resume her lessons."

Mrs. Field was not the type of woman, however, to retire before misfortunes into helpless inactivity. Indeed, the very desolation of her grief spurred her on to renewed efforts for the future. She was left with a theatre company on her hands, with debts caused by Mr. Field's loss in the burning of his theatre in St. Louis, and other misfortunes that had involved him in obligations which he was expecting to clear off by the season's work. The only property was a life insurance for $3,000, and this Mrs. Field felt must be held intact for their daughter's education. She turned immediately to her work on the stage, keeping the company together and facing the public each night with smiles and radiance, however heart-breaking were the lonely hours when she returned from the evening's performances. To a friend who wrote suggesting a benefit night for her in St. Louis, she replied: —

" My husband was very sensitive, but never shrank from what he conceived to be his *duty*. I will endeavor to imitate his example, as far as light is given me. I owe already so many obligations to my friends that they almost overpower me. If my dear husband's name was free from debt, I would decline your kind offers ; but as I am situated, I do not think it would be right or just to others in doing so."

To her sister, Mrs. Sanford, Mrs. Field wrote: —

" I would not have my dear, dear husband back if his suffering were to continue, as the doctor said. I could not be so selfish. It is a great consolation to me that my own darling child is with you, and you will do all in your power to comfort her, to console her."

To her daughter, Mrs. Field writes, saying: —

MY OWN DARLING, — My sweet comforter, I feel your sympathy, and now we will both endeavor to be less selfish than we have ever been before, and if ever we have any unkind or uncharitable feelings rise in our hearts towards those we mingle with, we will watch ourselves closely, and believe that the loving spirit of your dear Father is ever with us, loving us so dearly, so happy if we are purely so. Let us, then, pray, my darling, that time may never wean us, but keep ever fresh in our hearts the sad but sweet memory of your beloved father. And I pray to our Heavenly Father that we may find ease of heart and cheerfulness in the thought of usefulness to others. We will even try to be happier, my precious daughter. This I will try to do ; this I would like my darling to practise. How far our weak endeavors will succeed, time must show. 'T is hard to give up those we love so dearly. I thought so when I lost your darling brother. I do not wish him back *now*. He would have been left so young without a father's care that I now feel that it was for the best. He was a boy; I could not have had him always with me as I could a daughter. How much greater (as far as I can understand) would have been my responsibility! Our loved ones are together, — perhaps with us often, — loving us more dearly than ever. The time will come, if we are good, that we shall be with them, — never, *never* again to part. My own darling, you are young, and if you are spared, the world is before you, — I hope a bright and happy future, — one of usefulness, of *love* and charity. . . . As you say, my pet, 'there is nothing so easy as to advise others.' Do not think, my child, because I can give good advice that I am good myself. *No ; far, far* from it. I wish I were. I can only say that I will endeavor.

Such angelic words have their universal message, and are too vital to be consigned to oblivion. Written only for the eye of her daughter, they are now, after a lapse of nearly half a century, full of counsel and help for the life of to-day.

Again Mrs. Field writes, two weeks after her husband's death : —

"We do not know what we are able to endure until we are tried. I have been sorely tried in the loss of my best friend, — so truthful, so unselfish, so high-minded in all his actions. My beloved husband possessed my *entire esteem* as well as my love. He has gone to a happier world, free from toil and suffering. Do not think that I have no strength, no belief, in the promise of our Heavenly Father. I feel that He alone can help me in this saddest hour of my life, that He alone can give me consolation. Although my heart is sore and I am very lonely, I do not despair. Life

is not a blank to me, even in this the first hours of my bereavement. I feel that I have much to live for; that I am
blessed with a dear, good child, — one who has always been
a comfort to her parents, and who has never caused us an
anxious thought. I was asked after my husband's death as
to whether my wishes were to go home or to go on with
the theatre as usual. My reply was that I wished, as far as
I am able, to carry out the engagements made by my husband; that this was my most earnest desire; for I did not
wish any one to suffer so far as I was able to prevent it."

About this time Kate writes to her mother: —

"Yesterday I took my first singing lesson. Signor Bendelari was very kind, and seemed very sorry for me.
Darling mother, I pray that we may never be obliged to be
parted hereafter. Signor Bendelari spoke encouragingly of
my voice."

Again Kate writes: —

AUBURNDALE, Feb. 26, 1856.

MY PRECIOUS MOTHER, — Once more at school. Oh,
how strange everything appeared here! Each object wears
a different aspect. So sad, so desolate, how different it
was when I left it! Well, well, it must be so. It was hard
for me to return, but you desired it, Aunt Corda and Uncle
Milton urged it very much, and I have come. I cannot as
yet fix my mind on my books, but I will try to overcome
my feelings and thoughts and fix my attention upon my
studies. I do not think I have yet told you of my lessons.
They are Geometry, Rhetoric, Kames' Elements of Criticism, and (perhaps) Geography of the Heavens. I have
no French or Italian now, so I can take more English
studies. I have concluded not to continue Algebra, from
the fact that I dislike it to such a degree that it positively
makes me sick to open the book. It is of no use unless

you intend to be a teacher, and if I am to be one, I can never attempt to teach mathematics. I have a natural distaste for all excepting Geometry. You know my propensity to scribble and read. I delight in studies of a literary nature. Father wished me to study astronomy, and so I wish to take up the Geography of the Heavens. Father's picture is hanging up before my writing desk, so that I am gazing upon his beloved face all the time. Oh, mother dear, I know that I am very ungrateful to complain. You, who have so much more cause, are making all efforts to gain the mastery over your feelings. I think I have done so too, but in writing to you I forget myself. Forgive me, and do not be anxious about me.

Like all persons of strong imagination, Kate had great practical power, and of their affairs she said to her mother: —

" With regard to father's debts, if it is a possible thing let them all be paid. Will not something be realized from the properties of the theatre and the disposal of the lease? You remember that father owns the Reveille building on Olive Street in St. Louis. If the debts cannot all be paid *now, collect them* if the parties are willing, and let us see what can be done in the future, if we live."

The speculative discussion of the day in regard to spiritualism appealed to Kate, and she wrote to her mother: —

" If spiritual manifestations are true, what a source of comfort they will be to us! We shall hear from father from the Spirit world, but we must not give our confidence too readily, but receive all such communications with great caution. Were I in New York, I should seek the Misses Fox. I know them to be honest and truthful in them-

selves. I do not speak on this latter subject to Aunt
Corda or Uncle Milton, for they are averse to it and consider such belief as fanaticism. Nevertheless I am one to
enquire and to believe that which my reason allows, — to
believe *facts*. My father's mind was too strong to be led
away by impositions or idle fancies and supposition. He
sought eagerly for Spiritual Truth, he studied earnestly,
he found that which he sought, in Swedenborg. I have
read but little of Swedenborg, but *that little* has satisfied
me. What noble lessons of humanity does he teach!
Charity and love are his passports to Heaven. But to be
liberal one should study the teachings of others, of the
established doctrines. One thing it seems to me I must
believe, — in the Trinity. Do you accord with the Unitarian
belief? "

Kate's self-analysis is almost startlingly frank at
times. As this : —

"What I attempt is well done, and it is by no means
easy music that I sing, but I have not a powerful voice, no
dramatic fervor, little expression, nor is my voice the most
flexible known to the world. It is medium, neither one
thing nor the other ; in consequence, I am not satisfied. I
would sing like Jenny Lind, like Albani, like Grisi ; all
these different styles I would have combined in one. As
I am incapacitated by nature for anything of the kind, I
am unhappy, for music is my passion, my love. I would be
wedded to it were I a worthy bride. How glorious to
interpret the inspired notes of Mozart, Rossini, Bellini,
Donizetti, and even the thundering Verdi ! Oh, how I long
to be a follower of this divine art, the art of Arts ; but no
humble servant would I be. Could I not stand beside
Grisi, I would not tread their path. 'T is impossible, even
ridiculous to think this, so my favorite desire must be relinquished. Have I another? Yes, to be a fine writer.

Could I be? No. Why not? Nature has not thus endowed me. Does not success in an undertaking need
hard study, work? Yes. Do I seek to gain this desire?
No. These are my two great desires, I have always
cherished more or less. . . .

"I awoke at 5 finding the storm continuing unabated,
much to my discomfort. Did not rise till 6¼, lying until
that time in bed wondering what the future might bring
forth. It is foolish to indulge in reveries I know full well,
but since my return to school I find myself dreaming very
nearly half the day. My thoughts are anywhere but on my
studies. I find myself planning for the future, thinking of
my dear mother, and then the truth will flash across my
brain that I have no longer a father, that I am fatherless.
Oh, it is terrible. I cannot realize it. My own darling
father that I loved more than any daughter can love a
father, whom I studied for and depended upon, whose
talents, and whose sensitive, noble nature I so well understood and appreciated, is gone to his Eternal home. I
must not despair, it is wrong; the thought of the long,
lonely separation of father and daughter is so sad, so very
sad. But ought I to say long? for might I not be taken
away at any moment? Am I prepared for death? Ah,
no, and this is what makes me feel how awful that hour
would be. Such were my reveries, and very dispiriting
they were. . . . People may think I have little feeling.
They little know my nature."

And again: —

"I have always felt that I was different from the other
girls with whom I have associated; that I had a mission of
some kind on this globe. . . . I am passionately fond of
reading, not trash, but literature of a high order. This
is one thing in my favor, and I think that literature is my
forte.

" . . . After dinner commenced the 'Spectator.' I expect a 'feast of reason and a flow of soul' from Joseph Addison, in which I pray not to be disappointed. Wrote journal and read until bedtime."

She hears Mozart, and writes: —

"Mozart's 7th Symphony was played quite well. What a glorious composition, — so purifying in its influence! The andante from Beethoven's 7th Symphony was conceived quite well by the performer, — perhaps it was executed too slowly. There is too great a predominance of light music at these concerts to satisfy me. Waltzes rule the day, to the evident satisfaction of the majority. . . . It is so very galling to see aimless, stupid, brainless school girls get up and sing in a manner so far superior to my own. Music requires soul, — have I none? I am a devoted lover of music ; I have the most exalted worship for the art, and still I am only what I am. Voice. The voice is indispensable in vocal music. The want of this is my misfortune, not my fault. . . . Arrived at the Seminary and studied my astronomy lesson, wrote in journal, and *thought*, — went to bed, fell asleep. . . .

"Practised the Opus Second. It is a noble composition, and one which I delight to sing, — it is so grand, so religious in its sentiment."

Music was the absorbing passion of Kate's life. In her dying hours, in Hawaii, she was asked if the singing of some of the natives under her window disturbed her, and she replied, "Oh, no, music is heaven to me!" — an expression that sustained to the last her most intense devotion. When taking her lesson one morning from Signor Bendelari, the famous Boston teacher of that day, he told her that her high notes were improving, and she records this in her journal with her intention to take severe study, and adds:

" Some people go through life as if it were a plaything.
I have very different ideas of God's creation." She
was born under a star that danced, and a lapse into
domestic industries fretted her. She confided to her
journal one day that " the entire family are sewing
themselves out of existence. I cannot afford a seamstress, and I ought to sew," she continues, " but it
seems to me such a waste of time, such a sacrifice of
life. What new idea has suggested itself during such
work? " Another day was more to the girl's taste,
and she records : —

" I have been reading Mrs. Browning's poems all the
afternoon. Read the 'Poet's Vow,' which pleased me for
its moral. I was agreeably disappointed in my rapid glance
of the lady's works. She is a remarkable woman, and the
only real poetess of the age."

In the May of 1856 Kate first saw Washington
in a trip made *via* New York and Baltimore, with
her indulgent uncle and aunt, the Sanfords. In a
picture gallery she saw a sketch of an old man's head
which she thought " showed the hand of a master; "
and she visited the Smithsonian Institute with eager
interest in the inventions displayed, and she writes in
her journal: " But the instruments for experimenting, — how I feasted my eyes on mammoth lenses,
electrical machines, monstrous air-pumps, and horse-
shoe magnets."

This attraction to scientific achievements deepened
into one of her most marked characteristics, and at
the Chicago Exposition of 1893 her press description
and comment on the electrical achievements led all
the rest. This trip to the nation's capital was another mile-mark in the girl's life, and stimulated her

innate longing for wider horizons. Thus unconsciously does one come to an hour of destiny that
is retrospectively recognized as a point dividing the
past from the future.

> " We cross an unseen line,
> And lo! another zone."

On the Sunday following her return she gave herself up to the newspaper reading, which was to be one
of the interests of all her after life, and in her journal
she alludes to newspapers as " friends of humanity."
She finds that a stranger has leased the Mobile theatre that her father had managed, and she writes : —

" Will they find him equal to my talented, brilliant, sensitive, unappreciated father? The world in general scorns
actors. Be it so, which is most to be coveted, money or
genius? Death will separate men from the one. Genius
is eternal. Do I regret that my father was poor? No,
indeed ; I glory in his memory as he was. Honest, truthful,
sharing with others his gains, acting by others as he would
wish others to act by him, hopeful, never complaining of
reverses, but trusting in Providence, scorning a low action,
he was all to admire. Verily, he will meet his reward
above. Abbott Lawrence is spoken of as a pattern to
young men, a merchant prince ; follow his example. How
it makes my blood boil to have it said, as I know it is,
' Poor Joe, he was a noble fellow, too generous to get
along in the world, always sharing his money with others,
had not much business tact, infatuated with all the isms of
the day.' Why? Because he was not a Yankee, did not
screw those he employed, and would not drive a hard bargain. He was a Christian, and followed the teachings of
Christ. In business he was talented and always showed
it. In the progress of the day he was always interested ;
he always read what would uplift and advance him."

5

That parting of the ways which youth must always meet in some form opened now before Kate Field. She had a capacity for exaltation of spirit that was not understood, and she began to encounter that spiritual tragedy which reveals itself when one who longs to lead a higher life than the average fails in the effort, and questions the reality of his own ideals.

The summer of 1857 was a period of mingled ferment. In those days the outlook for women was limited, and Kate's inborn independence was urging her on to a life of her own, free from the sense of obligation that often burdened her. Mrs. Sanford was of a highly nervous and excitable disposition, and her ill health resulted in a lack of mental balance that made Kate's position in her aunt's home one that at times tortured her sensitive nature. Under the date of Aug. 24, 1857, the girl writes in her journal: —

" I sometimes think it is a great misfortune that I was not born a boy, for then any and every employment would be open to me, and I could gain sufficient to support my mother and self. I cannot, as it is, much longer lead my present idle, unsatisfactory life. Ever since the death of my dear father, there has been a something weighing, weighing, weighing upon me. A feeling of dependence, a knowledge that I was poor, that I was a drag upon my dear aunt and uncle. Still, I returned to school, but the death of the only one whom I adored, one whom I only knew and who only knew me, would ever rise before me ; and although I persevered in my studies, I made but little progress. I gave school up; money was too precious now to spend in vain. I left, however, with a sigh, for it is sad sometimes to see the plans of your youth frustrated. Dear Aunt Corda and Uncle Milton were then so good as to take me with them upon a visit to New York, Philadelphia, Baltimore, etc. A trip which I most thoroughly enjoyed and appreciated, for with me the sight of great cities never before visited could not fail to interest me and divert my mind from its dark channel of thought. I was very grateful to my aunt and uncle, although I did not express the same in words upon my return home. I met my mother for the first time since our bereavement. She had borne her trials bravely, had suffered more than I had. My poor mother's eyes failed her, her engagement is thrown up, not to be renewed, her eyes had not improved, she cannot work, it is my duty to do my best, and what is that? I have so little talent for writing, but provided I had the material within, it takes years of ill success before even a good writer makes a living. I have sometimes thought of the stage, I love it dearly ; it is a great profession for making money where an actor's efforts are crowned with success. But have I any talent? I fear not. Were I not talented, my ambition would soon bring me to the grave. Oh, God, what shall I do? Would that I had some one to advise me ! My father, if it be true that spirits are near the loved ones of earth, oh, listen to me, thy child who reveres thy memory as none other can revere it : listen to my prayers that God will lead me to the path in which I shall tread through life : and if it be in thy power, impress me with the advice which thou wouldst give if once more on earth."

Meeting a lady who had been making a trip abroad, Kate writes : —

" She has just returned from Europe, and almost disgusted me with the unexcitable manner in which she descanted upon the Old World. I can conceive of anything on earth except taking Europe coolly."

This was the time when the girl's tendency to intolerance should have been repressed, for the only true attitude toward life is to see each person in his higher possibilities and recognize the ideal in him. " Emerson's beautiful manners," says his friend Mr. Charles Malloy, " were the result of his seeing each man in his ideal self, and to that self Mr. Emerson always addressed himself." There was no wise hand to point this truth out to Kate Field, and she suffered all her life from a too keen sensitiveness to defects, — a fault which her father foresaw, and from which he had vainly endeavored to guard his tenderly beloved daughter. Adverse criticism is a deteriorating element in character. Nothing is more injurious to the spiritual quality of life than to discern the worse, rather than the better qualities of others. This tendency of Kate's was a result of an exceedingly fastidious and delicate temperament, whose inbred refinement and artistic exaction dominated her in these early days. Yet, withal, she was generous to a fault, and had her mother's exquisitely kind nature; but this keen perception of defects always remained with her to a degree, and to those who did not discern the real Kate Field under the outer semblance, often misrepresented her. A rare sweetness of nature was always hers, however, and she grew more and more devoted to her enthusiasm for music.

"Bendelari gives me every encouragement that I can become a prima donna," she writes. " There is a magic charm in the two words, ' I will,' and though I dare not utter them in this connection, I yet act upon that principle."

Kate's isolation of temperament revealed itself in her earliest girlhood, and she had, too, a curious tendency to that depression of spirits from which all her

life she suffered.   In her seventeenth year she writes
in her journal : —

"Oh, if I were a man ! I pity myself, indeed, I do.
There is not an ambition, a desire, a feeling, a thought, an
impulse, an instinct that I am not obliged to crush.   And
why? because I am a woman, and a woman must content
herself with indoor life, with sewing and babies.   Well,
they pretend to say that God intended women to be just what
they are.   I say that He did not, that men have made
women what they are, and if they attribute their doings to
the Almighty, they *lie*.   The time will come, but my grave
will be many centuries old. . . . Well, Excelsior, time will
work a cure for all things but the heartache.   It seems to
me that one of the greatest delights of life to a thinking
mind must be a study, — a room religiously your own, the
open sesame of which is a charm to be broken by none
else ; a sanctuary to which you retire to ponder, think,
weep, write, read, *pray*, knowing that there you may indulge
your feelings as the emotions and passions dictate, and no
one will dare intrude — no one will scrutinize you, save the
All-wise, Omnipresent God.   For such a retreat have I ever
sighed. . . . When at home I like to be alone, to collect
my thoughts, to read and write.   The presence of another
person renders me so nervous that I am almost ready to
fly ; it grates so upon my feelings that I am completely
upset and can do nothing.   The more I attempt to fight off
these feelings the fiercer is the battle, and I at length have
decided that I am constituted thus, and that it is entirely
useless to 'kick against the pricks.'   What person is there
that does not sometimes desire to shut the door upon all
mankind ? "

Visions rose before her of a life that flashed in
brilliant mirage and then vanished, leaving her with
a present that seemed ignoble and dull by com-

parison with her dreams. Yet the girl was full of tender household affections, as shown in this record : —

" Oh, I love my aunt and uncle very, very much ; now that my father is dead I have no one to love but my mother and them. For the last three years they have done everything in the world for me, and what have I done in return? Nothing. I have been conceited enough to look upon Cordaville as a home, as something to which I was entitled, expecting kindness from Aunt Corda and Uncle Milt rather as a right than as a favor. This is not as it should be. However much I may love and be attached to them, I cannot expect equal feelings from them. It is not natural. Everything they do for me is a kindness, and consequently increases my affection. Not one thing do I do for them that can cause a similar feeling. On the contrary, I am perfectly useless. I am selfish, have a very disagreeable temper and manner, and of no use about the house, and consequently in the course of time they will become weary of me, for I cannot expect them to make allowances for me as my mother does. Uncle Milt has a great many dependent upon him now. Mrs. —— intends to educate her children to earn their own living ; and how disgraceful it would be that while Uncle Milton's own nieces are at work, his wife's niece should be dependent on him. Mother is disabled, and she feels a burden on her friends ; she looks to me and asks to what my tastes lead me ? Oh, my dear father ! What shall I do ? The grave gives not up its dead. I cannot teach ; I have a little talent for singing, but even if my voice improved it would take years of study before I could dream of realizing anything from it."

Through all her girlhood and indeed through all her life, Kate suffered intensely from that feeling which William Watson well describes as " World-Strangeness," in a poem to which allusion has been made. There was always in her a certain detachment from ordinary life. She had her own world, one not easily adapted to alien atmospheres. To literature she turned with almost the same enthusiasm as to music, and the reading of Mrs. Jameson's " Diary of an Ennuyé" interested her, but she criticised its dolorous tone and longed for " less recorded grief and more Italy." After writing several pages regarding it, she asks : —

" I wonder if what I have written is in the least a criticism ? If my darling father were only alive, what a friend and instructor I should have in him ! It seems very hard to me sometimes that I should be separated from the only one I reverenced on earth.

. . . .

" Received a letter from Little Mother. She has visited Mount Auburn and says the iron railing is all that she could wish. Dear Father, if there is no monument to mark the spot where lies all that remains of so glorious a nature, at least his grave is protected from all harm. It is sad to think the absence of gold causes the poor to neglect their angel ones. The love is the same, though the world sees no monumental evidence of it. And, after all, what are appearances? This world ' is but the baseless fabric of a dream.'

" Dear ' Little Mother,' she is so sensitive too. Hers is a sad fate, a life of constant self-sacrifice, the death of her adored husband and darling little son, swindled out of thousands of dollars, deprived for the most part of sight, unable to follow her profession, naught of consolation but me, and I am a selfish, disagreeable creature. I ought to be her stay and support ; good daughters are of benefit to their mothers. I am a burden and an expense. My reproaches are many, and yet there is something that hints to me that I must wait awhile ; a scheme will be developed. Now perhaps this is all dream work — that I ought not to listen to anything but present duty; and yet I am almost forced to pay attention to this unknown pleader, perhaps a siren's voice to lead me astray. Mine is a hard alternative, either to remain as I am, depending upon the bounty of aunt and uncle with mother likewise a dependent, or try my fortune upon the stage. This is all I can do if I am in the least capacitated for success. It seems to me that I was not born to be poor or to earn my living in a miserable plodding manner (another dream) ; my tastes, desires, ideas, ambitions, and positive existence are so diametrically opposite. And then I love my darling Aunt Corda so very, very much, I cannot bear to be separated from her ; it seems to me impossible to live apart from her. But then there is Uncle Milt, I love very much, but I fancy lately that he does not care for me ; to-day especially I have noticed how little notice he has taken of me."

The revealing journal of a girl's hidden life runs on : —

" Oh, poor me, I 'm the victim of fate, fortune, circumstances, everything. Aunt Corda and Uncle Milt close the house on Tuesday, and mother and I straggle off to Charlestown there to remain perhaps for the remainder of our natural lives. Well, so much for being a lazy, stupid, conceited, selfish idiot. If I had the determination of a mouse, I would be independent of all relatives. But I 've just talent enough to make me despise humble occupations and long for that which it seems to me I can never attain. My talents are those apropos to a wealthy amateur born to gratify her tastes in literature, art, and science all over the world. Situated as I am, my talents are my bane, and it is my firm belief I shall be an unhappy creature as long as I am on earth. No one has the faintest idea of the thoughts

human and celestial that course through my brain. I wonder if it is so with every one. My outer and inner self have
not the least sympathy save in affection for those I love. I
feel as though my life were wasting away, leaving naught
behind to mark the days, hours, minutes, seconds. What
was I created for? Oh, how wicked to make God account-
able for my own misdeeds. I was born for a purpose.

. . . .

" It is not the love of one who has been benefited ; it is
a love apart from that. Had she the same love for me, she
could not part from me and be happy ; but her husband is
the receiver of this love, and I am loved slightly as a niece.
I must not expect more, so must plod on without the *star*
of my existence. Oh, my dear father, I am not forgetting
my love for thee when I write this ; no one can ever supply
thy place. I love Uncle Milt because he has been kind to
me ; he will not let me go farther."

Again Kate records in her journal : —

" Later in the evening we met Mr. Nat. Hale and passed
a very pleasant half-hour with him. He is a man of positive genius in some respects."

" We were introduced to Rev. Edward Everett Hale and
Dr. Hedge. Dr. Hedge enjoys a fine reputation as a theo-
logical writer, as a man of great talents, but his face is by
no means a pleasing one to a stranger. It is strong, hard,
unyielding, not good-natured, unsympathetic. His manner
is not winning. I should like to have heard him converse,
but had not the opportunity. My verdict on his face may
all be wrong."

" *Gertrude* is a difficult rôle, — one of great vivacity and
affection, of light and shade. I know how it should be
done, but I am unable to carry out my conception. Heretofore I have rehearsed the part awfully ; I trust to the

inspiration of the moment if there is such a thing in me as inspiration. Why cannot I do it as well as other girls of my age? Inability is the reason. Well, well, Katy, you are a poor, miserable little thing, fit for nothing but to brood over her uselessness in this world and unfitness for the next!"

" If I ask myself this awful question, 'For what do I live?' I can give no answer save 'self.' Knowing this, why do I not reform? It seems to me that I am the incarnation of all that is evil. There can surely be no one so little affected to good works as myself. Alas, alas! the angel does not smile on me!"

" I suppose I am ridiculously sensitive, but the least apparent slight affects me and makes me dolorous lachrymose. If Uncle Milt were only a little different, if he would treat me more as a father treats a child, if he would let me love him in a fatherly way, — I should feel so much better. I miss my darling father, — oh, so much, so much! no one knows how much I miss him. If I could only fill a little of the void his loss has left in my heart, it would be such a relief to me. But no; no longer can I look for a father on earth; I must seek higher. I have two in heaven: my earthly and my Heavenly Father; and this thought that I have two such spiritual guardians should make me better. Life is not everlasting, and I shall be with them by-and-by. Oh, my revered father! if thou canst see thy poor Kate now, pity her! and if it is according to divine law that the spirit out of the flesh may commune with the spirit in the flesh, infuse thy counsels into my soul in such a way that I may know they are thy teachings! Alas! I fear there is no truth in Spiritualism!"

" . . . be a heavenly union; but it never is, therefore where shall I seek for aid? Alas, I know not! No one to instruct me ; no one to tell me in what channel to direct my powers ; no one to point out my talents ; no one to say to me, 'Well done !' or the reverse. It is my misfortune to live among those merely equal or inferior to me ; I can learn nothing from them ; whereas could I be surrounded by superiors my steps would be quickened in following in the path of people of knowledge. Oh, my dear father ! you alone are the one to instruct me ! My aspirations are so vehement, surely, surely they must be based upon some little talent ! Shall I never meet with sympathy thorough and entire? What happiness when found ! Am I treating my dearest, kindest friends with injustice or ingratitude in writing thus?"

"Uncle Milt is very, very kind to me ; and, oh, how I wish he were more like my darling father, that I might love him in his place ! But, oh, there is a space in my heart that is always yearning to be filled and yet never will be ! for where shall I find a second father? Oh, how I need his counsel ! He alone could tell me what my life should be. Sometimes I long that I could treat Uncle Milt as a father, but he will not let me. Oh, I feel very lonely ! "

"Starr King occupied the head of the table opposite us. He is a very pleasant man, of winning and genial manners and ready repartee."

"That 's the best I can do to-night, and I am sure it is very bad. Nothing I despise more than bad poetry, and I cannot help rhyming, though knowing what a fool I am making of myself."

"The fact is, Aunt Corda is becoming decidedly misanthropic. I know not sometimes what is the matter with her. There is nothing sunny and joyous about. She is indifferent to every one. I love Aunt Corda passionately ; she is very, very kind to me. . . ."

" I trust then to begin a course of History, — one thing needful in a person who pretends to the least education, and something in which I am wofully deficient. I think that I am more interested in Biography and Metaphysics than any other styles of reading. Philosophy in any form is delightful to me. Poetry is gradually winning a good-sized place in my heart.

" I am losing all my taste for the languages. The longer I live the more I desire to become acquainted with homely English and its army of invincible writers. I find that these furious students of the modern languages devote so much time to them that they neglect their mother tongue. The system is all wrong ; I for one shall not follow it. Were I able, I should continue Italian."

" Uncle Milt is talking rather seriously about Europe ; but if he goes I do not know that he will take me ; or if I should be invited I do not know that I ought to go, leaving poor little mother all alone. I feel that this climate is injuring me, that I cannot be well here, and that the East winds may kill me. But to go to the South or West, live and be slighted, as I know I should, without the least sympathy or appreciation, would be as fatal as the East winds. There is nothing left me but Italy ; and that is a doubt, almost a myth. I hope for the best, and do nothing. This is not right ; I ought to scribble daily, and see if I cannot bring forth something worth being the author of. It is difficult to get up any enthusiasm here where no one is interested or spurs me on, and writing ought not to be mechanical. The other day, upon returning from Boston, after having become excited over Miss Cushman, I shut myself up and wrote some verses to her in a very short time, copied them, showed them to Aunt Corda, who said they were the best I had ever written ; sent a copy to Mr. Clapp of the ' Gazette ;' and next time I called upon Miss Cushman left a copy in her room. I did this to find out whether they were good or bad. Miss Cushman tells Mrs. Mears that the verses are very clever indeed ; the 'Gazette' publishes them ; Lincoln Emerson, a finely educated man and teacher, says they are good ; Mr. Spofford, I hear, acknowledges something approving ; I hear something else. What am I to infer? That they are trash, or good enough for me to try again? 'Alas ! poor Yorick !' I will persevere in spite of everything, and wait for time to bring approval. I cannot think that I have all this desire for authorship, all this love for it, and yet no glimmering of talent. I should be perfectly miserable if I thought that I could never write. I can better bear the thought that I can never sing, and this makes me think that I can or will write better than I can sing. After all, I prefer the fame of an author. The singer or actor, if successful, reaps golden harvests, is fêted for the time being ; but death knocks at the door and drives away friends, fame, all. No sooner dead than forgotten. A few remember the genius ; but the next generation know of no such person, save that the 'Cyclopedia' devoted a few lines to her, and some author may refer to her as having been great. How fleeting, how sad, is such fame ! But the author, how different ! He makes not a fortune, perhaps, his life may not be so great a triumph ; but his brain-work is strewn all over the world, he is everybody's friend and companion, everybody loves him, he is a universal benefactor ; and death, instead of ending his career of good, gradually increases it, until his name becomes most sacred. No fame is so lasting as that of a great author. Marble crumbles, canvas defaces, the voice is hushed, action still, but thought is eternal ; books must be renewed. Viewing it in this light, there can be but one choice ; but if I could be both, this is what I long for. Are the two incompatible? I think they minister one to the other. And then it must be so glorious to inspire thousands of people instantaneously with the same feelings by which you are excited ; to sway so many human beings by a power superior to them. Oh, it must be sweet to taste, as delightful as it is fleeting ! If I must make a choice, it will be for authorship, — that is, if I have the necessary materials to work with. I wonder what the future will bring forth. It is well, perhaps, that I cannot read it."

Tuesday, June 22d. This morning I received a cunning little note from Charlotte Cushman. She says she will write again. Oh, if I could only have a European correspondence with her, how delightful it would be *for me*, probably a bore to her. I intend to reply to this note to see what it may call forth on her part. She has a bright mind.

I feel that I ought to write for myself. I cannot keep this sensation out of my mind. It worries me that I cannot decide upon any one thing as a profession, and I know not whether my indecision is owing to my want of character or the undeveloped state of my faculties. No one could render me a greater service than to inform me if my powers are in the zenith or no. If they are, I am a very ordinary person, and can do nothing but teach a primary school. If not, I ought to wait and see what time unfolds. Without knowing which, I am waiting for time and so impatiently that I become almost crazy with misgivings now and then. But work is the only improver. If I do not study, I cannot improve. Sometimes I think that God would not endow man with such vehement aspirations if he did not intend to have them fulfilled. This is my theory, but if every one had this feeling then it is overthrown, for they are rarely realized. Will some friendly spirit impress me with the truth? I have often thought that if Spiritualism were true, my dear father would make himself manifest in some way, but he does not, and this is one reason why I doubt its truth. He was so interested in the subject when alive, that he would endeavor to make us believers. We do not seek mediums, to be sure, for it is too expensive ; but when we did, I, at least, was not satisfied with the communications I received. Spiritualism is strange and more than "passing strange."

Strangely introspective is this for a girl of eighteen. Bettina's letters to Goethe hardly reveal more intricate depths. But the way out of the labyrinth always reveals its clue to eager, aspiring youth, and that of the Cretan designed by Dædalus was not more intricate and involved than the labyrinth of life was to prove to be for Kate Field.

FLORENTINE DAYS

"And day by day the mountains seem to grow
Enwrapt more royally in robes of state
As with the sight of thy young face elate;
And the sun's flush is brighter, so to show
It kissed thee first, to all the world below,
And mounteth guard at noontide as to wait
And know thy happy footsteps are not late."

6

CHAPTER III

O Florence, with thy Tuscan fields and hills
And famous Arno, fed from all the rills,
The brightest star of star-bright Italy.
AUBREY DE VERE.

FLORENTINE DAYS. AT VILLA BELLOSGUARDO. ENTHUSIASM
FOR ITALY. GEORGE ELIOT AND THE TROLLOPES. WALTER
SAVAGE LANDOR. AT CASA GUIDI WITH THE BROWNINGS.

THE open doors that suddenly reveal themselves
in life as one approaches a wall, apparently
blank and forbidding in its positive limitation, are
among the most vivid intimations of the divine
leading. There is no absolute fate or destiny super-
seding the individual will; but the life of aspiration has
its attendant angels, who, while unseen, lead the way
and reveal an ideal existing in the realm of thought
which may be actualized in daily life. Kate Field's
spiritual nature always dominated her outer personality. She was not what the world calls religious, —
she had, indeed, not sufficiently realized the divine
aid that pours itself through form and ceremonial
when genuinely sought; but she had lived the life
of the spirit in its larger sense of intellect and aspiration. She was always in a curiously close relation
to unseen influences whose causes she had not
learned to recognize, but whose effects she felt
wonderingly. There was something in the girl too
fine for the world's coarse uses; and who shall say but

that the father who idolized her was not more potent
to aid in shaping her course from the unseen world
to which he had passed than he could have been
even in the human life? The potency of invisible
causes ran as a strand through the entire earthly experience of Kate Field. Her life was a spiritual
drama. The realm of ideals always lies behind the
realm of action, and to discern those ideals is the true
purpose of life. The stress and storm period which
all young people of keen sensibilities experience to
a greater or less degree in earliest youth had passed
by and left Kate none the worse, perhaps, although
a certain inborn tendency to an almost morbid
sensitiveness always lingered in her. She was alive
in every fibre of her being, and every touch and
tone thrilled, whether the response was discord or
harmony.

There now rose before the girl enchanted visions
of song and Italy. It was suddenly decided that the
one intense desire of her heart should be granted,
— that she should go to Italy to study music. The
Sanfords were going abroad, and the decision was
made to take their niece with them. Kate was in
the first flush of girlish loveliness. One evening
about this time she is described by a friend as appearing in a lilac gown, *décolleté*, sleeveless, revealing her beautiful arms and the fine poise of the head:
the clustering auburn curls tied back in the fashion
of the time, her luminous blue eyes shining, and the
faint rose tints deepening in the animated face.
Florence, that Flower of all Cities and City of all
Flowers, beckoned her on. What wonder the girl
danced on air and gave herself up to the long, long
thoughts of youth!

For always is it true that,—

> " Something sweet
> Follows youth with flying feet,
> And it never comes again."

Dreams of the lyric stage again rose around her like an incantation. The promise of definite musical study under a master caught her away to new life. And still one sad strain persisted, — the parting with her mother, who was then playing an engagement in the South. " Were you only going with us, darling mother," she writes, " but courage! it may not be so long before we meet."

Although music was her first love, literature was her second; and the eager girl, with something of that executive capacity that distinguished her in after life, made an arrangement to write for the Boston " Courier," then edited by Mr. Lunt, a brother-in-law of Dr. Parsons, the poet and translator of Dante. Mr. Lunt was a cultivated man of letters, and a recent tour abroad had brought him into contact with many eminent persons. He offered to give the young girl letters to the Brownings and Trollopes, and also to the Hawthornes and Ex-President Franklin Pierce, who were then in Rome. And thus companioned Kate set forth upon the journey which stamped upon her at this most impressible age images of beauty which sunk deep into her nature, pervading it forever after with that indefinable charm and exaltation which was always felt and which can no more be defined than can the fragrance of a rose. Such experiences in the happy hours of youth lie in character, moulding life.

It was on Jan. 8, 1859, that Kate with her uncle and aunt embarked on the steamer " Fulton," sailing from

New York to Havre. Going directly to Paris, they
stopped at the Hôtel Louvre, opposite the magnificent palace of art whose galleries held Kate under a
spell of enchantment. The Paris of that time is hardly
to be compared to the wonderful city of to-day, and
still, newly transformed as it was by Napoleon, it
appeared in great splendor to the American travellers. The drives through the boulevards, the visits
to celebrated churches and monuments, filled the days
with delight. With her inborn dramatic feeling Kate's
first longing was to see the interior of the Théâtre
Français, the scene of Rachel's triumphs, and on the
evening of January 30, — an evening that made itself
a date in her life, — this desire was gratified. Curiously the play happened to be one which her father
had translated (under the title of "Gabrielle") and
adapted to the American stage. The characters of
the Marquis and Marquise were played that night by
M. Bressant and Mlle. Augustine Brohan with that
marvellous perfection of art that always invests the
Théâtre Français. These fine comedians played with
the naturalness of life in a drawing-room, and with
the entire freedom from the rant that at that time too
largely pervaded the American stage. One morning
Kate passed in the Chapelle Expiatoire erected to the
memory of Louis XVI. and Marie Antoinette, which
is on the site of the old cemetery of the Madeleine.
In this cemetery, as will be remembered, the bodies
of the ill-fated royal pair had lain, from the time of
their execution, to 1815, when they were removed to
the royal vault at St. Denis. "This is one of the
most interesting places I have ever seen," wrote Kate
to her mother of the Chapelle. Mr. Sanford took
his wife and niece to the Morgue, but permitted them

too brief a glimpse to satisfy the girl, who, with a
foretaste of the independence that characterized her
womanhood, took a cab alone the next day, and
had herself driven there, only to flee from a horrible
figure newly brought, which was too much for her
endurance.

One evening in February was made memorable
to Kate by seeing Déjazet, the great French comé-
dienne who had retired from the stage some twenty
years before. By some good fortune for the American girl who was so eagerly absorbing Parisian life,
Déjazet reappeared for a brief season at this time to
astonish the world, and herself as well, with her performance in "The First Arms of Richelieu," in which
she played the rôle of Richelieu himself at fifteen.
Her make-up was so perfect that people forgot
she was a woman. Her costume was exquisite, her
manner boyish, but full of the courtly grace of the
character; and while her singing voice was slightly
worn, she yet held the house with her song, with that
finished power of the great artist.

At the Vaudeville there was then running, as a new
play, "The Romance of a Poor Young Man." Kate
was impressed by it, and wrote to her mother, saying:
"Oh, such a beautiful subdued play! But all for the
man. It would suit Mr. Davenport. And such a
wonderful actor as La Fontaine, who personates the
hero." The perfection of the *ensemble* in French
theatres surprised Kate, as she had never before seen
minor characters perfectly played. On another experience, she thus wrote to her mother: —

"To-day I have been to the Hôtel des Invalides, where
repose the ashes of the first Napoleon. I can give you no
description of the grandeur of this chapel and of the splen-

dor of the new sarcophagus, in which the remains are to be placed, but not for two years. Louis Napoleon is a great man, without doubt. He is determined to leave the Napoleon stamp upon every great work in France. I do not see who is so well fitted to govern this nation as himself. The French need a master. Yesterday the Legislative Session opened with a speech from the Emperor. Not one word in reference to America."

Another Parisian experience was in going to a ball given by Mr. Mason, who was then the American Minister. Kate's gown for this festivity was of white tulle and the traditional blue sash of the *jeune fille* of the day, with her curls tied back with blue ribbon, and she enjoyed the evening with all the zest of a girl who loves to dance, and for whom partners were eager. The treasures of art in the Louvre held her through long mornings, and she was half averse to leaving the brilliant city, when after a few weeks the travellers set their faces toward Rome, embarking from Marseilles and sailing on the blue Mediterranean, with constant views of the Alps, to Civita Vecchia, where they landed and took a coupé in a diligence for Rome, a distance of forty-seven miles, which it took eleven hours to accomplish. The railroad from this point to the Eternal City was completed in the May of that year, but on this second day of March, when the little party whose fortunes we are following set out, the diligence was the only conveyance. They entered the Eternal City by St. Peter's and the Vatican Palace, under a blue cloudless sky; and in the luminous Italian air, the purple hills gleamed like an encircling ring of amethyst. Kate was enraptured with the beauty. " Not Rome," she exclaimed, " but the seventh heaven." She was always keenly alive to the beauty of nature; and from the Italy of her first youth to the marvellous glaciers of Alaska and the wonders of the Yellowstone which she visited in her later life, she was always " alive to gentle influence " in landscape loveliness. " Rome is a thousand times more beautiful than Paris," the girl wrote, feeling at once that intense love for Italy that always remained in her life. The enchantment of early spring, bursting into bloom and fragrance, was over Rome, and the girl breathed the air in mute ecstasy. That wonderful view from the Pincian hill where the sunset splendor is seen beyond the dome of St. Peter's; the long and picturesque flight of steps that led up from the Piazza di Spagna to the Via Sistina; the glory of alabaster and gold in the rich temple of St. Paul's outside the walls; the Italian landscape with all Rome in the valley below, as seen from the heights of the Janiculum, — all these held Kate as under a magic spell. There were drives on the purple Campagna with its air of sublime desolation; there were descents into the catacombs of St. Calixtus; there were the pilgrimages to churches and paintings. There was a morning in the impressive Coliseum, with its oval glass windows for a roof, where one gazes into the infinite depths of blue sky. Oh, that first experience in the Eternal City! Can any other word or moment in life ever efface it from its supreme rank in memory?

The Sanfords were fortunate in securing a furnished apartment at No. 61 Via del Babuino. The Carnival was just ending, and Kate participated in the shower of confetti on the Corso, and in the opening days of Lent they all made a flying trip to Naples and Vesuvius. Returning, they began to find out old and new friends, of whom, among the former, were Charlotte Cushman and Harriet Hosmer, who, with Miss Stebbins, were all occupying an apartment together at No. 38 Via Gregoriana. This was one of the most beautiful locations in Rome. The street ran up to the Pincian, the house being hardly ten minutes' walk from that famous promenade, and the outlook from it at that time included a grand view of St. Peter's, with all the picturesque outline of the city and purple Campagna stretching away into azure distance. In front lay the Mignanelli Gardens, and the sculptured Madonna of the Column of the Immaculate Conception was silhouetted against the deep blue sky. The vista included the Castle of San Angelo, the far away heights of San Pietro, and the famous sculptured gateway of the Villa Pamfili Doria. These, with the gray old Coliseum and the lofty tower of the Capitol bathed in the golden sunshine, shot through with azure lights, made up a picture which held Kate in a rapture of enjoyment.

Miss Cushman welcomed Miss Field and the Sanfords with characteristically warm-hearted cordiality. " Miss Cushman rushed down upon us the moment she found we were here," wrote Kate to her mother. " She looks as bright and well as possible." Invitations to social festivities poured in upon the travellers, and Kate writes of the charming way in which Miss Cushman sang some English ballads and a brogue song at an evening party. " Hattie Hosmer came in last night about midnight," Kate writes, " and later we drove her home. She is praised by every one here, — a universal favorite. . . . The air is so delicious. Now I am off for St. Peter's with

Miss Cushman." The great actress was noble in her
friendships as well as in her art, and in all her after-
life Kate never forgot the kindness that made her
first experiences in the Eternal City so beautiful.
Young as she was, Kate's distinctive individuality
made itself felt by every one. " She was always a
personage, even as a girl of sixteen," Mrs. Edwin P.
Whipple has said of her; and she united the somewhat paradoxical qualities of being very womanly in
her early girlhood, and of retaining the freshness and
simplicity of the girl in her later womanhood. Life
was new every morning and fresh every evening to
her. She lived always in that region of spiritual
progress where perpetually new experiences keep
life in freshness and exaltation. On one of these
evenings, in Rome, Kate saw Salvini for the first
time. The play was " Othello." " He is superb,"
writes Kate to her mother, " very tall, handsome,
and a superior tragedian."

Kate became wholly enamoured with Rome. She
writes : —

" I like it, I love it, and I only wish I could remain here
for months. The weather is charming, the sky is so blue.
The carnival was glorious, and I was in it all the time, and
what fun I did have. I was in a carriage with a boy's hat
on, the only one in the Corso. I have just sent a letter in
rhyme to the 'Courier.' I am having singing lessons of
Sebastiani, and if I only enjoy these for a month, it will
still be a great gain. . . . Last Sunday I went with Miss
Cushman, Miss Stebbins, Hattie Hosmer, Mr. Ward, a
young sculptor, and Mr. Ned Cushman, to a picnic at
Hadrian Villa (six miles out of Rome). We had a glorious
day among the ruins, the mountains, and the wonderful sky.
The country around Rome is made for drives and rides."

Again the girl writes to her mother : —

" Miss Cushman wants me to go to England this Spring, but I want to study with Romani in Florence. Miss Stebbins is a noble woman, and has certainly a great talent for sculpture. The Brownings are here, and have been all winter. Hawthorne and President Pierce have just arrived. Rome agrees with me so much better than Paris. Then the green fields, the ruins, the paintings, the sculpture, all the life I love so much. If only you were with me, darling mother. There may be a bright future for us."

One evening Miss Cushman gave a musicale for Kate, who was herself asked to sing. The famous hostess had no idea of anything more than a schoolgirl's performance, and her friend Miss Stebbins said of the surprise she felt in Kate's voice and expression : " I wish you could have seen Meg Merrilies open her eyes. ' Why, I am completely amazed, Kate ! You sing beautifully. You have charmed every one,' she exclaimed." Among Miss Cushman's guests that evening was Levasseur, the famous comedian of the Palais Royal in Paris, who sang some acting songs in a manner that delighted the company with his inimitable art.

" Miss Cushman says Garcia, in London, is the finest teacher in the world," writes Kate to her mother, " and urges uncle and aunt to leave me in England. I am crazy to be at work. I want to see what effect the change of climate will have on my voice, and I am so anxious to be independent, and have my dear little mother in a position worthy of her tastes and talents. I shall never feel comfortable until I am my own mistress and have an occupation. Not that I do not enjoy the present ; not, indeed, that I do not appreciate my opportunities ; but I feel that if anything is to be done now is the time, and Aunt Corda has become willing that I should go on the stage as a profession. I am afraid there's no chance for me, but I hope for the best. Rome is no place for music, Naples is better, but I want to study in Florence with Romani. . . . President Pierce called on us yesterday. He was very polite, but does not seem to be a man of much fun."

The Brownings had arrived in Rome in the late December of 1858, and had been for some three months settled in their apartments at No. 43 in the Bocca di Leone when Miss Field and the Sanfords reached the city. On New Year's Day of 1859, Mrs. Browning, writing to Ruskin, said : —

"What would this life be, dear Mr. Ruskin, if it had not eternal relations? For my part, if I did not believe so, I should lie down and die. Nothing would be worth having, certainly. But I am what many people call a mystic, and that I myself call a realist, because I consider that every step of the foot or stroke of the pen here has some real connection with and result in the Hereafter. I believe in a perpetual sequence according to God's will, and in what has been called a ‘ correspondence ’ between the natural world and the spiritual."

In these words is expressed something of the beautiful and helpful influence which was about to come from Mrs. Browning into the life of Kate Field.

There was then living in one of the villas at the height of Bellosguardo a very interesting and accomplished English lady, Miss Isabella Blagden (" always called Isa by her friends," as Mr. Trollope says in his reminiscences), who was the most intimate friend of Mrs. Browning. The villa overlooked the Valley of

the Arno, and Florence, set gem-like amid the purple
hills. Looking over the city and its cypress-covered
slopes Fiesole was seen, and the view is one of the
most enchanting in Italy. From the bleak New England winter to this fair loveliness of the Italian spring,
which intimates its approach as early as February,
made a rapture of delight to the young girl. With
her passionate love of music she was inclined to
measure every one from the standard of musical culture, and one smiles to read, in one of her letters to
her mother, this mention of Mr. Browning: —

"Mr. Browning is the person whose good opinion I am
most anxious for, and to whom I am already very much
attached. He feels music, and I should like to sing before
him. There is something about him that I fancy marvellously. Last night he said to me, ' You are very ambitious ;
you are the most ambitious person of my acquaintance.' I
laughed and asked him how he had arrived at such a conclusion. ' Oh, I can tell by your eyes,' he said. ' How
so?' I asked. ' I can detect it in their glisten,' he replied.
' Well,' I said, ' it is no great crime to be ambitious, is it?'
' No, indeed,' he returned ; ' I admire it ; I would not give a
straw for a person who was not.' "

A little homesickness came over the girl at times,
and she writes to her mother: —

"You are mistaken when you think I can take care of
myself. I don't like to ; I want some one to love me, to
take an interest in me, some one to whom I can say, What
do you think? some one to kiss and tease and scold me."

It was fitting that love should first come to her in
the romantic atmosphere of Italy. Here she met a
young artist whose presence thrilled through her

days and dreams, and a new chapter opened in her life, not less determining, it may be, although it did not end in marriage. Neither ever married, and curiously both died within the same year.

Kate threw herself ardently into her press letters and writes to her mother that she has never shown any of them to Mr. Browning, but that Miss Blagden has told him of her efforts. " I could not possibly show one to him, he is too great," she writes. " But to show you what kind hearts Mr. and Mrs. Browning have, I send you two notes that they sent me yesterday with Landor's autograph. I wrote them a few lines thanking them for a letter of Lytton's. To Miss Blagden Mrs. Browning writes of me as '*dear* Miss Field.'"

Under the celebrated Italian master Romani, Kate made progress in her musical study. She entered with ardor on "Don Pasquale" to learn it by heart, with absolute assurance, and to express the words in her countenance. " If I can once break through the ice of my face," she writes, " I shall be rejoiced." She made constant advance, but she was as self-distrustful as she was earnest. The effect of so passionate an intensity for any form of art is to produce inevitable self-distrust on the part of the student. In one of her letters from Florence she says : —

" Every Monday evening we go to the Trollopes and there meet a half dozen Italians, politicians, literati, etc. Dall' Ongaro gave me his new book of poems and looked unutterable things at me, but he can't make an impression to save his life. Last Monday slavery was attacked, and I, an American, in the mingling of Italian, French, and English, had to maintain my country against seven adversaries. Foreigners cannot understand the ' peculiar institution,' and that it is no child's play to free 4,000,000 blacks. The English, the very creatures who forced it upon us, are most bitter against us. Mr. Trollope is such a fine man. His wife is promiscuously talented, writes for the Athenæum, composes music, translates, etc., but does not go very far in any one thing. What do you think Mr. Jarves said the other day? 'It is impossible for you to lie. You have a tell-tale face.' And then again, 'I should like to see you when you are thoroughly smashed' (meaning in love). 'Why?' 'Because you will love with so much earnestness and passion.' We were all talking about love. I could not but laugh and think how different you viewed me, as one devoid totally of sentiment and passion. People here think me so full of passion and truth."

This judgment of Kate was the true one. Her nature can only be described as that of fire under ice, or as flame through alabaster. She had the intensity that can only be compared to that rate of vibration which is so far beyond the vision of the eye as to appear motionless.

During the past two years of this period, her range of reading had been of a character to stimulate and develop her powers in a lofty way. Her note-books show her citations from Dante, Shakespeare, Coleridge, Cervantes, Mazzini, Carlyle, Heine; and she had entered into a speaking acquaintance, at least, with the great Latin poets through translation, before Mr. Landor's offer to teach her Latin led her into a fairly adequate familiarity with them in their own tongue. Often does the selection of a quotation unconsciously offer a key to the inner life, and in the line, —

" O, they love least that let men know their love,"

which Kate copied from the "Two Gentlemen of
Verona," there is more than a hint of her own nature.
Again, on a page of these note-books, which are
rather remarkable in their range as representing the
intellectual life of a girl of seventeen and eighteen,
one finds this selection: "Hesiod as quoted by
Aristotle divided the world into classes: the first
have sense of their own; the second the sense of
their neighbors; and the third have neither the one
nor the other."

Emerson was to her opening life a vital inspiration,
and her note-books show hosts of pages copied from
his essays and then translated into French. She
read George Sand's "Consuelo" in the original, and
records the curious impressions that it made on her.
Emerson's poems, too, — the noblest poetic work
that has ever been produced in America, — appealed
deeply to this high-souled girl. She had copied such
passages as these:

> "Give all to love!
>   Obey thy heart;
>   Friends, kindred, days,
>   Estate, good-fame,
>   Plans, credit, and the Muse, —
>   Nothing refuse."

And again: —

> "I hold it of little matter
>   Whether your jewel be of pure water.
>   A rose diamond, or a white;
>   But whether it dazzle me with light."

Another quotation from some classic author runs:
"Honor and virtue are ornaments of the soul, without
which the body, though it be really beautiful, ought
not to be thought so."

7

There are hundreds of pages full of the choicest
selections from choice literature, which she copied,
and out of this mental food the girl's mind assimi-
lated a store of what became transmuted into her
character.

> " The high that proved too high,
>   The heroic for earth too hard."

Fortunate is youth when it feeds on such thought
as that represented by the note-books of Kate Field,
for it becomes " music sent up to God," and is constantly creating for the one who possesses it the
larger and fairer world into which the soul enters
and lives.   It is since Kate Field has gone from this
part of life that the wonderful poem from Stephen
Phillips has appeared, with its tragic portrayal of
the death of a soul: —

> " She felt it die a little every day,
>   Flutter less wildly and more feebly pray.
>   Stiller it grew ; at times she felt it pull
>   Imploring thinly something beautiful,
>   And in the night was painfully awake
>   And struggled in the darkness till daybreak."

Yet something of the instinct to guard against this
spiritual suicide stirred in the young girl, and she fed
her soul on the loftiest literature of thought.   Reading is largely the fibre of which the mind creates its
quality, and the choice made is an unerring indication
of the inner life.

Into the cause of Italian liberty Kate entered with
all her heart.   In allusion to the varying fortunes of
her American press correspondence, she said, " I
want to write in a paper which does not assert that
Liberty is too good for Italy."

In the late winter of 1860, Mrs. Field joined her

daughter in Florence. " I am almost happy," writes Kate to her Aunt Corda; " I believe at last I have a mother." The idolized young aunt was necessary to complete her happiness, and in reply to a letter explaining an unforeseen delay in Mr. and Mrs. Sanford's arrival Kate wrote to her aunt: "Your letter gave me more than one twinge about the heart, but I must, I must, I must submit to destiny, so I'll no longer implore for that which will not be granted. You know how I long to embrace you — here let it end." She explains further to her aunt that she is in no need of new clothes, as she is not going into dress society, and adds: —

"Mrs. Jarves has asked me to go to the masked ball at the Veglio, which I hope to do, as much to see to write a letter about as anything. James T. Fields and wife are here, and I have made their acquaintance. She is very pretty and has been more than kind. He tells me he knew dear father, and speaks of the pleasure he had in reading my letters. Learning that I no longer write for the 'Courier' he said, 'You're just the person for the "Transcript." Dutton must have you. Suppose you send him twenty letters for $150, and later on you can ask more?' I agreed gladly. How good he is. I write twice a month for the 'Picayune' at $5.00 a column. Mr. Fields is an inimitable story-teller. They go to Rome to-morrow, as do the Stowes. I like Mrs. Stowe the more I see her. Robert C. Winthrop and family are here. Americans are always the belles of the occasion. Not yet singing, I am obliged to learn self-denial; not a bad thing for me, as I expect my life to be anything but a bed of roses."

All through Miss Field's earliest youth there ran this vein of sadness, a kind of prophetic recognition that life for her was to be a ceaseless struggle; that

her destiny was " to wrestle and not to reign." Yet
who, even of those who hold her in deepest tenderness, can regret that she never chose inglorious ease,
but, rather, the unfaltering pursuit of those ideals
toward which the road winds upward all the way?
Once in later life she exclaimed with her characteristic impetuosity: " I 've no patience with the selfish
women who evade every feeling and emotion. Give
me activity and struggle, — yes, even if it means
wrinkles at twenty."

Mrs. Field's gentle loveliness was instantly recognized by Kate's Florentine friends, and Miss Blagden
wrote of her in a note to Mrs. Browning comparing
Mrs. Field with her daughter as a dove who had
hatched an eagle.

It was in this spring that Miss Frances Power
Cobbe came to Florence and took up her abode with
Miss Blagden in Villa Bellosguardo. Mrs. Field and
Kate had rooms in the city almost opposite the Trollopes, and one of their near friends was a gifted young
man " to fortune and to fame unknown," whom the
world now recognizes with acclaim in that transcendent genius, Elihu Vedder. To her Aunt Corda
Kate writes, —

"There is a young American here, Mr. Vedder, very
talented and very poor, to whom I do wish somebody
would give an order. I have translated a sonnet of
Nicolini into blank verse; very blank, I fear, as it is
my first attempt. It is about the Pope and Rome, of
course. I 've sent two letters to the 'Transcript' under the
nom de plume of 'Fie.' Do you think it good? I was at a
loss for a name; mother thought it as good as any. I
think you will be delighted with Milan — people so fine —
Cathedral so beautiful — La Scala so grand — and Liberty

so new there. But poor Venice ! It would make my heart ache to visit Venice while the white coats of Austrians hover over her like birds of prey. Last evening we were at Miss Blagden's, — mother and I meeting Miss Cobbe, Hattie Hosmer, Emma Crow, and young Cushman, the great Charlotte's nephew ; and we all laughed immoderately at nothing, as people always do whenever Hattie Hosmer is present. Emma Crow tells me that Mr. Browning paid me a tremendous compliment the night before she left Rome. I was dying to know what, but modesty forbade. Still this much is pleasant to me and may be to *you*. The Brownings return in May. Miss Cushman does not visit Florence *en route* to England, so they say. Miss Stebbins is at work upon her Lotus Eater, and has completed a 'wonderful' bust of Miss Cushman."

The last day of May of this 1860 was made forever memorable to Kate by her first meeting with George Eliot. To her Aunt Corda Kate writes : —

" Last night we went to the Trollopes and there met the authoress of ' Adam Bede,' and Mr. Lewes, the Life-of-Goethe man. Miss Evans, or Mrs. Lewes, is a woman whose whole face is of the horse make ; but there is something interesting about her, and you feel impressed with her importance. They say she converses finely, she is very retiring — and talked all the evening to Mr. Trollope. I liked Mr. Lewes, who is a very ugly man, but very charming in conversation, so that you forget his looks, and Mr. Chapman, who is a regular good-natured, obstinate John Bull though a young man. I thought to myself, ' Shall I ever have the pleasure of looking upon you in the light of *my publisher ?* ' The Leweses intend to make Florence their home, returning here in the autumn. I hear that Dickens is making more money than ever, has provided handsomely for his wife, and lives very quietly indeed. It is reported of Mrs. Stowe that, having desired to know Dickens, he gave a large dinner party for her, and received her acceptance. Later the Duchess of Sutherland desired her company and Mrs. Stowe went to her, leaving Dickens out and sending him no apology. She called upon him afterwards and he refused to receive her."

Under date of June 6 Kate writes : —

" Miss Cobbe left to-day, to our great sorrow and Miss Blagden's great grief. She is a charming woman, though not so interested in Italy as she should be. In my desire to give her something, and with the limitations of my purse, I bethought myself of the black and yellow Austrian scarf you purchased for me in Rome. I cannot wear the colors of Austria, but Miss Cobbe can, — she feels no compunctions of conscience in this respect, — and she promised to tie it about her neck whenever she preaches unto the ragged schools. I asked her to write me something before leaving, and, behold, she gives me this note : ' Dear Kate, — You have asked me to write something to you. What can I say but that I like you very much ? I believe in you and think you are of the stuff of which realities are made, — if it must be out of Life's hard marble — It is meant to last. Good-bye, etc.' A very aggravating parting gift I call this, for I can't get at the meaning, but I suppose if she believes in me I ought to be content. Do *you* believe in me ? How can any one believe in *me ?* It would be impossible were I known *as I know myself.* Miss Cobbe went to see my portrait[1] and says there are a great many clever things in it. Vedder has introduced a distant view of Florence with Palazzo and the Duomo. This idea pleases me very much."

[1] This allusion is to the portrait that forms the frontispiece of this volume, the original of which is in the Museum of Fine Arts in Boston. It is very representative of Kate Field in her dawning womanhood.

Florence itself captivated Kate's imagination. "What traveller has not mused before Dante's stone," she wrote, "and lingered in Palazzo Buona-rotti?" She welcomed a pleasant opportunity that came to her in being invited by Mrs. Trollope to accompany her on a round of visits to Florentine studios. Mrs. Trollope had contracted to write a series of art papers, and to this end she planned this round. Mrs. Browning was at this time absorbed in writing her "Poems before Congress," which English critics censured while admiring her courage.

Theodore Parker's death had recently occurred, and of memorial portraits of him we find Kate saying: —

"I have seen a photograph of Story's bust of Theodore Parker, which I do not like in the least. Young Hart, the sculptor here, is, they say, making a much better likeness of him. Miss Cobbe has a cameo medallion of Parker, and Mr. Trollope one in plaster. The Brownings have returned, looking well and like angels. What think you, dear? They brought me a beautiful pair of Roman gold sleeve buttons, a copy of 'Poems before Congress,' and photographs of themselves, also a large one taken from Hamilton Wild's pretty painting of Penini on his little pony. Is this not dear of them? They have received mother very kindly, and last night we took tea with them in company with Mr. Landor. Mr. Landor, they say, was quite cross until I came. They also say I always put him into a good humor. In going to the table he came up to me and said, 'Now were I a young man, I should offer you my arm.' 'Why cannot you as it is?' I asked. 'With delight, if you will accept it.' And so we marched to the table. In taking our seats, Mr. Chapman came forward to occupy the place next me, whereupon Mr. Landor exclaimed, 'Don't come between me and Paradise,' and down he sat. It's the first time I was ever told I was *Elysium* Field. Do you take? Dear Mrs. Browning whispered, ' I hope you appreciate the compliment, Kate.' The old man, speaking of years, said, ' I wish I were dead and buried.' ' Buried or not, Mr. Landor, you will always live,' cried I, very much to his amusement. Miss Blagden and I noticed that his beard was cut. ' Yes, I cut it myself. Ah, willingly would I exchange my hair for yours,' said he to me, mine being curled. ' Most willingly would I exchange the outside on *my* head for the inside of *yours*, Mr. Landor,' retorted I, and again he laughed heartily. ' Pray tell me, Mr. Landor, how many times does a man fall in love during his life?' ' Well, every time he sees a pretty woman,' and at this witticism he shouted lustily, then resuming, ' Not that I ever was as fickle as that. Oh, no, I never loved but *twice*. I married to get rid of love, but found *this did not answer at all.*' Once speaking of women, he said, ' Women are all good. I never knew but two bad women in all my life — ah, stop, stop, — I mean *three — I forgot my wife.*' "

About this time these notes reached Kate.

SIENA, August 21, '59.

DEAR MISS FIELD, — Thank you heartily for your kind note. I enclose an affecting little poem, — Mr. Landor's last on his domestic misadventures. It seems perfect as far as it goes, but my wife fancied rhymes would have beseemed so short a composition, and I tried my hand accordingly. Between ourselves, I think my arrangement the happier of the two, for the devil's name is legion in this business. Wife, daughter, and son emulating each other in all that entitles people to the horrible epithet, and you will see I take Mrs. L. by the horns.

Ever yours faithfully,

ROBERT BROWNING.

My dear Miss Field, — I thank you for your excellent words, and also the vision of your bright, earnest face given in the sight of your handwriting. Do observe that the amnesty full and entire, spoken of in " La foi des traités," is just given in France. This is the second phase of the Empire, and to be followed by a larger measure of liberal concerns, which confirms and verifies the book, for the writer, Napoleon, walks under as well as on the earth. Now in Italy he is walking under, but walking surely, and we may congratulate one another in hopes again.

Then for lesser hopes we shall meet on the dear terrace, all alive, I hope, and I also hope you will accompany Miss Blagden, my dear Isa (I can't leave a Miss Blagden so), when she comes to pay us a visit; it will give us pleasure, dear Miss Field, if you do.

Yours affectionately ever,

Elizabeth B. Browning.

A spark of fire may be struck, but if it fall on nothing inflammable, no result will follow. It will simply vanish and leave no trace; while if it fall on tinder, a conflagration may ensue. Thus, with the effects of opportunities and privileges accorded to the individual whose mind is impervious to them. Practically, they do not exist. Opportunity is, indeed, as boundless as the atmosphere, and it is conditioned chiefly by the degree to which the individual faculties are able to appropriate it. By temperament Kate Field was singularly calculated to enter into the most sympathetic and responsive *rapport* with this stimulating life. She was the artist born, and she was so endowed with a straightforward honesty, an uncompromising demand for truth and sanity, that a merely meretricious art would not have enthralled her. She would have had no affinities with a passionate Brompton; she had, even, at this early age, a keen intellectual judgment, and her range of reading had, as we have seen, brought her into close sympathy with classic thought and literature. Her luminous blue eyes looked out frankly on life demanding of it that which was sincere, fine in quality, and of the upward trend. With Landor's Hippomenes the young girl might have said: —

> " the Gods have given me strength
> And confidence; one name for victory."

One June evening Miss Blagden had invited the Brownings and Mr. Landor, together with Mrs. Field and Kate, to tea. The other guests were already present when Mrs. and Miss Field arrived on the entrancing Bellosguardo heights, and as Kate entered she was embraced and kissed by the hostess and by Mrs. Browning. She was radiantly lovely that night, in a pale blue gown, her auburn curls tied with blue ribbons after the fashion of the hour, and a cluster of roses in her belt. As she kissed the ladies Mr. Landor exclaimed, "What, do you intend to stop there?" To the amusement of every one the girl turned to him and kissed him, and he proudly asserted, with the pardonable exaggeration of chivalry, "This is the happiest day of my life. I know now the advantages of being old, and for the first time. Let me hope it is not the last. Had I been sixty years younger, you would not have kissed me, I am sure." Then he laughed immoderately and complimented the girl in Latin phrases. For the lonely old man, with all his classic lore, his elegance of scholarship, his infinite intellectual resources, was still very human and very susceptible to the kindness and

affection which in some moods he affected to despise.
Emerson, visiting him in 1843 at his Florentine villa,
describes him thus: —

"I found him noble and courteous, living in a cloud of
pictures. . . . I had inferred from his books, or magnified
from some anecdotes, an impression of Achillean wrath, —
an untamable petulance. I do not know whether the impu-
tation were just or not, but certainly on this May-day his
courtesy veiled that haughty mind, and he was the most
patient and gentle of hosts."

The tea-table that night was a veritable banquet of
the gods. The reader will recall when Ixion ban-
queted with the gods, he remembered only the pattern of the table-cloth. With the girl who had been
permitted this privilege there was no failure to appreciate the high meaning of this beautiful occasion.
Mr. Landor confided to Mrs. Browning as they drove
homeward that night down the winding slope of the
hills into Florence, lying still and fair under the
golden moonlight, that Miss Field was "the most
charming young lady he had ever seen." Mrs.
Browning told this to the girl the next day, "and
you know, dear Kate," she added, "that he has seen
a great many." Kate listened to this while a sudden stillness swept over her, and she replied, "Dear
Mrs. Browning, there is something of heaven about
him." A night or two later, Miss Blagden dined with
Mrs. and Miss Field, and that evening they all passed
with the Brownings in Casa Guidi. The atmosphere
of sympathetic friendship was very sweet to gentle
Mrs. Field, who had already become a favorite in this
enchanted Florentine circle. Kate carried with her
that night Miss Prescott's 'Granadian Girl's Song.'

Harriet Prescott — now Mrs. Spofford — was then in the dawning recognition of her fame, and her work was watched with critical interest. Of this 'Song,' which Kate carried that night for the Brownings to see, Mrs. Browning said it was poetry, but not comparable to Miss Prescott's prose. "So it seems to me," replied Kate; "I am always thirsty for ideas, and I find few in this; but her 'Amber Gods' has the greatest charm, and she has a wealth of imagery. I long to see her write for great ends, great principles, on subjects where one is not only pleased with beauty of idea, but where the cause of humanity is likewise espoused. She has the beauty of feature and the beauty of flesh in her writings; but she needs, back of these, the all-conquering power of a great truth to be taught."

This girlish criticism held its prophetic keynote of Miss Field's own future work. "Art for Art's sake" never seemed to her a complete aim; but art for humanity's sake; art for truth's sake; art, never limited by mere actualities, but uplifting them to the nobler plane of spiritual realities. Nor was she unappreciative of the brilliant gifts and charm of the writer whom we now know as Harriet Prescott Spofford; she only demanded the highest service for gifts so fine.

About this time Kate read the new novel of George Eliot's that had recently appeared, and of it she writes: —

"I have just finished 'The Mill on the Floss,' and am perfectly content with it. It is vastly superior to 'Adam Bede' in my eyes. The ending has really made me melancholy. It seems to me there is much in my character like Maggie's, and that I shall have just such a struggling existence, I mean morally and mentally."

The June days ran on, and these pleasant little reunions of the *cercle intime* continued almost daily. To Landor Kate went each day for her Latin lesson, and his rugged expression softened, and he became what his pupil called "chivalry incarnate." If he paid her compliments, they were imbedded in the *sauce piquante* of a *bon mot*. One day he dropped his spectacles, and as she picked them up and handed them to him, he exclaimed, " Oh, this is not the first time that you have caught my eyes." A bit of playful verse that he wrote, in reference to the memorable night that she kissed him bears the date, in his own hand, of July, 1860, and is entitled

TO KATE FIELD

Kisses in former times I 've seen,
Which, I confess it, raised my spleen;
They were contrived by Love to mock
The battledoor and shuttlecock.
Given, returned — how strange a play,
And both are, even when night sets in,
Again as ready to begin.
I am not sure I have not played
This very game with some fair maid.
Perhaps it was a dream ; but this
I *know* was not; I *know* a kiss
Was given me in the sight of more
Than ever saw me kissed before.
Modest as wingèd angels are,
And no less brave and no less fair.

She came across, nor greatly feared
The horrid brake of wintry beard.

Regarding this bit of verse, Mr. Browning thus wrote to Kate : —

SIENA, VILLA ALBERTI, July 16.

DEAR MISS FIELD, — I have only a minute to say that Mr. Landor wrote these really pretty lines in your honor the other day. You remember on what circumstance they turn. I know somebody who is ready to testify to double the extent at the same cost to you, and do his best too. And you also know

Yours affectionately,

R. B.

Kindest regards from Ba, as well as myself, to Mrs. Field. The servant waits for this, and stops all expansion of soul.

Italian politics was the absorbing interest of this little group of poets and poet-lovers. Mr. Russell, an English M. P., came to Florence, and was a guest at Casa Guidi. He had much to report of the English attitude. Mrs. Browning, writing to Miss Blagden, said : —

" You are an angel, dearest Isa, with the tact of a woman of the world. . . . I shall agree with you as to Prince Napoleon if it were not that I want the Emperor's disinterestedness to remain in its high place. . . . Out of all, I rescue my fact that Napoleon made the English government acknowledge the Tuscan vote. Don't let Kate put any of this in the American papers, because Mr. Russell was our guest and spoke trustingly to us. He had just arrived from England, and went on to Rome without further delay. Our love to Kate, and mind you give our regards to Dr. Gresanowsky."

This reference of Mrs. Browning's introduces another person who became a factor in the life of Mrs. Field and her daughter.

Dr. Gresanowsky was a Prussian who, for political reasons, had left his country and domiciled himself in Florence, where he became one of the habitués of Casa Guidi. Mrs. Browning frequently had long talks with him as they both sat on Isa Blagden's terrace on Bellosguardo, and to Kate and her mother this liberal and cultivated Prussian became a valued friend.

Landor's friendship for the young girl, whom he distinguished by his regard, increased as the days went by.

" I have always deeply regretted that I never met Shelley," he said to her one day. " It was my own fault, for I was in Pisa the winter he resided there, and was told that Shelley desired to make my acquaintance. But I refused to make his, as, at that time, I believed the disgraceful story related of him in connection with his first wife. Years after, when I called upon the second Mrs. Shelley, I repeated to her what I had heard. She assured me that it was a most infamous falsehood."

Another day he gave Kate the Introduction to his " Gebir " to read, following it, the next day, by a revision, which he sent to her with the following note:

" Again the old creature comes to bother you. The enclosed is to take the place of what I wrote yesterday, and to cancel, as you will see, what a tolerably good critic " (Southey) " thought *too good to be thrown away*, etc., etc. I do not think so, but certainly the beginning of ' Gebir ' is better with

' Kings ! ye athirst for conquest,' etc.

You are not *athirst* for it, but *take it coolly*."

Another little note from Landor which Kate treasured was this revision of a line in his " Gebir ": —

" ' Gebir ' should begin thus : —

'Hear ye the fate of Gebir!'
Not
'I sing the *fates* of Gebir.'"

As the summer grew warmer, Kate and her mother
left Florence for Leghorn, where they were domiciled
in the Casa dell' Ardenza, from which Kate writes to
her Aunt Corda vivid transcripts of the days.

In Leghorn, Kate passed an idyllic summer life, yet
one full of ardent work and purpose. To her aunt
she writes: "Lincoln elected, and you write of eternal ruin. My opinion is just the reverse, — eternal
salvation."

The tendency of youth to proffer advice was not
lacking in Kate, and to some remark of her aunt she
replies : —

"It really is dreadful to think of your not thanking God
and enjoying the many blessings by which you are surrounded. You have health and wealth, and the power to
make yourself friends without number, and also the ability
to be useful. Interest yourself in things of universal interest, — schools or hospitals, or something carried on by
women, and which will call forth your energies and sympathies. You can do any amount of good, and your love to
me is almost as needful as daily bread. Your state of mind
grieves me beyond measure."

Mr. Landor sent to Kate while in this summer retreat a copy of his "Hellenics," with an autograph
inscription not yet faded from the leaf, presenting
it to his "amiable and intelligent pupil, Miss Kate
Field," and she comments on it to a friend : —

"Amiable? I wish I were. Just now I'm being re-
proved for not doing justice to ―― in my last 'Transcript'
letter ; but when I think of worthy Mr. Ball in Boston, and
of unworthy ――, with his pockets full and his head empty,
I get indignant."

The impetuous, high-souled girl had the defects of her qualities, and, like many another enthusiast, in early youth she looked on a far from ideal world with the exclamation, " That ever I was born to set it right! "

There is a tinge of both Hamlet and of Don Quixote in most young persons who have in them the stuff of which character is made.

Mrs. and Miss Field found in the Casini dell' Ardenza a pleasant group of people, — Count and Countess Rusponi, the Marchesa Romagnoli, and near was the villa of Mademoiselle Talvo, a vivacious French actress. In one of Kate's letters this sketch of their days is given : —

" Before breakfast we walk a little ; after it comes the mail, that always brings me papers and letters from almost the four quarters of the globe, which are duly read and digested. Then, perhaps, write a little, or perhaps I chat on the steps. At 12 M. we bathe ; but I have got tired of bobbing up and down under cover, so in a few days I shall begin to take swimming lessons. I am very curious to know how my courage will deport itself. Perhaps ill, as it always does on great occasions. After bathing we sit all in a pile upon the terrace built out in the sea, and laugh and talk there until 3. At 3 we dine ; after dinner, perhaps I write or read or do nothing. At 6 P. M. we make ourselves somewhat decent, and promenade along the ' passeggiata,' as it is called, watching the myriads of carriages from Leghorn and the surrounding villas containing gayly dressed men and women, — for you must know the Ardenza is the termination of the fashionable drive, — or we walk to Antignano, the charming village a mile beyond."

There were frequent dances, and there were evenings when Miss Field was asked to sing ; and a beau-

tiful bouquet was one night offered her as a tribute.
Of this night she writes : —

"We have had another concert, at which Giovacclini
Ricci played the violin most exquisitely. La Talvo sang a
romanza from Donizetti very well. There was a scherzo
for piano ; Madame dell' Imperatore sang a duet with an
officer and 'Mira la bianca luna' with me, but the latter
went badly. I sang 'Ma voce poco fa' and 'Ah ! fors'è
lui.' They seemed to think I sang very well, but I did not
think so. Principessa Argirapolo (a Greek girl) played remarkably well on the piano. We had among our audience
Princess Batellini, first cousin to Napoleon, who is a fine,
talented, and noble-looking woman, though immensely
stout ; her two daughters, who looked like servant girls ;
a Countess who is a second cousin to Napoleon, and who
lives near here, and is very pretty : to me, indeed, decidedly
distinguée. . . . Since then we have made an excursion to
Monte Nero (near here) with a large party. We had a
nice breakfast halfway up the mountain and sang lustily.
Two balls have taken place this week ; the last was the
winding up of the season."

To another concert Kate thus alludes : —

"We had been lingering late in the moonlight, and coming in a rush was made for the piano. The 'Croce di
Savoia' (written for caro and soprano, dedicated to Picca-
lomini, whom I heard sing it last winter) was produced and
played through by three good amateurs, two gentlemen and
a lady, — two at the piano and the third at a broken-down
tin pan formerly a piano. Then the young men sang the
choruses ; but such sticking at the solos ! What was to be
done? I mustered courage and exclaimed, 'I 'll sing
them ! ' This offer was gladly accepted, and 'Croce' was
bised and bised, and da capoed, da capoed ; and when all
was over everybody was very gracious and eternally obliged.

Every evening we are to practise, and every Sunday we give a concert, when all the visitors of the town assemble. 'Una voce come un campanello — perfettamente intuonata,' and many more such compliments I had. This morning everybody bows, so you see I am on the road to favor. It is perfectly delightful to sing in the hall, it is so nice and high, the voice rings through it, and I feel very happy at having so good an opportunity to sing. Mrs. Hanan was the prima donna last year, but this year no one has a voice except myself."

The victories of Garibaldi were thrilling the air, and Kate was in ardent sympathy with the liberty of Italy. A Southern cousin remonstrated with her on some expression in one of her letters to the "New Orleans Picayune," and hoped, as Kate said to a friend, that it "'did not spring from my own convictions, but from the opinions of others.' She little knows me if she thinks I could write contrary to my own convictions," added the girl.

The idyllic evenings of the *dolce far niente* days ran on, and a picture of one of these is suggested in this paragraph from a letter of Kate's to her aunt: —

"Last Monday night twenty-two of us had a grand supper at the famous restaurant near Leghorn. The courses consisted of macaroni made with butter and cheese, oysters, fried chicken, fruit, and fine ice-cream, champagne, and wine of the country. The table was beautifully decorated, and we had a nice time. We sang Brindisi, and at twelve o'clock broke up. We walked home, singing national songs the way along. . . . Miss Cobbe writes me a charming letter," again Kate records, "and says she is very well and very busy, so that her happiness is complete. Miss Blagden writes me that Mrs. Browning is quite overcome by the news of a sister's ill health. Have you read Mrs. Browning's last poem, 'A Musical Instrument,' that appeared in the 'Cornhill Magazine'? It is very pretty."

The August of this summer (1860) was made memorable for Kate Field by her first meeting with Ristori, the great Italian tragédienne, whose friendship was destined to enter as a controlling force and influence all her future. Of the first sight of the great artist, she says: —

"We have seen Ristori in Judith, Mirra, Medea, and in farce. Our delight is intense · a more fascinating creature I never saw, and her comedy is as fine as her tragedy. You could not have seen her to advantage, for I prefer her to Rachel. She is more melodramatic, I grant, but she has greater passion; her love is real love. Rachel was not so superb in the softer passions, nor had she the beautiful figure and lovely face of Ristori. A more mobile expression I never saw; her blue eye looks any color to suit the feeling of the moment, and when she smiles, disclosing pearly teeth, she is angelic. I am transported with her, and regret that we are not able to see her again. What a glorious effect would be produced with Ristori and Salvini in the same tragedy! We have no actors in America; we have no criticism. Italy produces both spontaneously; but a bad Italian actor is the most atrocious conception on earth. Ristori looks more like an American than an Italian, — she is so exceedingly fair and feminine off the stage. I hope Edwin Booth will study the French and Italian schools of acting, and will remember to be natural. Give my love to Miss Cushman when you see her next, and tell her that I sympathize in her admiration for beautiful, good Ristori."

The meeting with the great actress, Adelaide Ristori, who in private life was the Marchesa del Grillo, was the unconscious initiation of Kate Field into a line of work that she was destined to make brilliantly effective, — that of dramatic criticism. To her this branch of literary art was of the highest importance. " A dramatic critic should believe as firmly in the nobility of his calling as the clergyman believes in the sacredness of his pulpit," she said. " If acting is an art, — and the greatest minds have placed it high among the fine arts, — if the stage has such tremendous power for good or evil, surely a critic should hold himself aloof from every influence that is likely to trammel his judgment."

To follow in retrospective completeness a strong individuality through the period of time passed on earth is to become dimly aware of the rhythmic nature of life: the symphonic nature, indeed, one might almost say. For in this life, here, as in a great symphony, one will find a motive introduced in the first movement recurring again and again each time. with different combinations, but still recognizable in its identity. So do the presence and influences of certain persons recur and reappear in a given lifetime. They appear at intervals, like characters in a play; they come and they go, but are always liable to re-enter into that personal drama in which they are evidently among the appointed actors. " We meet — at least those who are true to their instincts meet — a succession of persons through their lives, all of whom have some peculiar errand to us," said Margaret Fuller. " There is another circle whose existence we perceive, but with whom we stand in no real relation. . . . Another circle is within this, one near and dear to us. . . . But yet a nearer group there are, beings born under the same star and bound with us in a common destiny. These are not mere acquaintances, mere friends, but are sharers of our very existence. The times of these meetings are

fated, nor will either one ever be able to meet any
other person in the same way."

It was thus that Ristori entered into the life of
Kate Field. The sum of that Italian summer by the
blue sea — the residuum that remained for Kate —
was this forging of the link that bound her to
Madame Ristori. The problem of fate is an intricate
question; still, life is not made up of blind chance
nor of automatic movements. Every outer event
has its inner cause.

The dramatic personality of Madame Ristori made
on Kate an impression that kindled her imagination
and colored all her future life. It was the source of
her distinctive and important contribution to the literature of dramatic criticism which found its fruition
in such papers as her monograph on "Adelaide Ristori;" her series of three papers on "The Hamlets
of the Stage;" a monograph, biographical and critical, on "Charles Albert Fechter," and others entitled,
"A Conversation on the Stage," "Fechter as Hamlet,"
and "Ristori as Marie Antoinette." All of these,
with the single exception of the latter, were published
in the "Atlantic Monthly," and in the same magazine
appeared Miss Field's "Last Days of Walter Savage
Landor," running through three numbers; her paper on "Elizabeth Barrett Browning," and the delightful transcription of Florentine days called "English
Authors in Florence." This group of a dozen papers
all appeared between September of 1861 and December of 1870. In the paper on Adelaide Ristori Miss
Field thus contrasted her with Rachel: —

"There is no common ground upon which Rachel and
Ristori can meet. Their conceptions of Phèdre may be
compared, but not their genius. Ristori makes a *tour de*

force of what with Rachel was bone of her bone and flesh
of her flesh. She is noble in it; her reading is beautiful,
as it ever is; and some of her points, particularly in the
fourth act, are fine; but we do not feel a character. Ristori's large humanity speaks through it all, and we heartily
wish that ' Phèdre ' had never been translated. Rachel was
fifteen years in mastering the idea of this wretched daughter
of the monster Pasiphae. How useless, then, to look for
an equal work of art from a foreigner, with whom the part
is a comparatively recent assumption! Independently of
predestined genius, Rachel's figure eminently fitted her
for the rendering of Greek tragedy. Drapery hung upon
her as it hangs upon no other human being, her very physical defects making her the more exquisitely statuesque.
Rachel's effects depended greatly upon her poses, — her
poses depended upon her drapery, the management of
which had been one of her profoundest studies. She
knew the secrets of every crease in her mantle. Every
movement was the result of thoughtful premeditation. A
distinguished painter once said to us: 'I never studied
my art more carefully than I studied Rachel. I watched
her before and behind the curtain, and so narrowly, that,
while one action was going on, I could see her fingers
quietly, and to all appearances unconsciously, making the
folds by which she shortly after produced a beautiful effect
in what the public considered a spontaneous pose.' This
is plastic art, and Rachel was mistress of it. Of course,
Ristori has little or none of it in 'Phèdre.' Impulse is death
to it, and no amount of pictorial genius will produce results for which years of practice, as well as of thought, are
required."

In her "Conversation on the Stage," Miss Field
struck the keynote of the dramatic dialogue which
she afterward used so effectively in producing her
comediettas. After the fashion of Landor's " Imagi-

nary Conversations" and Mr. Story's pleasant "Conversations in a Studio," Kate expresses her own speculative views and observations in the discussion of two characters whom she calls *Vif Esprit* and *Sang-froid.*

The influence of Landor stimulated Kate's literary inclinations as that of Ristori did her dramatic tastes. Charles Caryll Coleman had painted for her a study of Landor's head, which, as the last portrait ever painted of him, has an enduring interest. Kate introduced the subject to Mr. Landor, and she afterward related the conversation as follows: —

" 'Mr. Landor, do you remember the young artist who called on you one day?'

" 'Yes, and a nice fellow he seemed to be.'

" 'He was greatly taken with your head.'

" (Humorously) — 'You are quite sure he was not smitten with my face?'

" 'No, I am not sure, for he expressed himself enthusiastically about your beard. He says you are a fine subject for a study.'

" No answer.

" 'Would you allow him to make a sketch of you, Mr. Landor? He is exceedingly anxious to do so.'

" 'No. I do not wish my face to be public property. I detest this publicity that men nowadays seem to be so fond of. There is a painting of me in England. I have been urged to allow my portrait to be inserted in my books, but never would I give my consent.' (Notwithstanding this assertion, it may be found in the 'Lost Fruit.') 'It is a custom that I detest.'

" 'But, Mr. Landor, you had your photograph taken lately.'

" 'That was to oblige my good friend, Browning, who has been so exceedingly kind and attentive to me. I could not refuse him.'

" 'But, Mr. Landor, this is entirely between ourselves. It does not concern the public in the least. My friend wants to make a study of your head, and I want the study.'

" 'Oh, the painting is for you, is it?'

" 'Yes. I want to have something of you in oil colors.'

" 'Ah, to be sure! The old creature's complexion is so fresh and fair. Well, I 'll tell you what I will do. Your friend may come, provided you come with him — and act as chaperone!' This was said laughingly.

" 'That I will do with pleasure.' "

The nobility of Landor's head is admirably depicted in this portrait.

October found Mrs. and Miss Field again in Florence in the Piazza Pitti opposite the Pitti Palace and very near Casa Guidi. Kate's health was improving slowly, but she had then, as all through her life, a delicate physique, upheld by a steel-like nervous force. " I don't know what it is to be free from — not exactly pain, but uncomfortableness," she writes; and the cause is not far to seek in the conjunction of an originally delicate constitution and the pervading order of un-hygienic living of those days. " I am not unhappy about myself, however," she wrote, " but about Garibaldi! His declaration that the two Sicilies shall not be annexed to Piedmont until he has marched through Rome sounds like a hot-headed boy. The sooner Italy is consolidated, the better will be her position with other Powers. . . ." The letter runs on : —

" I 've finished the first two volumes of Gibbon, and am quite fascinated with him. I am beginning to wake up to a sense of my enormous ignorance, and perhaps if I live I may know something in the course of a few years. After all, considering that I could not do anything in July and August, my time has not been entirely thrown away, for besides carrying on a large private correspondence I have read 'Aurora Leigh,' 'Men and Women,' 'Bacon's Essays,' 'Transformation,' 'Tom Brown's School Days,' 'Three Clerks,' 'The Bertrams,' 'Scenes in Clerical Life,' 'Idées Napoléoniennes,' and the two volumes of Gibbon's, besides dipping into various other books, reading Italian newspapers, writing twelve letters to 'Picayune,' that account of watering-place life that I sent you, and thirty pages of a *something* at which I am now experimenting. I know this is nothing, but it is an improvement on the Kate Field of old. Three months of last year commencing to-day I did nothing except lie on a sofa and be miserable."

Dr. Gresanowsky had become a warm friend of Miss Field, and it was he who secured their apartment in the Piazza Pitti. The prices in Florence then were not high; several well-furnished rooms on the first piano were but twenty-two dollars a month, and two flights higher were four dollars less. But stairs were a serious consideration. His letters playfully recount the details of apartment-finding, and in one the learned Doctor writes: —

"I think it is high time for you now to come back to Florence, as the sea water seems to have a very exciting effect upon you. Such a mania for Ristori, as if she were a solid angel. Oh, womankind! Oh, youth! And what do you say of Garibaldi? And what of King Victor's war proclamation? Miss Blagden has wrapped herself in complete silence."

Finally in November Mrs. and Miss Field changed their abode for a first floor opposite the Trollopes in the Piazza Independenza.

"We are to furnish the rooms ourselves," Kate writes, " the Trollopes kindly volunteering to lend us some furniture to start with, and it is by far the most economical way to live in Florence. The furniture soon pays for itself and the remarkable decrease in the rent for unfurnished apartments is a consideration. Our situation, so near the dear Trollopes, will be a great comfort to us, and the Piazza is by far the healthiest locality in the city."

In these autumn days Kate began her study in music and Italian with renewed zeal. Her health was much better, and the gentle mother's companionship and care were her best safeguards. Florence was thronged with Americans that year, but the little circle of the Brownings, Trollopes, Dr. Gresanowsky, Mr. Landor, Miss Blagden, and Mrs. and Miss Field held their intimacy rather apart. To her Aunt Corda Kate writes: —

"Anthony Trollope is a very delightful companion. I see a great deal of him. He has promised to send me a copy of the 'Arabian Nights' (which I have never read) in which he intends to write 'Kate Field, from the Author,' and to write me a four-page letter on condition that I answer it. The Brownings returned day before yesterday. I sent her a bouquet yesterday and intend calling to-day."

The Christmas of 1860 dawned in Florence in a cold driving rain. Kate and her mother dined with the Trollopes, Miss Blagden and Dr. Gresanowsky being of the party, and she records among her gifts an album from Miss Blagden, and a picture — "a perfect gem" — from Mr. Vedder.

"I made only two gifts," she writes, — " one to Beatrice Trollope and a camellia to Mr. Landor. The old man made us a visit the next day and presented me with *the only copy he possesses* of his works, in two large volumes. They are filled with his corrections and doubly valuable on this account. Was it not kind of the poor old man? A few days previous he sent us some very fine grapes. The world may say what it pleases of Mr. Landor. I cannot but feel a sympathy for him, and certainly his errors have fallen most heavily on himself."

The New Year of '61 was inaugurated by a grand ball given in the Palazzo Vecchio by Signor Recasdi. A magnificent suite of rooms was thrown open and the scene was a brilliant one. Miss Field, with whom dancing was a passion, appeared for a little while in a white tulle ball gown garnitured with silver lilies, but the still delicate state of her health did not admit of long indulgence in festivities. A young American artist, Mr. Greene, left Florence about this time and made a parting gift to Miss Field of a sketch which she thus describes : —

" It is a moonlight scene ; the stars are out, and a meteor tracks the heavens. A troubadour with guitar in hand is serenading his lady-love, who is listening at an open window. The house and figures are in shadow, and fire-flies glow in the dark. The frame is very appropriate, and on the top are carved two bars of music from the serenade in ' Trovatore,' ' non ti scordar di me.' Is not the idea ingenious? Greene is a fine fellow and deserves success. His crayon of me excited universal commendation. I send you a photograph of it that does not of course do the crayon justice. Green took a sketch of Beatrice Trollope also that he presented to her mother. It is an admirable likeness, and Mrs. Trollope is delighted with it. There still remain three young artists, Baldwin, Coleman, and Oliver Lay, all three New Yorkers. Mr. Baldwin will never be an artist, but he is a noble character and very well educated. His father is very wealthy. Coleman is poor and has great feeling for art, — he is very clever in landscapes. Oliver is one of the handsomest and most charming young fellows that I have ever met. He is remarkably mature for his years, is well educated, talks well, argues with originality, is well read, and very imaginative. He has the most wonderful and yet practical dreams that he relates with glistening eyes and in romantic language. They are almost always allegorical. Oliver reads exceedingly well. What he will do in art I can't say, as I have seen nothing that he has done, nor have any of the students; besides, he is a beginner. He is going to Paris to study very shortly. All I know is that he is a singularly interesting boy, and when you see or write to Aunt Charlotte, please tell her the same, that it may be repeated to his mother. He has dined once with us and drops in every now and then. The Trollopes, through me, have invited him to their house, but he has not gone yet. He is eminently calculated to take care of himself. His mother need have no fears for him."

Under date of March 31 of this year, Kate writes to her aunt: —

"Is it really true that Miss Prescott is engaged to Mr. Spofford? . . . Well, I've read 'Sir Rohan's Ghost' and am disappointed. I don't think it nearly as good as her stories in the 'Atlantic.' There is an entire want of anatomical knowledge, if I may so speak. She has a great deal of gorgeous coloring, showing that she possesses to a great extent the first requisite of a writer, imagination, but character-drawing so far she utterly fails in. Then there is an effort and straining at saying clever things in the dialogue which shows she makes her people talk with difficulty. This criticism of 'Sir Rohan' does not take away from my firm belief in her talent, and if she only has the proper advisers

I doubt not a few years will cure her of her faults. The misfortune in America to a young author is that the general tone of conversation is *slangy* and that the least promise of talent calls forth enthusiastic praise unadulterated with that sound criticism so necessary to stifle self-conceit and promote the improvement of the writer. I do hope Miss Prescott will not be spoiled. If she could only come to Florence she would be on the road to salvation. Her technical knowledge of different subjects is perfectly wonderful, and foreign travel would open to her a mine of thought. . . . Miss Blagden's book has arrived, but I have not seen it yet. She is a good creature as ever was. Lady Ashburton got down on her knees to Hattie Hosmer the other day, and gave her a magnificent ring, a ruby heart surrounded with diamonds. Why she went on her knees is a mystery. Is not Hattie lucky? She is fortunate in everything. Is it true that Miss Cushman is to pass the summer in Florence? I hope so."

The Brownings go for a little visit to Rome, and Mr. Browning thus writes to Kate : —

ROME, VIA DEL TRITONE, 28, March 29, '60.

DEAR MISS FIELD, — Do you really care to have the little photograph? Here it is with all my heart. I wonder I dare be so frank this morning, however, for a note just received from Isa mentions an instance of your acuteness that strikes me with a certain awe. " Kate," she says, " persists that the ' Curse for a Nation ' is for America and not England." You persist, do you? No doubt against the combined intelligence of our friends, who show such hunger and thirst for a new poem of " Ba's," and when they get it digest the same as you see. Write a nation's curse for me, quote the antislavery society five years ago, and send it over the Western seas. " Not so," replied poor little Ba, " for with my heart sore for my own land's sins, which are thus and thus, what curse can be assigned to another land when heavy sins are mine?" "Write it for that very reason," rejoined Ba's botherer, "because thou hast strength to see and hate a foul thing done within thy gate," and so after a little more silly rallying and shilly-shallying she wrote and sent over the western sea what all may read, but it appears only Kate Field out of all Florence can understand. It seems incredible. How did you find out? Besides the meaning of all these puzzling phrases, which I quote in the exact words of the poem, that the people who have broken their own chain and climbed a nation's height yet thence bear down with brand and thong on souls of others, are not precisely the English, but those who have a claim to honor in the Old World's sight are likely to live in the New World. In short, you are not only the delightful Kate Field, which I always knew you to be, but the perspicuous creature to whom I am suddenly found bowing down before you as the sole understander of Ba in all Florence. Kate persists, etc. I can't get over it.

To be sure, the Athenæum pretended to make the same blunder for a private pique, but then it had the instinct of its kind, the crawlers, and took care to leave out of its quotations every word of the explanatory prologue I have been laying under contribution. But I thought the friends you "persist" against would read in plain English, and were inclined to pay a moderate attention to that of the divine Mrs. Browning. They precipitated themselves upon this excruciatingly expected work. They read, marked, and thoroughly digested those precious words above cited. They devoutly thanked God they were not called to discuss any of the unintelligible Browning, the husbands stick Jew jordellian stir about, and they came to a conclusion which Kate Field persists against. Browning, the husband, means to try increasingly and grow somewhat intelligible to all of his intimates at Florence, with the sole exception of Kate

Field, to whose comprehension he will rather endeavor to rise than to stoop henceforth ; and so, with true love from Ba to Kate Field, and our united explanations to all other friends, that the subject-matter of the present letter is by no means the annexation of Lombardy and Nice, she will believe me,

Hers very faithfully,   R. B.

Mrs. Browning also writes : —

ROME, Tuesday.

Indeed, my ever dear, kind Kate, you gave me a great fright with the first page of your letter, but from writing herself to you as a shade better, I take heart again and trust it may simply be an attack of grippe. Isa catches cold easily. I am glad she has . . . and do hope that you will be ministering angel enough to let me have a word before I leave Rome. Only if it is n't done spontaneously, don't write because I say this. We shall be gone before a letter of yours could arrive here. We go on Saturday, creeping along the road by Siena, and expecting earth-quakes and banditti as travelling companions. Would that we could hold some magic in our hand which by thinking of a party we hear where you are. At Rome it is very hot and oppressive. In fact, we have overstayed our time. The winter has been mild, and I have had repose for the most part. Now the necessity for effort which comes with the summer frightens me, yet I am better and stronger in body and soul.

My dear Kate, never say that I have cursed your coun-try. I only declared the consequences of the evil in her, and which has since developed itself in thunder and flame. I feel with more pain than many Americans do the sorrow of her transition time ; but I do know that it is transition ; it is crisis, and you will come out of the fire, purified, stainless, having had the angel of a great cause walking with you in the furnace. As to England, a late article in the " Post " has quieted the worst of my fears, and, in fact, the government could scarcely cover itself with apologies up to a certain point.

It has been bad enough, what we have read in the "Times" and elsewhere, of ignoble selfishness on this subject, and listened to Lord Brougham, but we may trust England as under her present political régime for being consistently interested as far as she can and dares. Why blame her? Is it not proved that the Boers murdered themselves, and that the Ionians would but for her tender care, and that the Suez canal is impossible because France and the Nation might get some good by it? Why talk any more after these things are evident? For me, I have done talking, I only groan. Have mercy upon us, miserable sinners, is my form of the National Anthem. So, Kate, you are learning Latin and communing with W. S. Landor, and he feels, as we all do, that you are clever, dear, and good, and that the more we have of you, the better. Give my love to . . . Oh, our photographs, how like you, and how glad we were of your words! And now good-bye till we meet next week.

Very affectionately yours,

E. B. B.

My husband sends his love. He may.

In reply to the urgency of her aunt, Mrs. Sanford, that Mrs. and Miss Field return to America, Kate writes: —

"There are all good reasons for returning home, but there are still more powerful ones for remaining here. I assure you we have not the money to live out of Italy. Here we can exist comfortably within our income, which were it tripled would not insure us a respectable living in America. Were I strong and healthy, and could submit to many inconveniences fighting my own way, it would be different; but I am equal to nothing of the kind, — the

9

greater part of my time is passed in an easy-chair. Distances are so great in New York that I never could walk; and where I pay a dime here for conveyance, I should pay a dollar in America. No, dear; much as I wish to see you, whom I miss more and more as I grow older, much as I wish to have mother surrounded with her own particular interests and family, we cannot leave Italy."

Patriotism was a passion with Kate Field; and most characteristic of her is this expression, written to her Aunt Corda, under date of June 21, 1861:

"You speak of 'feeling apathetic.' Is it possible that any American in times like these can dream of such a thing? You must be ill, or you would be more alive than you ever were before, — invigorated, strengthened, by the grand attitude which America has taken before the world. '*Un grand peuple se relève*,' to use the title of M. Gasparin's good work upon America. The one thing that makes me happy in my far-off exile is the patriotic pride which positively makes me glow with satisfaction. Our house is very hot, our money is almost oozed out, our doubts about reinforcements are great, our sanitary state is none of the best, yet we joy on, content; and if we must starve to save the Union, then let us starve. What are individuals in comparison with the nation's welfare? And you, who are so fortunate as to be a witness to the American regeneration, feel apathetic! Go, armed with the thimble, needle, and thread, and offer your services at the Evans House where the Sanitary Commission is toiling. Quicken your blood by pricking your fingers in the making of drawers and shirts, or even work at home. Without an object in life, no one can be happy; and there are so many calls made upon philanthropy, that no one can say there is no opportunity of being of use. It is my only salvation that I can find food in the politics of the world; they fill up the vacuum that otherwise would yawn for want of friends and activity. On my couch, with no visitor hardly from one week's end to another, I find enough to do to be interested in, and time flies so rapidly that I am terrified at the wicked manner in which I let slip my opportunities. Yet I am not absolutely idle. You want to know what will be the end of this war. I don't think we have any right to look into the future. What we *do* know is that the Union has been betrayed, government property stolen, and the flag disgraced. What we know is that traitors should be punished, property recaptured, and the national flag rescued from dishonor. These three things we know; these three things are right; these three things therefore must be done. What will be the consequences? The consequences of right are *good*."

Kate's patriotism, indeed, cost her what most girls would have held to be too great a price. Her uncle, who was then a millionaire and childless, had announced his settled purpose to make her his heiress. But his sympathies were conservative. He had not the breadth of mind to welcome sacrifice, loss, or ruin if it meant the triumph of principle; and Kate's spirited espousal of the radical side of the war in her press letters, brought upon her his censure and his command to cease. She, however, had the courage that could hold fast to a forlorn hope and assert, " One with God is a majority." He reversed his decision; and the girl who had been encouraged to feel that the ways and means of life were provided, was thus left — in ill health, in a foreign land, a girl of twenty-one — to face the future as best she might, and provide for her mother and herself. Yet was she steadfast and magnanimous always. Her spirit is revealed in this passage from a letter to her aunt about this time: —

" You are good enough to say that if we are in need of the *necessaire* you will accommodate us; but you forget that your money is in reality Uncle Milton's; and you forget that he would not respect me, nor I respect myself, did I become still more indebted to him when his feelings towards me are as they are. Put yourself in my position and ask yourself if I am not right. Were we able to live independently of you in America, and there was a hope of my being able to refund the sum advanced, the inducements to return home would be so great that your proposition would be accepted; but there is no such hope, I am sorry to say. *You* know that my feeling towards Uncle Milton has ever remained the same."

These family matters are not literary material, and this reference is only made as it involves a fact bearing on Miss Field's life. Mr. Sanford, although conservative and devoid of the heroic nature, was a man with many admirable qualities; and the development of the future of his gifted niece was nobler and greater in that she was left without his inheritance.

Of Landor at this time she writes: —

" Mr. Landor comes to see me every day, bringing me flowers, books, etc.; and although I have the very highest respect for his intellect and derive advantage from his visits, yet I do grudge passing every morning to such comparatively small profit. I console myself by thinking that I am pleasing an old man, and therefore making myself useful. He sent me yesterday all the manuscript scraps in his possession, which I am to edit and publish after his death. What will Mr. Forster's biography say to this? I endeavored to persuade him otherwise; but he insisted, and I was obliged to accept them in self-defence. Mr. Landor's praise of me is too extravagant and absurd to mention. Let us hope that I may never offend him, and thereby become quite as black as I am now white, as is the case with his attached friend Forster. But, Aunt Corda, Mr. Landor is a great man, the cleverest mind I have ever encountered, as well as being the most wayward, — wayward in temper and fancies. There is much good in him. His latest donations to me are a Virgil, a fine Latin dictionary, and Aubrey de Vere's poems, that I fancy greatly."

As the summer again came on, it became evident that there was little improvement in Kate's health, and she began to look, not hopelessly, but certainly with serious questioning, at the future. She loved the dreamy air and the poetry of the golden sunsets as seen from Villa Brichieri, where Miss Blagden dwelt on Bellosguardo; but a haunting fear that she was doomed to invalidism recurred to her and would not be silenced. She was learning, too, that between the two arts that beckoned her with almost equal attraction, Literature was more her own than Music.

With her artistic temperament there was another that responded to affairs; to activities and to a certain universality of interests to which the artist *par excellence* must sometimes close his eyes. As the poet says : —

> " Who loves the music of the spheres,
> And lives on earth, must close his ears
> To many voices that he hears."

That Kate loved the music of the spheres there was no question ; but neither at this time nor increasingly in her after life, could she ever succeed in closing her ears to the many voices. While the art-life is enriched by all possible breadth and extension of interests, there is yet in it a demand for a degree of absolute concentration ; and the nature of Kate Field was one that responded in too many directions to ever permit her to centre her forces on a single line. In her after life this fact was sometimes regretted by her friends; but when the period of years passed in this world is regarded in its true light as the preparatory and experimental stage out of which a more positive and definite life of achievement is to be evolved, it can hardly be other than encouraging to see a nature keenly responsive to progress in more directions than one. Kate's girlish ambition for the lyric stage was, at this period, modified, and she said: "If only I had strong health and no disposition to write, I could give myself to lyric art unreservedly; as it is, I feel that writing is my only hope."

If heredity is a force with which we must reckon, this complication of the girl's inclinations and gifts is not strange when the mixed conditions of the drama, of literary work, and of practical and executive matters that filled the life of both her parents and the ancestry back of them, are remembered. Her father's versatility was to her an inheritance.

The June of 1861 found Mrs. Browning's strength failing, although, until the last day of her life, she did not consider herself sufficiently ill to remain in bed. On the last evening of her life she read the "Athenæum" and the "Nazione," and when her little son kissed her good-night she smiled and said: "I am better, dear, much better." Her death brought to Kate a loss that made upon her an impression never to be effaced. In two letters to her Aunt Corda, dated June 29, 1861, she thus tells the touching story: —

FLORENCE, June 29, 1861.

DARLING, — I am sick, sick at heart, for dear Mrs. Browning is dead. The news was as sudden as it is dreadful, for though she has been quite ill for a week past, yet her health has always been so feeble that I firmly believed she would rally as of yore. I believed that God had more work for her on earth before he called her to fill a glorious place in Heaven. During her illness I have not seen her once, as she was unable to converse, but I went every day, and always the report has been more encouraging. Two days ago we saw Mr. Browning, and he like myself deceived himself by founding hopes upon her powers of endurance. Yesterday Mrs. Browning said that she felt better, read a little in the "Athenæum" and saw Miss Blagden as late as eight o'clock in the evening, who left her with but little misgiving. This morning, at half-past four, she expired unconsciously to herself with the words, " It is beautiful," upon her lips. Poor Mr. Browning was entirely unprepared for the terrible blow. When she raised herself to pronounce her dying words wherein she expressed the glorious life which was opening upon her, he thought it was simply a movement premonitory to coughing. I have not seen him, but Miss Blagden, who is constantly with him, says he is completely prostrated with grief. The poor boy wanders about the house, sad and disconsolate, hardly realizing that his angel mother is no more. We went to the house the moment we heard of Mrs. Browning's death, but could be of no use. All that we did was to buy flowers and consecrate them by placing them around all that is left of one who was too pure to remain longer in this world. They have cut off all her hair, and the emaciated form was heart-rending to look upon. I almost regret that I have seen her in death, only that I do not wish to shun the house of mourning. I am sufficiently callous as it is. Her last act to me was one of kindness, insisting upon our going up to Villa Brichieri with Mr. Browning in a carriage. Almost the last thing that I did in her presence was to kneel before her, and say that when near her, I always longed to be at her feet — and she was so gentle and kind, so loving and unassuming. Her character was as perfect as God permits in the flesh. What Mr. Browning will do, I don't know. His nature is so excitable that at first I fear the consequences ; that in the end this terrible loss will chasten and perfect him, I trust and pray. He who has never had any heavy affliction is now to feel its rod of iron, iron that remorselessly enters the heart and lacerates in the name of the Highest. I cannot realize what has befallen us and the world. The almost last link that binds me to Florence has been sundered, and I long more than ever to be away. Mr. Browning will surely leave Italy, and I should not be surprised did he seek a home elsewhere. Italy and his angel wife are one. Or perhaps for this very reason he will be the more ready to remain. I doubt this. Now I know nothing more than that she is dead, to-morrow we are to learn if anything can be done, and are to do it if called upon. I cannot help perceiving that Dr. Wilson, who was called in owing to the absence of Gresanowsky, and who is most forbidding in physiognomy and is said by some to be a humbug, has hastened Mrs. Browning's death by resorting to a violent practice which her weak body was thoroughly incapable of enduring. He began by frightening her, telling her what a fearful state her entire system was in, — a fine way to treat an imaginative person. Gresanowsky knew her constitution, and it does seem most unfortunate that he should have been absent. Since the medical murder of Cavour, I have begun to distrust all doctors in Italy. Dear Mrs. Browning had reached the age of fifty, and had labored long and nobly for humanity, therefore we must be resigned, and think that her release from a long-suffering diseased body is Heaven's reward for a pure, religious life, religious in the truest sense. I can never forget her, and hope that her memory may lead me to better things than have yet been my aspiration. I thank God that I was permitted to know

her, that I can claim her as a friend, that I may look upward for one more tie binding me to a life hereafter.

FLORENCE, July 1, 1861.

DEAREST AUNT, — I have been completely upset for the
last three days, — the death of Mrs. Browning has unfitted
me for doing anything. We have just returned from her
funeral. We have seen all that is mortal of her buried in
the beautiful Protestant burial-ground outside of Florence's
walls, where lies Theodore Parker. The service was according to the Episcopal form. No discourse. Her life had
been a sermon; she needed no other. It was agonizing to
look on Mr. Browning — he seemed as though he could
hardly stand, and his face expressed the most terrible grief.
The poor boy stood beside him with tears in his eyes, and
when I glanced from them to the pall where their loved
one's remains lay, it seemed as though the sorrow was too
much to bear. I yearned to go to Mr. Browning and weep
with him that wept. The scene was made impressive in
spite of the minister; it was very short, and we were
hurried away by Mr. Trollope. A lovely wreath of white
flowers and a laurel wreath were placed upon the coffin.
The funeral was managed by a friend of the Brownings,
and so managed that no one knew anything about anything.
Orders were given in the greatest confusion during the three
days, and up to this morning I was told that no ladies were
to be at the grave. However, Mr. Browning expressed a
wish that Miss Blagden should be present and all other
friends that desired to; therefore at the last moment I
sent word to those whom I knew would wish to attend,
and in this way there were sorrowing women to mourn for a
great woman. The funeral would have been meagre without them. I thought that Mr. Landor ought to have been
there, and had I known that the service would have been
so short would have gone for him. The Storys came up

from Leghorn ; young Lytton, Mr. Trollope, the Powers, and others paid the last tribute to her memory. There were very few Italians; they were invited to attend, but with their usual indifferences abstained from doing so, indifferent to one who loved Italy with her whole soul and labored for it with her whole intellect ! England and America will mourn if Italy does not. Mr. Browning is almost heartbroken ; last night he did nothing but rush through the house. He says that he will sell everything, settle up everything, and leave Italy forever, — only return to be buried beside his wife. He will probably go almost immediately to Paris, where his father and sisters live. God be with him ! My hold upon Italy has gone. The Brownings were dear to me ; she was a guiding light, and will ever remain so, wherever I may be.

With the breaking up of the Browning household the glory of Florence vanished for the girl who had so deeply loved and revered Elizabeth Barrett Browning. There was for her in the air that subtle feeling so exquisitely expressed in the lines of Bliss Carman : —

> " The old, eternal Spring once more
>   Comes back the sad eternal way ;
> With tender, rosy light before
>   The going out of day.
> The great white moon across my door
>   A shadow in the twilight stirs ;
> But now forever comes no more
>   That wondrous look of Hers."

Yet, withal, while Kate grieved for the inspiring friend who had vanished from mortal sight, and while obstacles and difficulties surrounded her, she was not depressed. In the heart of the artist

> " There's always, always something sings,"

and her preponderance of the ideal nature was her saving grace. Youth and its boundless exhilaration were with her; and although her press letters to America were neglected (the war not unnaturally crowding out all other interests) she took matters with a certain serenity that was doubtless the effect of unseen ministries.

> "We see not half the causes of our deeds,
> Seeking them wholly in the other life,
> And heedless of the encircling spirit world
> Which, though unseen, is felt."

Looking over Kate Field's life as seen in retrospect, one cannot fail to recognize how her father, from the Unseen, guarded and directed his idolized daughter more effectively, indeed, than he could have done on earth.

Mr. Browning and his little son, accompanied by Miss Blagden, left for Paris. Casa Guidi without *her* presence was intolerable to him.

> " Places are too much
> Or else too little, for immortal man."

Just before leaving Mr. Browning sent to Kate this note: —

July 6, 1861.

DEAR FRIEND, — God bless you and yours for all your kindness, which I shall never forget. I cannot write now except to say this, and beside that I have had great comfort from the beginning. I know you are truth itself in all you profess to feel about her. She also loved you, as you felt. I hope to see you soon and talk with you. Meantime ever remember me as

Your affectionate   R. B.

I speak to Mrs. Field also, you understand.

Goethe's mother affirmed that whenever her son had a grief he made a poem of it. The impulse to record the deepest feeling in literary expression is with all writers, and Kate found in the writing of a sketch of Mrs. Browning a channel for hers. This article, which appeared in the September number of the "Atlantic Monthly" for 1861, has long since been conceded to be the finest interpretation that was ever given of Elizabeth Barrett Browning.[1] It will forever remain the one perfect interpretation of Mrs. Browning in its portrayal of the sympathetic divination that so peculiarly characterized her, and as the authoritative transcription of the exquisite life in Casa Guidi. Mr. Trollope read the article in manuscript and surprised Kate by pronouncing it the most adequate and perfect sketch of Mrs. Browning that he had ever seen. Kate wrote to her aunt: "I have sent it to the 'Atlantic,' but of course it will not be accepted, notwithstanding I said I would take no money for what was written as a tribute of love." However, it was accepted, and as in those days the "Atlantic" did not allow its contributors to sign their work, this paper was often erroneously ascribed to Mr. Story, who was a well-known contributor, and whose literary talent and well-known friendship with the Brownings gave probability to such authorship; the circumstantial evidence being as misleading as such evidence has been known to be on more serious occasions than this. However, the semi-annual list of contributors which the "Atlantic" gave establishes this paper on Mrs. Browning as Kate Field's, even to those who do not know the fact from the personal side.

To her aunt Kate wrote: —

[1] A Study of Elizabeth Barrett Browning.

" Mr. Browning has a very severe cold, and the other night he thought he was dying, being attacked by a fit of strangulation. Miss Blagden says the change in his face is marvellous. God help him ! I love him more now for *her* sake. He has just written a reply to my note of sympathy, which I copy for you. ' God bless you and yours for all your kindness, which I shall never forget. I cannot write now except to say this, — and, besides, that I have had great comfort from the beginning. I know you are truth itself in all you profess to feel about her. She also loved you, as *you* felt. I shall see you soon and talk to you ; meantime and ever remember me as your affectionate R. B.' It is a great comfort to have this note, — to be told again that she *loved* me. Oh, Aunt Corda ! hers was such a beautiful spirit that the tears flood up from my heart whenever I think of her, which is very, very often. We went to her grave two days ago. I could not feel that *she* was there. I hope she will think of me sometimes in the other world, and out of her love for humanity influence me for good. I did worship her as a glorious type of woman-hood, — unselfish, suffering, loving, grand. She is not dead to me ; but the absence of her dear face is hard to bear. I am trying to write upon her, but feel how unworthy I am for such a task. We shall probably go up to Miss Blagden to-day. She is very gloomy, of course. To me Florence is one vast Campo Santo ; my hopes in it are dead. It seems as though there was to be a break up of everything.

" We passed several evenings at Villa Brichieri before coming away. Mr. Browning is very subdued, very dear, and has been more than kind to us. He gave mother a favorite shawl that belonged to dear Mrs. Browning, and me a locket that she had before she was married, and of which she was very fond. In the centre is a crystal, in which is her hair shaped in two hearts. The gold around it is a serpent emblem of eternity. I cannot tell you how much I value this souvenir. We went to Casa Guidi to take a last farewell of it. Everything was just as she had left it, — the half-opened fan, the last ' Nazione ' that she had read, the open desk on which she had written all her poems. It was sad, very, very sad ! I felt far worse than when standing at her grave. An artist here has sketched the drawing-room in oils, and has made a most satisfactory picture, not as a painting, but on account of the minute detail. He has put in everything, and the sketch brings the dear room right before you. Mr. Browning is to have it photographed, and has promised me a copy of it. He, Penini, and Miss Blagden leave to-day for Paris if all the furniture of Casa Guidi can be packed or sold in time. Miss Blagden has gotten release from her villa, stored her furniture with Mr. Trollope, and intends to pass a year at least in England. Mr. Browning does not think he shall ever return to Italy, — at least not to Florence. He says he shall never have a home again, but rove about the world. He said he might come to America some time or other. So there is nobody left in Florence but the Trollopes. You can fancy how changed the place must be to me. Dr. Gresanowsky, however, returns in the fall. I have met Lytton, the poet, several times. He talks exceedingly well, and is by no means a snob. I like to hear him converse, for there is no doubt about his being exceedingly intellectual, and he puts forth his best powers before Mr. Browning, whom he adores ; but I don't like the man as a man. Although under thirty, he has the broken-down appearance of a *blasé* man of fifty. You can read dissipation in his face and in his stooping figure and shuffling gait. He is weak in character, and this one sees most readily in his poetry. There is nothing vigorous about him, nor is there anything lofty in his aspirations. There never was greater contrast in persons, as well as mind, as between him and Mr. Browning. I pity Mr. Lytton, for he has misused his life ; but there is an inherent

want of truth and candor about him that prevents him from
ever obtaining the respect of honest, earnest natures. He
has lately written a review on Mr. Browning."

Out of this apparently dissolving fabric of life new
combinations were to arise. Friends are taken from
us; circumstances change like the baseless fabric of
a dream; the skies fall upon the ruins of our personal world, and then out of this wreck and ruin
suddenly arises, like a dream of enchantment, a new
world that brings with it, in essence, all that is best
of the old. "The flowing conditions of life," says
Emerson; and how true to actual experience is that
description.

" Who thinks at midnight morn will ever dawn ?
　Who knows, far out at sea, that anywhere is land ? and yet a
　　shore
　Hath set behind us, and will rise before."

The truth of these words was to fulfil itself to Kate
Field. Her Florence had crumbled before her eyes;
her health was very uncertain; the financial reliance
she had been encouraged to feel had been withdrawn
because she had given full expression to her ardent
espousal of the cause of the Union; the war closed
for the time the literary market; the dreams she
had cherished of lyric art were abandoned; the one
beloved friend, Mrs. Browning, was taken from her,
and the beautiful life in Casa Guidi was no more.
Yet something whispered to the girl to be of good
cheer.

" Mortal, they softly say,
　' Peace to thy heart.
We, too, yes, mortal,
　Have been as thou art,

Hope-lifted, doubt-depressed,
    Seeing in part,
Tried, troubled, tempted,
    Sustained as thou art.' "

Out of the chapters of experiences that make up
life there always remains a certain residuum. The
outer events vanish; the ideas and purposes developed remain. In Kate Field's life the Florentine
influences were to germinate and grow. They entered
into her mind, moulding her character. They were
to find their inflorescence in a certain exquisite grace
that always invested her; in a purity of purpose and
nobleness of quality which became the very fibre of
her being.

In the purely literary sense, also, this period had a
rich fruition in her grasp of the themes embodied in
her series of papers in the " Atlantic Monthly " between 1861 and 1868, comprising her article on Mrs.
Browning; the three entitled " Last Days of Walter
Savage Landor; " the charming sketch, full of color
and character-drawing, entitled " English Authors in
Florence; " and others, including " A Conversation
on the Stage," " Adelaide Ristori," and " Fechter as
Hamlet." All her life was she to draw sweetness and
inspiration from this charmed period of her youth in
Bella Firenze.

LECTURING AND WRITING

"Thought is the wages
For which I sell days."

Duty, freedom, truth, a divine life, what are they? They are the real things of God, for which all poor temporalities of fame, ease, and life are to be cast to the winds.

THEODORE PARKER.

"Around the one who seeks a noble end
Not angels, but divinities attend."

Kate Field.

From a Photograph, 1865.

CHAPTER IV

O young Mariner,
Down to the haven,
Call your companions,
Launch your vessel,
And crowd your canvas,
And, ere it vanishes
Over the margin,
After it, follow it,
Follow the Gleam!

TENNYSON.

LECTURING AND WRITING. INTENSE ENERGY OF PURPOSE. JOHN BROWN'S GRAVE. RISTORI, FECHTER, AND THE DRAMA. PLANCHETTE'S DIARY. DEATH OF ELIZA RIDDLE FIELD.

ON returning to America Mrs. and Miss Field passed some years in Boston, New York, and Newport without any very settled conditions of life. The summer of 1863 they spent largely at Sharon Springs, and in La Rue Cottage where they were boarding, there was a very interesting and accomplished Catholic priest, Father Fiarotti, between whom and Kate sprang up a warm friendship. The political state of the country interested Kate deeply. The policy of Governor Seymour of New York was then attracting attention and denunciation from the supporters of Lincoln; and in a private letter Kate says: —

" A fine state of mob in New York. How my blood has boiled the last two days! Thank God! Boston has behaved better. Our Governor has not addressed murderers and house-breakers as 'friends.' 'The fact is,' said a New York gentleman yesterday, 'our city is controlled by venal politicians; in Boston there is a government.' Abraham Lincoln can not have sunk so low as to be frightened out of drafting by Seymour and 'the left wing of Lee's army,' as the mob is called. The rioters only help on the good cause of union and liberty."

During that summer Mr. Vedder and Charles Caryll Coleman made sojourns at the Springs, and the pleasant comradeship of Italy was renewed.

Mrs. Field and her daughter changed their location frequently within the succeeding decade. Kate was thinking and writing and planning, and living her daily life with intensity and with purpose. Her circle of nearer friends included many of the most interesting people of the day. Boston was then in the golden age when Emerson and Lowell and Longfellow, Sumner, Dr. Howe, James T. Fields, and Edwin P. Whipple were to be met under the overarching elms of the old Common; when Curtis, Phillips, Garrison, and Lowell were to be heard from the platform; when Mrs. Julia Ward Howe was one of the younger matrons, — a brilliant presence greatly sought and admired; when Louisa Alcott first enchanted the juvenile world with her "Little Women;" when Louise Chandler Moulton was in the early dawn of her poetic fame; when Edmund Clarence Stedman inaugurated his exquisite criticism; when Henry Ward Beecher was the great preacher of the day, and Horace Greeley, Prof. and Mrs. Vincenzo Botta, and Phœbe and Alice Cary were prominent figures in New York life. From these days during her entire lifetime Mr. Stedman was one of the nearest and most deeply prized friends of Kate Field, giving to her appreciation and counsel and sympathy in a measure of which any mere mention conveys little idea of the fulness and strength of the inner current.

It was somewhere about this time that Miss Field became the Boston correspondent of the Springfield " Republican," then edited by that brilliant journalist, Mr. Samuel Bowles. The friendship between Miss Field and Mr. Bowles continued during his life, and one of the most finely appreciative of the memorial tributes to him was written by Kate Field. For a number of years Kate's letters to the Springfield " Republican " were signed " Straws, Jr.," in imitation of her father's signature of " Straws " in his press correspondence. In playful allusion to this pen-name is the following note from Mrs. Annie Fields : —

DEAR KATE, — Three cheers for " Straws, Jr." The letter is capital, — full of spirit from end to end. How glad I am you wrote this letter about Mr. Dickens ! It is such a relief, somehow, to say a little when we feel so much. He told me of the pretty basket of flowers on his desk, and I believe I felt almost as much pleasure as you in the reading. A. F.

Again is there this pleasant note from Mrs. Fields : —

DEAR KATE, — I have just read Miss Blagden's romance, " Agnes Trevor," which, in spite of inaccuracies of style, has fascinated me by bringing all Italy to my wintry fireside and filling the common world with lovely pictures of *un*-common character, yet such as we see slumbering under the mask which too many think is human, Christian — perhaps necessary to wear. . . .

The great Fair held in New York in 1864 for the benefit of the Sanitary Commission was one of the subjects vividly handled in Miss Field's letters, in one of which she says: —

" General Frémont and Mrs. Frémont were there, he looking very intensely out of that eagle eye, and she the embodiment of a strong, brilliant, impulsive woman.   General McClellan also was there, creating a little curiosity and indeed a vastly interesting study to the impartial critic. It were not possible for such a head and face to save a country.   Salvation is not written on a hair or a line, but there are symptoms of incompetency everywhere."

And again, of the art of the day as represented in the donations to the Fair: —

" By far the most hopeful and promising pictures among the rising men are the little interior 'Repose,' by George H. Boughton ; the 'Post Boy' and 'Working for the Fair' by Eastman Johnson ; the 'Prayer' by Hennessy, and a sunny 'Interior' by Charles Caryll Coleman.

" The two hundred pictures that have been donated to the Fair represent almost as many New York artists, and demonstrate not only that art is patriotic, but that it is growing powerful in numbers as well.   Church, Bierstadt, Dana, Vedder, Winslow Homer, Gifford, Samuel Coleman, Kensett, Beard, Whittredge, and Gray have contributed the best work."

Miss Field's letters from Italy revealed her trenchant incisiveness of expression, and her press work of these years shows the growing development of her pungent phrasing.   It was an effervescent style, — arresting at the moment and not unfrequently enriched with a vein of thought and epigrammatic expression worthy of a less ephemeral medium than the

daily press. She had an unusual power of presenting scenes vividly with terse condensation. Abounding in a sense of humor, she served up many a
phase of life with *sauce piquante ;* and her letters
setting forth a dress reform craze that swept over
New York and New England, a Fourth of July in
Boston, the great Peace Jubilee held on the Common, and various features of the season at Newport,
are like a series of instantaneous photographs of
the times. The contrast between the Newport of
1864 and that of to-day is a commentary on the
development of " the leisure class " in America which
might well enlist the attention of Mr. Thorstein
Veblen. One of these letters bears the very Kate-
Fieldian heading, " The Miseries of Pleasure : " while
another invites the reader to " Richmond and Religion," a keen bit of reflection on Jefferson Davis. Of
Mrs. Howe's country house, near Newport, Miss
Field thus writes : —

"Six miles north of Newport, on what is called the West
road, is a charming bit of nature known as Lawton's valley.
It is a most decided valley, steep and narrow, bounded
north and south by rather high hills. Through it a brook
trickles, forming quite a pretty water-fall, above which there
stands an old mill, long unused, which, from the valley
below, looks like the remains of a Swiss chalet. This
valley runs down to the sea ; and here many a *fête cham-
pêtre*, many a pleasant informal picnic, many an æsthetic
tea, have been given by the lady whose cottage and whose
hospitality have given celebrity to it. Here French officers
have danced on the green, youths and maidens have wielded
the mallet of that apparently inexhaustibly fascinating game,
croquet ; grave and reverend seniors have hobnobbed over
great questions, and all the clever men and women visiting

Newport have found their way hither. The valley, attractive though it be, would have few worshippers were it not for its presiding genius, Mrs. Julia Ward Howe, whose name is too well known to require aught but its mention. A recent tea-party there recalls pleasant memories of Henry T. Tuckerman, who, as passionately and rationally in love with Newport as your special correspondent, never fails to pass the summer here, thereby laying the large supply of health required to endure the remorseless demands of a New York winter; of Miss Sarah Freeman Clarke, the artist, whose cosy cottage in the harbor is frequented by all the bright lights that shine steadily or flash occasionally on Newport; of Miss Margaret Foley, the sculptress, who has lately returned from Rome on a visit which will terminate in November. While here, Miss Foley was engaged upon a medallion of Mrs. Howe."

Miss Field writes long letters, too, on the Academy exhibitions in New York in those years. A New York critic had attacked William Hunt, and we find Miss Field — who was one of his truest appreciators — saying: —

"Most incorrect, too, is the statement that Mr. Hunt is a slave to Couture's manner. That he studied with Couture for a time is true enough, but his style of painting is thoroughly un-Couturian. If he must be likened to any former master it should be Millet, with whom he naturally sympathizes, though we believe that Mr. Hunt is an original man, and always thoroughly himself. One artist may resemble another without being an imitator. There is a little sketch in Boston so like Millet in manner that for a moment we attributed it to him, until told that it was by Vedder. At the time it was painted, the artist had never seen anything of Millet's, nor did he know there was such a painter living.

"But these three pictures are Mr. Hunt playing with his brushes, and we blame him for doing himself injustice, in not allowing New York to see his finest work. He has hardly treated the Exhibition with sufficient respect, for though the Academy is absurd enough in many ways, still it is the national institution, and every artist should make it a point of honor to contribute his very best. Though Mr. Hunt's worst may be better than many a National Academician's most pretentious effort, he at least, is too true an artist not to be more exacting with himself than any one else can be. A want of earnestness is not one of Mr. Hunt's faults. Could the critic of the 'New Path' visit Hunt's studio, he would see there works superior to 'Marguerite.' He would see a portrait of a mother and child that, unfinished as it is, would have represented the artist's power far more truly than anything of his in New York. He would see a life-size 'Hamlet,' that ought to have been completed for the exhibition. He would see the portrait of a blonde, beautiful in pose and drawing, Titianesque in color, such a painting as does Hunt credit. He would see, too, a composition called 'Night,' which, though only rubbed in, is fine in idea and vigorous in execution. What the public ought to demand of Mr. Hunt is, that he should finish the work he has begun, and not allow critics to mourn over 'rich possibilities.' Mr. Hunt is great in suggestion, and it will be sad indeed, if he does not carry out his noblest inspirations. But he will."

In this early estimate of Hunt, we find Miss Field agreeing with the later, and the mature and authoritative estimate made of him by his favorite pupil, and afterward his co-worker, Miss Helen M. Knowlton, whose biography of the great master in American art is one of the ablest interpretations of life and genius.

John Weiss was another whom Kate truly appreciated, and of him in this brilliant press correspondence of her youth, she wrote : —

"John Weiss is always in earnest ; therefore whether you agree or disagree with him, he commands your liking and respect. He is saturated with his subject ; he has convictions ; he believes in his opinions. The fire in his soul never burns low. It is always bright and ready to warm the cold, faint-hearted wayfarer. Therefore his essay on the ' Law of Marriage ' inspires, though it does not prescribe a panacea for happiness. He believes that marriage is the best wine of life, and his eloquence makes converts of the willing. To some his theories are too radical ; to others not radical enough ; to the few they are inadequate ; to all, many passages of the essay are beautiful. The scoffer dares not show his colors in the presence of so much genuine enthusiasm. The reader of French novels breathes an atmosphere impossible when under the influence of morbid thought. Mr. Weiss does not describe matrimony as unadulterated bliss, but he does assert it to be the nearest approach to individual completion."

Of Vedder we find this finely critical estimate : —

"By far the most promising artist in America is Elihu Vedder, a native and resident of New York, whose picture, ' The Lair of the Sea Serpent,' is the most prominent work on exhibition at the Academy of Design. After wandering through a wilderness of mediocrity, it renders one speechless to come suddenly upon so much originality of idea and power of execution. At last the myth of the sea has found an interpreter. Criticisms on this painting are loud and various, and though many are repelled by the steel-gray monster that is the only bit of life in a wonderful landscape, all are obliged to allow the exceeding ability of the artist.

Fancy a background of silvery-blue sea and soft, transparent sky which is a reflex of the water, a dead calm pervading, allowing scarce a ripple of the water even where it nears the land, — a warmth so tropical that you feel as though you stood on the equator. In the foreground lies a sandy, sultry waste, stretching out into the sea with a wonderful effect. Tufts of grass, burnt yellow by the scorching noonday sun, show how dead is vegetation, and a cluster of scrubby brush is the centre around which is visible the serpent's trail. Back of this, on higher ground, lies the sea-serpent, coil on coil, his head resting upon the sand with a dilated eye as glittering and sultry as the still life around it. Critics have exhausted the passions of hate, revenge, etc., etc., in describing what they consider to be an 'evil eye.' To us, that eye expresses nothing more terrible than insatiable, impatient longing. Here is a creature drearily alone in his lair, the last of his kind, doomed to roam the sea, another species of wandering Jew, no likeness to other monsters of the deep, no recognition from them, — a friendless thing that sees itself unlike all nature in its solitude, that seems to ask in a dumb, passionate way how many ages more existence must be prolonged. To us this picture is the tragedy of solitude. Many are disappointed that the sea-serpent is not painted in gay colors ; such a serpent would be contrary to nature, which gives dark coloring to the largest animals of both sea and land. Others maintain that Vedder's serpent could never find its way to Barnum's or be recognized by Agassiz. If Agassiz or Barnum knows how a sea-serpent looks, they are wise, and should establish the reality of what the artist has imagined to be a myth. Real or unreal, the sea-serpent is going to Boston, having been purchased at the private view by Thomas Gold Appleton, the well-known art patron. Mr. Vedder has still another picture at this exhibition, — a bit of Venetian coloring, that is exceedingly powerful."

These press letters of Kate Field's through the years of 1863–69 contain material that is not without value in permanent literature.

The following interesting letter from Thomas Adolphus Trollope came to her : —

CHRISTMAS DAY, 1864, FLORENCE.

DEAREST KATE, — How can I sufficiently thank you for all your abounding kindnesses, moral and material, your pudding and your praise, and what a wretch I am for not having written to you sooner ; but if you know what it is to be struggling on to do the daily tale of bricks against interruption of every possible kind, and how necessary it is that I should have completed my history of Florence in time for publication in May, you would be disposed to forgive me. I have just reached the death of Savonarola, and hope, having all my materials ready, to be in time ; but I have two more months of hard labor before me.

Thanks a thousand times, dear Kate, for the " Atlantic," and for the only too kind things you have said in it. Your article contains the only correct account I have ever seen in print of the circumstances that led to the publication of the domestic manners of the Americans. As I write the title, it strikes me that the most objectionable part of the work is that title. It implies generality, where particularity should have been expressed. Isa tells me that she has written to you all she could tell of Landor's last hours. I met by chance old Mrs. Landor the other day. She was very curious about the will which he has made. There is no mention in it of any of his children. What little he had to leave he has left to his nieces, but you know that he had long since given up the bulk of his property to his eldest son. She told me what I did not know before, that her son had been obliged to pay the damages, $1000, awarded by the jury in the case of libel to Mrs. ——.

I presume that she has been able to put her hand on some property in England to which she had a claim. She was very furious against Browning, who is executor to the will. It seems to me unnecessary. She told me that when he (Landor) heard that Mrs. Gestone had succeeded in getting his money, he tried to starve himself. Many thanks for your notices of Landor. The book has done very well in England. . . . The book of engravings is yours, and remains in my hands. What am I to do with it?

. . . .

Mrs. Browning's monument has not yet been erected, but will shortly be so. Leighton, who was intrusted by Mr. Browning with the design, was exceedingly and very reasonably angry on coming here in the autumn to superintend the erection of the monument, to find that the sculptor had most unwarrantably changed divers parts of the design. Some of these departures from his plan Leighton insisted on having restored, as far as was possible, to what he had intended, and this has led to considerable delay. And I should fear that the monument, when it is put up, will not be wholly satisfactory to Mr. Browning or Mr. Leighton.

I am delighted, truly delighted, to hear of the literary progress you are making and the evident opening of a career before you. Would to God that it were possible for you to get something that should involve a residence here as its means of execution ! Surely many of your papers will require a correspondent in the Capital of Italy? It would be a very great delight to have you here.

It really does seem at last as if Sherman and Thomas are making important steps towards the final crushing of the Rebellion. But of course it is difficult here to form any accurate opinion of the exact probable result of their operations.

Did you see what the "Daily News" said of Seward's answer to Lord Horncliff ? Seward's letter was by no means a bad one, but I am inclined to think with the "Daily News" that it would have been more dignified to have replied by a simple and haughtily cold refusal. The impudence of the proposal was so outrageous that it needed no remark to point it out. I almost think that I would have given no answer at all. . . .

I am very fortunate in the moment at which my history of Florence will come out, next May, just at the time when general attention will be called to the subject by the coming of the capital. If you do not make haste to visit the old place again you will not recognize it, so great are the changes that are in prospect and in progress. . . .

I suppose you have heard all about Mrs. Ritchie's dramatic drawing-room; thirteen representations have been given with a very encouraging amount of success, and now a short carnival season is about to begin of six nights, — *i. e.* six Saturdays. Really, Mrs. Ritchie's enterprise has done a great deal for Florence, and has made the late autumn much gayer than it would have been otherwise.

Pray tell me how in case of need any book might be sent to you better than by the post. I finish this letter, dear Kate, at three-thirty A. M. on Monday the 2d of November. We have no ball this capo d'anno the first time in Florence for more than twenty years, and I must be back at my desk at nine A. M. this morning for my new day's work, so you may judge that it is not without difficulty that I find the time to write. I am really working very hard. Give my kindest love to your dear mother, and be sure, dearest Kate, that I am and shall always be,

Very affectionately yours,

T. A. TROLLOPE.

A letter from Mr. Vedder gives this intimate view of the great artist's life at this early period : —

PARIS, 22 June, 1866.

FRIEND KATE, — You have doubtless received the letter I wrote when feeling very discouraged, and when I should not have written at all. But I suppose it is my fate to lose my best friends and then work out my salvation in sorrow and alone. Since then, I have read your letter over and over and fully appreciate the thorough kindness in it, and I thank you for it and am determined to set to work and profit by it. That it made me angry is a good sign, although I must continue to think that spurning is more apt to make me balk than anything else. I am just what I am, so shall write no more on that subject. Only I would say once for all, that I desire sincerely to be your good friend and to always have you as such. I was delighted with your article in the "Galaxy" and am glad you sent it. I have been look-ing out for good articles on the Exposition here to send you, but I could not bear to send such trash — not to put too fine a point on it — as came under my notice. I have given up reading criticisms on art. I like that person telling Hunt to try some "tints from Story's palette." Coleman is here, and I have settled him and his mother in a good house for the present; a most unsettled settling it is in Charley's case, as he is vibrating between furnishing rooms and going into the country. I have had a busy time getting Inman, Hitchcock, and Charley in running order, but hope they can now take care of themselves. . . . I should like to know when the stream of American immigrants to Paris will stop. I have n't the faintest idea of your not being among them in due time. I am glad of it. I feel more like working already. Charley How has been in Paris, but did not call. Are you still of the opinion that the Italian is not worth thinking of as a commission? I have no letters of introduction except to Colonel Hay — and one to Lawrence in Florence. I have not money enough to move with independence in society here, and lack the desire. May repents bitterly all the time he has wasted in that way. I give that for what it is worth. The state of my funds is low, but not eminently dangerous. I have nearly finished a nude picture, which will be good at least. I am very glad that Mrs. Sanford sent my picture to the exhibition. . . . Be kind enough to thank her for me. Hope you will improve in health and not remain in Boston.

Sincerely, E. V.

The first exhibition of Harriet Hosmer's " Beatrice Cenci ; " the first appearance of Tennyson's "Enoch Arden," which seems to have made a great sensation ; the Bryant Festival in the early part of 1865, when Emerson and Mrs. Howe went over from Boston, and of which, in describing, Miss Field speaks of the " charmed hearers," who listened to Mrs. Howe's reading of her poem ; Edwin Booth's Hamlet ; the lyric genius of Adelaide Phillipps and the philanthropic work of Clara Barton, — all the range of which these themes are typical is represented in Kate Field's press letters through these years. Of Adelaide Phillipps we find her saying : —

" Miss Phillipps knows how to sing. What nature could not do, art has accomplished. Her style is the purest Italian, her execution exceedingly fine, and her versatility unusual, for she is equally at home in intensely dramatic, comic, and sacred music. Her rendering of Orpheus' great song ('Che faro senza Euridice') by Gluck, is second only to Viardot Garcia's, and the manner in which she sang 'Una voce poco fa' from the 'Barber of Seville' at a concert given here recently, was superb. In Europe it would have created a furore."

To the Academy of 1865 Vedder contributed eight pictures, of which Miss Field wrote : —

" All are admirable ; two of them are remarkable. 'The Girl Feeding Chickens' is a poem, such as dear human Hood might have written. . . . 'A Lost Mind' is another name for a lost love embodied in a woman more fascinating through her magnetism than her beauty. . . . The woman is of the intellectual style, — a sort of Romola, who, too human, too broad-visioned to enter a convent, wanders into the world in search of her old self. She is one of those few women capable of a 'grande passion,' who has loved with body, heart, and soul, and has waked to find the lover lost. The mind is not gone, it is simply eclipsed by hopeless grief ; therefore we seriously object to the name of this picture. It is the story of a broken heart, and although hearts cannot be broken without stunning the intellect, still, in this case the mind sits enthroned even in its stupor. The majority of people, interpreting the painting by its name and not by the idea conveyed, insist upon seeing a fit subject for an insane asylum. However ideal a picture may be, we do not believe in leaving its name to the imagination, for names, as Hamerton says, 'are almost as necessary to works of art as to living persons, for it is inconceivable how any work should become celebrated without one.' It is best not to indulge in misnomers.

"The greatness of 'Lost Mind' consists in suggestion. It shows that Vedder is rich in ideas, and that with proper study and growth he may attain to the first rank among poets. In execution the picture has shortcomings. The nose of the face is too long, the hand is not harmonious, and the whole picture denotes the fact that the artist worked without models. This is his misfortune, not his fault ; for models in America are rarer than angels' visits, and the art student groans in spirit at the lack of proper tools for work. Should Vedder go to Paris, as is his intention, and study faithfully under the influence of the French school, with the example of such men as Gerome, Millet, and Corot before him, he will, in a few years' time, be able to paint a ' Lost Mind ' that will be a glory to American art.

" Many object to Mr. Vedder's recent pictures because of their sombre tone ; and a critic verges on complaint because in looking at the ' Lost Mind ' every beholder feels sadder for it. Would it not be as sensible to demur at ' Hamlet ' because every reader or spectator of it feels the sadder for it ? Must every painting be a species of jig in color? People don't look at tragedies to be amused."

This criticism made on Vedder when he was so young an artist is curiously interesting as embodying a prophetic verdict that the years since have more than fulfilled. Equally prophetic, too, was her instant vision of the place Lincoln would hold in the heart of the nation when, on his assassination, she wrote : —

" Abraham Lincoln was removed at the flood-tide of his fortune. He is now all-wise and all-powerful, and will live in history as a grand sacrifice to the cause of human progress. John Wilkes Booth has made a hero of the honest backwoodsman. The crucifixion of the last Good Friday has canonized its victim."

As a critic of the arts, — music, painting, and the drama, — Kate Field ranks among the best the world has known, in our own country, England, or France. Her literary criticism, while always effective and often adequate, has not quite the completeness of judgment and unerring insight that marked her critiques of lyric, dramatic, or pictorial art. Her literary judgments, while formed from able standards, — for her mind was stored with the choicest quality of literature, were occasionally colored by her eager and impetuous temperament, and a certain vehemence in her nature demanded a corresponding quality of vigor in any expression. The productions of a certain American story-writer whose work is, in its way, fine, were always obnoxious to Miss Field, who had little patience with the elaborate carving of cherry-stones. Still, as a rule, her literary criticism is of value, its defect being, perchance, in that it is more trenchant than sympathetic.

Her Shakespearian criticism is a classic. In her own lofty and heroic temperament she intuitively responded to the greatest of English poets, whom she loved with an absolute devotion. A criticism running through three numbers of the "Atlantic Monthly," on "The Hamlets of the Stage," is one of the most valuable contributions to modern dramatic literature. In it she compares the long line of actors who have played this rôle, and speaks of the Hamlet of Edwin Booth as one of rare grace and tenderness, of an electric swiftness, and an even more even, finished, and scholarly beauty than that of the elder Booth. Another paper in the "Atlantic," "A Conversation on the Stage," is one of the keenest critical insight, in dialogue form, full of *esprit* and sparkle.

Among many letters from authors are the following from Miss Phelps, now Mrs. Herbert D. Ward. In reference to Miss Field's criticism on her "Gates Ajar" she writes: —

MY DEAR MISS FIELD, — Thank you; you have spoken some very pleasant words about my book. I certainly was very much in earnest about it, and it is pleasant to find earnest readers. I am in haste, but

Very truly yours,

ELIZABETH STUART PHELPS.

In reply to a question of Miss Field's regarding the story called "The Day of My Death," Miss Phelps replies: —

DEAR MISS FIELD, — The phenomena recorded in the story occurred, every one, about fifteen years ago, in the house of a friend of mine, — an honorable Christian gentleman. Testimony sufficient "to hang a regiment," he says, could be brought to sustain his individual witness. I never saw the manifestations myself; but I believe in the fact of their occurrence precisely on the principle by which I believe in the pyramids of Egypt; and am,

Very truly yours,

ELIZABETH STUART PHELPS.

About this time Miss Field discovered her gift in the writing of comediettas, which she afterward developed to a marked degree. She began by translating little plays from the French and Italian. One of the latter, from the Italian of Baron Cosenza, a little comedy in five acts, she translated under the title of "Mad on Purpose;" and it had some little vogue as it was played by Adelaide Ristori, who impersonated the character of Novina, while her daughter, Bianca del Grillo, appeared as Mademoiselle Cristina.

It was in 1866 that Madame Ristori (the Marchesa del Grillo) first visited America, and this event inaugurated for Kate Field her distinctive work as a dramatic critic, which became a leading feature among all the varied achievements of her after life. It is impressive to see how when a great work is prepared for an individual in the future that he is meantime being prepared for the work. A life that has been nobly lived looks in retrospect almost like a mosaic, so marvellously do the parts fit into one perfect whole. The pattern of life, Phillips Brooks used to say, is on the divine side, and Emerson, too, affirms that

> " There is no great and no small,
> To the soul that knoweth all."

Miss Field's life in Italy; the strong impression that Madame Ristori had made upon her when first hearing the great tragédienne in Leghorn; her own temperamental magnetism toward the stage and her familiarity with the Italian tongue, all combined to make her the ideal critic for the appearance of the Italian actress. The New York "Tribune" at once engaged her for the Ristori season in New York; and during Madame Ristori's playing in Philadelphia and in Boston, a leading journal of each city secured Miss Field as the critic of what was justly felt to be an important dramatic event. Miss Field's criticism on each appearance were articles of from one to three columns in length, and were exhaustive in their noble presentation of the art of acting and of the genius of Ristori. Miss Field had the traditions of the drama at her finger-tips. She had the most intuitive grasp and recognition of dramatic quality. Beside her voluminous newspaper criticism of Ristori, she wrote the paper on the great Italian artist which appeared in the "Atlantic Monthly" for April of 1867, and which contains such passages as these : —

" There is no surer test of grandeur of character than a readiness to acknowledge and respect the individuality of all God's creatures. This is the crowning grace that brings Ristori so near to the hearts of her friends. Her social ease makes you wonder how she can ever be transformed into the classic statue of Mirra. Rachel was so complete a Pagan princess — 'Elle pose toujours,' said her best friends — that she never succeeded in being herself. Both she and Siddons were first artists and then women. Ristori is first a woman and then an artist. . . .

"It is not enough that an actor know how to wear a toga. To live in his own age, and love and laugh with his contemporaries, is as necessary as to suffer, hate, and murder after the fashion of the past."

And of her Lady Macbeth, Miss Field wrote: —

"Ristori's sleep-walking scene is a wonderfully solemn vision of retribution. The twenty-two lines of the dramatist become a five-act tragedy. It is the thrilling, terrible picture of a guilty, heart-broken woman on her way to the grave. There is none of the horrible and conventional gasping, but just sufficient hardness of breathing to denote somnambulism and approaching dissolution; for Ristori evidently, and we think properly, believes that Lady Macbeth died by no suicidal hand, but of that disease to which none could minister. There never was such a washing of the hands; there never was queen so quickly transformed into a spirit of Dante's hell; there never was more fearful remorse, more pitiful, heart-rending sighs. And her final exit is the fatal flicker before the going out of the candle; it is the summing up of all the horrible past, a concentration of superhuman power into one moment of superb action. Ignorant of English, with no knowledge of Macbeth but what she has obtained from an inferior translation, Ristori has made the part of Lady Macbeth her own. It is the interpretation of Shakespeare's soul."

This paper on Ristori was followed by others of a dramatic cast, — all of which Miss Field contributed to the "Atlantic Monthly," — as "The Hamlets of the Stage," "Fechter as Hamlet," a biographical paper on Fechter, and the "Conversation on the Stage" as heretofore mentioned.

Press and magazine work and social enjoyments filled the time. The summer of 1865 was passed by Kate in Newport, her mother being among the northern hills; and in one letter to her Kate speaks of a delightful tea at Mrs. Howe's, where she met Hamilton Wild, the artist, and another friend whom she had last seen at the Brownings' in Florence. Colonel Higginson was also present, and the Storys from Rome were, she noted, expected the next week. Mr. Caryll Coleman, the artist, and Mr. Vedder both appeared at Newport at this time, and the old friends made excursions to Paradise, and walked on cliffs, and enjoyed that old, poetic Newport which is now so rapidly disappearing in its transformation into a city of palaces whose splendor more than rivals the courts of Europe. Colonel Higginson was the always delightful presence ; Miss Sarah Freeman Clarke, the artist sister of James Freeman Clarke, had a cottage at Newport that summer, and had as her guest Miss Margaret Foley, the sculptor. Miss Lina Warren, a charming New York girl, now Madame George Nonné, of Paris, was one of Kate's nearest friends, and the two girls had a boat called "The Mermaid," in which they rowed. Miss Warren was the captain and Miss Field the mate, and the former being asked one day if she were not afraid of her companion, — for there was a vein of *hauteur* and of sarcasm in Kate which sometimes overawed the unwary, — to this question Miss Warren replied that she was not in the least afraid, for if Miss Field, as the mate, showed any signs of insubordination, she, as the captain, would throw her overboard at once. The Frothinghams were also among the Newport visitors that summer, and of Mr. Frothingham — whom, in later years, Kate was to know so well — she writes to her mother: " He is very sweet in his manner and is a charming and cultivated companion."

Mrs. Field's noble counsel to her daughter relates itself, in a universal way, to life. " Remember you cannot be too careful, my child," she writes; " the world is not always just or kind. Yet never say fail! The world is before you. You are blessed with more ability than the average, and you must be true to yourself, and to all that your dear father would wish you to be. Oh, my child, how I long to be with you! But we must sacrifice our feelings, and be prudent, and simply do the best we can in our circumstances."

Kate already felt indeed the responsibility of caretaker. She was earning money, and to her mother she writes: —

" I made you no Christmas present and now I make it — the product of two letters to the ' Post,' twenty dollars, — and I want you to spend it on excursions. First, I want you to go to the top of Mount Washington, if it takes that and more still to do it."

Miss Field was always a social favorite, being accorded a certain distinction wherever she went. Her little vein of hauteur could not conceal the kindest heart in the world; she was sincere and truthful to the very highest degree, and always perfectly honest with herself and with others. There are persons who cannot bear the honest daylight of sincerity and prefer contemplating themselves in some arti-

ficial atmosphere of hypocrisy more flattering to
their self-love. To such persons as these a sincere,
straightforward nature is an offence. Yet, happily,
this class of humanity does not abound, and the
sincerity of the good-will of the world in general
is more conspicuous than is the reverse.

> " There are nettles everywhere,
> But smooth green grasses are more common still."

The social world in which Kate mingled was exceptional in its grouping of noble and remarkable personalities, a society unsurpassed in character and brilliancy, to whose stimulus she was keenly responsive.

Mrs. Edwin P. Whipple, meeting her often and
knowing her with that inner clairvoyance of kindred
natures, gives many a vivid word-picture of Kate
through these years of her young womanhood. " I
shall never forget," says Mrs. Whipple, " the sense
of freedom and largeness of life that she gave me.
The fine poise of her head, with a wealth of clustering auburn curls drawn back from the broad, fair
brow; the changeful, luminous blue eyes, — now
starry and sparkling, now full of serene calm that
indicated depths upon depths of feeling and thought.
She used to come to our Sunday evenings," continued Mrs. Whipple, " in a little pale blue silk gown
under white lace, with Maréchal Neil roses, of which
she was very fond, in her belt. There would often
be with us Mr. Emerson, Mr. Longfellow, Mrs. Howe,
Louisa Alcott, Prof. Benjamin Peirce who was our
great friend, Charles Sumner, and other interesting
people of the time, and Kate was a personage among
them, young as she was. Clever men liked to talk
with her and draw her out. Edwin, my husband, was
always very fond of her."

Miss Sarah Holland Adams, the distinguished German scholar and translator, and a sister of Mrs. James T. Fields, says of Kate at this time: " She was beautiful, with her mass of flying curls, and her exquisite voice, and then her brilliant intellect charmed every one."

In the early days of the April of 1868 Miss Field was the guest of Mr. and Mrs. James T. Fields for a little time, and from their house she thus writes to her mother in New York: —

" Here I 've been ever since Saturday evening, but there was no Charles Dickens to dinner. Of course not. Of course he had to have a dreadful cold and go to bed. Such is life. We were dreadfully disappointed. Mr. Dickens has a serious attack of catarrh and is obliged to reserve all his strength for reading. Perhaps I may meet him, but now I doubt. However, as the Fields go on to New York with him, there may be a chance there. Friday p. m. I attended a concert; Friday evening I never heard Dickens read Doctor Marigold so well. The audience was the most sympathetic that I have seen, and Dickens was inspired, although he had been ill in bed all day. Saturday Mr. Osgood gave me some items. Loring thinks very favorably of the Pacific Railroad, and I have written to Lombard. Mr. Fields has given me items and books about Dickens, but I am afraid I cannot write much.

" Yesterday, of course *it snowed*, and to-day is wintry, cold, and blowy, although fine overhead. Last evening we took tea at Mrs. Beal's (Mrs. Field's sister), who lives in a fine house on Beacon Street, and after tea we went to Josiah Quincy's. There the Women's Club was discussed, and it meets with great favor, I assure you. Everybody thanks me for my book on Dickens. All read it."

Soon after this a farewell concert was given to Miss Adelaide Phillipps before her departure for Europe in June of '68, Signor Bendelari, the famous musician of the day, conducting it. The programme was made up from Mendelssohn, Handel, and other great composers, and then one number of Signor Bendelari's own composition, a "laughing song," which Miss Field sang, and also "Auld Robin Grey," — which she rendered with pathos that brought tears to the eye. Miss Phillipps herself appeared in two numbers, from Handel and Schubert, and again with Madame Gazzaniga in the Sappho duet from Pacini. While Miss Field had definitely renounced her girlish ambition for the lyric stage, she was yet a musical artist of a high order. She sang classical music *con spirito;* and in ballads, such as " Twickenham Ferry " and " Kathleen Mavourneen," her voice had a wonderfully sympathetic *timbre* that entranced the hearer.

In the mean time her friends abroad did not forget her throughout these years. Under date of May 5, 1866, from Warwick Crescent, No. 19, London, Robert Browning wrote to Kate : —

DEAR KATE FIELD, — Do let me ask you, please, in regard to old times, when I might have done it, but did not. I know well enough that there is great stupidity in this way of mine, this putting off a thing because I hoped and felt some other thing as here, for had you not asked for some photographs, which I suppose I could soon find, and in condition to get, I should have thanked you at once, as I do now indeed, and with all my heart. But the review article is wavering and indistinct in my mind now, and though it is inside a drawer of this table where I write, I cannot bring myself to look at it again, not from a motive which is disparaging to you, as I am sure you understand. The general impression is enough for me, and enough for you also, if you care in the least about how I feel toward you.

The boy has certainly the likeness to which you refer, and an absolute sameness almost in feature as well as look with certain old portraits here older and younger. There is not a trace of me in him, thank God.

I know that dear, teasing Isa and how she won't answer your questions, but sometimes for compensation she tells you what you never asked for, and though I always or very often ask about you, yet I think it only may have been in reply about the price of Italian stock that she lately described to me a photograph of you yourself, and how you were, . . . what, ever and ever, and moreover how you were your old self with additions, which, to be sure, I don't require.

Give my true regard to your mother, and thank her for her goodness in remembering me. How you can give a thought, even to old friends, is strange in this terrible state of yours. But I wrote only to have a cordial minute's chat with you in the balcony, looking for fireflies in the garden under between us and the slanting Pitti-façade. Now that it's warm and May-like in Florence, and I won't spoil it now it's ended. God bless you.

Yours ever truly,

R. B.

Again, Mr. Vedder wrote : —

ROME, June 4, 1867.

DEAREST KATE, — You are the best and truest woman I ever knew. I am trying to leave Rome for the country and work. Your letters have been read over and over again. You did just the right thing at the right time. It is needless to say how much obliged, nor how much I thank you, nor how noble I think you. I have written this letter to

Mr. —— and send it through you, thinking you would wish it so. If I can only manage to paint the many things I have on hand (exhibition pictures) and have a number finished in my studio for the winter season, I shall do splendidly. I am full of hope, but impatient. You suggest more work than any one man can do and do well. Indeed, you are a friend, a better one than I deserve, but I will try and be somewhat worthy of you.

Yours,

Elihu Vedder.

Miss Field's diary of 1868 offers a condensed commentary of the times, and from it the following extracts are presented.

January 1, 1868. Last night Dickens read "David Copperfield" and "Bob Sawyer's Party" with great effect. During the afternoon I became possessed with the idea to present the Great Charles with a New Year's offering in the shape of a bouquet. Told Fanny Ashley of my idea. She seconded it warmly, and out we strolled in search of flowers. Dashing wildly into every flower-shop in Broadway, and being told that only previous orders would be fulfilled, our ardor received numerous shocks, but finally we discovered a young German who had violets for sale, and who would arrange them in a pretty little basket.

"It is impossible to make the bouquet now. I'll send them to you."

"I want them now." (It was then 5 o'clock.)

"I'll let you have the basket by 7 o'clock."

"No, I want it now."

"I'll send it at 6 o'clock."

"That will not answer."

"In half an hour."

"Now or never."

"Well, then, now," replied the young German, desperately, and away he went at the flowers. Fanny and I sat on the end of a box and watched the German and the shades of night stealing upon us. At last the basket was completed, and off we sped.

Upon arriving home I began to feel nervous, and tortured myself by imagining that Mr. Dickens might think me very impertinent. But finally I said to myself, " If Mr. Dickens fails to appreciate my motive in offering that basket, so much the worse for him, and so much the better for me, as I shall then know what manner of man he is. On the contrary, if he receives it in a proper spirit, the flowers will prove him to be all my fancy paints him." Thus inspired, I tied some pretty ribbons of red, white, and blue around the handle of the basket, and on one end I fastened a card on which I wrote, " Wishing Mr. Dickens ' A Happy New Year ' in America. ' God bless him ' — *every one.*"

Griswold and I went off to Steinway Hall together, I wondering whether I had bought an elephant and what I should do with it upon reaching the hall. Fortune, however, favors the brave. I had no sooner entered the building than Mr. Dolby came to me, saying, —

" I 've a message for you from Dickens."

" Indeed ! Pray, what can it be ? "

" I asked him whether he saw you in the audience, to which he replied, ' See her ? Yes, God bless her ! She 's the best audience I ever had.' "

Of course I was surprised to hear that Mr. Dickens had noticed a person whom he did not know and could not have ever heard of ; but without confessing as much I answered, " And *I* have something for Mr. Dickens."

" Really ? "

" Yes, I 've a little nameless basket of violets that I want to have placed on his desk unknown to him. Won't you please see that this is done ? "

Mr. Dolby hesitated: he thought it was too late for anything to go upon the platform; that it would be better to carry the basket directly to Mr. Dickens, and, moreover, tell him whom it came from, as he would be infinitely more pleased to know the giver. After much demurring, I allowed Mr. Dolby to have his own way, and Griswold and I took our seats, — on the left side, two from the front.

Great was my horror when, the gas being all on and the reading about to begin, I saw a man mount the platform and deposit my basket on the desk, letting the card fall in front, so that those on the front seat could read it. I felt as if the eyes of Europe were upon me and was quite ready to go through the floor. Then out came Mr. Dickens, smiling *profusely*, and when he reached the desk what did he do but pat the basket as if to assure me that it was all right, and give a pleasant nod to Dolby behind the screen, as if to say, "I hope Miss Field is pleased with my way of receiving her flowers." Then he read "David Copperfield" finely, and at the conclusion of Part I. he bore off the violets.

At the close of the readings he addressed the audience thus: —

"Ladies and gentlemen, from my heart of hearts I wish you a happy, happy New Year."

"My flowers did that," I said to Griswold. "It is the first speech he has made in America." I came home in great glee.

January 2. Heard Dickens in Doctor Marigold for the first time. I was delighted.

January 3. Adelaide Phillipps went with me to hear Dickens in "Christmas Carol." Going up the hall steps Mr. Dolby gave me a letter from Mr. Dickens. It is charming. The most neatly worded note I ever read. I feel one inch taller. It is very sweet of Mr. Dickens to take so much notice of my little offering.

January 4. Lippincott published my "Ristori as Marie Antoinette." "The Philadelphia Press" calls it *the* sensation article. "The Tribune" stigmatizes it as written in bad Carlylean. Thank you, Mr. Ripley, I know nothing of Carlyle, so must be naturally depraved. That article will live to be noticed yet, if I ever succeed in putting my "Ristori" together in book form.

"The Public Spirit" prints my first story, — "Love and War." Springfield "Republican" copies it entire.

January 9. Went with John Russell Young of "The Tribune" to hear Mr. Dickens a second time in Doctor Marigold, — was more pleased than ever. Had seats immediately in front. Caught Mr. D.'s eye on one occasion, and felt that he saw way down into my boots. His eye is a dissecting knife. Took supper with Mr. Young at The Westminster. Had a long talk about newspapers and people.

January 18. My letter on Dickens in Springfield "Republican."

January 19. Sunday. Ristori celebrated her *fête* with a dinner to her company, and a *proverbe*, "Un Mari dans du coton," acted very cleverly by Bianca and Giorgio. Giorgio was particularly good, — as easy as an old stager. Ristori stood behind a screen, and directed everything with as much interest as if worlds depended upon it. My present was two copies of "Marie Antoinette" article, — one for Ristori and one for Giacommetti.

January 22. Ristori sent me an exquisite full-length photograph of herself (French), on which is written, "To my dear and noble friend, Kate Field. A remembrance of sincere affection, from her true and grateful friend, Adelaide Ristori del Grillo." I prize this highly. For Ristori to acknowledge herself grateful is more than I expected. Artists do not often make this confession and concession. Took leave of Ristori to-day. She is tired and ill, but always good and uncomplaining.

January 23. Ristori sailed for Havana with all her troupe. Success and glory attend La Diva.

January 27. My article on Adelaide Phillipps appeared in "The Tribune." Has excited much remark. Hope it will do her good. No critic has ever done justice to her genius.

January 29. Addie made her *début* in "La Favorita," —a great success. Her acting and singing beautiful. *The* operatic sensation of many years, from an artistic point of view. Of course, Strakosch won't let the critics praise her as she ought to be praised. What a horrible life it is to be before the public, and at the mercy of unprincipled managers and ignorant or vile critics! How I wish I had control of an art organ! I'd have the truth told.

February 3. Wrote Dickens. Dined at Mrs. Botta's with Helen Hunt and Mr. C. W. Elliott, the author. I invited them all to opera; also the Frothinghams. Addie in "Don Pasquale." All were pleased.

February 4. Wrote on "Pen Photographs of Dickens," —the hardest task I ever set myself. Hope they will repay me for the trouble when issued by Loring. Shall I ever be independent in pocket?

February 5. Breakfasted at Mrs. Botta's with George Ripley, Helen Hunt, Major De Forrest, Mrs. Elliott, a Frenchman, and Du Chaillu. Mr. Ripley was my right-hand man, and by far the most brilliant person at the table. Returned home at 2 P. M. Wrote on Dickens.

February 10. Wrote on Dickens. Will finish to-morrow, thank Heaven! Then I'll stop writing for a fortnight and breathe. Oh, if I could only go to Europe, take care of my physique, and study! Heaven's will be done! I must not complain. It will all be made clear one of these days.

February 13. "The Public Spirit" for this month publishes my essay on "The Wisdom of Masks." I see that the newspapers have made extracts from it. I wonder if I

12

ever shall write anything to be proud of? Life is a curious puzzle to me.

February 15. Notice in " The Tribune " of my book. Calls me " brilliant," and my pen " facile." No compliment, because everybody is called brilliant and facile nowadays.

February 18. Received a letter from Mr. Osgood saying Mr. Dickens had seen a notice of my book about his Readings in " The Tribune," and proposed to have it republished by Chapman and Hall, in England, if I would furnish advance sheets. I have written to Loring. Amazed at Dickens's proposal.

February 19. Correcting proof. Telegram from Loring. Won't delay publication, but will send me a second set of proof. Telegraphed to Osgood at Providence.

February 21. Mr. Osgood called at 9.30 about the " Pen Photographs." Said book was smaller than Mr. Dickens supposed it would be, and it might be too late to obtain English revenue. Decided to let Mr. Dickens be the judge. Corrected proof and left it with Mr. Osgood.

February 23. Called on Adelaide Phillipps. Long talk. She had a great ovation in " La Favorita " yesterday, and at the Philharmonic in the evening at Brooklyn. Wrote in the evening.

February 24. Awful day. As blue as any indigo. Could n't fix my mind on anything. Began Lockhart's " Life of Scott."

February 25. Saw " Norma " in evening.

February 26. Lippincott will give me three or four pages, and $25 for my Kemble article. Sha'n't have it.

February 27. Mr. Fields will take my article on " The Tombs." Is doubtful about Kemble. Dickens praises my " Photographs " very warmly. So do Boston papers. Mr. Dickens says it is too late for English republication. Delighted that he is pleased.

February 28. Mr. Frothingham called. He will write an article on "Photographs" for "The Nation," if editor permits. Busy mailing "Photographs" to different persons. The book is a success. Have received complimentary letters. Loring wants me to enlarge it.

March 2. Went to gymnasium. Heard Mrs. Kemble read "Coriolanus" in evening.

March 3. Mrs. Kemble in "Midsummer Night's Dream." Delighted with Bottom. Voice beautifully musical in some of the poems.

March 4. Loring wants me to enlarge my Dickens book. Will do so at $10 per page. Had I foreseen its success, I would have fought for a percentage on sale. He will make money, and I not a cent. Alas! Fanny Kemble in "Tempest," — not good in Prospero and Miranda. Great in Caliban. Excellent in Stephano.

March 5. A very flattering notice of my book in Boston "Transcript;" also in Portland "Press."

March 6. Forney's "Press" gives me more than a column of praise. Amende honorable! Called on Mrs. Kelley. Gave her $10 to pay her rent. They say she makes desperate efforts to get down on her knees and pray for me, but she fails from physical inability. Poor woman! And I have done so little.

March 7. Springfield "Republican" praises my book. Read "Lear." Heard Mrs. Kemble read it in afternoon. Was exceedingly fine in some portions. Fails in Kent.

March 9. Fanny Kemble in "Julius Cæsar." Fine, but open to criticism. Brutus was not Brutus. But it is a terrible test.

March 10. Wrote letters, read Boaden's "Siddons." Note from Mr. Osgood, suggesting calling at his office. Down there P. M. Had a charming talk about my book, Dickens, etc. I like Mr. Osgood. He is true, manly, and considerate.

March 11. " Herald " has flattering notice of my book. Heard Fanny Kemble read " Merry Wives " in the afternoon. Perfectly delighted with every character, Falstaff excepted.

March 12. It appears that it was with greatest difficulty that Mr. Phillips could arrange an article about my Dickens book, that Bennett hates Dickens, and it was only by peculiar wording that the notice was allowed insertion.

March 13. Heard Fanny Kemble in " Measure for Measure." Cuts immensely. Reads well, but gave false interpretation of Isabella. She does not psychologize me as Dickens does.

March 15. Carrie Rosencrans spent afternoon with me, and told me about the Gilmore drama.

Wish I could travel.

March 18. Dr. Barker delighted with " Pen Photographs." Colonel Higginson writes to " Independent " that I have " extraordinary talents." Hurrah ! I 'll try and do something.

April 21. Worst snowstorm of the season. Did not stir out. Read.

April 22. New Orleans " Crescent " says my book is an insidious attempt to injure the genius of Dickens. De Gustibus. Called on Carrie Rosencrans P. M. Went with Addie Phillipps to concert in evening. Gazzaniga bad.

April 23. Mrs. Fields asks me to visit her in Boston. Ay, ay ! Read and wrote letters.

April 24. Wrote letters. Finished " Martin Chuzzlewit." Dined at Mrs. S. G. Ward's. Large party. Young Ward for my companion. Is a strange, but agreeable and well-educated fellow. Like him. A young Frenchman came to me without introduction, and we had a sympathetic *tête-à-tête*.

April 27. Party at Mrs. Ripley's ; played, etc. Addie Phillipps sang. Give me the voice for soul. Mrs. Henry

Field has promised to join our Woman's Club. Hassard of "The Tribune" present. At last he has written against the indecencies of Offenbach. I thanked him.

April 28. Read "Nicholas Nickleby." Henry Sayles of Boston called.

May 1. Went to Boston. Got tickets for Dickens' Readings.

The Longs called. Visit to State's Prison. Intensely interesting. Shall make article out of it, I hope. The Warden polite.

Read "David Copperfield." Saw Loring. Fall into my idea of writing about Pacific Railroad Excursion. Dickens in Doctor Marigold and Mrs. Gamp (first time of Mrs. G.). The finest audience I ever felt.

Called on Mrs. Claflin, who says I must visit her. Met Mr. Osgood by appointment. He is a noble fellow. Told me things about Dickens. Came to visit Mr. and Mrs. Fields.

A horrible snowstorm. In house all day. Browsed among Mr. Fields' books. Copied extracts about Dickens. Took tea at Mrs. Beals'. Passed evening at the Quincys'. All receive my idea of Women's Club most cordially. Mrs. Fields will support it. Am to meet the Boston Women's Club just started in idea.

Blowing a hurricane all day. Thought I was out at sea. Read "David Copperfield" all day, and heard Mrs. Fields talk about Dickens. David Copperfield and Bob Sawyer in the evening. Dickens weak owing to illness and exhaustion. Dolby wants him to stop reading, so do Longfellow, Charles Eliot Norton, and Fields.

By way of variety, it rained pitchforks. Did not stir out. Copied articles about Dickens. Lombard says I can go to the Pacific. Dickens read Dombey and Pickwick. Presented to him after reading. Said he was delighted to make my acquaintance. I replied that I owed him so heavy a debt that I never should be able to pay the interest. "Then I will give you a receipt in full," he replied.

Dickens last night. Dr. Marigold and Mrs. Gamp. Great house and great enthusiasm. Mrs. Wales, florist, sent an exquisite basket of flowers; Mrs. Fields a palm leaf inlaid with flowers; I a lovely little basket of pansies. On the card I wrote: —

> A little western flower
> That's for thoughts.

It was a memorable night.

Copied Thackeray on Dickens. Took leave of Mr. and Mrs. Fields and went to Mrs. Claflin's. Took tea at Dr. Angell's, and made the acquaintance of Perabo, — a positive, *entête* fellow, who plays remarkably well, and who made me dream sadly as he passed from one Schubert composition to another. Schubert is divine.

A dreadful snowstorm. Mr. Dickens and the Fields went on to New York. Also Addie Phillipps. Mrs. Claflin invited me to go to Washington for impeachment trial. Shall do my best to go. Must work, though.

Ordered a beautiful laurel wreath for Dickens last night. Received an engraving from Dickens, on which he had written.

Left for Washington with the Claflins. Saw the "Russia" getting up steam, and bade Dickens "Godspeed" as I crossed the ferry.

May 23. Beautiful day; first taste of spring. Went to Capitol. Not captivated by my first glimpse of Washington. Saw Congress assembled; a clever-looking body of men. Met Henry Wilson.

May 24. Drove out to General Lee's house, Arlington Heights. Evening at Senator Pomeroy's. Met Stanton, Butler (a sharp, clever lawyer), General Howard (good), Colfax (an amiable politician), Senator Wilson, and others.

May 25. Went to Capitol. Heard Grossbeck. No orator, and I could n't endure the atmosphere. Met Anthony Trollope. Same as ever. Interviews with General Banks, Spofford, and Stillson. Latter took me over building and to Vinnie Ream's studio. Trollope called in evening. Met Chief-Justice Chase, a fine-looking man.

Sunday, May 26. Wrote all the morning. Called on the Pomeroys.

May 27. Visited the White House ; like a big hotel, then to Treasury ; Spinner very polite and showed me everything. Had a charming visit at Charles Sumner's house ; he was very cordial. Then to Capitol. Stevens and Williams spoke. Met Anthony Trollope again. Walked over Patent Office. Friends at dinner. The Boutwells called.

May 28. Anthony Trollope called and went with us to Capitol. Williams finished, and Evarts began his speech after skirmish between Butler and Nelson. Took my last breath of Capitol air. The Spoffords and Mary Clemmer Ames called. Left for New York in night train. Not one wink of sleep. *Sleeping* cars, are they?

May 29. Heard Mrs. Kemble read "As You Like It." Touchstone, Audrey, and Jacques admirable. Rosalind affected. Called on Addie Phillipps. Did not get to bed until midnight. Tired to death.

May 30. Called on Ristori. Found her tired and worn. Great season in Cuba. In the evening, Fanny Kemble in Mary Stuart. Bored to death. She was exaggerated and stagy. No idea of Mary Stuart's character.

June 3. Visited Mrs. Botta.

June 6. Mr. Trollope came and remained an hour or two. Asked me to write a story for his St. Paul magazine. If I can it will be a feather in my cap. If I can't — well, we shall see.

June 7. Saw Ristori in Medea and Teresa. Good house. The play does not wear.

June 9. Ristori's last appearance. Goes to Boston. I called on Mrs. —— to consult about the club, but I saw there could be no understanding between us. We belong to different spheres.

June 24. Ristori has returned. She says she is over-worked, and will not act after next season.

This summer of 1868 Kate passed largely at the Isles of Shoals, and on September 3 she chronicles: " My first letter on the Isles of Shoals in ' The Tribune' to-day."

She soon returned to Newport, and a few days later notes going to a tea-party at Mr. Samuel L. Ward's, driving there with Colonel Higginson and meeting La Farge; she meets Mr. Lawrence (a son of Sir Henry Lawrence), and other people of note.

The next day the diary tells of a call from Mr. La Farge and Henry James, Jr., as he was then, the novelist, and she records her impressions of his power and his refined charm of personality. Miss Field's book, called " Pen Photographs of Dickens' Readings " was making quite an enviable success, and Charlotte Cushman wrote to her that the work was the most perfect criticism she had ever seen and urged Miss Field to come and stay with her at Swampscott. In the mean time, another alluring invitation came to Miss Field from Miss Carrie Rosencrans of Glen Falls, N. Y., the *fiancée* of the artist Vedder. Miss Rosencrans and Miss Field were already warm friends, and Kate records in her diary the wish that she might accept this invitation; " but I can't," she says, " and they must do their love-making without my moral support."

Helen Hunt, the poet, who was an *habituée* and an ardent lover of Newport, was one of the intimate circle in Kate's life at this time. Mr. La Farge had then a studio in Newport, and Miss Field writes in her journal of a very interesting landscape of his called "Paradise." It was in this September at Newport that Miss Field and Mr. Howells first met, and she writes that the young poet "is very sweet in disposition and so sympathetic." She felt at once that rare charm of Mr. Howells' personality. The Perry monument in Newport was unveiled on October first, and John Russell Young commissioned Miss Field to describe the event for "The Tribune." Thus she was enlarging her field of press work.

The autumn of 1868 found Mrs. Field and her daughter located for the season at the St. James Hotel in Boston, now the New England Conservatory of Music. Kate hears Wendell Phillips lecture one night on "Events after Grant's Election," and she records: "He was great and suggestive, but not hopeful. The issue is momentous."

James R. Osgood, the noted Boston publisher, the noble man and the ideal friend, had previously to this time come somewhat into Miss Field's life, and during this season of '68–69 their lifelong friendship was formed. His counsel and influence were most valuable to Kate, and were always deeply appreciated by her.

In her "Pen Photographs" Mr. Osgood took a keen interest, and about this time thus wrote to Kate: "Mr. Dickens spoke of the little book very warmly and in terms which show that it pleased him very much." This little volume, now entirely out of print, is, as its title indicates, a series of vividly pictorial impressions of Charles Dickens in his American tour of reading from his own works.

The days brought to Kate various pleasant experiences. One entry in her diary records this incident. "When in the publishing-house to-day, Mr. Fields called me aside, saying that he had recently looked over my Landor papers, finding them to be very valuable, that I had been paid too little for them, and gave me a check for $88.50, making in all now $300, for the three articles. I could not speak, but I smiled my thanks to him."

The famous Radical Club of Boston had been recently formed, and it seems that Kate had already written of it in press letters. One entry in her diary notes that she called on the Sargents (Rev. John T. and Mrs. Sargent, at whose house this Club met) and that they were delighted with her report, and told her that Wendell Phillips liked the way in which she opened the subject. Her first letter regarding it begins as follows : —

"Now that I have been admitted to the inner temple where the gods forge their potent thunderbolts, I wonder how Boston ever existed without the Radical Club, and why it never was born until last year. Last Monday saw the second meeting of the second year in the commodious parlors of those well-known friends of humanity, Rev. and Mrs. John T. Sargent. There were present Emerson, Wasson, Alcott, and Weiss ; Morse and Marvin of 'The Radical ; ' the Whipples, W. J. Linton, the most graceful of designers, the young and noble Gen. Edward M. Hallowell, who fought beside Shaw at Fort Wagner, and took the command left vacant by the death of his friend and colonel ; Julia Ward Howe, Louisa M. Alcott, Louise Chandler Mouiton, and other potentates in literature and society.

The chair was occupied by John Weiss, who read an essay on the old yet ever young subject of woman, — an essay so beautiful, so earnest, so appreciative of the best womanhood, so generous, so chivalric, that there was not a woman present whose eyes were not moistened, whose heart was not softened, whose intellect was not inspired, by this tribute from a man to the latent worth of her sex. 'God bless John Weiss and all men like him!' murmured more than one woman who saw the glorious vista opening for another generation of women. Yes, God bless John Weiss! If ever there comes a time when all men think as he thinks, every woman who comes short of the possibilities awarded to her will have no excuse to fall back upon but that of total depravity. May that time come quickly, for who is not greater and better for being believed in by the true and good? Who that sees her niche in the Panthéon will not strive to be a goddess? To attempt to report John Weiss's essay would be as futile as to attempt a description of Beethoven's heroic symphony. It is a heroic symphony, breathing in every page the poetry of humanity, and I could no more tell you what it was like without giving you the whole than I could take the sparkle out of a diamond."

Mr. Edwin P. Whipple delivered his great lecture on "Jeanne d'Arc" before the Parker Fraternity on the evening of Nov. 1, 1868, and Kate records of it: —

"Mr. Whipple was so earnest, and impressed me so much that I fairly cried, and when I met him and Mrs. Whipple after the lecture I could not speak for the tears. It was noble and suggestive and made one feel strong to do and to dare. All my life I shall henceforth be indebted to Edwin Percy Whipple."

One of Miss Field's best newspaper articles at this time was one on the new publishing house of Fields,

Osgood, and Company for the Springfield "Republican." She had breakfasted with Mr. and Mrs. Fields
in their home on Charles Street, where the library
windows command that Venetian-like view of the
river, and afterwards Mr. Fields gave her the data
for the article, which was full of information and not
without its hints of keen powers of characterization
in its setting forth of such strong individualities as
Mr. Fields and Mr. Osgood. During the preparation for Miss Field's article on the Fields and Osgood
house, Mr. Osgood drove Miss Field out to the
University Press in Cambridge, which she went all
through with keenest interest in every department.

Edwin Booth played an engagement in Boston
that winter giving Macbeth to Madame Janauschek's
Lady Macbeth, and seats were at a premium and
the theatre crowded to the doors. It was in the
November of this year ('68) that the idea of lecturing first occurred to Kate. Mrs. John T. Sargent
thought favorably of the project, and offered to herself speak to Wendell Phillips who encouraged it.
Kate speaks also of a beautiful and helpful conversation with Mr. Whipple. Emerson gave this winter
his lecture on "Hospitality," and all Boston heard it
with delight. Mrs. Siddons came, bringing a letter
of introduction to Miss Field, who heard her read
and felt her power, but found her "bad in 'King
John.'" The Boston life of 1868–69, on which Miss
Field was fairly launched, was as usual deep in
interest. Kate attended the Symphony Concerts;
heard Emerson again, this time on "Greatness,"
and in company with Mrs. Moulton, with whom she
took long walks, it seems, discussed poetry and art.
Miss Field finds continued interest in the Radical

Club meetings, where she meets the most brilliant group of that day. Of one occasion Mrs. Julia Ward Howe says: —

" I can remember neither the topic nor the reader of the essay, but the discussion drifted in the direction of woman suffrage, and John Weiss delivered himself of the following sentence : ' When men and women shall meet at the polls and he shall hold out his hand and say to her, Give me your quick intuition and accept in turn my ratiocination — ' A ringing laugh here interrupted the speaker. It came from Kate Field."

There were in Kate's life at this time undercurrents which were as all-determining as they were undreamed of by her friends, and whose nature might be suggested by these lines from " Aurora Leigh": —

> " Even so we let go hands,
> And in between us rushed the torrent world
> To blanch our faces like divided rocks
> And bar forever mutual sight and touch
> Except through swirl of spray and all that war."

The 31st of May of this year was a fateful day for Kate Field. It was a warm golden Sunday in New York, and in the morning she called upon Madame Ristori. That afternoon she wrote a letter which, accompanied by a little explanation, will be given in full in these pages. A biography is not a romance. If it exist at all, it exists as a truthful interpretation of the events of the life it commemorates. There was never a woman's life with less in it to conceal than that of Kate Field. She had her share of defects ; she made mistakes; she made errors of judgment, but it still may be said that she was so essentially noble in her temperament and character that nothing ignoble was ever possible to her. This is not saying that hers was a perfect character; she needs no special pleading, and it is not the wish of her biographer to assume any attitude of the apologist, but rather to present, with the same frank simplicity that characterized Miss Field herself, the story of her life.

Into this story came more than once the romance of a girl's life, — the approach of love and lovers. She was very fond of the companionship and comradeship of men. Other things being equal, she enjoyed their society more than she did that of women. This enjoyment was largely a *camaraderie* quite removed from romantic ideas: but while in Florence there came into her life a young artist between whom and Kate there sprang up a warmer interest than that of friendship. As he died in the same year with herself, it is possible to allude quite frankly to him, and to say that he was the victim of a vacillating temperament. He was one who would and who would not in the same breath. His nature — slow, hesitating, uncertain — was the very reverse of that of the ardent, impulsive girl, whose vehemence of temperament often led her into mistakes and unwise decisions. For some seven or eight years the friendship between this young artist and Kate Field had persisted through a variety of stages. A large package of his letters are among the voluminous records of her life. And with this little explanation a letter that she wrote to him on the last day of this May will be given in full, as it portrays the strength and clearness of her mental attitude regarding this influence upon her. She writes: —

NEW YORK, May 31, 1868.

It is five months since I received your last letter, and you undoubtedly imagine that my silence has been owing to disgust or indignation. Neither. I was at first disgusted, naturally, and therefore put your letter aside until I should be perfectly cool. The coolness came much before leisure. I have been so engrossed in business, people, and things — Dickens, especially, about whom I have written a series of photographs in book form — that I have never seen the moment until now that I could sit down and tell you my opinion of you and your letter.

First let me tell you that I renewed our correspondence after a year's cessation because I heard you were very ill, and because I at that time could write to you, having no other feeling toward you than that of a friend. I supposed you would understand this from the fact of my writing at all. It seemed to me consequently that your letters were anything but friendly, even brutal at times, but I so believed in your honesty and principle that I gave you the benefit of the doubt and laid all the shortcomings to bad health. We are the slaves of our nerves.

The letter you wrote last December ought to have been written in 1862. You were a moral coward not to have written it then. Now you know you were ; therefore I shall say nothing further because I don't care. That episode has passed out of my life, and is as dead to me as if it were buried six feet under ground. The friendship I entertained for you is very sensibly diminished by knowing more of your real character, but I have, at the same time, a certain respect for a man who even at the eleventh hour will voluntarily enter the confessional and show himself in his true colors.

By not writing that letter you made me fancy that I had allowed myself to be much more interested in you than you were in me. This is what made me so indignant *with my-self* that ever since I have been trying to make the *amende honorable* by showing you that I was, after all, nothing more than a friend, that I had recovered from the delusion, after considerable mortification. Now I know that I was no such fool, that you were deeply interested in me, as I had reason to suppose at the time. I was young then and inexperienced, but not so inexperienced as to fancy myself admired without any foundation. This has always been the mystery to me, — that I, who never imagine I am making impressions, who give men the widest possible margin and rarely believe a word they say — when it comes to sentiment — should have made such an idiot of myself.

Your tardy letter assures me that I was not this idiot, and my regard for my own common sense is much greater than it has been for six years. I thank God that you did not remain longer in Florence and that I did not tarry in Paris, for had you offered me your hand, I should have accepted it, believing you to be other than you are, — and been cured. When my eyes open they open very wide. I am not one to submit tamely to wrong, and separation if not divorce would have been the inevitable consequence of such an ill-assorted union. You do well to say that you will never marry. No woman should be subjected to such a miserable fate. As a single man, infidelity hurts no one but yourself, provided you have honor enough to confine your flirtations to those who are educated in the art. I have no sympathy with flirtation. It must be a very cold nature that can play with fire. Neither do I admire fickleness. But your nature in no way concerns me, and pray don't imagine that I am lecturing. I am simply giving my opinion of you and your letter. It is unavoidable, and is given for the very last time.

I am not the Deity and having no claims to perfection do not intend to visit anathemas upon your head. You undoubtedly have many admirable qualities, and so long as you live I shall have hope of you. I believe that the time will come when you will be tired of your present order of exercises, and will care for more earnest friends. If you desire to retain me as an earnest friend, you can. I shall never flirt with you, never entertain you flippantly, *never go down to your lower nature.* You must come to me with the best there is in you. I will never tolerate any more cruel, unkind letters. Now we understand each other. If you choose to accept my terms, you can. If you do not care to do so, why, we will part. If ever I meet you it will be in the kindliest manner, for I shall always wish for you health, happiness, and ultimate regeneration. There is something of divinity in you, and the sooner it develops the better for you. You may laugh, but if you have a heart it will be more inclined to weep that a beautiful dream has vanished into such thin air.

                            Yours earnestly,
                                    The Once Mistaken.

Later, in allusion to this episode in her life Kate recorded : —

"In 1871. This man has made a long journey to ask my forgiveness and declare his love, and I have refused him. How strange is life ! "

The man's reply to this is dated Dec. 4, 1868, and runs : —

" It is five months since I received your letter. Had I written at the time, I should have written much that I shall now leave unsaid. I will merely observe that I could not have written my last letter in '62 because my affection for you did not begin to wane until the summer of '63. As soon as I had made up my mind to abandon all pretensions to your heart and hand, I wrote an ungracious letter to that effect. That was in April, 1864, since which time I cannot be accused of having encouraged you to continue the correspondence. In my last I think I attributed my change of feeling to 'inconstancy.' I ought to have told you *why* I was inconstant to you. It was because I could no longer shut my eyes to the fact that there was great incompatibility in our natures; that we had many traits of character, habits of thought, tastes, whims, or prejudices — whichever may be the proper term — that were too antagonistic to blend or to harmonize by contrast. Your offer of 'earnest friendship' is magnanimous; but permit me to observe that friendship can only exist between *equals*. If I ever attain to your level, I shall eagerly accept your generous offer."

But this was not the end. Can anything, indeed, in this part of life be ever said to be the end in our human relationships? At all events, these two young people had not lived their lives out, even on earth, at this time: and in the story of Kate's life he is to reappear, as the reader will find, later on. Each had an intense feeling for the other, however paralyzed into coldness at times, and however successfully disguised or concealed.

In the June of '68 Anthony Trollope, Kate's ardent friend, wrote asking her to secure rooms for them in New York. Adelaide Phillipps sailed for Europe, and the Trollopes arrived. It was during this summer that Miss Field found that Planchette would write for her, — the little mechanism that was then new and attracting a great deal of attention. Kate Field had the electric temperament. She had a vast preponderance of what latter-day scientists (who are also psychic researchers, like Sir William Crookes and Prof. William James) call "luminiferous ether." And it is said to be by virtue of this ethereal quality that persons possessing it are more or less mediumistic. Certainly Kate was intensely psychic. The clue to her whole life on earth is to be found, indeed, in the fact that she was intensely susceptible to unseen influences, and that these acted upon her powerfully in ways which science in those years had not begun to reveal. Her experience with Planchette grew to be so marked in the significance of the writing that she collected the matter into a little book called " Planchette's Diary," which was sent to Redfield, the publisher who was to bring it out. He accepted it on her own terms, — $100 paid in advance, and ten per cent copyright on all the sales. This book is a literary curiosity. Planchette wrote under Kate's hand, and the voluminous communications received were so curiously significant in character as to incite her own analytical study. The modern intimations from the Unseen were then in the early stages, and this little book will always hold a place in the historic record of a progressive movement of psychical re- search, which Mr. Gladstone, some years before his death, pronounced to be the most important move- ment before the world. Space does not here permit citations from " Planchette's Diary," and all that is of special interest or importance in it has already been reproduced in a recent book,[1] the original volume being out of print.

What with Ristori, Charles Dickens, Fanny Kemble, and Adelaide Phillipps, that spring was a memor- able one. The Cary sisters were then living in New York, and Kate knew them well. A playful little

---

[1] The World Beautiful: Third Series.

note from Phœbe Cary to Kate, after the style of a " Herald " " personal " comes to light, running as follows : —

If the young lady who spent last Thursday evening at No. 52 East Twentieth Street will meet her friend at the same time and place, she may hear something to her advantage.

PHŒBE CARY.

P. S. — This establishment does not advertise in the " Herald."

Of the opening of the year 1869 Kate's diary graphically records a running story : —

Friday, Jan. 1, 1869. The new year began on an unlucky day, Friday, and carried out the old superstition. It was most intolerable, and not to be endured. The night before, I went to bed, rather believing that there never would be snow again ; I awakened to assist at the greatest snowstorm in several years. It snowed and blew furiously all night, which state of things aggravated my melancholy at the death of another year. I have just gotten used to '68, and now I am called to throw myself into the arms of unknown '69. I am sick at heart with the fleetness of time, and have almost determined to close my shop-windows until Eternity, when the absence of almanacs will enable me to accomplish something in the course of cycles. My discontent with *status quo* undoubtedly arises from disgust of self. I am wasting time. I know that I do not accomplish all that I should. But I am not thoroughly well, and, moreover, have no one to spur me into new fields. My lecture hangs fire for the reason that I am afraid to touch it. Alas and alas ! I wrote letters and practised all day. Then at five o'clock Mrs. Fields sent a carriage for us. In we stowed ourselves, and were driven through the pitiless snow to No. 148 Charles Street. There we found Whittier, who has a lovely spirit, but is not entertaining at a dinner. In fact, I should have preferred to see Fields alone, and to have heard his literary news and comment. Whittier nibbled at his food, and scarcely touched his wine. After dinner there was conversation such as Mr. and Mrs. Fields know how to lead and inspire. I was beguiled into using Planchette. Mr. Whittier said he had read my " Diary " with interest, and was really quite earnest in watching me as I wrote. The communications were pertinent, and some of them about Thackeray and Landor were clever, but there was nothing in them to astound one. I demand tests. Mrs. Stowe is to write an article on Planchette for the Atlantic. She believes in it. After Planchette I produced my Ristori and Vedder drawings. Both interested Mr. Whittier very much. Being particularly struck by one of Vedder's beautiful drawings, I asked him if he would not write a poem about it. " It is already a poem," he replied. He was right. Many people cannot appreciate Vedder truly. He is too great for the time in which he lives. Later Mrs. Fields read an interesting private letter from Charles Dickens. He gave a graphic account of his trying his new reading, " Oliver Twist," on his family and then on his friends. " If that's what you are going to do," said his daughter Mary, " I suppose it ought to be seen and heard, but it is awful."

" The world has been waiting for a sensation for fifty years," exclaimed Mrs. Keeley, the actress ; " now they have it."

I believe in Dickens thoroughly, and I 've no doubt that his new reading is great. Nevertheless, I do not forget that Rachel and Ristori have lived within fifty years. Perhaps Mrs. Keeley believes in nothing that is not English. I 'd give an immense deal to hear the new reading. The Fields were enthusiastic over a new story of Dickens, " The Star in the East." It is a clever photograph of life. Finally we came home in a worse storm even than that in which we set out, and I went to bed wondering who and what I was? Where the money to live on is to come from, and whether I ever shall do anything worthy of myself or of the world?

January 2. Cessation of storm. Wrote out "Luminara of Pisa" with a view to publication, and practised. Went down town and stopped at the Women's Club, where I met Mrs. Sewall. I called on Mrs. Moulton, walking home.

January 3. A mild day. Read all the papers and wrote with Planchette. Returning, we dined, and I finished my "Luminara." Mrs. —— called and was very flattering, as usual. I wish she wouldn't say such extravagant things to me, for she makes me doubt her

January 4. Copied sentences from Mrs. Julia Ward Howe's essay with view to a letter for "Health and Home." Walked down town to meet an appointment with Mr. Waters of the "Advertiser," and met Mr. Perabo full of enthusiasm over some pictures. He said that Emerson's reading at Chickering's was great. To-night Weiss lectures at the Club, on "Woman." On my way home called at Fields, Osgood, and Co's., and there were Howells, Aldrich, and Fields, all together, and the latter gave me two autograph poems, — Lowell's "Two Rabbis," and Whittier's "Ember Picture." I left my MS. of "Luminara" with Fields, which I dare say he will return. I doubt its being good enough for the "Atlantic." Then went to the station to see Aunt Corda off, and then I met Mr. Weld. Walked home and began reading Mary Wollstonecraft's "Rights of Women."

January 5. Gilmore has issued the programme for a Grand National Peace Jubilee for the 15th, 16th, and 17th of June ; 1000 orchestra and 9000 chorus. Coliseum on Common. What next? Took notes from "Les Femmes," and practised for two hours. Went down town and left Mrs. Howe's essay on "Polarity" at her house, not finding her at home. I'm just as downhearted as I can be, but nobody knows it. I feel as Mrs. Browning felt when she wrote that pathetic poem, "My Heart and I."

> "How tired we are — my heart and I, —
> We seem of no use in the world."

What a game life is! And is it worth the candle? When I'm alone, —

> "I am the doubter and the doubt."

Father, be near and help me. Let me be useful if I cannot be happy. To expect recognition or happiness is folly. I have many who call themselves friends, but — oh, I wish not for much, but more than I shall ever get. This is my cross. I must learn to bear it without murmuring. Amen.

January 6. A warm, spring-like day. Mr. Fields sent me word that my "Luminara" article is capital, but not important enough for the "Atlantic." Just as I expected. I've sent it to Lippincott, and have begun a letter for "Hearth and Home" about the latest Boston notion, a grand festival in June. In the afternoon went to the Symphony Concert and heard Camilla Urso, who manipulated the violin as beautifully as she alone does. I had to miss Mr. Alcott's Conversation on "Beauty" to-night, because of no escort. Read Mrs. Dall's "College, Market, and Court."

January 9. Read Mrs. Dall and practised. Bought "With Verdure Clad," a great study. To-night, at Mrs. Waterston's, where I met Dr. Langmaid and General Gordon, both very clever men, Addie Phillipps sang, with the greatest effect. I was then urged to sing, but refused, saying it would be as absurd for me to sing after Adelaide Phillipps as for one who had supped upon canvas-back ducks to call for a thin beefsteak. Addie laughed and said she was never called that before. " Why," I replied, " you have often been called a duck, and you know you have been extensively canvassed, and frequently backed." Poor sort of wit that.

But —— had n't any sort of scruple about singing after a great artist, not she. So a thin voice brought forth a mouse, and people exclaimed, " How charming ! " Society is such a humbug, and the bad often seems to have the advantage, because it is brazen and has no feelings. I remained until eleven. Addie gave me a very pretty little English ballad, " The Danube River," and made me happy by saying I had made a conquest of Mrs. Waterston. I am glad if this is true, for she is most kind. They have a wealth of books, and are so good as to promise me the run of them. The Waterstons have heart, and are lavish in grace and goodness.

January 10. Again read from Mrs. Dall. Miss —— called, and we found her a bright, clever woman, — a little anxious, perhaps, to be up to her reputation in what she says, but nice for all that. In the evening we went to Mrs. Moulton's and there met Mrs. Corbin, who has written a novel on the woman question, called " His Marriage Vow," and D. R. Locke, the author of the widely known Nasby papers. I liked him. He is defiant of pronunciation and of elegance, but he is so shrewd, frank, and good-hearted, that I fancied him immediately. He addressed his conversation to me, and we kept on talking till midnight. First women's status, then Grant, Wendell Phillips, the press and personalities. He was very funny about his interview with Olive Logan and Sikes, — she sending Sikes out of the room, and then exclaiming to Locke, " That man is the Thackeray of America." And he, taking Mr. Locke for a walk, exclaimed, " Do you know there is not a woman on earth who writes like Olive ? " I should hope not, indeed ! Locke has made $40,000 in one year's lecturing ; and by his Nasby papers he has gained nothing but reputation. Such is life. I shall lecture.

January 11. Addie Phillipps called to invite me to the opera. A letter from Redfield saying that 1300 copies of "Planchette's Diary" remain unsold. All speak well of it, however, even the most intelligent. The Diary is nothing, and as I expected nothing from it, I am not disappointed, but I *am* sorry for my publisher. I have tickets for Alcott's next Conversation, and I secured mother's photographs to-day, which are beautiful. In the evening went to the Club, where was laid an æsthetic tea, Mrs. Howe presiding. Among those present were Mrs. Lodge. The members are all efficient and strong in their way.

January 12. Read, practised, wrote, and received a long letter from Elliott Coues, who speaks with great praise of "Planchette's Diary," and says that he, too, writes with Planchette. An invitation to a party at Mrs. Waterston's, and I shall go. A letter from Carrie Rosencrans, who says that Vedder is threatened with pleurisy. [Miss Rosencrans, now Mrs. Vedder, was then the *fiancée* of the great artist.] I returned Mrs. Dall's valuable book to the Library and took out "Histoire Morale des Femmes." Henry James repeated his essay on "Women" at Chickering Hall for the benefit of the Club. Annie, an old servant, whom I had such a bother getting off to Ireland last June, writes beseeching me to send her money to return. She is out of work, has spent all her money, and knows not what to do. How I'm to get the money, or what I'm to do with her when she gets here, Heaven only knows. It must be accomplished, however, in some way. We are the only persons in the world to whom she can look for help, — poor thing. I visited Mrs. Waterston and Addie Phillipps to-day, and told Addie I'd do all I could to rouse the press and make Maretzek engage her if she would say the word. Addie is rather in favor of it, and Mrs. Waterston promised her aid. . . . In the evening, mother and I went to Alcott's Conversation on "Theism and Christianity." My first experience in these unique entertainments. Mr. Alcott is to me incomprehensible. Henry James told me the other day, when he called, that Alcott once said to him: "There are but three men who never strayed from the Divine Centre: Socrates, Christ, and myself." I think that is saying about as much for himself as a man can. Carlyle calls him "the acorn-eating Alcott," and Emerson, when Mr. James told him of Alcott's assertion, replied: "But, after all, he is the most spiral flame New England has produced." When Carlyle heard this he went into fits of laughter. I dare say Alcott is a spiral flame, only I don't know what that means. These Concordians are too much for me. However, Alcott was interesting in his monologue, with his serene, benignant face, his thin white hair looking like spun glass, and his curious gesticulation with his left hand, as if brandishing something at an imaginary enemy. He made a strong distinction between personality and individuality, saying we were persons not individuals in another world, the former being the soul, the latter body. His interpretation of Christ's words, " I and my Father are one," was very satisfactory. Mr. Alcott came to me later and courteously expressed his regret that I had not been present at the Conversations on " Plato " and " Beauty," and he added that " this to-night was rather dry." I do not think so.

January 14. Read Legouvé and practised. "Hearth and Home " returned my article on the Peace Jubilee as likely to be stale before they could publish it, and I posted it to the " Republican." A letter from Willie Winter. Mrs. Russell called, then Lizzie Boott and Dr. and Mrs. Angell, who liked my little room very much. Mrs. Waterston, too, made me a little visit, and said that Addie Phillipps was averse to any demonstration in her favor. So like the great artist that she is.

January 15. Still not well and in the house all day. Mr. James Murdock called and we had a long talk. I told him of my lecturing idea and he seized upon it immediately. He has very good ideas, and he gave me more encouragement than I have ever before received. He said he would come on and help me make my first appearance if I would let him know. He thinks I can be successful. Mr. Murdock told me that only ten months ago a friend of Anna Dickinson's asked him to prepare her for the stage. A party in the evening at Mrs. Waterston's, and I met Gen. Horace Binney Sargent. There was music, and Addie sang.

January 17. Wrote notes on Legouvé's book, and letters, letters, — among them a non-committal one to ——. Other women may glory in scalps ; I won't. If he will be a friend and nothing more, all right. Mother went to hear Weiss on " The Evils of the Day." Says it was great.

January 18. At the Radical Club Colonel Higginson read a paper on the " Greek Goddesses," and there was a vigorous discussion by Mrs. Howe, Mr. Alcott, Miss Peabody, and others. John Weiss, whom I ventured to stir up, was eloquent in praise of the women — not goddesses — of to-day, and even I dared to say a word which turned out a strong blow to the pretty theorizing. I said, " After all, Colonel Higginson, I do not believe there is a woman present who would return to the Greek civilization," — a remark received with applause. Something was said by Mr. Alcott about Plato and women. When I ventured to say that Mr. Alcott must remember Plato's declaring that women were not capable of Platonic affection, he grew excited and denied that anything of the sort had ever been said by Plato. I had only read this in Legouvé, so I could n't prove it. I 'll read Plato now and find out for myself. The meeting was interesting. We met there Mr. Robinson, the " Warrington " of the Springfield " Republican," and later mother and I called on Mrs. Fields. On our way home we stopped at the Library, where I took out Grote's "Plato."

January 20. Another wonderful day. What this weather means, Heaven only knows. I hope it has nothing to do with the earthquakes that are performing with great effect in various parts of the world. A letter from ——, who says she heard my "Moving Tale" pronounced very clever, and that I was called "very beautiful." I laughed. Better be thought a beauty than a fright. I am reading Aimée Martin's "Éducation des Mères de Famille." At the Symphony Concert Haydn in D and Beethoven's Eighth Symphony were as pure and refreshing as mountain spring water. At breakfast Dr. —— got into an argument with mother about women, and declared that any woman who spoke in public was unfeminine, *et cetera*. And this man is now speaking and preaching, — a man of less originality, of less breadth, of more conceit, of less dignity, I never met in my life. He is an insufferable bore, and is never happy save when talking of himself. I wish he'd vanish. How long, O Lord, how long?

Mrs. —— called, and in the course of conversation I said that I held the post of honor to be a private station ; that a home, a loving husband and children, were the real satisfactions of a woman's life.

"Strange that *you* should say this," replied Mrs. ——.

"Why?" I asked.

"Because you strive for just the opposite."

"I am trying to make a living, certainly."

"The world says you care for nothing but fame."

"The world tells many lies."

"Ah, but there is never fire without smoke," she replied.

Polite, to say the least. I scorn to vindicate myself to such people. I am misunderstood.

January 22. A bright cold day. Got Rousseau's "Émile"

from the Library. . . . An invitation from the Longs to a German on Friday. Read all the evening. A letter from Juliet Goodwin saying that Henry James was enthusiastic in my praise. " Barkis is willin'." Letter from Putnam desiring me to send on my " Luminara." I 'll oblige him. He 'll return it " with regrets." Read in Plato's " Republic " and Rousseau's " Émile." Plato does not confound me with his wisdom, and I don't see what Mr. Alcott meant by advising all young girls to take Plato as a guide. Mrs. Moulton's report of Colonel Higginson's address on the " Antislavery Standard " is very good. It looks queer to see my little remark in print. Down town and called on Mrs. Ballou. The photographs of father's picture are good. It is the finest face I know.

January 24. A lovely day. Rose late ; read " Émile," and just as I was going out Mrs. Homans came. A charming woman. While talking, Addie Phillipps came, anxious to have me go to Chicago with her to-morrow. She is engaged for several concerts by Parepa Rosa, who is laid up with rheumatism. I felt much like going, but health and duty say stay at home, and I resign the pleasure. Later I went to Horticultural Hall to hear Mrs. Howe on " Religion," her first professional appearance. The hall was well filled with the best people, who appreciated the many fine things she said. I borrowed a Bible (all ours are packed), for I want to study it for myself. In the evening Addie Phillipps came for me to go with her to Camilla Urso's testimonial concert. Urso was delightful in Beethoven's concerto. Addie sang " Lascia ch' io pianga," and " O Lord of Hosts " from " Samson." She was fine. Addie and Mrs. Waterston left me at home, and I slept the sleep of the just.

January 25. Read " Émile " and practised. Miss Frothingham called. Dropped in at Club but found —— mouthing poetry, and I beat a retreat. Called on the Bracketts, who told me that I'd made a deep impression on Nasby (Locke). Very glad, as I like him. A letter from Lina Warren containing a little picture, — New Year's gift. Encountered Mr. Osgood in the street, who stopped me and wanted to know when I had returned from New York. Seemed surprised that I had been in town so long, and wanted to know why I had not advised him. *Nous verrons.*

January 26. A bitter cold day. Finished " Émile." Rousseau therein gives a few good ideas, which he drowns in an ocean of turbid sentimentality. A sweet picture he draws certainly of a perfect man and woman. False, false, false ! Rousseau's conception of woman is as wrong as it can be. A fine man, he, to instruct the world.

Practised, went out and called on Madame Bendelari. Came home soon, nearly frozen and as blue as possible. Tomlinson sent me the money for my article in Warren's " Advocate." A letter from Carrie Rosencrans enclosing one from Charley Coleman in which he calls me " Dear Cousin Kate, — the tonic of the earth. I swear by her, and would fight for her any day." Ah, well, perhaps I'm of some little use to somebody. Perhaps by leading an honest life I may help to raise the standard of my sex. But, oh, I am weary, weary.

Read Plato. Dr. Lothrop called. He is interesting, although Weiss called him a clerical Silenus.

January 27. Charming day, warm as May. Rose early, and by half-past ten o'clock I was off for Mrs. Sargent's to assist at the supplementary meeting of the Radical Club. Mrs. Linton read a very interesting paper on the " Religion of Organization," and the conversation that ensued between Weiss, Alcott, Robert Dale Owen, and Mrs. Foster was better than usual. Mrs. Sargent begged me to report the meeting, and to oblige her I took notes. Mr. Linton gave me his MS. I was introduced to Mr. Parker, a clever radical and a lawyer, and Mr. Powell, editor of the "Anti-slavery Standard." They were both very kind in what they said to me. . . . I had a pleasant chat with Mrs. Dale Owen and Mrs. N. P. Willis. The latter told me that she had received but $60 on the copyright of her husband's books. . . . After the Club dispersed, fourteen of us, including Wendell Phillips, Mr. Weiss, and Mr. Linton sat down to a lunch. I sat beside Saint Wendell, who was as lovely as a June day. He is very sympathetic to me, and if I saw much of him I should love him, I am quite sure. He is so truly a gentleman. He told me that he had never studied oratory; that it came to him by nature, but that he had had his failures. I walked toward home with Mr. Linton, who stopped at Fields, Osgood, and Company's, and on reaching home found that Mrs. Whipple and Mr. and Mrs. Fields had called. In the evening to Mrs. Howe's reception. A crowd; met Mr. Morton again, Governor Claflin, and others. Mrs. Howe in low neck and short sleeves. She is a most charming hostess. . . .

January 28. Another charming day. Read "Republic." Mrs. Anthony and Mr. Linton made us a long call. Lunched at Mrs. Moulton's to meet Mrs. Bullard, — an interesting woman with a beautiful Greek profile. In the evening we attended the antislavery festival. Reformers are the queerest-looking people I ever saw. "Here is the angel who records our sins," said Mr. Phillips, when he shook hands with me. He spoke admirably, so did Weiss. Then Mrs. Howe read two of her poems. Mrs. Sargent says $5000 will be made for the "Antislavery Standard." No need of such an organ? Slavery dead? When not an hotel or a boarding-house will receive Menard and Simms, the colored members of Congress, who are now in the city. Mrs. Sargent has herself taken them. "They shall be accommodated if I go into the streets myself," she bravely said; and then, crowded as her house is, she found room for them.

January 30. A rainy, dreary day. After breakfast wrote off résumé of Linton's essay. Dined with the Anthonys, where were Mr. Linton and Mr. Osgood. Dinner very pleasant. I like the Anthonys extremely. Mr. Osgood is a fine fellow and a genial companion. The more I see of him, the better I like him. He walked home with me, and a glorious night made the distance much too short for my inclinations. I could have walked miles. Going to the Anthonys in a dull, feverish condition, I returned home in the best of spirits. Such is the effect of being with people one enjoys.

Sunday, January 31. A horrid east wind day. I lay in bed dreaming until one o'clock, and took my breakfast and dinner combined one hour later. John How called, and I sang for him. He was followed by Frank Boott, who engaged me for Tuesday week for a séance, with Mrs. Tappan and myself as mediums. Took tea. Read a pile of newspapers.

February 1. A cold, fine day. Took notes from Rousseau's " Émile." Practised. Went to the Library, returning " Émile " and took out " Corinne." Called on Mrs. Moulton and saw Mrs. Bullard, who is very interesting. Sang all the evening.

February 3. At the Woman's Club to-night Mrs. —— read a paper. I did not go. They say she looked all around the room for Kate Field and not discovering me said, " Then my manuscript is safe." It would have been " safe " in any event, so far as I am concerned. I can't blow a horn whose notes are not music. In a letter from Aunt Corda to-day I learn that Junius Henri Browne has put me in his subscription book, — " The Great Metropolis." I am one of the " distinguished women," Mrs. Calhoun and Mrs. Mary Mapes Dodge being among them. Here is the damning with faint praise and praising with faint damns : —

" Kate Field, daughter of J. M. Field, the actor, and a bright writer for the ' Atlantic ' and other magazines, is rather small in stature, a pleasant blonde. Seems to be in excellent spirits always and delights in epigrammatic conversation. [Do I?] She was a friend of that cultivated and peculiar brute, Walter Savage Landor, whom she knew in Italy. She gained considerable fame here by her elaborate ' Tribune ' critiques, or, rather, eulogies, upon Ristori when she first appeared in this country. She is frequently at Miss Cary's receptions."

Sat down to my lecture. Tried all day Saturday and not a word came. Just as I began to screw my courage to the sticking point Mr. and Mrs. Howells came. I was very glad to see them, and we had a charming visit, grumbling over the miseries of authorship. They remained for a long call, but too short for me. Later I went down town and called on Mrs. Severance, situated at the top of Belleview with a view over all creation. In the evening I sang to callers. Shall I have courage to write to-morrow? Munson sent me his photograph, and Tom Sturgis, from the wilds of Missouri, writes me, enclosing a letter for "The Tribune." I doubt whether "The Tribune" will publish Tom's first effort, but I'll do what I can for him. He is a manly fellow, and has no end of pluck. How many more men am I to take in tow? Formerly I had my hands full of artists ; lately I seem to have been getting into business channels. How queer a kaleidoscope is life !

February 4. As vile a day as one desires to see. Snow and then rain. Walked down to Pinckney Street to invite the Anthonys and Mr. Osgood to dine Saturday. Found Mrs. A. ill with a headache, but she said they would come if Mr. Osgood returned from New York in time. Borrowed "Aurora Leigh." By the time I reached home, I was afloat in my own boots. In the evening Mr. and Mrs. Sloane called and asked me to sing. Mr. Sloane was enthusiastic over "The Danube River." After they left I ran through "Aurora Leigh." How I see dear Mrs. Browning in every line ! Helen Hunt's encyclical letter reached me. It is clever, but somehow I don't relish a private letter written for circulation among fifteen or twenty. It looks like posing, — not easy enough. She says some good things, though. . . . There comes a grand account of the opening of Booth's Theatre in New York. I expect the acting was bad, scenery fine. Such is our stage.

February 6. Wakened with a sore throat. Wrote beginning of lecture, and practised with some difficulty. By afternoon I was worse, and at night my throat was very sore. Mrs. Governor Smith of Vermont came in, and said she had a plot for a novel in a Husband of Fact and a Husband of Fancy. She said that when she was first married she lived two lives, — on the plane of fact, she met her husband ; on the plane of fancy, she met an ideal man entirely different. As years went by the two became less distinct, until finally both blended and she found all she craved in her own husband. She had grown to his fact, and he had grown to her fancy. A capital idea that might be elaborated — by one who has brains. It is too much for me, I fear.

February 7. Passed a restless night and wakened with a very bad ulcerated sore throat. Lay on sofa and did nothing. Mrs. Angell called and presented me with a ticket to Listermann's quartette concerts. In the evening I felt a little better. Memorized Hood's "Song of the Shirt," which mother read to me with great feeling. *Was* to have had the Anthonys and Mr. Osgood to dine, but had to write them to postpone it.

February 8*th.* A lovely day. Throat better, but still ulcerated. Kept my room. Still no appetite. Read the paper and wrote on my lecture. John How came and brought me two songs, —Wallace's " Winds that waft my

Sighs to Thee " and Archer's " Alice." Henry James, Jr., soon followed and remained until night. We had a good long talk about everything under the sun and some things above it. I lay on the sofa rather exhausted. When I am excited I do not realize how much vitality I throw off.

February 8th. Throat better, but still ulcerated. Read and wrote a lecture. I actually begin to see a little light. McGlenen sent me an invitation to visit Selwyn's Theatre at any time. Very polite. The first courtesy I ever received from a theatre, Ristori excepted. Of course did not go to the social tea at the Women's Club. Cards from Bessie Frothingham and Walter Brown. May they be happy. Shall not be able to go to write with Planchette to-morrow night where we were to have a Planchette séance.

From February 8 there is a blank in this journal till November of the ensuing autumn. Miss Field then writes: —

November, 1869. A long blank of some months, in which I have lived years, and why I have not grown gray under the pressure, the excitement, and the misery seems strange to me, who know myself so well. Oh, if there were some one who knew me half as well!

Ill for a month previous with an ulcerated sore throat, on March 3d I made my *début* as a lecturer at Chickering Hall, before the most critical audience that Boston can assemble. James T. Fields says it was the most successful début that he ever saw. The papers next day were very eulogistic. I was more dead than alive at the time, and had not the remotest idea what sort of an impression I produced. Mr. Whipple's notice in the " Transcript" was very fine. I was invited to repeat my lecture, " Women in the Lyceum," by the best men in town. It was again given with the same success. On the 22d of April I appeared at Newton; on May 4 at Brooklyn, where I was introduced by Mr. Beecher, and on May 10th at the Union League Theatre, before a crowded house of fashionables. "The Tribune" gave me an editorial, and all the papers treated me well.

In June I reported the Peace Jubilee for "The Tribune," and received the kindest courtesy in the press room. It was one of the pleasantest experiences of my life. On July 5th I started for the Adirondacks with mother, and the Rev. Mr. Murray was of our party.

What came of that excursion has been printed and spoken. Returned August 1st, joining Aunt Corda at Saratoga, where all attended the races, and had nine days of Congress water. While there I wrote four columns for "The Tribune." While there, Mr. Osgood invited me to stop at Lanesville on my way to Newport, which I did, passing three days with the Anthonys, the Partons, Mr. Osgood, and T. B. Aldrich. On August 16 found myself again in old Newport.

Mr. Osgood thought well of a caricature book apropos of the Adirondacks, and told me to write out my sketch for illustration, which I did, but the artist who came down to get my ideas was so bad that the plan was deferred *sine die*. I wrote another letter about the Adirondacks to "The Tribune," and by August 26 had an article called "In and Out of the Woods," written for the "Atlantic Almanac," which Mr. Osgood says is the best thing in it. Then I began my lecture, which it was hard to write in the lazy atmosphere of Newport. Between the sentences I rowed, and made Ida Lewis's acquaintance. On September 4th I saw a tremendous gale, the worst since 1815. Correcting proof with one eye, I watched vessels break away and drift from their moorings with the other. It was a terrible spectacle, and the damage to the town was great. September 17th Mr. Osgood and the Anthonys visited us. On the 27th mother and I returned to the St. James, Boston. On October 1st I again started for the Adirondacks, where in company with the Farquets, Mr. and Mrs. Emmons, Mr. E. F. Parker, and Mr. Arthur J. Landon, I passed a very jolly week, ascending Whiteface only to get caught in the rain, and visiting Elizabethtown and Ausable Chasm. Owing to the terrible freshets and breakage on the road, I was obliged to return from Plattsburg *via* Albany. To Troy I got on very well, Smith M. Weed, the democratic politician, being my escort, but on arriving at Greenbush my troubles began, for at Albany in a strange hotel, in the pouring rain, I was stranded for forty-eight hours, my only consolation being in work. I wrote all day Sunday.

Previous to leaving for the Adirondacks the last time, I wrote a biography of Mr. Osgood for the "Advertisers' Monthly." Then I sat down and finished my lecture, and on October 15th took it to Mr. Osgood to read. He returned it the next day, praising it highly, saying that it would go far toward making my future, but advising me, as a matter of policy, to leave out the peroration on John Brown. Leave out the only portion that was a matter of conscience? How wretched I was on that Saturday! I shall never forget it the longest day I live. I sobbed like a child, and wanted to die. Then conviction took possession of me and said, "Retain the peroration if you die." So I wrote a letter to Mr. Osgood, telling him that my conscience forced me to hold fast to John Brown.

The series of circumstances that arise through a lifetime by means of which moral fibre is tested and developed offers an interesting problem. The kingdoms of this world are forever being offered to those who accept the terms; but to those who pray "Give me new wisdom and knowledge," these gifts are granted. Kate Field was not one to sell her soul for a mess of pottage. As this record has revealed, there arose one crisis in her life when the choice was between the inheritance of a large fortune or the free and full expression of her patriotic ardor in the hour of her country's peril. She unhesitatingly chose the latter and renounced the wealth that might have been hers. For in the time of the Civil War party spirit ran so high that it was very possible for a man who had many admirable qualities and impulses of lavish generosity to yet be so intrenched in his prejudice as to be exasperated by direct opposition to his views, and this, too, on the part of a young girl whom he had warmly befriended and whom, being a woman, he did not recognize as possessing any right or title to hold political convictions. Again before Miss Field arose circumstances when she must choose between the politic, the merely expedient, and the eternal right. "You will ruin yourself as a lecturer if you insist on eulogizing John Brown," said —— to her. "Then let me be ruined," was her reply.

Yet she was facing the problem, not only of self-support, but of caring for her delicate mother. To earn a living for two at the point of a pen, especially in those days when literature was far less remunerative than now, and when there was much less demand for literary productions, was not unlike the task of Sisyphus. On the other hand, the lyceum lecture of that time was the most remunerative of the professions and attracting many of the finest intellects of the age. George William Curtis, Wendell Phillips, Henry Ward Beecher, Edwin P. Whipple, Anna Dickinson, Starr King, and Mary A. Livermore were sweeping the country with their eloquence and communicable ardor. Emerson,

Lowell, Whipple, and Mrs. Howe also occasionally went far afield; and although with them the lecture never became an exclusive profession as with the others mentioned, yet their appearances on the plat-form contributed signally to the diffusion of the higher culture. One must have grown up from a child, in the middle West, to be able to quite appreciate what the lyceum lecture system did for the people through that decade of the seventies. It is not now held as an article of faith by the people of the East that the inhabitants West of the Alleghanies differ in essential characteristics from those on the other side of this mountain range. Customs and fashions and even the finer culture follow the star of empire westward, and the settlers of the great middle West were very largely the flower of New England enter-prise and energy. The succeeding generations were their children, and they have never revealed them-selves, as a whole, without a very fair share of those virtues and aspirations which so signally mark the distinctive New England character. But inner as-piration does not, alas! immediately create outer advantages. Education in the scholastic way has never lagged superfluous in the middle West; but education in the sense of artistic culture requires museums and galleries and many aids that this region is, even now, only beginning to acquire. In the sense of literary culture the advantages were less impossible. A great picture or statue may only be seen in one place at the same time; but books and periodicals have wings, and are rather mag-netically attracted to their lovers. Thus it was that the people of this region were very conversant with the literature and thought of the day, and were

prepared to welcome, with the most intelligent appreciation, the lyceum lecturers who appeared through
the cities and towns. Families living in the country
would willingly drive ten miles and back at night to
hear Emerson or Phillips, Mrs. Livermore or Anna
Dickinson, and it was to this enticing profession
that Kate Field began to incline. It was very
remunerative. Miss Dickinson has said that for
several years her income averaged $30,000 annu-
ally from her lecturing. Mrs. Livermore — in case
her generosity ever permitted accumulations — must
have had a similar experience; for the infinite number of people whom she has helped and placed on a
foundation to proceed again, is something of which
only the Recording Angel could give accurate statistics. The lecture audiences of those days were people
who could seldom enjoy pictorial, lyric, or dramatic
art. The lyceum platform was their theatre, their
art galleries, their balls and dinners as well. The
arrival of the lecturer was an event.

Kate Field made her initial appearance on the
platform in March of 1869 with a lecture entitled
"Women in the Lyceum." She had made an instant success with a witty and thoughtful paper
on what was then a comparatively new theme.
A press notice, describing her appearance on this
occasion, said: —

" Miss Field was costumed in a blue and white silk, with
flowers in her belt. Her hair, which is sunny brown, was
looped up at the back of the head by a comb, and fell in a
cascade of shining curls down her neck. She is slender,
and eminently graceful. For the rest, she has blue eyes, a
rather prominent nose, a generous mouth, whose expression

is wonderfully improved when she smiles, a well-developed forehead, and a chin that indicates a good deal of will power. As a whole, the face cannot be called a handsome one, yet there is a bright intellectuality about it which makes even a more grateful impression upon the beholder than mere beauty could. Her elocution is — well, it is super-latively Bostonian ; and that means as proper as proper can be. She sits as she reads, manages her inflections very artis-tically, and charms you with the music of her voice no less than with the piquancy of her thought."

Rev. O. B. Frothingham wrote congratulating her : —

NEW YORK, April 5, 1868.

MY DEAR FRIEND, — Accept my heartiest congratulations. I was confident of your success, but such a brilliant success did surprise me a little. More anon, when I see you. Good-by. With kindest love to your mother, believe me,

Faithfully yours,

O. B. FROTHINGHAM.

Henry James, *père*, thus amusingly narrated an expedition he undertook on behalf of Miss Field:

MY BLESSED CHILD, — I went, as you bade me, to the " Advertiser," but learned Mr. Waters was out of town. Where was Goddard? Three stories up ! I proceeded, when I discovered he was out ! 'T was ever thus. 'T is true, 't is pity ; pity 't is, 't is true. But Mr. Goddard had authorized his colleague to inquire of the fugitive Waters, What could *he* do? What could *we* do? Prosecute? Nay, forgive him once, but only this once. So I came home to think what a dear, industrious, good little girl you had been to occupy your fair fingers with my crabbed in-tellectual fancies, and to tell my wife and daughter that not even they should be henceforth more sure of my tender and most respectful homage. But in reading over your Report, blessed child, I could n't help seeing that my crooked intellect had stifled the free movement of your spirit for the time ; and I at once sat down to rewrite my paper with less of myself and more of your lovelier self in it. And this I send as a substitute for your gracious gift, leaving you to retouch it as you please, and make such use of it as you will, — stipulating only that you cover and conceal from your lovely eyes my masculine conceit in the drapery of your own womanly forgiveness. Forgive me, but not forget me, and believe me,

Your friend,

HENRY JAMES.

Another letter from Mr. Frothingham runs : —

January 2, 1867.

MY DEAR FRIEND, — If George Bancroft, or George Ripley, or any other of my learned acquaintances, had sent me a handsome copy of " Michelet," I should have been surprised at nothing but the kindness of the remembrance. But when Kate Field sent it I was impressed, not by the kindness merely, but by the kind of kindness. Are you a pundittoo or a pundette? Do you deal with Muckle, with Mickles, and people of that ilk? Do you lend a hand at large . . . as well as at magazine and newspapers? I shall begin to be afraid of you, through the very cause that should make me think of you with more affection than ever. I shall take you for a universal genius, and always some remote and private sanctum, where you pass studious hours over the great poets and sages . . . the vain world is forgetting. I will spare you all that ill opinion, however, until further evidence for my suspicions, and only thank you heartily for thinking of me in holiday times, as well as in times of trouble, and your taking the pains to bring me a gift, which must have some associations of a tender character connected with it. Pray don't forget to remember me again in times of perplexity and trouble, when you think my poor advice or influence may be of the remotest service to you.

With kind regards to your mother, who is well, I trust, by this time, and with best wishes for the New Year, believe me,

Faithfully yours,

O. B. FROTHINGHAM.

Mrs. Elizabeth C. Kinney, the mother of Mr. Edmund C. Stedman, thus writes to Kate : —

DEAR MISS FIELD, — How your name — so often seen in print as the lecturer or author, and in my son's letters as the *friend* — takes me back to old Florence, and to some of our mutual literary associates there who are now no more. But I have not taken up my pen to speak of Italy, or the days of auld lang syne. I want rather to thank you for your beautiful, able notice of Edmund's collected poems. I feel a twofold pride for " Pan in Wall Street," first, as a mother, and, secondly, for my fair country-women, who so graciously and aptly brought home the poet's theme. Your " Hap-Hazard " is by me as I write, and I congratulate you alike on the piquancy and point of its pages and the felicity of its title. With warm wishes for your success in this and every venture, I am,

Sincerely,

E. C. KINNEY.

Immediately after her first appearance, Miss Field had the compliment of being invited by a number of eminent men, among whom were Hon. William C. Claflin, Henry James, *père*, Dr. Holmes, T. B. Aldrich, and James T. Fields to repeat her lecture, this testimonial bearing the date of April 3, 1869. Of this second effort Mr. Wasson wrote to her : —

CUSTOM-HOUSE, BOSTON, April 13, 1869.

DEAR MISS FIELD, — I felt just like quaffing a glass of your sparkling wine yesterday, but the fates had decreed that I should remain thirsty. "Official duties" detained me until thirty minutes past the hour. I was willing to be guilty of the barbarism of coming a quarter late rather than lose the entertainment altogether, but twice that was manifestly too much. I thank you for the ticket you were kind enough to send me, and congratulate you with all my heart on your success.

Yours with much regard,

D. A. WASSON.

Mr. Hilliard also wrote: —

BOSTON, April 13, 1869.

MY DEAR MISS FIELD, — "But with the morning cool reflection came." But with the cool reflection of the morning I will say that your lecture was a success. In the first place, it was well written, with a style simple and yet pointed, with good thought and good rhetoric. In the next place, your manner was good, your enunciation is very distinct, and the quality of your voice will enable you to fill a much larger space than you occupied yesterday. But as I am nothing if not critical, I make two slight qualifications to my commendation. First, I should omit hereafter what you say of the novel of St. Elmo as being somewhat out of harmony with the rest of your discourse, and also because the game is hardly worth such good powder and shot as yours. And next you occasionally, in speaking, fall into a slightly artificial tone or cadence. This was, perhaps, the result of embarrassment, and will probably pass off with time. Cultivate, in speaking, the easy, natural tone of conversation. This is the charm of Mr. Phillips's speaking, and with him, as with all finished orators, such ease is the result of exquisite art, and not a gift of nature.

You observed, yesterday afternoon, that my countenance was shorn of a portion of its usual charms. I was suffering from an angry and inflamed eye, and on this account I am obliged, in addressing you, to use the hand of a secretary, and let me add, in honor of woman's rights, that it is a feminine hand.

With warm congratulations and hearty good wishes,

Yours faithfully,

G. S. HILLARD.

A request to lecture in Plymouth Church brought the following response: —

MY DEAR MISS FIELD, — If the Plymouth Church was mine, you should have it just as often as you wanted it, and free too. But except to preach in, it is not mine, alas! but is held by trustees, who have to extend to the secularities, and who must be bargained with, even with filthy lucre. But two facts it behooves me to mention: first, that, as I believe the church has engagements for lectures on the dates you specify; and then lectures are a dead failure in Brooklyn, — not a single one has begun to pay expenses. Are you rich? Do you deal in superfluous money? Do you want to use some of it? Yes, Dickens sent me word after speaking in our church never to build another, as I should not get so good an one. I mean to take his advice. I have noticed the very favorable words of you and your lecture in the papers. I congratulate you.

I am very truly yours,

HENRY WARD BEECHER.

It is incredible that barely a period of thirty years lies between the days when a woman's appearance on the lecture platform was in the nature of social phenomena and the present, when it is a matter of daily and universal experience.

Although Miss Field was a very earnest woman, and would have been quite capable of going to the stake for the sake of her convictions, she was yet extremely sensitive to public opinion and appearance. However engrossing might be her theme, she never forgot that she was a lady by birth and breeding, and she was hampered by conventionalisms in a way that other women on the platform at the time were not. Mrs. Livermore had the married woman's freedom and prestige, with a marvellous greatness of experience, too, lying behind her for her noble work in the Sanitary Commission; Lucy Stone and Miss Anthony were totally absorbed in their cause of the political enfranchisement of women; Anna Dickinson, with her ardor and eloquence, was a law unto herself, and all these women in varying ways had the gift of the genius that well cuts its own channels. Miss Field had the divine gift, too, to a very remarkable degree; but she was younger; she had been for ten years an acknowledged favorite in the choicest, the most exclusive and not unfrequently conventional social life, and she shrank with a nervous dread that no words could describe from a public career. Yet she obeyed the voice that called her to go on. She wrote two other lectures at this time, — one on Charles Dickens, and one drawn from her experience and observations in the Adirondacks. The press notices of these lectures, which extended over two years, — from the spring of 1869 to that of 1871, — hundreds of which are preserved in her scrapbooks, are curiously glowing in their praise. On her appearance in New York with her second lecture, " The Tribune " said: —

"Miss Kate Field appeared in Steinway Hall, last evening, and, in a happily devised and smoothly written narrative, described her personal experiences in the Adirondack woods. The occasion was uncommonly agreeable, and was enjoyed by a large audience, in which the intellect, culture, and fashion of the city were well represented. Miss Field has but recently adopted the lecturer's vocation. Her brilliancy of mind, however, and her soft, gentle, refined, yet piquant manner of delivery, have already gained for her a high professional rank.

. . . .

"Miss Field's discourse closed with a touching mention of her visit to John Brown's grave in the Adirondack country and a tender tribute to his memory."

For a column and a half this pleasant appreciation ran on in unqualified praise. This period of her lecturing resulted, therefore, not only in a success of estimation, in considerable financial profit, and in a great gain for herself of endurance and poise, but her work also contributed materially to the breaking down of prevailing prejudices regarding women's part in the affairs of life. Although over thirty years of age at this time, Miss Field looked ten years younger. Not strictly beautiful, she had the effect of beauty, and she had grace, distinction, and exquisite taste in dress. She appealed to the eye as well as to the ear. William Lloyd Garrison once remarked that it was worth an admission fee merely to see Kate Field on the platform. Then, with these incidental advantages, she had vigorous ideas, exceptional charm of literary quality, and a voice of rare beauty.

It is not possible, without employing terms that would, in this day, savor of exaggeration, to record adequately the enthusiasm that attended Miss

Field's lecturing experiences. As a speaker she never equalled Mrs. Livermore in spontaneous and impassioned power and the magnetism of genius; nor was she ever calculated to make the peculiarly vivid and electric impression that Miss Anna Dickinson made during that period. Still her place was unique. She had great social prestige, and she went out from Boston with the stamp of approval from men and women whose names were held in national esteem. To have the indorsement of Wendell Phillips, Mrs. Julia Ward Howe, Dr. Holmes, Edwin P. Whipple, and Henry James was to carry a letter of unlimited social credit everywhere, for the Modern Athens has always been a recognized Mecca of social and intellectual power, and its *cachet* rather absolute.

There is no such absolute interpretation of spiritual quality as the voice, and in this was Kate Field's most felicitous gift. Her enunciation was pure, her English was choice, her use of language perfect in its values. The scholarly Boston "Advertiser" said of one of her early appearances: —

"Miss Field's voice is exceptionally musical, sweet, and agreeable ; and it is but the simple truth to say that she manages it admirably. With a little practice she will find it easy to deliver her lecture in the largest hall, and we prophesy that, if she goes on in the path upon which she has entered, her refined and modest manner, her artistic perception of the power of light and shade in speech, and her native gifts of mind, will make her everywhere acceptable."

It was an impressive hour when Kate Field stood in Music Hall and told to an audience that crowded it to the very doors the story of John Brown. In this lecture she said: —

" I could not leave the North Woods without making a pilgrimage to John Brown's grave. What ! that humble, unpainted farmhouse John Brown's home? I stood upon the threshold and knocked in vain. Trying the door, it opened ; and venturing to enter, I saw signs of habitation, but none of comfort. There seemed to be no angel in the house. A portrait of John Brown, a few memorial wreaths snatched from some recent grave, were the only visible remains of sentiment. Several men were pitching hay in a field near by, and when I hailed them, one sad man came forward to bid me return. He was the owner of the farm, for John Brown's homestead is no longer the property of his family, although it was his wish that there they should remain.

" ' I am Alexis Hinckley,' said the thin, sad man. ' My sister married John Brown's son, Salmon, who went West and is now in California. Mrs. Brown was very lonely without any of her children, and in order to join Salmon, sold the farm in 1863 for $800. She did not want it to go out of the family, and so I bought it. But I do not feel like staying here any longer. I buried my wife last winter. The place is not what it used to be, and, in fact, I *must* sell it. I have offered it for $2000.'

" ' Does that plot of land go with the farm ? ' I asked, looking from the window where ' John Brown's body lay mould'ring in the ground.'

" ' Oh, no. That is reserved by Mrs. Brown. There are two hundred and forty-four acres, and $1000 worth of timber.'

" So John Brown's farm was for sale."

Telling this story, the $2000 were, within forty-eight hours, subscribed, twenty persons, of whom Miss Field was herself one, and Mrs. Waterston (*née* Quincy) another, giving each $100, and thus was

John Brown's farm purchased to be held as historic
ground; this act of national justice being entirely
due to Kate Field.

These two years of lecturing carried her as far west
as Illinois and as far south as Virginia. She appeared
in hundreds of the smaller cities and towns, under-
going the inevitable fatigue and hardships of travel,
but making hosts of friends, acquiring very valuable
experience and also making a considerable amount of
money. On her arrival in Chicago, Anna Dickinson
met her at a dinner at Robert Collyer's and thus wrote
of Miss Field: —

"Witty, pungent, concise of speech, hating shams with a
royal hatred ; with beautiful blue eyes that penetrate deep,
while they reveal depths, and firm mouth that dominates
the delicate face, and seems to say to it and to any weary-
ing that lies beyond it, 'Advance ; you have your work to
do, your plan to accomplish ; do and accomplish them.'"

In Washington, where she appeared on Dec. 10,
1870, members of Congress and several Senators
listened to her. " They gave me undivided attention," writes Kate to her mother, "but less applause
than anywhere. I thought they were not pleased,
but I am assured that they were delighted and did
not applaud because they were listening intently."

Constantly was she sending money to her mother
and urging upon her every indulgence. " You are a
darling, and I'm not half good enough for such a
mother," she writes in one letter. The rush of life
through this period is indicated in her letters to Mrs.
Field. She lectures in New Haven and takes the
eleven o'clock train afterward for New York, where
she arrives in a driving rain and is up and off on an

eight o'clock morning train for Buffalo. She speaks
in a small town in New York, and after the lecture
drives ten miles to Batavia and takes the train for
Albany. On this particular journey she says: —

"Then at West Point Mr. Bigelow, formerly minister to
France, came in, and we had a very interesting talk about
Mexico and France."

At another time she reaches Poughkeepsie at five
P. M., where she is to lecture in the evening, and in
the interim drives to Vassar College. From Madison,
Wisconsin, under date of Feb. 23, 1871, she writes to
her mother: —

"An excellent house last. The University and Legislature turned out, and Lieutenant-Governor Pound, a very
nice man, presided. This morning I visited the Capitol
with Governor and Mrs. Pound."

Sometimes the houses are not excellent, after all
this midnight travelling and rush and effort, but she
accepts things as they come. All the time she is
sending money to pay debts and for her mother's
comfort.

"I enclose draft for six hundred and fifty dollars.
Make it payable to Uncle Milt," she says. "I hope
this spring to pay him entirely." . . . And later:
"Of the $250 I sent you yesterday pay Uncle Milton
$50. That squares things with him. . . . In next
letter I'll remit $650, the profits of last week." And
again: "Yesterday I sent you $250 from Auburn."
And again referring to a relative, she says: "I
gave —— $20 for clothes the other day, and shall
give her $20 more for Christmas, and there stop."

Finance is a very important matter. The spending

and apportionment of money is an unerring index
to character, and Miss Field's accuracy, promptness,
and moral integrity, as well as the generosity which
always so signally characterized her, is revealed in
this glimpse of the constant conduct of her finances.
She was as prompt in repaying an advance from a
wealthy relative as she would have been to a relentless creditor. Invariably, in every relation she was
the soul of honor. She was always very easily
touched by kindness, and of a lecture season in
Washington she writes to her mother: —

"The Washington people treated me in the most affectionate manner. One landlady would accept no payment,
saying that the pleasure of my company was sufficient compensation, while the other (where I lodged) made me a
present. Both of course were women who had seen better
days. The Southern women are deeply interested in the
women movement."

Her lecture on Charles Dickens was one of the
most artistic and beautiful of literary lectures. She
repeated it with great effect in Boston, New York,
Chicago, Washington, Brooklyn, — in Henry Ward
Beecher's church, Mr. Beecher himself presiding, —
and the lecture is one that was not only impressive as
oratory, but which may well be embalmed in literature. On her delivery of this lecture in the Globe
Theatre in Boston, Mrs. Louise Chandler Moulton
wrote to the New York "Tribune": —

"One saw among this audience the poet Longfellow, in
company with his friend, James T. Fields of 'The Atlantic,' the Hon. George S. Hillard, David A. Wasson, Dr. L.
H. Lothrop, E. P. Whipple, the Rev. Petroleum V. Nasby,
and others.

"The curtain rising, a slight, graceful girl is disclosed, with floating hair, ' outwardly brown but inwardly golden,' and clear, honest eyes, which insure her welcome before she opens her lips. The applause which salutes her is only less enthusiastic than that with which she is summoned before the curtain after it has fallen upon her brilliant peroration. She wore blue silk, with an overdress of misty white lace, and made a pleasant picture as she stood among the flowers with which admiring friends had made the scene beautiful."

Miss Field continued to give this lecture on Dickens throughout her life, its last delivery being, indeed, in Honolulu, where she gave it only a few months before her death, for the benefit of a kinder-garten. Somewhere about 1883 she gave it in New York before a notable audience. Very lovely she looked, in a costume of dark-blue velvet and silk, which brought out the pure, perfect brightness of her face, — that spirituelle beauty which held one with its irresistible spell, — as she stood by the little table laden with rarest flowers, where great baskets of scarlet roses and calla lilies, with bending sprays of mignonette and cluster of violets gleaming through trailing greenery, made beautiful the place. It was the last of a matinée course that she had been en-gaged in giving in New York at the pretty little University Club Theatre, where delighted audiences listened to her.

In this interpretation of Dickens Kate is unsur-passed in her swift, subtle insight, her epigrammatic vigor, her fine touch, and her appreciation of the values of life. One found in her lecture on Dickens two separate aims: one to present a living, lifelike portrait of the great genius in her consideration of him as the actor, dramatist, journalist, novelist, — as the merry-maker, the poet, the friend of humanity; the other fulfilment of the lecture, and one that seemed an outgrowth rather than a conscious aim, was to give a most inspiriting, vital, and suggestive presentation of thought, in a manner that ennobled all who listened. In it she said: "Great genius is only great good sense;" "The price of success is industry;" and "Who that is head and shoulder above his fellows escapes misinterpretation?" she questioned. Again: "They who have great ideas fight for them," and somewhere in passing she spoke of "the blessed trinity of love, devotion, and self-sacrifice." Of Dickens she said: "The watchword of his life was duty;" and one silently thought how truly the same words might be said of herself, — this woman in her simple elegance standing before her audience, — with the earnest, beautiful eyes; the spiritual loveliness of face and form; the graceful, exquisite refinement that surrounded her like an atmosphere. Rarely does one find such an hour of spiritual uplifting as was this in hearing Kate Field in a lecture in which she touched the deepest chords of humanity.

Her lecture on Charles Dickens closed with this paragraph: —

"Dickens, the uncommercial traveller for the great house of Human Interest Brothers, has made his last journey. The light of Gad's Hill has gone out; the light of the world is dimmed. . . . He lies with England's best and greatest, with tuneful Handel gazing heavenward above him, with Garrick by his side, with Johnson at his feet, with Dryden, Chaucer, Spenser, and Milton near by; with a mighty congregation of kings and queens, philosophers and generals, to sing hosannas as they welcome him to this city of the dead. But mightier is that congregation of living, humble souls silently filling the sombre abbey from noon to night, treading lightly lest the dead be waked, casting flowers into the still open grave until the dark void is made bright and beautiful as if with the bloom of everlasting peace and hope. Last to linger is a woman, listening to the voice of Memory as it repeats the words of him who lies so silently at her feet : ' O woman, God-beloved in old Jerusalem ! The best among us need deal lightly with thy faults, if only for the punishment thy nature will endure in bearing heavy evidence against us on the day of judgment.'

"This world's day of judgment has come to you, Charles Dickens, and this grateful woman casts humble flowers upon your grave for your loyalty to duty, for your loyalty to literature, for your loyalty to the drama, for your loyalty to friendship, for your love of humanity, for your love of truth, — loving it better than Shakespeare and Shakespeare's country, better than Irving and Irving's country, — for your love of children, for your tenderness towards the outcast of her sex. And as she lets fall the last pansy in her hand she murmurs : ' The old, old fashion. The fashion that came in with our first parents, and will last unchanged until our race has run its course, and the wide firmament is rolled up like a scroll. The old, old fashion — death ! O, thank God, all who see it, for that older fashion yet of immortality ! and look upon him, angels of young children, with regards not quite estranged now the swift river bears him to the ocean.'"

These three lectures — the one on Dickens being most in demand — filled the time, and yet with all the rush of life Kate found days for occasional writing. One article, called " Woven of Many Threads," appeared in the New York " Herald ; " and she suggested to Mr. Whitelaw Reid a paper for "The Tribune" to be called "Leaves from a Lecturer's Notebook," to which proposition he replied warmly, accepting it.

The sense of movement conveyed by Kate's letters to her mother can only be compared to the whir of wings through the air. Seldom is she in one place for two consecutive days. One night in Buffalo after the lecture an intelligent quadroon came up, saying she must speak to Miss Field, and exclaimed: "God bless you for what you have said of John Brown! It was sublime, and it was as much as I could do to keep from shouting." Miss Field records the fun of a Buffalo sleigh-ride the next day "with the avenue as gay as the Corso in Rome." Lecturing once under Mr. Daly's management in New York, the success was so assured that Mr. Daly wished her to repeat it on Christmas night of 1870, which she did. "I am very sorry not to be at home for Christmas," she writes to her mother, who at this time was living in Joy Street, Boston, at No. 21, "but I must think of our business interests first." Lecturing in Hartford, she was entertained by Mrs. Jewell, — the wife of the Governor, to whom Miss Field was much attracted. In all these tours she was quite by way of being a guest at the home of the Governor, the College president, or the chief magnate, in some way, of city or town. Occasionally her travelling experiences included a night like this, — to return from her lecture to be called at three A. M. for a train; change cars at six and reach her next destination in the afternoon, with her evening appearance before her. There was no complaining at all of these hardships. In one town there was a very small audience, and Miss Field insisted on returning one third of the fee. " It surprised and touched my good friend," she said, " but he was a teacher, and I could not bear to take money out of a teacher's pocket."

From Cincinnati she wrote : —

" Murat Halstead, Editor of ' The Commercial,' to whom Mr. Reid gave me a letter, has been very kind. To-day he drove me to see the sights and then took me to dine with some pleasant wealthy people living at Clifton, a suburb of beautiful residences."

In February of 1871, she lectured in St. Louis, and she writes that as she went to church and heard Rev. Dr. Eliot, " the old times quite came back listening to his gentle voice." Hon. Wayman Crow introduced her on the evening of her lecture, and drives and a number of festivities marked her stay in her native city.

In New York City about this time she sees Fechter, whom she finds, " passionate, natural, and in earnest. He is always sympathetic and *knows how to make love*, which is a luxury," she adds.

Lecturing again in Washington, she writes : —

" Chief Justice Drake of the Court of Claims came up to me, told me that he was an old friend of my father's and that I looked and acted so like him as to almost bring him to life."

Through all these years and, fortunately for the world, continuing until the autumn of 1893, — there was a serene star shining in the firmament of progress whose influence was marvellous in its penetrative and permeating power, — a star that radiated a light not only of illumination but of energy. This

great power for human progress was known to the
world as Lucy Stone, — a woman who was a very incarnation of heavenly forces and who builded better
than she knew all through her long and beneficent
life. She lived with her face toward the dawn, and
while her own specific work was for the political
enfranchisement of women, her power was so great
and so united with the divine energy that it operated
in other ways, producing results on lines which Mrs.
Stone did not, at the moment, mentally define.
George Eliot suggests that by desiring what is perfectly good, even when we don't quite know what it is
and cannot do what we would, we are part of the
divine power against evil, widening the skirts of light
and making the darkness narrower. This deep truth
was signally illustrated in the life of Lucy Stone and
a group of noble women of whom she was one, — a
group originally represented by Lucretia Mott, Lydia
Maria Child, Lucy Stone, Julia Ward Howe, Susan
B. Anthony, Mary A. Livermore, and Elizabeth
Cady Stanton, — a constellation that will shine forever in the records of womanhood. To this group,
individually and collectively, is due the opening of all
the larger life of women in the industrial, the educational, and the professional lines. To opportunities
that these women had made possible, Kate Field
owed an infinite debt and one that, in the later years
of her life, she came to fully comprehend and acknowledge. Noble as were all these women, it would not
yet be possible for a writer who had enjoyed the ineffable privilege of dwelling in the same city with
Lucy Stone and seeing, in the sweet atmosphere of
friendly proximity, this morning star among women,
not to pause in the record to offer special tribute of

gratitude to the serene, resistless, and ever-ennobling influence of her personality.

Miss Field's unique individuality impressed every one, and a little reflection of this is seen in some playful letters of her friend, Richard Watson Gilder, now so widely recognized as a poet of exquisite gifts, and the editor of the " Century Magazine." The success attending Kate's lecture on Dickens had led her, as we have seen, to prepare a book under the title of " Pen Photographs of Charles Dickens' Readings," which she called " the inspiration of gratitude " for twenty-five of the most delightful and instructive evenings of her life. After the death of Dickens the work was republished in London by the Trübners. Miss Field opened this with one of her vivid, electric transcriptions of the welcome to Mr. Dickens in Boston and in New York, passing on to a truly photographic picture of " the desk of the reader," as he appeared before his audiences, describing through some dozen chapters his different readings. In closing this volume Miss Field says : " Thank God that morals have something to do with art, and that the genius of Dickens has realized this solemn fact."

After the appearance of these " Pen Photographs " Mr. Richard Watson Gilder wrote to Miss Field :

Miss Kate Field.

Dear Individual (As if it were Mr. Kate Field, Dear Sir), — I want to thank you for your " Pen Photographs," and to apologize, in a manner, for what I send you by way of acknowledgment. And this is the apology : that there is no other book wherein is name or initial of mine than the Howarth poems, wherein I perform the humble part of organ-grinder to the show. As to your book . . . I must prolong my note enough to tell you that nothing of the kind, since Dickens, has had the same effect upon me. I confess to a happy period upon the boat " Providence " this morning, of intermingled giggles and moistenings of the eyes, as on that memorable night when I heard and saw that man of blessed memory. Henceforth, O woman ! the world owes *you* a debt as well as it does Dickens' family. If that is your Naples — die.

I have an insane desire — being full to overflowing of my little glimpse into the Newport Paradise — to say many things to you here with this pen on this paper. But as I have no excuse for screeding, I will put in the stopple, only adding this : before being critical on the little volume, read again the last paragraph of the preface, and see the possible prevarication that lies so near the surface. Ah, do not misunderstand me ! I refer to the last clause, and only mean that to stand up before the critics, these, as a whole, need the bolstering of circumstances. The " Daily " will take the liberty of saying something, however insufficient, about the photographs, and this " we " will always be only too happy to climb into any windows, through any pig-pens, after any oars, that are to row " K. F." to any haven where she would be.

Farewell, Witch. I like you, and I 'm afraid of you.

RICHARD WATSON GILDER.

Another characteristic letter from this delightful poet and wit, dated " The Place of Abominations, otherwise the Capitol," ran as follows : —

DEAR K. F., — For the reason that you shall not forget me, I write unto you. What a glorious, interesting, " grand, gloomy, and peculiar " letter was the last you wrote me. Missing such missives, I awake to the consciousness that, if I expect to receive the same, I must deign replies thereto. I have sent you one or two pointed reminders of my existence, which I hope you received. One was the St. James paragraph; the other was — well, I guess you "waked and remembered and understood," did n't you?

You said something about having a fine photograph taken when you were in New York. I did n't dare then to hint a desire, but since then I have waxed bolder, to wit : —

> My darling Miss Kate,
> If it is n't too late,
> May I aspire
> So high and so higher
> As humbly to ask
> For a pho. of the mask,

"which I mean to say," of your face (all faces are masks, nevertheless). Rhyme and unreason aside, you see what I am trying to muster courage to say, "and your petitioner will ever pray," etc.

Questions.

1. How are you in body and soul?
2. How is your mother, ditto, ditto?
3. What are you doing?
4. What are you trying to do?
5. What do you want to do?
6. When are you coming to New York again?
7. When shall we two meet again?
8. Will you show your generous forgiveness of my not having written lately by answering this soon?
9. Will you be horrified to learn that I write monthly for Scribner's " Hours at Home "?
10. Will you please not try to find out what I write therein until I can send you a proof-corrected copy thereof?

Please believe me your sincere friend,
R. Watson Gilder.

Among the words of encouragement she prized were these from the poet and novelist, Mrs. Elizabeth Stoddard: —

DEAR MISS FIELD, — Mr. Stoddard says he will do all he can to further the growth of William's . . .

How wonderful that you have the interest, courage, and energy to do such things as you do do ! How do you do it? It is fine, I think, and I like to see the meaning and intention in your face. It would be a nice thing if you and I could become friends, — friends in one sense ; that is, the whole *double* sense is a lost art, — to mean, I mean.

We should both be pleased to see you here, and I hope you may find time to come without ceremony.

Yours,

ELIZABETH STODDARD.

To the " Atlantic Monthly," Kate contributed a paper on Fechter about this time, which incited several pleasant letters from literary friends, among which are the following: —

Mrs. Botta wrote : —

October 29, 1870.

DEAR KATE FIELD, — I am not going to write you a letter, but only a line, to say how delighted I am with your " Fechter " in the " Atlantic." It tells just what one would wish to know, and yet many things are already known by instinct, that he was the true Prince, noble in all his sentiments, a gentleman in all his instincts. He is happy in having such a biographer. . . .

Always affectionately,

ANNE C. L. BOTTA.

And Mrs. Moulton also wrote : —

September 1, 1870.

DEAR LITTLE QUEEN KATHERINE (Queen of Hearts), — I kiss in respectful admiration the small hands of your gra-

cious majesty, for I have just been reading in the September
" Atlantic " " Charles Albert Fechter," and admire you and
him through you immensely. I believe I know what is
good. It does n't take much for that, and this article of
yours is very good. I am proud of you! They tell me
that your ease, self-possession, and knowledge of stage business were a surprise to those who know you best. Laura
has a great deal more faith in you than before she saw you
play. She says she knows you can make a theatrical success, as you have already made a literary one.

Affectionately,

LOUISE CHANDLER MOULTON.

A characteristic letter from Mr. Samuel Bowles,
the distinguished editor of the Springfield (Mass.)
" Republican," — one out of dozens from him which
Miss Field had preserved, — runs as follows : —

SPRINGFIELD, MASS., June 15, 1870.

MY DEAR KATE FIELD, — This note is from one of your
distant and unseen admirers. He is an indescribable sort
of a chap, well enough to know, but not well enough to be
on very intimate terms with, — a child of nature and the
mountains, with an occasional weakness for the distillations
of corn ; irrepressible in his enthusiasm ; harmless enough,
so far as I know, but not quite holding the respect of the
best society in Colorado. Thus I give a character for your
new " brother."

Yours very truly,

SAMUEL BOWLES.

From Mr. Charles G. Leland, then editing " The
Philadelphia Press," are also preserved a great number of letters, of which one — which suggests its own
commentary on the journalism of that period — thus
runs : —

What does Miss Field mean by saying that she cannot write funny articles? I have just read for the first time your " Shadows of Christmas Eve," and am charmed with it. It is melancholy, — of course I do not suppose there is a lady writer in America who knows what *cheerfulness* is, — but it is well adapted to please our readers, and *respice ad finem* should be every editor's motto. The idea of a series of living pictures as you have sketched them is very good, and might be again employed and applied to fashions, as in describing ladies as they "shop" along the street, or to celebrities in New York, going by or to the public build-ings. However, I am not prescribing — only gossiping on my own private account. Whenever you want your reward in money, make out your account and draw on our cashier, J. G. L. Brown, giving him a day or two notice.

Yours truly,

CHARLES G. LELAND.

Miss Field's connection with " The Tribune," which, virtually, continued during her life, seems to have been initiated with the following letters from Mr. Greeley and Mr. Reid: —

NEW YORK, June 27, 1869.

The bearer, Miss Kate Field, who has long been con-nected with " The Tribune," is to represent us this summer at various watering-places, and other summer resorts. Any courteous kindness that may be extended to her will be gratefully appreciated by this journal.

WHITELAW REID, *for* MR. GREELEY.

Mr. Whitelaw Reid writes: —

NEW YORK, August 12, 1869.

MY DEAR MISS FIELD, — Coming back yesterday from a week's visit West, I found your last two letters here, one in type, the other waiting on my desk. You will see probably before this reaches you that they have been given the place

of honor in eight columns of correspondence which we publish to-morrow morning.

I was on the point of writing to Ticknor and Fields to find
out whether you had committed suicide up in the Adirondacks, or what had become of you. We should have been
glad to have had the Adirondacks letter two weeks ago;
still I take it for granted your sufferings up there were too
great for earlier expression.

What are your plans for the rest of the season?

Faithfully yours,

WHITELAW REID.

This letter follows: —

NEW YORK, September, 1869.

MY DEAR MISS FIELD, — Yours of the 7th came to-day on
the heels of a note I had sent you last night. I'm delighted
to have you growl. Do so whenever you please, and I'll
keep on cutting you up just as I please, and just as I promised you at the outset. Is it a bargain?

You know somebody warned me not to engage you.
"You never can get along with her unless you give her her
own way in everything, and that you couldn't do." I
thought we might succeed better than the false prophet
predicted. After a summer's work, of which there hasn't
been half enough, I'm satisfied. If you are not, you ought
to be. That's all.

Of course I knew when I saw the letter about your "tog-
gery" that there was something wrong, but I confess I
hadn't thought it deserving of quite so serious epithets as
you apply to it. You will have to learn, my sensitive little
friend, that people in public or quasi-public positions get
all sorts of criticism, and must quietly bear it and make no
sign. Witness our own angelic meekness under the not
always absolutely considerate criticisms of our dearest ene-
mies of Twenty-Third Street.

Cordially yours,

WHITELAW REID.

Again Mr. Reid writes: —

NEW YORK, Sept. 29, 1869.

MY DEAR MISS FIELD, — I am a little sorry about your decision not to "do" Ida Lewis, and still you are quite right in not attempting to keep too many irons in the fire. Perhaps you will be glad to know that your Adirondacks letters were a success, the first one particularly. The second happened to please the publisher of "The Tribune" and some other people who take a commercial view of such things. But I was immensely amused by your innocent suggestion that since we took out the first-class notice of somebody's hotel, we ought to take out the first-class notice of "The Tribune" also, on the ground that both came under the general rule against gratuitous advertising. Bless your innocent heart, do you suppose that we have any rule against advertising ourselves in the paper?

I don't believe I shall tell you now the person who gave me the advice about you against which you remonstrate so characteristically. It has proved untrue, and so is not worth minding, but some time when you are here I may tell you.

Your complaint that "The Tribune" does n't pay enough is sound on abstract principles. I think the same myself, and should n't make the slightest objection to its doubling my salary; but there is a view of the question which in spite of my having already given, you won't look at. You forget that though our rates are below those of the magazines, we can furnish you fifty times the market the magazine can. For example, if you had written during the season, we would have taken a dozen Adirondack letters. Where 's the magazine that would print more than one article?

Hoping that you may have the best and most remunerative lecture season ever heard of, and that you may come out of it not too strong-minded, I am,

Always very truly yours,

WHITELAW REID.

In some hour of enthusiasm to assist John Brown's family, Kate apparently wrote to Mr. Emerson for sympathy, and received the following reply: —

CONCORD, Oct. 28, 1869.

DEAR MISS FIELD, — Forgive me for not answering your note in time. I am in these days enchained by an engagement to my publishers, which just now hardly leaves me a respectable degree of freedom. I do not know enough of the present condition of the Brown family to judge of the desirableness to them of your project. I once passed by the farm when it did not look attractive to a settler. One of the daughters was for some weeks in my house, and I do not recall any expression of attachment to the place. It would be graceful from the State or from individuals, — this gift, — but I believe their removal was their choice. The land has already John Brown's mark indelibly on it. So I wait to be fired by hearing your speech, which hitherto has been denied me.

With kind regards,

R. W. EMERSON.

All during this period Kate and her mother were living in the historic old West End of Boston. The simple, refined home that Mrs. Field made in Joy Street was one quite in accord with the spirit of the best Boston life of that day, — the true New England spirit of high thinking and plain living. The Whipples lived just around the corner in Pinckney Street; Dr. and Mrs. Howe were living in Mt. Vernon Street; Miss Alcott, coming in from Concord for east wind and the inspiration of seclusion, had rooms in Hayward Place, cheerfully christening her abode as " Gamp's Garret." James Freeman Clarke was earnestly preaching his gospel of love; Emerson was to be heard now and then of an evening; Mrs. Livermore's great lectures were events of the day; Mr. and Mrs. James T. Fields made their hospitable home a literary centre. Left stranded now on Charles Street, from which the tide of fashion has ebbed, the rear of the house commands an enchanting vista up the Charles River; and no one who has seen it can wonder that Mrs. Fields clings to this home where so many notable people have been entertained, Thackeray, Dickens, Arthur Hugh Clough, Miss Martineau, Emerson, Hawthorne, Longfellow, Lowell, Dr. Holmes, Matthew Arnold, Whittier, Elizabeth Phelps, Kate Field, and many another whose name is a part of the world's treasures, have lingered under this hospitable roof. In the chamber above the library Emerson wrote his " Voluntaries," and after breakfast called his host and hostess into his room to read to them the new poem, which was flying around the room in loose pages. After reading it aloud, he questioned them as to what its title should be, and Mrs. Fields suggested the perfect one it bears.

The social life of the Boston of these days was of a quality unsurpassed in any city in the world. Mrs. Howe, to whom the choicest circles in the cities of the Old World have opened, and whose range of comparison is so widely inclusive, has never, as she says, found any society superior to this which included the famous men and women who made what may well be called the golden age of Boston. Among the most pleasant of the social occasions were the Sunday evenings of Mr. and Mrs. Whipple, which were reunions of the most brilliant people. Prof. Benjamin J. Peirce, Prof. and Mrs. Agassiz, Dr. Holmes, James Freeman Clarke, Dr. Parsons, Charles Sumner, when he was in Boston, the noble John A. Andrew, Mr.

and Mrs. Fields, the Alcotts, Emerson, John Boyle
O'Reilly, Gen. Francis A. Walker, the beautiful
Mrs. Anagnos, the lovely elder daughter of Dr. and
Mrs. Howe, and Mr. Anagnos, whose work for the
blind is so eminent, — these and others of note were
among the guests. Mrs. Howe and Henry James,
père, were always brilliantly sparring, with the wit
that characterized both and the easy familiarity of old
friends whose acquaintance dated back to the time
when both were residents of New York, and when
Mr. James often called upon the brilliant Miss Ward
in her father's house. Into this charmed life Mrs.
Field was welcomed. " She was more suave than
Kate," Mrs. Whipple says of her in describing those
days. " If ever a woman suggested the very ideal of
the word *lovely*, it was Mrs. Field." The Hawthornes
were mostly abroad at this time, but the great-
hearted Elizabeth Peabody was usually to be found
in the Boston she loved ; Mr. Howells, as a young
poet and romancist, was, with his charming wife, then
living in friendly touch with Longfellow and Lowell
and the elder Henry James ; and the great Agassiz
was teaching and lecturing. The home of the Whipples was the constant scene of the most refined and
liberal hospitality. The brilliant gifts of the husband
were fully equalled by the exquisite culture and personal charm of the wife. Mr. Whipple stands to-day
as the greatest literary critic of this century ; the critic
whose sympathy with excellence was as swift as his
discernment of error, whose criticism was constructive
and creative, and who was the friend to whom Hawthorne, Whittier, Lowell, and Longfellow constantly
expressed their indebtedness for that sympathetic
interpretation of their work which insured their

recognition by the general public. Mrs. Whipple, the most gracious of hostesses, has always made of society a fine art. Her influence was potent for the sincerity and simplicity of life. Mrs. Field could offer her guests of an evening a cup of tea or its simple equivalent, and the little dinners she gave, to which not more than two or three guests were bidden, were as delightful as they were simple and refined. Adelaide Phillipps was one of the *habitués* of this home, as were a group of the many artists of the day, including Foxcroft Cole, William Hunt, and Oliver Lay.

During Kate's lecturing tours in the West it chanced that Mr. Stedman, while travelling, was stopping over the night in a town, where, seeing the town hall lighted up, he rather aimlessly drifted into it. He found the hall crowded with an audience who had gathered to hear a lecture. The lecturer proved to be Kate Field. The incident was embodied by the poet in his " Hypatia " : —

'T is fifteen hundred years, you say,
    Since that fair teacher died
In learned Alexandria
    By the stone altar's side.
The wild monks slew her, as she lay
    At the feet of the Crucified.

Yet in a prairie-town one night,
    I found her lecture-hall,
Where bench and dais stood aright,
    And statues graced the wall,
And pendent brazen lamps the light
    Of classic days let fall.

No civic crown the sibyl wore,
    Nor academic tire,

But shining skirts, that trailed the floor
   And made her stature higher;
A written scroll the lectern bore,
   And flowers bloomed anigh her.

The wealth her honeyed speech had won
   Adorned her in our sight;
The silkworm for her sake had spun
   His cincture, day and night;
With broider-work and Honiton
   Her open sleeves were bright.

But still Hypatia's self I knew,
   And saw, with dreamy wonder,
The form of her whom Cyril slew
   (See Kingsley's novel yonder)
Some fifteen centuries since, 't is true,
   And half a world asunder.

Her hair was coifed Athenian-wise,
   With one loose tress down-flowing;
Apollo's rapture lit her eyes,
   His utterance bestowing, —
A silver flute's clear harmonies
   On which a god was blowing.
   .   .   .   .   .   .

The rose-tree has its perfect life
   When the full rose is blown;
Some height of womanhood the wife
   Beyond thy dream has known.
Set not thy head and heart at strife
   To keep thee from thine own.

Hypatia! thine essence rare
   The rarer joy should merit;
Possess thee of that common share
   Which lesser souls inherit.
All gods to thee their garlands bear, —
   Take one from love and wear it!

This poem appears in a volume of Mr. Stedman's,
but few readers know the origin of his "Hypatia."

It reveals how Kate's personality always suggested the classic and the nobler trend of life.

Mrs. Field's health was evidently failing: in the spring of 1871, Kate decided to take her mother abroad, feeling that an ocean voyage would be for her the best restorative; and it was to this end that Miss Field had been working in this almost super-human way, on the lecture platform, and in her literary work. Her papers on Ristori and on Fechter, which appeared in the "Atlantic Monthly," had added to her literary reputation, and she had served "The Tribune" in New York as the special critic of Fechter, as she formerly had of the great Italian tragédienne, Madame Ristori. Her literary contributions to a great number of periodicals had been incessant, and she herself seemed in need of change, although in solicitude for her mother's health she forgot her own. It was on May 17, 1871, that Mrs. and Miss Field sailed from New York on the steamer "Russia," for England. The voyage opened pleasantly, notwithstanding Kate's momentary depression. Madame Rudersdorf, the talented *artiste*, was among the passengers, and to her Miss Field read aloud from the poems of John Hay, which were then just appearing; and she read also, on this voyage, the early stories of Bret Harte, which were the sensation of the hour. *En voyage* she wrote as follows to her aunt, Mrs. Sanford: —

STEAMER "RUSSIA," May 25, 1871.

DEAREST AUNT CORDA, — I never loved you as much as I do now, and if it does you any good to know that you are missed perpetually, know it. You see how the ship's motion interferes with writing, and will forgive brevity. I will write from Liverpool or London. We may remain over in

Liverpool for a few days. Now we are making Queens-town, and I send these few lines to let you know that so far the voyage has been an excellent one. Only one rainy day, and no great motion. Passengers well enough. Madame Rudersdorf and Mr. Cummings a blessing. God bless you. I hope we shall hear in a few days. Mother sends love.

YOUR KATE.

Kate Field was made of very impressible stuff. In later years she used sometimes to remark laughingly: "I am neither a prophet nor the daughter of a prophet, so how can I tell?" in reply to some question of politics or affairs; but she certainly had a curiously prophetic cast of mind. In a reading of her hand by Heron Allen many years after this period, he recorded of Kate's temperament: "You always know more or less beforehand what is going to happen to you, or when any misfortune is to occur," and this highly sensitive condition always characterized her. In the light of later psychic science it is not phenomenal that she thus received swift and direct impressions of the future. Her nervous and mental life was intense, and was lived more on the spiritual plane of causes than on the physical plane of effects.

And so, when she saw the gray shores of New York fade away through mists of tears, as she wrote at the time, her inner self undoubtedly perceived dimly the cloud of sorrow into which she was unconsciously entering; the loss that for the time was to leave her so desolate, and yet, in the guise of this sorrow and loss, a new door of life was to open before her and she was to be led forward in undreamed of ways. Even in her deepest grief she was not to prove too weak to master "the flowing conditions of life." Now another crisis in life was before her. She was to learn to

> " Scorn trifles and embrace a better aim
> Than wine or sleep or praise.
> . . . .
> The soul
> Shall have society of its own rank."

By what mystic mooring fared forth the "Russia"? Who knew when the Angel of Death drew near to summon gentle Mrs. Field away to that fair country we shall all one day know? Who shall say that the husband whose withdrawal from earth she had borne so bravely for fifteen years was not now with her, the first to welcome her to the unseen realm?

> " At last to be identified,
> At last, the lamps upon thy side,
> The rest of life to see.
> Past midnight, past the morning star,
> Past sunrise. Ah, what leagues there are
> Between our feet and day."

Mrs. Field's illness was not thought of as serious until the very last. Three days before reaching Liverpool she had gone to the life beyond. Her daughter's first letter recording this event is so re-markable in its power of self-control that no complete idea of her character could be given without presenting this narration in part : —

LIVERPOOL, May 28, 1871.

DARLING AUNT, — For my sake, dear, be calm. Accept the inevitable. We did it all for the best. I acted on the advice of physicians. You have of course received the telegram. I sent it to Mr. Long last night, because I did not wish you to be shocked suddenly. . . .

Giving the full details of her mother's illness, Kate continues : —

At Queenstown I telegraphed to Mr. Hennessy to meet me at Liverpool. I saw the beginning of the end. The doctor stood by, and Madame Rudersdorf, who had been kind from the first, came to me. From eight to quarter past ten, May 26th (Friday night), I watched her as she gradually faded away. There was no suffering to her. . . . At Liverpool dear, gentle Mr. Hennessy joined me, and is with me now. Do not imagine that I am without friends. The doctor has been as kind as a man could be. Many of the passengers volunteered their services, but nothing was to be done that they could do. Miss Williams and friends in her house called immediately, and the Barney Williamses and Florences, who arrived in the previous steamer, came to-day to offer their aid and express their sorrow. I am well provided with friends and (as you know) money.

May 29, 5 P. M.

The embalming will be completed to-morrow, and then I shall visit the darling. A cast of the face has been taken to-day, that I may have material for a marble bust. The face was so sweet, the features so delicate in repose, that I determined to have them preserved in marble as well as in my memory. All arrangements have been completed to have her body sent on the Cunard steamer "Siberia," leaving here next Thursday. Do not let the funeral take place until you receive another letter from me. If the face is fair, I shall want you to see the darling once more, and will leave the curls on the forehead, which you will have cut off before the casket is closed for the last time.

Remember this.

Let the casket be removed to Mount Auburn Chapel, and the services be performed there. No funeral cortége. Let a few carriages be in waiting for the few friends asked who will desire to go from the Chapel to the grave. The darling is to be buried beside my father, *to the right,* and I hope all the graves will be decorated with flowers on that day, especially the bed over my father's grave. And before the earth is filled in, cast upon her all these loving flowers. If possible, I desire Mr. Frothingham to officiate, and I should like Mr. Weiss to offer prayer. Mr. Frothingham knows more of my mother's character than any other clergyman, and can do her greater justice. I have written to him, and do you also on receipt of this. Failing both these friends, call upon Rev. C. A. Bartol.

I have written to Whitelaw Reid to have the notice of her death published in New York, Boston, St. Louis, and New Orleans. Give out no public notice of the funeral. Notify such friends as I shall name and such as you desire to be present, that on a certain day and hour the funeral services will be performed in the Chapel at Mount Auburn. I should like Mr. Anthony, Mr. Long, Mr. Goddard, and Mr. Whipple to be pall-bearers. Before the funeral go and look upon the face (if Mr. Long and Uncle Milton think best), have the dear curls cut, and then let all be closed up. I do not wish those who did not love my mother to see her when she is so sacred. Telegraph me the day of the funeral, that I may be there in spirit. I do not return because I cannot. The strain upon me crossing that wide ocean alone so soon after the blow would be more than I could bear. To-morrow, P.M., after completing all arrangements, I expect to leave for London, and the Hennessys will take good care of me. Do not worry about me, darling; I am trying to be resigned. I feel that dearest mother gains a dear husband and son in leaving me, and in putting aside a tired, worn-out body will be so much happier than when here. Her death would have been impossible had she not been on the verge of eternity before sailing. There was no strength to bear up against the slightest shock, and perhaps God has been kind in taking her suddenly rather than to have her linger in suffering for some years more. Dear, the separation is only temporary. Even now I feel her influence, and giving myself up to it, she tells me that it is for the best. Could I have foreseen all, no power on earth could have induced me to set sail. I acted up to my light; and God, I hope, will not blame me for doing what every one thought so excellent for her. Would we have the sweet darling back to suffer? Even now, with my heart so very, very heavy, I say "no." She will be with us, and her sweet example will help us to grow better and more worthy of her future companionship. Be brave, and grow strong, dear, that I may look to you to supply the void in this life. You know how mother would implore you not to grieve. If you love her, heed her prayer. Give my love to Uncle Milton, say that all bills are paid, everything is settled in a thoroughly business manner. There will be debts incurred on the other side, which for the present I must leave to him. . . . The darling's wedding ring I wear upon my little finger. Go to Harves and secure the three negatives of the photographs he has taken of mother. The last is the best ever taken. I have one with me. I think I have said all that I can to-day. I will write again, for Thursday's mail, as soon as I arrive in London. I will write to New Orleans also. God bless you, dear, take good care of yourself, and believe me,

Ever your loving

KATE FIELD.

Alone in all this grief and desolation, Kate entered England, yet still sustained by an unfaltering trust and by earnest purposes.

LONDON LIFE

" And for success I ask no more than this :
To bear unflinching witness to the truth."

———————————

" And what gift bring I to this untried world ? "

———————————

" Nor stony tower, nor walls of beaten brass,
Nor airless dungeon, nor strong links of iron,
Can be retentive to the strength of spirit."

CHAPTER V

I pray you, let us satisfy our eyes
With the memorials and the things of fame
That do renown this city.
                                        SHAKESPEARE.

London, that great sea, whose ebb and flow
At once is deep and loud. . . .
But in its depths what treasures!
                                        SHELLEY.

EUROPE REVISITED. AMONG LONDON CELEBRITIES. IN SPAIN
WITH CASTELAR. MUSIC AND DRAMA. PROFESSOR BELL AND
THE TELEPHONE. THE SHAKESPEARE MEMORIAL.

WHATEVER degree of success Miss Field achieved in the sense of fulfilment of definite purposes was largely due to her power of adaptation to the environment of the moment. She was rather swift to discern the line where the attainable became the unattainable, and she was not apt to waste her forces to any great extent in fighting windmills. True as steel to a moral conviction, she had, withal, a very liberal endowment of common sense, which is a gift less freely bestowed on man than is often believed. When Guizot termed common sense the genius of humanity, he felicitously phrased the results of a very fine balance of power and purpose.

For the moment, however, on arriving alone in London, Kate was desolate almost to the verge of despair; and under date of June 8, 1871, in Aubrey House, Notting Hill, she thus writes in her journal: —

" God help me, for I do not now seem able to help my-self. My own darling mother gone, and I alone in this great, heartless city of London among strangers. It all seems a terrible dream which I can in no way realize. It seems as if I had left mother in America, and should rejoin her on my return, — if I live to return. The sooner it is all over, the better. And how the predictions of that clair-voyante have been fulfilled. . . . Just before we started, dear mother consulted a clairvoyante, who told her she was going to England and approved of it. I, too, went and was told the same thing. Determined to leave no stone unturned, I went to another clairvoyante, reputed to be quite wonderful. I in no way pin my faith to this kind of people, but I be-lieve in the possibility of second sight, and never turn my back upon light, if it seem to be light. The woman soon went into a trance, and gave evidence of much suffering. She seemed to go through the gaspings of death, and finally said : ' She has come. It is she,' pointing as she spoke to a ring on my right hand made of Aunt Sarah's hair. I rec-ognized the manner of her death in the gasping of the medium, who then said she saw a large grave near me, — that of a chief who was near to me. She said that I was enveloped in black ; that she should say I was about to die were it not for light beyond ; that there was work for me to do ; that I had endurance ; that I was going away and away off across water ; that I should wade through black, but it would be all right in the end. The woman kept me over an hour, when I was entitled to but one half of that time, and begged me to keep my own counsel. When she awakened she assured me that she had never been so fear-fully influenced, and asked me to please let her know if anything did happen. She told me at the beginning that if I would only give myself up to the influence around me I should be a medium ; that there was no necessity for me to seek others.

" All this made no special impression on me. The main point, crossing the water, seemed to be decided upon favorably, both by the regular and irregular faculty. The grave made no impression upon me, and the 'wading through black' became associated in my mind with struggles for position. The whole interview passed out of my mind. On May 11th, fifteen minutes before I left Boston for Northampton, where I was to lecture that night, previous to going on to New York, G —— came and gave us a great shock by telling us that his father had just died. Here was the grave filled already. . . . I had believed —— to be beyond the reach of physicians, but I had thought he would die gradually of softening of the brain. God was good in saving him and his family this long trial, and I did not grieve. . . . Before we left I remarked that dear mother was more easily fatigued and more forgetful of where she laid things than usual, and when she packed a trunk I said to myself, 'Dear, that's the last trunk you shall ever pack. Henceforth you, who have so long taken care of others, shall be taken care of, if it costs me every dollar I have in the world.' It was, indeed, the last trunk she packed."

On June 16 the casket containing the body of Mrs. Field was placed in Mount Auburn beside her husband and their little son, after a poetic and beautiful service in the Chapel. Of this Rev. Dr. Bartol wrote to Miss Field in the following letter, giving a pictorial narrative of the last rites: —

DEAR MISS FIELD, — I am asked to sketch for you what I have just said over your mother's bier. I may add or omit, I cannot perfectly recall, but am most happy to repeat the line of thought: —

This is the hour when we know not whether to speak, or be dumb and listen to the voice which is silence. Is there any light or hope? Can aught be said? The answer

seems to come, nothing but the hope itself God's spirit
makes to " spring eternal in the human breast." Evidence
of faith? Faith is the evidence. He that makes us believe does not play false with us in our very nature. His
inspiration, beyond verbal declaration, ghostly apparition,
or bodily resurrection, is our conviction. But is not our
immortality too much to credit? Mr. Channing said the
only argument to his mind against a future life was the
greatness of the conception; and friends have said to me,
The idea of living again is too wonderful. But I have
had my surprise already. To live at all is the marvel, the
strangeness, the almost impossibility. *This*, lying here, the
sister and mother, our friend? You call her dead? Was it
spirit that once animated this form? *Dead spirit?* As well
say dead life or dead God ! Spirit is that which does not
die. As we live and believe in infinite Being, and know we
are, ourselves, we cannot cease to be.

I am glad to see no heavy pall, but the bright flowers,
God's language of love to us and our language of love to
each other. Their cheerfulness tells yours, — you could
not lay them here on this lid if you did not believe and
hope. They are not brought in the hands of despair. But
the real flower is not on the coffin, but in it, the flower of
gentleness, the flower of sweetness, the flower of courtesy, —
or the broken vase from which God has taken that flower of
the soul's beauty to set it out elsewhere for perfect bloom.
It is her tenderness that impressed others, I am told. But
there is no true tenderness without strength. What was her
power and courage to pursue her worthy vocation, in times
when it met frowns so dark from whatever was called religious in the church? I would not be uncharitable to my
own profession; but, with its opposition to the theatre,
however presumably sincere, is it not possible there mingled
unawares something of that jealousy and rivalry natural
between those two great arts of expression, the pulpit and

the stage? Be this as it may, I am free to bear witness to
my own receiving from the actor an instruction as well as
comfort beyond what preaching has already supplied. But,
thank God, a better day is coming — has come — of be-
holding religion as no insulated element, which any temple
can hold, but a service wide as life and deep as the God-
given faculties of the human mind.

In one thought more these mourners and sympathizers
will join, to cross the sea to her who did her pious duty so
thoroughly, who still pursues her steps, with the heavenly
approval and the satisfaction of that mother she was so
devoted to, — a mother that would have been proud of her
had she been proud of anything, and who, were she here,
could not, through flowing tears, look more earnestly and
fondly on these sacred relics — than she looks.

. . . .

The Benediction I send you, may I have from you? In
all love,   Yours,

C. A. BARTOL.

At the grave I thought how much better was the silent
pouring in of flowers than talking about the death of the
body, when the soul is joyous already, and I felt what a
great saying that was, " I am the resurrection and the life ; "
how high Jesus must have been, how greatly he must have
seen, to be able to say that. May I excuse so much paper,
with one sentence more? The half-humorous, wholly kind
look from you at Mr. Sargent's house, where I last saw and
talked with you about the North End Mission, — in answer
to my almost uncivil gaze, — has stayed with me ever since,
and I think will not go. May not less, but more happiness
come into face and heart, with the grief, prays

C. A. BARTOL.

It was hard to turn to the activities of life again,
but there are natures that must press onward with
ever renewed energy.

"Life is ever lord of Death,"

and to Kate Field, still in her youth, with her varied talents and keen interests, life called with many voices. Friends were kind, and she felt the consciousness of unseen companionship sustaining and encouraging her. Leaving Liverpool on May 30, with her friend Mr. Hennessy, the well-known artist, he took her to his home, and she began at once to look forward and not backward. It was she who put aside her own grief and endeavored to comfort the other relatives, and to her Aunt Corda she wrote:

"Dear, let us believe it to be for the best, and let us show our love for her by doing all in our power for those who are left in whom she was interested. Every harsh word I ever uttered comes to me as a reproach, and I ask forgiveness many, many times a day. I pray God this grief may chasten me."

There was, however, no occasion for self-reproach. Kate had been to her mother not only a most devoted and tender daughter, but, as we have seen, in her untiring work she had assumed all the cares of life for both.

Miss Frances Power Cobbe was among the first to call on Miss Field in London, and her kindness was full of cheer. Mr. Browning was another friend who brought her comfort; and with Miss Mathilde Phillipps, the younger sister of Adelaide, who was then in London, Kate renewed her friendship, and through Miss Phillipps met Garcia. Mrs. Taylor, the wife of a Member of Parliament, living in an exquisite old house on Notting Hill, a part of Kensington, persuaded Miss Field to remain with her for a time. "She will not allow me to seek a boarding-house," writes Kate, "declaring that I need rest and must not worry about material existence. Her house is charming, surrounded by a garden, and her friends are clever and liberal."

Mr. and Mrs. Moncure D. Conway were most hospitable to her, and at a dinner at their house she again met Robert Collyer. Robert Browning called on her frequently. "Gradually I shall find some place to fit into, I suppose," Kate writes; "but nothing in the world can take the place of love. . . . I shall not put on mourning. I don't believe in it, and darling mother understands. I shall realize that she is with me, free from pain, happy in the possession of husband and son, and not lost to me. I am going to be strong. I shall mourn as little as possible. I shall try to be cheerful and try to do good, and so please her who has only gone before."

The first letter that Kate received from her aunt was written before the news of Mrs. Field's death had reached her, and it began, "Dear Ones." The expression almost overcame Kate, after all she had gone through, and she wrote: —

"You can imagine how I felt. Yet the other dear one was near me. She who loved me so dearly will not leave me in the spirit."

Hon. Whitelaw Reid wrote to Miss Field this letter of sympathy: —

226 East Eighteenth Street,
New York, June 3, 1871.

My dear Miss Kate, — I do not know what to write to you; and so it would doubtless be better if I did not write at all. But I cannot find it in my heart to be silent when such a distressing grief has so suddenly and terribly come upon you. At least let me send a single word, to show that if your friend *is* silent it is through no lack of sympathy or saddest pity.

I am doubly troubled about you because I know you depended so much on Smalley's kind offices. If, as I have thought not improbable, you decide to return at once, this will make no difference ; but otherwise he could and would be of great service were he on the spot. I was not quite sure when he was going to take his vacation, and so said nothing to you about it. His letter came very soon after you sailed.

If anything I can do here can help you, pray command me ; and meantime accept my sincerest sympathies, and count me always

Your friend,

WHITELAW REID.

From that beautiful spirit, Charles A. Page, came a letter in which Mr. Page said : —

Your sweet, beautiful mother dying at sea ! — and you with her ! Little as I knew her, you will let me say that I loved her.

" I am here, — and *alone*," you say. No wonder that you add that you feel in a nightmare dream.

My eyes are watery — but that won't comfort *you*.

I want to see you.

If you want to be quiet for a little while, there is a room and two good women at my house.

Yours in sympathy,

CHARLES A. PAGE.

Oliver Lay, the artist, wrote, expressing his remembrance of Mrs. Field in the rooms on Twenty-Seventh Street, where he would find the mother and daughter with an open fire and a loaded desk, and all the pictures and quiet loveliness. "How beautiful she appears to me now!" he continued; "how inestimably precious is every thought of her! I can never forget her dear face, and voice with such soft and tender intonations, and the sweetest smile; and how sympathetic she was! so noble-hearted, so ready to listen to another! and how she forgot herself in helping any one who appealed to her!"

Miss Field's cousin, Mr. George Riddle, the distinguished reader, wrote to Kate an exquisite letter, in which, of his aunt, he said: —

"When I think of her beautiful, holy character, which seemed to grow more spiritual every day till God took her, I endeavor to embrace that faith which supported her sweet life."

Mr. Thomas Adolphus Trollope wrote from Florence: —

FLORENCE, June 10, 1871.

MY DEAR KATE, — I cannot refrain from writing you a word of sympathy and condolence, though I know but too well how fruitless all sympathy and condolence must seem to those who suffer from such sorrow as you are now suffering from. I know well and perfectly remember how close the tie was that united you and your dear mother, and I know the feeling that makes all the world seem one great blank and wilderness when so large a part of oneself has been torn away. Your letter to me you put perhaps by mistake in a cover addressed to Isa Blagden, and I received it open from her. She no doubt will have told Mrs. Jarves of the unhappy tidings it contains. Jarves is in America.

We leave this place for Venice on Monday, the 19th, with the intention of remaining in Venice all summer. We have been recommended to give Bice a course of sea-bathing, and it seems to us that Venice is the pleasantest place at which this can be done. Leghorn is detestable, but at Venice there is always at least something in the city to interest and occupy one. We propose being back here about the 20th of September. Do you know that I am seeking to sell my villa? The fact is, that I cannot afford to live in it without working, and I am tired of work, having in my day done a fair share of hard work; and if I could sell this property we should be able to live as we wish to live without the necessity of working for money. There is a lady here from New Orleans who talks of buying it, but must wait before she can decide, for the arrival of her husband from America. Now that Paris as a residence for wealthy pleasure-seeking people is a thing of the past, we are likely to have a great influx of American residents here as well as others. Of course we shall be glad to hear as soon as you know what your immediate plans are likely to be, and of course Fanny joins me in assurances that we sorrow with you in your sorrow. You could not doubt it even without any such assurance. My brother Anthony sailed from Liverpool for Australia on the 24th of May, intending to be absent from England about eighteen months. Believe me always, my dear Kate,

Affectionately yours,

T. Adolphus Trollope.

And Robert Browning wrote: —

19 Warwick Crescent W., June 5, 1871.

Dear Miss Field, — I am profoundly grieved at your misfortune, — most sad misfortune. I shall not attempt to speak about it. I was away when your letter came, and I waited two days in order to try and get information about a place of abode. Yesterday I went to Edwardes Square and found you had already left. I then proceeded to your present address. I know enough of Mrs. P. Taylor to feel at ease so far respecting you, and the kindly hands into which you have fallen. It is quite useless now to mention what was recommended to me as a particularly comfortable boarding-house, but I can refer you to it if necessary.

I should be very glad to know the time when you are most likely to be met with if I call. I will do your commission at once to Isa B., and through her to Mr. Trollope. I would gladly be of any sort of use to you. I hope you need no assurance of that, but I hope to see you, and we can talk together.

Ever affectionately yours,

R. B.

Miss Field sought instruction from Garcia, who heard her sing, and then said to her: —

"My dear, I must tell you the truth. You have passion, you are sympathetic, you have musical intelligence, you interpret rightly in intention, your voice is sufficiently powerful and the quality is good, but it is an exhausted voice. You have not the muscular power to carry out your intentions. If you were physically strong, you could sing perfectly well, but you are tired out. You need rest, amusement, care. You should consult a physician, receive treatment, and if you regain your strength I shall be most happy to give you lessons."

Commenting on this, Kate said: "Yes, Garcia told the truth. Now that the motive for constant exertion has gone, now that I can no longer care for mother, I find how tired I am." She wished to give up their house in Joy Street. "I don't feel that I can ever live in Boston again," she said. And in reply to her aunt's expressions regarding Mrs. Field's death, Kate wrote: —

" Dear, don't say you are never to see mother again. If I did not believe that the separation is merely temporary and that the darling must be happier than were she suffering on earth, there would be no sunshine in life. I miss her tender love and care so much. No one can have the faith in me she had, but I try to believe that it is right, and that the good God who took her away will make me strong to endure. I can't think yet of the future. I seem a waif now. . . . But I try not to grieve for darling mother. What could I offer her in comparison with what my father and brother and freedom from pain can give her? But I miss her, and I am so tired and do so long to have some one know what ought to be done for me and to do it. Everything seems impossible, and yet the old story of supposing I am able to bear all, goes on. Dear, you tell me to spend the remainder of my life with you and to give up work. You ask whether I have not had enough of public life, and say that mother worried at my work. I have never overworked from desire. Necessity has been my master ever since childhood. I have never known freedom from care. I have never seen that I could be idle until now. Now I am alone and have sufficient money to authorize devotion to my best interests, which at present are assuredly health and relaxation. I certainly desire to be with you, but it is neither right nor expedient that I renounce my public career just as it is beginning. To do anything while I am ill is impossible. To work reasonably should I recover my tone is absolutely required of me. No one desired me to do certain things more than mother, and now if I live I long to realize her desires. But I long for home life, and I have no wish to repeat the experiences of the past two winters. Incessant travelling is most distasteful to me. I want to return to America, but as the physicians say ' no,' I ought to turn Europe to the best possible account. I am hedged in by the fact of loneliness. If I only had some

one with me, I might do what now seems so difficult. The
doctor says I am generally better, but I feel far from well.
I sleep very little, and old troubles make me good for nothing. I am told to go up the Rhine to Wiesbaden, there to
drink the waters which are prescribed, and then to go on to
Switzerland. How I am to do this alone I can't see, yet if
no one can be found, I must go alone. In Switzerland I
shall be with Lina Warren, and the Trollopes want me to
spend October with them, and the Vedders write urging
me to go to them wherever they are, and then spend the
winter in Rome.''

The two months passed in London at this time in
the utmost retirement had still revealed to a keen
observer like Miss Field something of the quality of
social life. The world in which she found herself
was made up of poets, journalists, artists, with members of Parliament, a few of the clergy, and here and
there a peer, and others of the nobility, — certainly a
social world of varied elements and of representative life. In this society she found herself at no
disadvantage. She had known in close intimacy at
home men and women who in culture and good
breeding were not surpassed by any in the Old
World, and she was herself a young woman of such
gifts, such distinction of presence and beautiful culture, that she was here, as elsewhere, *persona grata* at
once. Withal, she had much of her mother's winsome power, and she made friends easily. Kate
believed in social life as one of the greatest sources
of development as well as of enjoyment. " Society
ought to be the best expression of humanity," she
would say; " one of these days it will be." She
always mingled freely in the more significant social
interchange.

Faure and Lucca were in London at this time. Garcia, who had no voice, was so great an artist as to make his art compensate for the loss; Lucca's dramatic force impressed Kate, and Faure she spoke of as admirable. She saw a few people quietly and heard good music; and for the rest she drove a great deal with friends, observing and studying the London she was one day to know so well. Constantly was Kate consoled by the conviction of her mother's close presence. "I do not believe the dear one has left me," she wrote. "I shall try to do the work left undone by her and by father and make myself useful until my last hour comes." And again speaking of her mother she said: "Her face told the story of youth and immortality. Spiritualists should be cheerful," she added, "and I try to be."

The following note from Mrs. Lewes (George Eliot) came very pleasantly to Kate: —

THE PRIORY, REGENT'S PARK, May 21, 1872.

DEAR MISS FIELD, — Your letter finds me still here, but in the midst of arrangements for our departure. The weather, our ailments, and various other causes have made us put off our flight from one week to another, but now we are really fluttering our wings and making a dust about us.

I wish we had seen you oftener. I was placidly looking forward to your staying in England another year or more, and gave way to my general languor about seeing friends in these late months, which have been too full of small bodily miseries for me to feel that I have much space to give to pleasanter occupation.

The present of autumn leaves which Col. T. W. Higginson has brought will be very gratefully accepted, if he will kindly send them to this house, so that I may find them on my return in our coming autumn. Pray thank him on my behalf.

If Mrs. Mark Pattison is still in town, and if you are seeing her, will you say that I expected her to come the Sunday before last? Since it has been agreed that if we left before the Sunday she was to have a card telling her the fact. I wish you had been here on that Sunday. There was some pleasant singing of men's voices.

Mr. Lewes adds his hearty wishes to mine that your future may be a bright one. We trust that your visit to England has been at least a good seedtime in your experience, and you are young enough to make each sowing all-important.

Good-by. Believe me always, whether you come back to us in the flesh or not,

Yours with sincere friendliness,
MARIAN E. LEWES.

Wishing to meet Charles Reade, Miss Field wrote to him, receiving the following reply: —

DEAR MADAM, — I beg to acknowledge your favor, and Mr. Osgood's. I do not know whether I am competent to advise you, but will try.

I am always at home, from eleven till two, and shall be happy to receive you any day you may feel disposed to honor me with a visit.

I am much concerned to think that you should have lost your mother on the voyage. It is a terrible bereavement, and under the circumstances truly pitiable. I am,

Yours faithfully,
CHARLES READE.

A letter from one of the prominent story-writers of America, Mrs. Rebecca Harding Davis, reached Miss Field during this summer: —

My dear Miss Field, — I know how many people there are in the world who ask favors, and are bores in consequence, and it is with a good deal of reluctance I add myself to the number. But I really wish some information, and can only think of you as the most capable person of giving it. I am sure you will be willing.

To plunge in . . . at once, I want to write for an English magazine — one of the best class, of course. How shall I go about it? I do not find the editors of our magazines disposed to help me in the matter. What magazine or what editor would be most likely to consider manuscripts sent? Secondly, I am going to begin a novel (running about six months) in July in "Lippincott's Magazine." Do you think it likely I could arrange to have it published simultaneously there, as Black's, Macdonald's, etc., are here? And, thirdly, how do the rates of compensation there compare with our own? You see, I am absolutely ignorant of the whole matter, and I know that in all probability you have the *carte de pays* of the literary world in your hand, and can advise me what to do.

I have been heartily glad to hear of your great success in England. Don't come home just now if you are happy there. You can have no idea of the stagnation of all business and life here. The country is like a man whom somebody is holding by the throat.

Once more, — don't think of me as a nuisance. I have a strong dislike to myself while writing this letter, for I know that I am one.

Very cordially yours,
REBECCA HARDING DAVIS.

Kate was, however, beset with anxieties for the future. She had on her hands the lease of their house in Boston — at $1000 per annum — for almost another year. With her characteristic executiveness she set to work to find some one to take the lease, to store for her certain designated articles of furniture, to have the remainder sold, and to send all her mother's wardrobe to a relative at a distance. To a faithful servant she designated certain gifts to be made out of the household stores, and all these practical details — so difficult to arrange at a distance — were attended to by Miss Field. Out of her three years' incessant lecturing and writing she had repaid to her uncle several hundred dollars that he had spent for her previously; she had supported herself and her mother, had been very generous to certain relatives, and had saved $2000. This indicates that she had very good financial abilities. On leaving for Europe her uncle, Mr. Sanford, insisted upon giving her a letter of credit for $2000 more, which she accepted gratefully as a safeguard, but with the hope not to draw upon it. So it was that she faced the future, and felt the two-fold pressure both of earning a livelihood and also of rendering whatever gifts she possessed of as much value as possible to the world. She was intensely ambitious, but it was always a lofty and a noble ambition. Although her finances were uncertain, she loaned thirty pounds at this time to a friend in need, whose prospects offered little assurance that it would ever be repaid. Miss Field carried with her to London letters to many persons of distinction, among whom was Lord Houghton, and a note from him runs: —

MY DEAR MISS FIELD, — I am very sorry to have missed you, and it would give Lady Houghton and myself much pleasure if you would dine with us next Saturday at eight o'clock. I am,

Yours,

HOUGHTON.

Mr. Browning was then in London, and called often to see her, renewing their friendship of a decade before, and with George Eliot and Mr. Lewes the acquaintance begun in Florence was continued. For the sake of the future, Miss Field desired to test herself in London by giving a lecture before an invited audience, and on July 23, in the Haymarket Theatre, she gave her lecture on Dickens before a select gathering, which included Mrs. Fanny Kemble, Miss Frances Power Cobbe, and other people of note, whose verdict was that the effort was a perfect success.

Miss Cobbe wrote to Miss Field the next day, saying : —

" Your lecture is brilliant and clever. A great many points of it ought to be quoted as epigrams. I think you have great literary powers which would not fail to be successful in pure literature. I think also you have dramatic powers."

A literary friend whom Miss Cobbe had invited wrote to her regarding Miss Field, saying: —

" I cannot allow the great enjoyment of yesterday to pass away without thanking you most warmly for the pleasure of hearing and seeing Miss Field. It is a very long time since I enjoyed anything so much. Although I heard Mr. Dickens read quite near the last time, the impression was far less pleasing of himself there than that of yesterday, which, speaking of him, reminds one of his whole life so well. I only hope the critics and privileged friends of such a lady were able to give her encouragements to proceed with the idea of favoring a larger audience."

Having made this experimental success, Kate dropped the matter for the time, and thought only of

regaining her health. With her father's effervescent
energy, she had also inherited his physical delicacy,
and the terrible strain of the past three years, culmi-
nating with the nervous shock of her mother's death,
left her in extreme exhaustion. Recommended to the
waters of Baden-Baden, she left London for the Continent the last of July, stopping at Brussels, where
she met Adelaide Phillipps, and they tarried one night
in Cologne to see the Cathedral. At Ems she joined
American friends, and one of the first letters she received was from a London manager, who assured her
she had "both fame and fortune" in her gifts as a
lecturer. While Miss Field could endure hardship,
if inevitable, with great fortitude, her tastes were
always for elegance and luxury. In Ems she occupied at the hotel the grand apartments that the Kaiser
always occupied, and she met some people of eminence among the Germans. She was perfectly conversant with French and Italian, but not with German,
of which she never acquired more than a superficial
knowledge. In the early September she left Ems for
Geneva, stopping *en route* at Heidelberg, Baden-
Baden, Strasburg, and Lucerne, where she was joined
by her old friend Lina Warren; and the man to whom
she had written that unique letter dated May 31,
1868, appeared and begged to escort them. Miss
Warren's sister and maid were included in the group.
The gentleman in question was again deeply devoted
to Miss Field, but while she found him chivalrous,
delicate in artistic feeling, and most interesting,
she felt no revival of a warmer inclination. But
to transform a lover into a friend was one of Kate
Field's possibilities. She was so frank, so unaffected,
she had so much of the comrade spirit, that these

rather unusual relations were possible. While no woman was more capable of passionate and deathless love, she had yet an instinctive distrust of marriage. In one of her letters to her aunt she says:—

"Dear, you say your only ambition for me is to see me *well* married. Do you think that so easy? I've had several escapes from matrimony, for which I thank God. A life of ambition is a terrible grind, you say. And how about most marriages? Are not they terrible grinds? Do you realize what would happen if I married and made a mistake? I do. I believe in love. I don't believe in being tied to a man whom I cease to love. Therefore the less said to me about marriage the better. If I marry, there's no knowing the misery in store for me, so don't think that the panacea. My observation makes me afraid of lifelong experiments."

And again in one letter she says:—

"You seem to think that ambition is the guiding star of my existence, and that I am sacrificing everything to it. Dear, it seems useless to argue the matter, yet you never were more mistaken in your life. . . . With regard to the acts of my life (outside of health) of course no one can decide but myself. If a human being possesses character and conviction, he or she is the best judge of what must be done. I *am* a person of convictions, and am as fervent in them as Charlotte Corday when she became a murderer, or Jeanne d'Arc when she braved everything to lead France on to glory."

This intense individualism may suggest the clue to the curious fact that a woman so attractive as Miss Field never married.

As the little group of friends were leaving Ems, a

letter came to Kate from Mrs. Vedder of which she writes : —

" Carrie Vedder writes, urging my going to them. Evidently they are very happy. Money has cheered them, and they are going into new quarters with new furniture designed by Vedder's self. I am very glad."

The trip to Geneva was most interesting. They paused at Worms and saw the statue of Luther, — a colossal bronze statue of the great Reformer, which was erected in 1861, in the centre of the square called Luther Platz; at Heidelberg, visiting the old castle; at Strasburg they passed some time in the Cathedral, which Kate did not find so fine as that of Cologne; and at Basle she admired the fine Holbeins in the museum, which she says are worth a long pilgrimage to see. Of Freiburg she says : —

"We arrived just in time for the concert on the celebrated organ. They give one daily (during the travelling season) at half-past eight P. M. The cathedral is dimly lighted, and the effect delightful. I never heard such exquisite tone before in an organ. The vox humana and pianissimo were wonderful. After the concert I sought the organist, and the next morning before starting for Geneva I had a private concert all to myself."

In this cathedral is the tomb of Berthold of Zähringen, who died in 1218. "He was the last of his race," Kate wrote; and added a vivid description of a beautiful old altar-piece by Grien representing the Ascension and Coronation of the Virgin. The ancient University in Freiburg also interested her.

During the summer Miss Field was writing occasional letters to the New York "Tribune," but with

this slight exception she undertook no work. The
meeting with her old friend Miss Warren was a great
joy, and she wrote: —

" I am as much attached to her as ever. She is full of
American energy, which is good to encounter in Europe."

In Geneva Kate had a room looking out upon the
lake with an enchanting view of mountains down to
the water's edge. She was an enthusiastic lover of
nature and enjoyed the open air with the abandon of
a poet. While in the city of Calvin, Kate sought out
the traces of the eminent men who had lived there, —
Sismondi, Rousseau, Merle D'Aubigné, the author of
the "History of the Reformation," and Necker, the
Minister of Louis XVI. She visited Ferney, Vol-
taire's residence, some five miles from the city. From
Lausanne Miss Field went to Paris, where she was
domiciled at the Chatham and indulged in shopping
to the extent of a street costume and two evening
gowns, and where two or three dinners were given
for her. Thence to London again, which she reaches
on November 1, going to an apartment in Bedford
Place that Helen Hunt, and later that Justin McCar-
thy had occupied, but not liking it she finds pleasant
quarters in Half Moon Street off Piccadilly. As
usual with the artistic and literary folk, the financial
problem haunts her, and to her uncle, Mr. Sanford,
she writes: —

" Five months only since I left home, and already I have
drawn the amount I started with, $2000. When I next call
for money, it will probably be on your letter of credit. I
am sorry, but I 've undertaken to regain my health and in
doing this I am obliged to spend a great deal — for me.
At this rate, I shall expend the remaining $2000 by next

February or March; consequently it behooves me to consider the future. I am going to try to lecture here, and if I succeed, I need give myself no concern about money. But if I do not, I must sell out some of my stock. What shall I sell? N. Y. C. Scrip or the Louisville and Nashville R. R. bonds? Please answer this question. Chicago may have killed stocks of all kinds, for aught I know, but as I need not sell before February, everything may revive before then."

This fine independence in money matters was a salient point in the flawless integrity of Kate Field's character. She could accept a favor when needed, but she was always sensitive to obligation and always met it at the earliest possible moment. London expenses she found very high. Her physician, Sir Morell Mackenzie, charged a guinea a visit. Garcia's terms for singing lessons were the same per lesson. But friends multiplied and life began in deeper earnest for her. One November night, dining at a famous house, she met Miss Elizabeth Peabody of Boston, who had then just gone over to care for her niece, Una Hawthorne. Meeting William Black, the novelist, he begs Miss Field to let him show her the old London, and about this time he writes to her this amusing note: —

"Why did you not tell me you were to sing after the lecture? You said 'a song and champagne thrown in,' and so I heard the song with the greatest pleasure and thought I'd better not stay for the champagne. Won't you bring the song of which I was defrauded, and sing it to me?"

And again Mr. Black writes: —

Gracious goodness me! the idea of going into the Park on Good Friday! We should be apprehended by the

police and sentenced to seven years' transportation for life !
If you wish to admire the trees and roam in sylvan solitude
by the banks of the Serpentine, this Barkis " is also willin',"
but if you want to see all sorts of Parliamentary swells a-
airin' of theirselves in the Row, we shall have to wait till
Parliament comes together next week.

In this awful dilemma I leave myself in your hands. If
you say the aimless wander, and that lunch to follow, well
and good ; if you say wait until we can see the swells a-
airin', good and well. Twenty-four hours' notice will suf-
fice, and I am

Yours to command,

WILLIAM BLACK.

Miss Field always believed in the gospel of good
gowns, and she writes that on one of her early consul-
tations with Sir Morell Mackenzie he exclaimed to
her : —

"'What a pretty hat you have on ! I 've tried to describe
it to my wife. It 's the prettiest hat I 've seen this season.'
Of course this led to my saying that I 'd be happy to show
it to Mrs. Mackenzie. He rushed upstairs, dragged her
down, and it ended in the wife's begging me to call on her
reception day. Here strangers call first."

" Was n't it funny ? " she adds. In her letter to
her aunt she expresses herself freely regarding Boston friends, — James R. Osgood, whose royal nature
was the counterpart of her own in generous goodness ; and of Mr. and Mrs. Edwin P. Whipple she
said : —

"The Whipples, — they are the sincerest of people, and
if they are cordial you may be sure they mean it."

Again she writes : —

" My friend Sir Charles Dilke has come out publicly as a republican. All the papers are howling, and some of his friends have cut him, but he has done a brave thing, and I honor him for it. He has merely anticipated events, and now becomes a leader. English monarchy is doomed within the next twenty years. Politics here are becoming interesting in consequence."

Miss Field grew to like Half Moon Street. It is in Mayfair, the parks are near, and she had a drawing-room and bedroom; and when she had a piano sent in and had arranged her household gods, she found herself almost happy again. The intimations from the Unseen continue to come to her, and consulting a medium she records a communication as written signed " Little Mother," — her own pet name always for her mother. The message ran : —

" I am always with you. I shall make every effort to impress you, so that we can communicate together alone. I know, my baby, that you suffer, but I try to impress you with our complete happiness. I can do more for you here, darling. You have work to do, and we will help you always."

" It was all so real," says Kate, " that the tears came to my eyes. Oh, if I could only *see* into the other world, what a comfort it would be."

The complete story of Miss Field's life could not be told without including her experimental interest in the relations between the Seen and the Unseen worlds. It was a matter which she never discussed save in special intimacy and sympathy, but the quest, the consideration, and the practical experimenting whenever possible, was always a part of her inner life. As the Christmas of this year drew on, her aunt and uncle wrote asking her to choose herself a gift and send the bill to them. She replied declining, and said : —

"You and uncle do enough for me all the year around. If you will transfer my present to —— you will do a charitable as well as kindly act."

With all her indomitable courage, Kate always had gravest anxieties when making a new venture; and her entire life was a series of new ventures. Fairly settled in her rooms, she begins writing leading editorials for the New York "Tribune" and making preparations for her first professional lecture in London. "If you knew how I feared results, you would pity me," she writes to her aunt. Yet was this only a momentary giving way in the atmosphere of high and heroic thought. Never lacking in sentiment, there was never a trace of the merely sentimental in Kate Field; and it was indeed in this December of 1871 that she struck the keynote of all her after life, — that breathless quarter of a century which still awaited her on earth, — in her insight and analysis of the political status of the day in England. While her literary work included criticism, sketches that verged on romance, narrative, and comment on almost every topic; and the dramatic comedietta, in which she was particularly happy, — it was yet the political significance in progress that became her leading interest through after years.

Republicanism in England was in its dawn in 1871. To Miss Field it appealed as a great cause; and she wittily says that although we are assured that truth is mighty and will prevail, there is no commodity which requires such liberal advertising to bring it into

circulation. The price paid for truth, she said, has
been blood, and she instanced that when John Brown
went to the scaffold, exclaiming, "I am persuaded
that I am worth inconceivably more to hang than for
any other purpose," he foretold the knell of slavery.
It seems that at a meeting addressed by Sir Charles
Dilke, where he argued in favor of a republic or of
true parliamentary representation, there was great
excitement, and one William Schofield, who espoused
the speaker's side, was killed. The event gave Miss
Field a text which she did not fail to elaborate in her
spirited way. Again she goes to the Royal Chapel
to hear Charles Kingsley, and writes of it one of her
inimitable press letters, under the caption of, "The
Divine Right of Kings — and Kingsley." The opening of Parliament and republicanism in Parliament
occupy her attention, and certain selections from this
very able and brilliant series of press letters are collected in a volume entitled "Hap-Hazard."

As usual, her days were filled with interests that
kept her in a state of nervous tension. One week full
of incident she thus recounts : —

"On Sunday I dined with the Chippendales. On Monday I went to the House of Commons, met several members, remained there until 6 P. M., then went to the Dilkes,
where I dined, after which I accompanied them to the
great republican meeting, where Dilke and Sir Henry Hoare
addressed their constituents. It was very fine and very exciting. Then at eleven Sir Henry drove me back to the
House, where I heard Gladstone and saw a division. The
whole thing I have written out in four columns for 'The
Tribune.' On Thursday I dined with the Peabodys (bank-
ers). On Friday I heard Henry Leslie, the composer, deliver a lecture on music before the Royal Institution, but it

was very bad. On Saturday I met Sir Henry Holland and others at the Schencks. And to morrow I go to the great show at St. Paul's. I dined this week with Mrs. Inwood Jones, — Lady Morgan's niece, — where I met several clever people, among them a brother of Lord Clarendon's and again at Sir Charles Dilke's. On Saturday evening I was invited to George Eliot's; but as I had previously promised to go to General Schenck's reception, — he has one every week, — I was obliged to decline, much to my regret. General Schenck is very polite to me, and is a clever man of the Western type. He is a good American."

Again comes an experimental test in psychic research. She writes: —

"The other evening I attended a spiritual séance at a private house. Kate Fox was the medium. We saw strange lights, but I was the only person who received communications. 'Dear child, I live and am happy.' I asked no question. This came. Then I inquired whether I should obey the request made in the letter received that day (Uncle Milt's letter). 'No,' was the vigorous reply. Of course I do not act upon such things. I only relate what happened."

In the early spring Kate's uncle urged her return to America, and she explains more fully than before the state of her health. She wrote: —

"The fact is, that I have been overworked all my life, and that I realized my condition last spring, but as I am not in the habit of talking about my ailments, and as my own dear mother occupied my thoughts, I have never until now done anything to more than stave off illness. My dear mother's death left me without nerve. All that I could do for myself last summer I did do. I am better, but I am far from well. Both physicians say that in justice to myself I ought to try Ems again. Am I selfish in what I write? Do you think me unreasonable? I hope you will see things as I do, and believe that I love you, although I desire to remain in Europe a few months longer."

So averse was Miss Field to any recognition of ill health, so full of spiritual energy and indomitable will, that not even her nearest friends ever realized how inadequate was her strength to her ceaseless demands upon it.

On May 6 of 1872, Miss Field gave her lecture on Dickens again in Willis's rooms, before an audience including General Schenck (then the American Ambassador), Mrs. Kean, Garcia, Sidney Colvin, the distinguished art critic, and many others of note. The lecture was preceded by an informal reception, in which Miss Field was assisted in receiving by Mrs. Mark Pattison (now Lady Dilke), who was at that time the wife of the rector of Lincoln College, Oxford, and who was always one of the more intimate friends of Miss Field. Mrs. Pattison was also a near friend of George Eliot's, and is supposed to be the original of the character of Dorothea in " Middlemarch." And the readers of that strange book, the " Memoirs " of Mark Pattison, which appeared in 1885 from the " Macmillans," will hardly need to go farther to find the original of George Eliot's wonderful portraiture of Mr. Casaubon.

The London critics were enthusiastic over Miss Field's success on this occasion. Mr. Sidney Colvin surprised Kate by saying there had been no such voice as hers on the English stage for many a year. Mrs. Kean was charmed, and she said that Miss Field could easily fill any hall. If genius is only the art of

taking great pains, the audiences who have enthusiastically recognized Kate Field's exquisite art in
speaking before the crowded houses of her later
years, will trace in these beginnings the unwearied
efforts she made to render herself worthy of public
approval.

Before leaving England for Ems again, she looked
about her with her customary thoroughness of detail.
" On Saturday," she writes, " I visited Oxford as the
guest of the rector of Lincoln College. I was invited to dine at Professor Jowett's, and there met the
Dowager Lady Stanley." Miss Field was very much
feasted and fêted on this visit, and soon after she
made another quite different little tour, — to meet not
the English aristocracy, as at Oxford, but the laboring
class. She writes : —

" I went to Leamington this week in order to see Arch,
the agricultural laborer, who has been the cause of raising
the laborers' wages from one end of England to the other.
He is an earnest, honest man. He got up a meeting on
purpose for me, wanted me to speak, but I was too great a
coward. Came to see me, and brought me a lovely bouquet, a bit of which I enclose. During this visit I went to
Coventry, Kenilworth, and Warwick Castle. I made
friends with the editor of Leamington 'Chronicle,' and
left highly satisfied with my expedition. This week is to
be devoted to lunatic asylums, agricultural congresses, and
sight-seeing generally. People want me to visit them in
the country, but I see no time. Engagements in London
at this season of the year are made six weeks in advance,
and I 've every evening filled up for a fortnight."

Just before her departure Miss Field was invited
by Sir Morell Mackenzie to a dinner of the Hospital

for Throat Diseases, and requested to return thanks for the ladies. Miss Field's speech came last, and it proved the sensation of the evening. It was received with tremendous applause, and Lord Clarendon and others pronounced it the best after-dinner speech they had ever heard. In her later life Miss Field became rather noted for her felicitous post-prandial eloquence.

Miss Field opened this speech as follows : —

"Several days ago an eminent physician tied a cord round my neck, put a laryngoscope into my mouth, applied a galvanic battery to my throat, fastened a glittering eye on me, and then, lifting up his voice, said : —

"'I should like you to speak at our biennial dinner for the Hospital for Diseases of the Throat. Will you?'

"Reduced to such a helpless condition, how could I refuse? This eminent physician combines Scotch pertinacity and Yankee energy with French tact. He has found the lost art of making people do precisely as he wishes ; and I honestly believe he has no friend who is not convinced that the salvation of the British Empire depends upon the financial prosperity of the Hospital for Diseases of the Throat. I do, for one ; and I shall tremble for Young Turkey, and the Balance of Power generally, if the subscriptions at this dinner do not cover the expenses of the new hospital building. Far be it from me to betray the identity of this persuasive gentleman. I will merely say that he sits with graceful but unconscious dignity at a neighboring table, and spells his name with an *M*.

"On the removal of the cord, laryngoscope, battery, *and* glittering eye, I asked, —

"'What subject?'

"'The Ladies.'"

It is little wonder that they laughed.

Mr. Stedman's letters, always full of sympathy with her high aspirations, with joy in her successes, with banter and fun and glancing wit, followed her everywhere. Here was a bit of rhymed nonsense which he sent her on a post-card : —

> " There is a young woman named Kate,
>   Whose vivacity none can abate !
>   The wits of all lands
>   Obey her commands,
> And she makes all the cabbies go straight."

At London entertainments Miss Field met Lady Franklin, who sent her a note that runs : —

DEAR MISS FIELD, — It would be so great a pleasure to me to have you, if only for an hour, in my own house before your departure that I have resolved upon the bold step of asking you at the last moment if you could not make it possible to look in upon us to-morrow evening.

We have some other friends coming to see the laurel-brow'd African lion, but what of the American lioness? I have not dared except to a favored very few to mention her name, and was then asked what relation she might be to Mr. Cyrus Field, so natural does it seem to men to take to themselves all the honors. Never mind their blundering ; my reply was that it was the Miss Field who ought never to be taken for anybody else, not even for the daughter of Mr. Cyrus Field of telegraph and other celebrities.

I had hoped to find a vacant place at our dinner table to offer you, but my party was already made up before Mr. Stanley appeared on the stage, and unless somebody should fail at the last moment, there is literally no space left for the most anxiously desired addition.

I have ventured to send a card to Sir Charles and Lady Dilke, trusting the latter might excuse my not having yet been able to call on her. Believe me,

Very sincerely yours,

JANE FRANKLIN.

Mr. Froude, the historian, apparently added to his other gifts a sense of humor, as evinced in the following: —

My dear Miss Field, — What possessed you to keep your veil on; and what possessed Conway not to tell me who I was speaking to till you had gone? I have always thought of you as the brightest of my American friends, and there you were, talking to me in your old way; and although the voice and the lower part of your face (all that was visible) seemed so pleasantly familiar I could n't conceive whom you could be.

Knowles is the most accessible of men. You have only to write directly to him. . . .

If you are so diffident that you want an introduction, you can use my name, but it is not the least necessary.

Will you not come here and see me and let me introduce you to my daughter? If not, when will we be likely to find you at home?

Ever yours truly,

J. A. Froude.

Mark Twain, being in London, writes: —

Dear Miss Field, — I see that it is n't your fault that you do not know me, and I 'm sure it is n't mine that I do not know you. Plainly, then, the party to blame is Providence, and therefore damages cannot be had in this vale. But we shall be glad to see and know you and likewise Lady Dilke; and since you give us the privilege of naming the time, shall we say Wednesday about 5 p. m.? I do not know that we have another disengaged day or hour for some little time to come, or I would of course offer a larger latitude. My small family of sight-seers keep themselves pretty busy; they have never been abroad before.

Very truly yours,

Samuel L. Clemens.

In the opening days of June Miss Field left London for Ems again *via* Paris, and her last three days were completely filled with the good-by calls of her friends. Her sincerity and frankness of nature, no less than her gifts and grace, had peculiarly endeared her to a very large and very varied circle.

One English lady, a peeress in her own right, wrote to Miss Field on her leaving: —

"I am almost sorry that you came. Had we not known you, we should not feel the loss. You have had a great success here, without seeking it or without paying the least court to people of position. You have treated everybody alike (this is a marvel to the English, who are sat upon by caste), and we all like your independence and respect you. I am sure you can go nowhere without making friends, for no American ever came here who made so great an impression and in so short a time."

Mrs. Julia Ward Howe, calling and not finding Miss Field, wrote her the following letter, which, though undated, apparently belongs to this time: —

Saturday Morning, 12 o'clock.

DEAR KATE, — My heart gave such a twinge when I received your farewell card that I flew down here this morning in a coupé, hoping to take tender leave of you. And you are not here. I am so sorry I do not know whether you have been in town all these days. I thought not, knowing of your trip to Cambridge. Then I heard of your going to the Derby, and then came your card. I have been miserably unwell with a cold. The London climate seems to promote such things. I shall be at home this P. M. from 4 to 6 — no company invited, but if you could call in, how pleasant! I expect to be at home all this evening, and would surely stay there if you could send me word that you

would come round (*Boston*). And I dare say you are
going to dine with some of the *grandees*. I go to Paris to-
morrow, to attend meeting " Alliance Universelle," — humbug, I expect. Thence to Bristol, back in town to-day
week. Expect to hold Sunday service at Free Masons'
Tavern Drawing-room to-morrow week — time, evening.
Kate, I like you. Farewell.

Affectionately,

JULIA W. HOWE.

Kate was warmly greeted in Ems by the friends she
had made the preceding summer. To her aunt she
writes : —

" In Paris I saw Ristori, who was delighted (at least she
acted so) to see me. She has a pretty apartment and looks
as well as ever. Louis Blanc called, but I was out."

Miss Field's newspaper work was now attracting
eminent attention. A little note from that nearest
and most prized of her friends, Mr. Edmund Clarence
Stedman, enclosing a press complimentary mention
of her, closes with these words: —

DEAR KATE FIELD, — If you will let me call you so,
to be so helped by a woman who seems to *me* so fair and
free-hearted as yourself, is enough recompense for any poet,
and I feel as much stirred by it as Rizzio could have been
when Mary Stuart said his voice had music and his lips
were sweet. I send you an exchange picture, which looks
as much like Governor Boutwell as the man 't was taken for,
and am

Faithfully yours,

E. C. STEDMAN.

A letter of similar import from her old friend, Mr.
Richard Watson Gilder, in which he wrote : —

" How are you getting along, My Dear K. F.? Often and often we (at our house) and your friends here talk about you. We have a half-dozen pictures of you over home; and you always look so pathetic (NOT *sentimental*) in photographs that I feel, on sight, like sitting down and expressing a great deal of interest in your affairs. I will not say that there is not the same quality in your bodily presentment; but it is accompanied by a — what shall I call it? — ' jasm,' electrical sparkles. I read your ' Tribune' letters with interest, and so do a great many people. We would like to have Dilke send us an article on ' Republicanism in England.' "

Mr. George Ripley writes, asking her to send "a luminous screed about London or the Brownings, or Miss Evans (George Eliot) or the great Lucifer, or any other worthy." A characteristic little letter of Celia Thaxter's runs: —

DEAR KATE FIELD, — Here is a lackadaisical picture, if you want it. I cannot get a picture that is not either idiotic or savage — what is the reason? for I won't confess to being a fiend or a simpleton *quite*. And I can't look up and show my little eyes, for then I seem most like a hag, so it is taken in this " maiden meditation fancy-free " style. Yours would be quite charming if you did not look so discontented; it carries a protest about the mouth, against all the world. But photographs lie, at least I know mine do. Thank you for it — most for the love you sent us with it. Take mine in return — as much as you like, pretty Kate Field. . . .

      Believe me ever truly your friend,

                        CELIA THAXTER.

James Parton writes to her this genial letter: —

NEW YORK, April, 1874.

MY DEAR MISS FIELD, — I wonder if you know how welcome to readers of " The Tribune " are your initials and all that goes before them. You ought to know for your own comfort, for no one of the scribbling temperament can keep on long without being petted and praised a little. You are an admirable journalist and much besides. You select the right things to tell and you infuse them with human spirit. All your letters from Europe last year, — your Spanish, especially, — your kind and good and wise letter this morning, delighted me, and I feel grateful to you for them. I hope you will regularly join " The Tribune " as its writing-whenever-you-feel-like-it-correspondent, at a salary that will cheer and not inebriate you.

Excuse my impudence, and believe me,

Gratefully,

JAMES PARTON.

A literary man in London wrote to Miss Field:

MY DEAR MISS FIELD, Dear K. F., My dear Kate, My Lovely Passion Flower, — I apostrophize you thus alternately in order that you may, like ladies in a draper's shop, select the article which suits you best. Your letter of September 6th has reached me, and has somewhat calmed my tempestuous wrath. I began to think that, like some fair siren, you had lured my footsteps to the Southampton Pier and then plunged all writing (I believe you *were* writing, though you ought to have been doing the other thing) beneath the Atlantic, vanished, in fact, altogether.

Another friendly word came from Mr. Richard S. Spofford, who said: —

" I don't know of any one who has been the victim of a more pronounced and progressive success than yourself, or who more fully illustrates the profundity of Emerson's assertion that the only way to be successful is to succeed ! "

Already Miss Field had achieved a distinctive recognition in the writing of dramatic dialogue, and her
sparkling comediettas were somewhat in demand in
both London and New York for holiday magazine
issues and other festive literary occasions. Mr. Stedman, whose genius for friendship rivals his gift of
song, wrote to her: —

"Naturally, after an evening with your letters, and reading
to-night your 'Tribune' works, I have been musing with
regard to its author and your hint that you had half a mind
to write a play. Why not make the half a whole, and do
it? I really don't believe that you can do anything else so
well (unless it be to win friends at sight). The fact is that
your education and career have been nomadic and versatile,
— you have coquetted, and something more, with literature,
art, lecturing, criticism, etc.; but if you love one thing
more than another it is, possibly, the stage, both from early
associations and instinct. Now I don't know any woman
who has your peculiar gifts and advantages as a dramatist.
You are a writer, to begin with, with sentiment, culture, wit,
sensibility. More than this, you know the stage, its effects,
limitations, and requirements. Lastly, you have natural
dramatic instinct. Write a play in prose, close, sharp,
epigrammatic, sparkling, but with scenes and passages of
real tenderness, pathos, passion. If the period is far in the
past, the story may be either foreign or American; but if in
the present, American by all odds. You will succeed, and
such a work in hand will give *point* to your ambition, and
you will be happy while engaged upon it. But write it *as
an artist;* that is, quit society for a time, throw your whole
heart into your work, let it absorb you to a certain extent,
do it for the love of it. It is too late for you to go on the
stage, and for you to stoop to pass through the several
grades of promotion — is it not? These few words come

wholly from my desire to see your fine temperament developed by an *adequate* task. You will succeed, if you try
honestly. Don't think that giving advice is the ordinary
habit of your friend,

E. C. STEDMAN.

This letter had a cumulative effect on Kate, not
only in the one direction suggested, but as influencing
her with added impulse toward the drama in its practical expression of stage appearances. Yet for the
moment this inborn desire of her life was to be held
in abeyance.

Among the many sparkling comediettas which
were the fruits of the future years of Kate's work, —
the original manuscripts of which are now in the
Boston Public Library — are those entitled: " The
Blind Side," "Extremes Meet," "Two Quarrel-
some Cousins," "Dead to the World," "The Wrong
Flat," "A Moving Tale," "Caught Napping," "A
Morning Call," and "The Opera Box."

These are instinct with dramatic movement and
inimitable sparkle and humor. The original manuscripts of these comediettas, together with a large
number of the letters written to Miss Field by some
of the famous people of the age, were presented to
the Public Library. These, accompanied by a repro-
duction of Vedder's portrait of Kate Field, painted in
Florence (the original of which is in the Boston
Museum of Fine Arts), were graciously accepted by
the President of the Board of Trustees, Frederick
Octavius Prince, Esq., Herbert Putnam, Librarian,
and the members, Messrs. Solomon Lincoln, Josiah
Henry Benton, Jr., H. P. Bowditch, and Rev. James
de Normandie, and by their courtesy form a "Kate

Field Memorial Collection," a permanent honor to
the memory of one of America's noblest women.

Mr. William Winter, the distinguished critic and
poet, wrote, under date of 1898, in reply to a letter
from the friend who presented these papers to the
Library, saying: —

"Your disposition of the letters of Kate Field seems
the most judicious that could be made. She often wrote
to me, and many of her letters remain among my papers.
With respect to letters of mine, addressed to her, I would
say that I have no reason to suppose them to be worthy of
preservation. It would, of course, be my wish that all letters of mine which may happen to touch upon matters of
private experience, and which were intended for her alone
(if any such there be), should be destroyed. She and I
were accustomed to write to each other with entire frankness. It was never my wish to contribute to the gossip of
the world, or in any way to minister to the taste of the multitude. I am, however, very sure that the choice of the
letters to be saved may confidently be committed to your
judgment and taste."

To Kate Field herself no form of memorial could
be more grateful than the honor of having her name
enshrined in the Public Library of Boston.

The London season of 1872 was no exception to
the usual brilliancy, and, as usual, there were no
lack of Americans to enjoy the great metropolis.
Two little notes from Mrs. Julia Ward Howe to Kate
were apparently written at this time, although the
first is undated: —

DEAR K. F., — We are here for a short stay after two
years of wandering, and shall be very glad to see you again,
if you are willing. If you will come to see us, or if we

shall come to see you, send a cheap postal to say. I suppose, talking of cheapness, that you have made your fortune by this time.

Yours always sincerely,

JULIA WARD HOWE.

The second runs: —

Monday, May 20, 1872.

Yes, dear Kate, I will come with much pleasure, for
much pleasure. Yours, just returned from the North,
very cold and old, but rather good-natured,

J. W. H.

Miss Field passed this summer of 1872 at Ems and
in the autumn returned to London. She met Bradlaugh and interviewed him for the New York " Tribune." At this time all London called him " Beast
Bradlaugh," and the tide of denunciation incited Miss
Field to hear and know the man and judge for herself.
" What's the matter with Bradlaugh? " she asked.
" The matter? " replied the British public: " everything! He's an atheist and, what's worse, a republican." Still unconvinced that the man was utterly
unworthy, Kate drove to the East End one evening to
hear him address an audience of working-men. " I
went again and again," she remarked later, " for I was
deeply impressed by an orator who would not have
had his equal in England had he not occasionally
dropped his *h's*. In physique he resembled Henry
Ward Beecher and Robert Collyer. Charged with
magnetism, he swayed his audiences at will and was
often inspired with an eloquence so spontaneous as to
be beyond his own recollection a few moments later."

Miss Field was not averse to giving *her* views of
Bradlaugh at Mayfair dinner-parties, quite to the un-

disguised horror of her listeners. " Sir Charles Dilke was the only exception," she laughingly related afterward in speaking of this episode in her life. " While Sir Charles was not altogether in sympathy with Bradlaugh, he did him justice, and said of him, ' Bradlaugh is the only man in England who has a following.' It was true," continued Miss Field, " his ' following ' could not be found in society, but it existed all the same."

Among Miss Field's papers is a letter from Bradlaugh, under date of Nov. 4, 1872, that runs: —

MY DEAR MISS FIELD, — I feared you had excommunicated me for my baseness. Really, it is very difficult to write about myself. I do not like always to boast, and yet to write my life really seems like a succession of boastings. I got a letter from the agents, and have written them in reply, asking them again to bother you.

I have gained a great victory over the authorities, who have backed down and have registered my paper. I am now very busy trying to bring the numerous republican clubs into one great organization, and believe that I shall succeed. The first edition of the Impeachment is nearly sold out, and I am occupied on another edition, which will be much stronger. Please choose my subjects for me for America, and I will be as gentle as it is possible for a bear like myself in all I say and write to you. The Bute of to-day is a descendant, the Earldom having become a Marquisate. If *wise*, — that is, for lectures in America, — I am well up in the facts as to Ireland, and I take very strong ground for the Irish against our past rule.

Thanking you for your praise, which one day I will try to justify. I am,

Sincerely yours,

CHARLES BRADLAUGH.

It was through Miss Field's influence that Bradlaugh came to the United States to lecture, making
very successful appearances. The last time Miss
Field ever saw him was in 1880 in London, one night
that she and Mr. John McCullough, the actor, were
dining together. As the door-bell rang violently,
Kate remarked to Mr. McCullough, "Whom do you
suppose that is?" "I have not the remotest idea,"
replied the popular tragedian. "Guess," tantaliz-
ingly continued Kate. "I am not good at guessing."
"Who is the most talked-of man in England?" she
questioned. "The Prince of Wales?" he ventured.
Kate's eyes sparkled with fun as she shook her head.
"Well, if not the Prince," said Mr. McCullough, "it
must be Bradlaugh." "Right," Kate replied; and
just then the hero of the hour was ushered in, and he
exclaimed, "Why, it's more difficult to get into your
lodgings than into the House of Commons, from
which, by the way, I can only be absent an hour and
ten minutes."

This was at the time when Bradlaugh had fought
his way into Parliament and three several actions had
been brought against him. At the end of his career,
however, the House of Commons expunged the resolutions that it had passed against Bradlaugh ten years
before, this reversal of judgment being advocated and
led by Mr. Gladstone.

Whatever appealed for freedom of thought always
inspired the interest and the allegiance of Kate
Field.

At this time Sir Charles Dilke was editing the
"Athenæum," which was then, as now, a standard in
English literary criticism, and through her friendly
offices Sir Charles asked Edwin P. Whipple to send

an article for the "Athenæum," and to Kate Mr. Whipple writes: —

BOSTON, Nov. 19, '73.

MY DEAR MISS FIELD, — I must decline Sir Charles Dilke's invitation, none the less because my eyes are pleased at the renewed sight of your bold, clear, and strong handwriting. We — that is, Charlotte and I, a plural unit — unite in sending our best love to "Kate." Shall we see you in Boston this winter? If you come, be assured that you can be welcomed by no more cordial friends than live in No. 11 Pinckney Street.

Very sincerely yours,

E. P. WHIPPLE.

The secrets of literary art are sometimes surprised by the student of literature, who even emulates the zeal of Sir Joshua Reynolds when he scraped a painting by Titian to discover the hidden power of his coloring. To such researchers a revelation of the methods of so great a critic as Mr. Stedman will be of no little interest; and the completeness of the unveiling of his art in the following letter to Miss Field establishes its claim to be placed on permanent record. Under date of Dec. 12, 1873, Mr. Stedman thus writes to Kate: —

DEAR K. F., — Your letter first before any other work. The manuscript I see is in no condition to print, owing to former marks, so I have n't scrupled to mark it still more. Have numbered the stanzas for reference's sake, but would not number them, if I were you, in a clear copy.

In this poem there is much of your characteristic original strength and vigor. Your very lack of poetic study keeps your mind clear of old or hackneyed phrases, and occasion-

ally you hit upon some most felicitous phrase. Again, you
put in something so grotesque or commonplace as to be
out of keeping — even in a grewsome poem like this. The
poem, on the whole, is too good to be lost; may be re-
vised and sold to Harper or Scribner, I should say."

The poem in question was evidently the following,
entitled, —

FORTY TO TWENTY

A DRAWING-ROOM DRAMA

TEARS in your eyes; and why? Because you find
That he you love is mortal, after all?
Dear silly coz, what else did you expect?
You met the man, and though you said no word,
Your eyes were eloquent and warmly spoke
The electric language of the universe.
You thought him brilliant; ay, he 's truly so:
Brilliant enough to know, ere many days,
What spell the magic of his genius cast
Upon a bright but untrained country girl.
Your fresh, frank ways, your eager earnestness,
Were revelations to the sated lion.
He looked on you as on a *nouveauté*,
A creature quite unlike the simpering dolls
Whose fans he flutters as he talks sweet lies.
You innocently touched his weakest point;
And that, as in most men, is vanity.
'T is writ in books, 't is said by wagging tongues,
That women are the weaker vessels, coz.
Our love of approbation is so great
We 'd sell our birthright for a mess of it.
Whene'er potential "he" pours in our ears
The honey kept on tap for our poor sex,
We melt as wax before the burning sun;
And being born thus weak, fulfilling fate,
We 're called to task if we walk not a crack;
Held up to scorn, make we but one misstep
And fall from earthly heaven to earthly hell.

(By heaven I mean, of course, society,
And woman's hell comes when it turns its back.)
Man, coz, — the stronger vessel, being strong, —
Jumps cracks and wanders at his own sweet will
In zigzag paths where morals can't keep straight.
He 's not responsible if his poor head
Is turned by winsome glance and loving speech;
Being strong, you see, he cannot help himself!
It makes a deal of difference in this world
Whether you 're born a man or woman, coz.
You 've been taught from your birth that it takes two
To make a bargain; when it comes to sex,
It takes but one, and woman is that one.
So has it been since chaos settled down
Into the muddy mush that we call earth.
Man ever is an Adam, woman Eve.
He asks to taste the apple in her hand,
And when he 's eaten it and is arraigned,
Exclaims, " Behold, the woman gave it me ! "
Not manly, think you, to thus shirk results?
You call him coward for betraying Eve?
You say such reasoning would never hold
In any book of logic? True enough;
But when you 've longer lived, you 'll surely learn
Though logic 's fact, fact is not logic, coz;
And you 'll be in your grave, as well as I,
Before society revolves around
An axis of right reason.
                                Weeping still?
You fancy, coz, yours is the only heart
That has been trifled with? You long for death?
You think the sun will never shine again,
That life will taste of naught but Dead Sea fruit?
Now look at me. I 'm envied by the world
Because I 'm handsome, rich, endowed with wit,
And tact enough to know just what to say,
And when to say it. My salon is thronged
With genius and with beauty, coz, because
I 've sense enough to listen to the men,
Acting as whip to each one's hobby-horse,
And art enough to advertise the charms

Of my own sex, whatever be their kind.
Because of this, some call me politic,
But all admit that I am popular,
And you, 'mong others, long to wear my shoes.

Why, silly coz, I 'd gladly change with you,
To lose the memory of earlier days.
At your age I loved madly, loved with all
The passion of a soul that loves but once.
I thought my love returned; his vows at least
Were warm enough to melt a colder heart
Than nature gave to me.   The man was born
Below my sphere, but genius knows no rank,
And I placed him above, beyond the herd
Of titled nobodies with addled brains.
I lived for this one man — for him alone.
We plighted troth; my parents threatened then
To cast me off, to disinherit me !
" Defy our will and you may beg for bread
Ere we will give heed to your misery,"
Said they who brought me into this kind world.
I loved, and so was ready to lose all.
Not so the hero of my one romance :
His face grew pallid and his speech confused ;
He kissed me hastily ; said he 'd return
To claim me.   How think you, coz, he claimed me?
He wrote a cold, brief note, in which he said
That he was far too proud a man to wed
In opposition to my family.
His grief had forced him to the Continent,
He hoped I might be happy, and then signed
Himself " Sincerely mine," etc.
None born with strong physique e'er die of love;
I did not even faint, or go to bed
Raving with fever, as girls do in books.
I sent back that man's note without remark,
Assured my parents their will should be mine,
Was taken to their arms, and soon betrothed
To the old lord whose name I 've so long borne.
He, to reward me for my sacrifice,
Died, after our most placid honeymoon,

Leaving me mistress of his large estates.
Then passed away my parents, blessing me
For reaping the reward obedience
So filial merited.   Restless, distraught,
I wandered to and fro for three long years,
Seeking to dull the pain about my heart
By change of scene and new acquaintances.
One day, 'mid Roman ruins, I came upon
The man I once adored.   He dared to speak :
Begged me to take him to my heart again,
Now death had broken down the barriers.
The devil in me got the upper hand ;
I lashed the craven creature with my tongue,
And sent him cringing from me.   " Nevermore
Let me behold your face," were my last words.
Full well have they been heeded.   Then I came
Back to my native land, took up the game
Society demanded I should play,
And faithfully I 've played it, though alone
I 've held the cards, no partner aiding me.
Such is my story.   Without love or child, —
The only longings of a woman's heart, —
I 'm pointed out as Fortune's favorite.
Perhaps I am !   Come, cousin, dry your tears.
Your wound 's skin deep.   Mine penetrated far ;
And yet I 'm not what people call a wreck.
You 'll have no appetite ; you 'll lie awake ;
You 'll sigh and sadly smile at merry jests.
This will endure for possibly a month,
During which time I promise to disclose
The true proportions of the demigod
You 've worshipped at the altar of your dreams.
I 'll prove to you, despite the charm of heads,
That in the game of life, coz, hearts are trumps.
Is it agreed ?   Then look up while I bathe
Your eyes in cooling spray.   Now you are like
Your dear old self.

I 'm hungry.   Let us dine.

KATE FIELD.

This poem was published in " Appleton's Maga-zine." While Miss Field had some degree of the poetic temperament, she was not a poet; yet now and then the rhythmic impulse took possession of her and she wrote some clever verse. As a child and all through her early girlhood the poetic impulse manifested itself and much of this versification remains among her papers.

Returning to America in the autumn, the following note from Mr. Reid indicates that Kate was with her aunt in Newport.

NEW YORK, Sept. 21, 1872.

DEAR K. F., — I 'm so startled at the alarming prospect of solitude that you set before me at Newport that I 'm com-ing at once, — that is, next Saturday, — unless the Political Fates should get the better of me. I 'm running away from them to-day, and I hope I may venture on a longer run next week. I 'll find my way to the house and the key under the door mat, to say nothing of the dining-room and the goodly array of comfort there, which you considerately promise.

As for Kennedy, No. We could n't print his work now if we had it. I do hope Mrs. Sanford is better. Her sad face, as I saw it last, haunts me.

Always very truly,

WHITELAW REID.

Again Mr. Reid writes : —

NEW YORK, Feb. 6, 1873.

DEAR K. F., — Very many thanks for your ringing article. Do you know that the excellent threatens me with libel suits? He 'd have a good time ! I waited till this P.M. about the Arion, because I wanted to see what I could be sure of about going. But it won't be safe, with the awful pressure I have, to undertake it. Suppose you do this : take the box as proposed (sending bill to us), make up your party to occupy it, and let me look in when I can.   I did n't get to the Infant Asylum ball, you know, till one in the morning, or to the Charity till two.

Will this do?   If so, I 'll arrange for having your copy brought early.   Here are half a dozen waiting to see me ; and the desk is covered with letters marked " Immediate."

Hastily and very truly yours,

WHITELAW REID.

In May of 1873, Kate again sailed for England, Rev. Dr. and Mrs. Chapin and Rubinstein being among her fellow-passengers.   Just before sailing, the great pianist was introduced to Miss Field, and he exclaimed : —

" Everybody has told me how charming you are, and have congratulated me upon sailing with you."

It was in the early June that Miss Field reached London, where she dined first of all with her old friends, the Hennessys, and the next night at Anthony Trollope's, meeting Wilkie Collins.   Lunching with her friend Mrs. Taylor, the wife of a Member of Parliament, she met a niece of Carlyle.   Mr. Browning called at once, and one afternoon read to her two books of his " Red Cotton Night-cap Country."   Ristori was playing, and Miss Field, seeing her in Marie Stuart, pronounces her as fine as ever.   Wilkie Collins took her to the Olympic Theatre to see " The New Magdalen," dramatized from his novel, in which Ada Cavendish was playing the title rôle.   " I like the play," said Miss Field.   " It marks an era in social thought."   Another afternoon Mr. Browning came and finished reading his new poem to Kate.   " He has killed a fine dramatic fact," she wrote of the work.   It is noticeable that the sympathy between

Robert Browning and Kate Field, so marked during her Florentine days, diminished as years went by. Miss Field was an enthusiast for clear, direct, terse, and simple expression. Mr. Browning's style grew more and more involved; and while friendship, certainly, is not made or unmade by literary style, yet it may be true that this style of itself is an expression of the mental attitude behind it; and then, while the poet became more exclusively a figure in society, Kate's sympathies grew broader and she became more and more engrossed with the world of affairs. *The best of each nature — both Browning's and Miss Field's — was hidden from each other. Their paths diverged, — doubtless to meet again in the truer life to come.

Soon after Kate's arrival in London in 1873, the following letter reached her from Mr. Reid: —

NEW YORK, July 17, 1873.

DEAR K. F., — I have delayed writing partly because it was not imperative, and I was doing nothing but the imperative things, and partly because I have been out of town a good deal, speaking first at Miami University, then at Dartmouth, and finally at Amherst. The speeches seem to have gone off well, have brought me all manner of complimentary letters from Professors, another degree of Master of Arts, ad eundem from Dartmouth, innumerable invitations and the choice attentions of our friends of "The Times." I believe I did not say op-ponents or in-quiry once. The audience were exceedingly nice and very responsive.

Smalley and yourself both speak of Mark Twain. I hear he says he has a quarrel with "The Tribune." If so, it is simply that "The Tribune" declined to allow him to dictate the person who should review his forthcoming novel. His modest suggestion was that Ned House should do it, he having previously interested House in the success of the book by taking him into partnership in dramatizing it. There is a nice correspondence on a part of the subject which would make pleasant reading; and if Twain gives trouble, I'm very much tempted to make him a more ridiculous object than he has ever made anybody else.

You do not need to be told that most of the stuff he has done for the "Herald" is very poor, because you have seen it. It won't hurt you to know that your letters, on the other hand, have received more praise than any you ever wrote for us before. That one on the naval review for the . . . was a model. The Rubinstein letter was also exceedingly good. Both have been very widely copied.

Your little book looks very fresh and pretty, is getting read, I know, a good deal in nice quarters, and bringing you fresh friends, and looks as if it were selling well.

You ask about Bradlaugh. Give him a letter of introduction, by all means. You spoke to me about him when here, and interested me in him not a little. As for Wilkie Collins, I will try to make it pleasant for him when he comes, but I have no particular fondness for this business of lionizing. Hitherto I have done what the club wanted. This winter I mean to take things a little more easily, and hope it may be easy and courteous when the time comes to decline peremptorily a re-election.

Thanks for the suggestion about purchases. I think of nothing just now that I want to get unless it is a Jules Jorgensen stem-winding repeater, and it would be hardly fair to bother you with a purchase of that magnitude, especially as it would not look particularly like your own on the steamer when you come back.

Faithfully yours,   WHITELAW REID.

P. S. Here are a few clippings I find on my desk. Not all nor the best I have seen. Poor Stedman did splendidly at Dartmouth, but has been ill ever since.

Your package is locked up in my box in the big cashier's safe at "The Tribune" office. It felt as if you had put a small consignment of ten-penny nails in it.

Thanks for the telegram about the "Herald's" work. I knew before that they had asked you, and am not likely to forget that you preferred the old colors. I only wish you had been at Springfield yesterday. Still our second edition looks well. But Bret Harte is n't used to the newspaper pace, and the storm made the telegraphic work beastly.

W. R.

To trace the record of Kate Field's life from the child who took her little friends to play in her father's theatre in St. Louis in the deserted daytime; from the young girl who at fifteen wrote to her father, "You don't know how I long to get hold of some one who will *strike fire;*" and on, — through her indomitable persistence in every year, — her experience thus reminds one of the artistic methods of Beethoven in producing his symphonies. While in his initial epoch he trod in the paths (with whatever variation) of Haydn and Mozart, long before he arrived at the creation of the Fifth Symphony he had achieved his own method; and the startling distinctness with which he announces his theme at the outset in certain emphatic repetitions of one note, the phrase being echoed later, in varying degrees, reminds one of the manner in which, in Miss Field's life, features appear, disappear, and reappear, on the scene. Her life was one of dramatic sequence from her infancy in St. Louis to her death in Honolulu and the final committal of her ashes in Mount Auburn, near Boston. Beethoven often announces his theme with unmistakable clearness, then abandons it for a time to strange uncertainties; the key in which it is to be finally set is still undecided, and the musician wanders amid harmonies; there is an atmosphere of vague apprehension, of intangible experiment, — a period of listening, it would seem, for some diviner melody in the air; then a phrase is boldly struck as if by chance; it multiplies itself in swift, rapid vibrations, and the theme is grasped. "It is as if a fearful secret, some truth of mightiest moment, startled the stillness where we were securely walking and the heavens were sending back the sound from all quarters of deep calling unto deep." And as the theme of that great musical creation, the Fifth Symphony, is that of a human soul endeavoring to escape the limits of pain and attain to inward joy, so in this life of a woman whose intense energy of purpose made almost a tragedy of existence, there is seen, under all the varying circumstances of her pilgrimage, the unity of the theme running through her entire experience on earth.

For now, again, in this London June, Madame Ristori once more appears in Kate's life; and the biography and the incomparable criticism which Miss Field had written of Ristori nearly a decade before is republished at this time in London. On a Sunday afternoon, Miss Field takes Mrs. Pattison to call on Ristori, and the Italian tragédienne, with the fervor of her country, takes Kate in her arms and envelops her with kisses and caresses.

Another element of destiny came just then into Kate's life. At a dinner-party she met Señor Moret, the Spanish Minister and his wife, the Señora, with Mademoiselle Gaetano and Monsieur Brosseau, the latter of whom assured her that he was a republican and wished to go to America. It was at this dinner that Miss Field, whose nature was as susceptible to an idea as tinder to a spark of fire, first conceived the thought of visiting Spain, and interviewing Emilio Castelar, the president of the Spanish Republic, whose political situation was at the time peculiarly interesting. Mrs. Mark Pattison was again in London this season, and Kate took her one night to Covent Garden, where they saw Patti in " Ernani," and Miss Field remarked to Mrs. Pattison that the prima donna sang admirably and looked like a fashion-plate. At a dinner soon after, Miss Field met a clever Frenchman whose hobby was coins, " and I believe he knows more about them than any one else in the world," she said. Sir Charles Dilke invited Sidney Colvin to lunch to meet Miss Field, and later they went to the Goodwood races, where Robert Barrett Browning came up to her and recalled the old time in Italy when she was in Florence and passed days with his mother in Casa Guidi. The season flashed by. Kate went with Mr. and Mrs. Mark Pattison to visit the Castilian collection at a museum, dined with them, and met interesting people. Anthony Trollope called often of a morning. She went to a private rehearsal of "King John" at the Queen's Theatre, and of Miss Clive, the actress, she said in her journal: " She is a very natural and original person, but I doubt her power, in spite of the enthusiastic predictions for her." She passed a morning with Mrs. Procter, who spoke at length on Fanny Kemble; she dined with the Smalleys and met again persons of note and drove with Mrs. Dorschemer to Drury Lane, where they saw two acts of Ristori's " Marie Antoinette." A note came from Charles Dickens inviting her to Gad's Hill, which she accepted with pleasure. Mr.

and Mrs. Clemens, otherwise the Mark Twains, were in London, and Miss Field greatly enjoyed meeting them. Mr. Samuelson, an M. P., meeting Miss Field at a dinner, invited her to a naval review at Spithead the next day, which she accepted; and reaching home after midnight rose again in time to make an early start the next morning. One noticeable thing in Miss Field's life was the way in which she always met the spontaneous opportunity; she had grown to be peculiarly *facile de vivre*. At this naval review she met Sir Vernon Harcourt, General Noble, and Sir David Wedderburn, and enjoyed a most interesting day. The young M. P., Mr. Samuelson, sent to Miss Field tickets for a review at Windsor, and it seems that she and Mr. Smalley set off together. Of that day she records in her diary: —

"Lunched with the Smalleys. G. W. and I started for Windsor at two, arrived at four. Took the Long Walk and found seats on House of Commons stand. A splendid sight! Got back at ten o'clock, dined with the Smalleys, and then returned home."

A collection of Miss Field's "Tribune" letters, with various revisions and additions, had just been published in Boston by Fields, Osgood, and Company under the title of "Hap-Hazard," and her copies reached her in London. Of the naval review she wrote a vivid description to "The Tribune." She heard Wilkie Collins read at the Olympic Theatre; Garcia, her master in singing, called on her frequently and they had long talks; Alfred Austin, now the poet laureate of England, was one of her callers, and she found him "sincere and agreeable." With a merry party of Americans she drove to the Crystal Palace,

where they had supper.   Du Maurier dined with her
one night, and she greatly liked him, and in the evening Kinglake and Lord Houghton called.   "They went
into raptures over my Japanese polonaise," she said.
Another morning Wilkie Collins made her a long
call.   She lunched with the Smalleys, and went with
them to see Aimée Desclée in " Maison Rouge,"
which she found "very clever."   A London friend
took her to Grosvenor House, where she enjoyed the
magnificent paintings.

On the July "Fourth" of that summer she was,
with the other Americans in London, at the reception given by the American ambassador, General
Schenck, meeting there President Roberts of Liberia.
That night Lady Franklin and her parliamentary
friend, Mr. Samuelson, dined with her; and while at
the table a telegram from the New York "Herald"
reached Kate asking her to go to Paris and describe
the visit of the Shah,— a commission she declined, as
she did not feel able to make so fatiguing a journey.
A July day was made memorable to her by spending
it on the Thames with a pleasant party which included Herbert Spencer.   Miss Field was asked to
sing, and she sang like a mermaiden, " all the way up
to Maidenhead."   She heard Bradlaugh lecture on
Republicanism in France, Spain, and England, and
found him " very eloquent."   The Marchesa del Grillo
(Madame Ristori) gave a little dinner for her, at
which she again meets the Morets and Lord Hay;
and later she makes an appointment for her friend,
Madame de Guerrebelli (Genevieve Ward), to meet
Mr. Chippendale.   She "lunched and drove" with
William Black, and went to a reception at Kensington
Museum in the evening.   On a "glorious day" she

drives with Mr. and Mrs. Hill and William Black to
Reigate on the top of a coach, and at night is at a
dinner where she meets Comte de Franqueville and
two Indian magnates: "the latter gave me a glimpse
of Brahmin life in India," she records, "very intelligently, too."

The succeeding day she sends a letter of thirty-
eight pages to "The Tribune," and calls on Adelaide
Phillipps and Mrs. Jewell, the wife of the ex-Governor
of Connecticut, who are in London, and renews her
acquaintance with Mrs. Jewell.

The next morning Kate makes one of a breakfast
party as guests of Mrs. Inigo Jones, and she goes
with a group of friends to St. Paul's. In the afternoon Mr. Smalley took her to the Royal Academy,
"and I was not impressed," she said, "except by
Watts and Millais." In the evening she sees Madame
Judic at the theatre, and she records : —

"Clever in the verbal rendering of her songs, but their
effect depends too much upon indecency. I believe in no
art that is based upon sensuality. There is divinity in the
senses."

This brilliant London season came to an end, like
all things terrestrial, and Miss Field's plans included
a trip to the South of France. This anticipated
journey to the Pyrenees was rendered full of delight for her by the decision of her friend Adelaide
Phillipps also to visit that region. Kate gives a
little breakfast for Madame de Guerrebelli, and later
shops in Regent Street with Mrs. Smalley ; assists
at Madame de Guerrebelli's rehearsal in Lewis Wing-
field's studio, meeting there a group of critics and
actors, and records that the new star (now better

known by her maiden name of Genevieve Ward)
"did Lady Macbeth admirably." At night she dined
at Anthony Trollope's, and finished the day with a
party from which she returned home at three in the
morning.

The next day Kate took a friend to visit Mr. Hennessy's studio, and later she writes : —

"Then we went to James Whistler's by appointment.
He was very cordial, showed me over his charming house —
delighted with his pictures. Hennessy said he had never
seen Whistler so radiant. We remained two hours. Dined
at Hennessy's, met Appleton of the Academy."

The journal later runs on :

July 26. Drove to Stafford House and went over it.
Paid visits. Dined at Madame Moret's, meeting Sir Thomas
Henry, Pellegrini, General Schenck, and others.

July 27 . Reading and writing all day. Madame de
Guerrebelli called, and we discussed Lady Macbeth. Lionel
Robinson and Moscheles called. The latter gave me a
Japanese fan. Browning and Kinglake to dinner, and later
on one of the editors of the "Times" came.

July 28. Went down to Mr. William Dilke's at Chichester
for the first day of Goodwood Races. Lovely day — five
hours *en route*. After lunch drove to Kingsley Vale and
saw a Fairy Ring for the first time in my life. Charming
landscape !

The last days of July came on, when the curtain is
rung down on the London season, and the 30th she
passed in writing letters, packing, and seeing callers,
and on the morning of the 31st Miss Field and Miss
Phillipps left London, Mr. Browning and other notable people seeing them off, " half smothered in
bouquets." She went directly to the Hotel Chatham

in Paris, where they met a French princess. Rev. Dr. and Mrs. Robert C. Waterston were in Paris, old friends of both the ladies, and especially the intimate friend of Adelaide Phillipps, whose life, later on, Mrs. Waterston's sympathetic pen was to chronicle. But that was still in the unforeseen future. The Waterstons, Miss Phillipps, and Miss Field drove to many places, lunched and dined together; and on the morning of August second — a brilliant, radiant day of that bewildering brightness known in sunny France — Miss Field with both Adelaide and Mathilde Phillipps left Paris for Bordeaux, where they passed the night, sleepless for noise, and the next morning in a broiling sun continued their journey to the Pyrenees, where they found beautiful scenery and began drinking the waters. Spanish contrabands abounded here, clamoring to sell their wares. Miss Field's records of these days are the usual ones of watering-place life, where prescribed walks, drives, and spring water, speedily become alike stale and unprofitable. " Sat in park nearly all day. Addie went to church in the morning and theatre in the evening. Both equally mad ! " so runs one day's diary record. *Ab uno disce omnes.*

" The clouds sit on our shoulders," Kate remarks in truly Kate-Fieldian dialect. The last of August the Misses Phillipps left, and Kate was indescribably lonely; but for two weeks she still persevered, made excursions to Lourdes and other points, and her physician still assured her she was gaining in health. On September 15 she departed for Biarritz, and of her day there she writes : —

"Took a walk in the picturesque town, saw many Spaniards, drove and talked with a Spaniard who spoke English.

Went to bed, but not to sleep. The dashing of the waves
on the beach kept me awake. Rose at 3 A. M. to prepare
for journey."

For the suggestion that came to Miss Field the
night she met and talked with Señor and Señora
Moret at a London dinner-party, — to visit Spain and
meet Emilio Castelar, — she was about to carry out.
So she fared forth. On the next day, September 19,
she records this not encouraging experience: —

"At 4½ A. M. started for boat in a drizzle. Arrived to
find 50 passengers crowded into a small and distressingly
dirty boat. I never had such a voyage. Never saw such
scenes. Weather good. Arrived at 7. Detained in quar-
antine two hours. Then allowed to go ashore without bag-
gage. Difficulty in securing room at hotel. At last found
a hole, with fleas in possession, at Hôtel d'Angleterre.
Supper and to bed."

Miss Field's experiences in Spain were as lively as
they were brief; and the story is related in full, in her
own inimitable way, in her book called " Ten Days in
Spain." She had been walking about, she explained,
" on the top of the Pyrenees, with a glass of luke-
warm water in one hand and an umbrella in the
other," and by way of a variation from this mild
amusement she conceived the idea of going to Spain
and Castelar. She procured a letter to him from the
American Embassy, — Kate always had the diplomatic service at her sovereign command, — and having been admitted to the presence of the President,
she characteristically proceeded to argue the political
question with him and to express frankly her own
views in favor of Cuba libre. She found Castelar
"an author and orator: I recognized the lovable

man," she said, "but not the born statesman. A leader should have profound knowledge of men," she continued. "I could not feel Castelar to be in any sense a man of the world."

Castelar's "exceeding amiability" impressed Kate, and she described him as "thoroughly unassuming" and as turning the conversation on America. He "regretted that he did not speak English. He could read it, and was very fond of Emerson, but to speak it was beyond his power." He spoke French, though not very fluently, and it was in that tongue that the conversation was carried on.

For her journey into Spain Miss Field employed a courier whom she christened "the Blinker." After concluding her visit to Señor Castelar she drove back to her hotel and rang for this extraordinary being. Her sole instructions to him had been to buy three pounds of grapes each day, and to spend his time in finding out what the tradespeople thought of republicanism. As "the Blinker" appeared in response to her ring, she said to him : —

"Well, what do Spaniards say to you about the government?"

"Madame, I have known the Spaniards twenty-six years —"

"Yes, I am aware of that fact," interrupted Miss Field. "Never mind what happened twenty-six years ago. Tell me what happens now."

The "Blinker" proceeded with an hopelessly entangled story, and Kate cut him short with the question : —

"Do you mean to say that there are no real republicans?"

"Parfaitement, madame."

" My search seemed to be as hopeless as that of Diogenes," said Miss Field afterward, recounting this experience.

The crawling trains in Spain suggested to Miss Field that the law of compensation prevails, as, had the train on which she was to leave started on time, she would have missed it. " Hereafter I shall never despair of catching a Spanish train," she observed, " for, although it may have started, I shall be sure to catch up with it by walking over the track, because it stands still much more than it goes ahead."

Of the Escurial she said : —

" I saw in its gridiron the bier of the past and present Spain. This is the country that once ruled the world, the country to which America owes its discovery ! Is anything so incredible as history? "

A little note from Kate to her aunt dated at Bayonne, Sept. 29, 1873, tells the story of her return from Spain. " I am safely through the Carlist lines," she says, " and in two days I shall be in Paris."

She returned to America that autumn, passing the winter in New York, located in Gramercy Park at No. 23, and entered with renewed zest into the American life. She was in the midst of a charming circle of friends, — the Gilders, Mr. Stedman, Prof. and Mrs. Botta, Hon. Whitelaw Reid, Prof. and Mrs. Doremus, and many others, to say nothing of the tide of cosmopolitan visitors that set toward New York, among whom Miss Field had a very wide acquaintance. As usual, her time was filled with interests and engagements of manifold character. She was almost equally interested in music, the drama, and in pictorial art. She was a social favorite, and was much in

demand as a dinner guest. Her reputation as a wit
was long since established; she was acknowledged to
be one of the most brilliant women of the day; and,
withal, Kate Field had a warm heart, a very ardent,
generous nature, and she was an almost ideal friend.
In one of her note-books is found copied, in her clear,
beautiful hand, this passage from Thoreau: —

"Is your friend such a one that any increase of worth on
your part will really make her more your friend? Is she
retained, is she attracted by more nobleness in you, by
more of that virtue which is peculiarly yours? Or is she
indifferent and blind to that? Is she to be flattered and
won by your meeting her on any other than the ascending
path? Then duty requires that you separate from her."

The words take on an even deeper significance from
having been stamped with her noble appreciation.
The theme is further played upon and carried out in
certain words of Emerson, and it would be easy indeed
to multiply quotations from poet and prophet since the
world began to enlarge still further the significance
of authority. For friendship in its true sense is
the divine part of life, and the communion with the
angelic is best learned by communion with friends —
for the human being is, primarily, as well as poten-
tially, the spiritual being even in this part of life. So
divine an experience as friendship should be divinely
lived. It is a sacrament, and should be held in living
faith and perpetual sweetness of spirit. Friendship
should be held amenable to an appreciation of high
qualities, irrespective of the fact of personal return.
It is good for the soul to love what is good; to estimate at its true value an illumination of spirit, even
though it does not especially shine for one's personal
benefit.

Kate Field's friendship was of this quality, and the rare truth and sincerity of her nature impressed all who met her.

During this winter of 1873–74 Miss Field was writing for the "London Athenæum" a series of letters called "Notes from the United States." In one of these we have a glimpse of the early impression made of the Wagner music-drama: —

"The very latest sensation is 'Lohengrin,'" she says; "with Nilsson and Campanini in the principal rôles; Wagnerites are ecstatic."

Of Mr. Howells she wrote that his story "A Foregone Conclusion" was by far the best thing he had ever done, and that it held a revelation of unsuspected dramatic power on the part of the author.

A graceful little note from Mr. Howells to Kate about this time runs: —

MY DEAR MISS FIELD, — It is most kind that you like my ditty and tell me so. I like it the better for its pleasing you.

Yours,

W. D. HOWELLS.

Miss Field was anxious to write for the Harpers, and the well-known critic, Mr. Henry T. Tuckerman, gave her the following letter of introduction to them: —

Allow me to introduce to you one Miss Kate Field, whose articles in the "Atlantic Monthly" and elsewhere you doubtless know have proved themselves highly acceptable to the public. A long residence abroad and a taste for art enables Miss Field to write with much geniality of spirit, and I am sure some of her personal reminiscences and local sketches will be very desirable for your magazine

or weekly. Please give any manuscript she may confide
to you your candid consideration, and oblige

Yours truly,

H. T. Tuckerman.

A little note by Miss Field, written on the blank
leaf of one of her scrapbooks, tells this story of one
year's writing: —

From June, '73, to July, '74, wrote fifty-seven articles,
making eighty-six columns, — about one and two-thirds
column per week, — six short magazine articles, not regularly engaged, and devoted the winter to dramatic study,
so that it did not seem as if I wrote at all.

Miss Field must have confided to Mrs. Helen Hunt
(" H. H.") a new purpose that she conceived in the
previous summer, as, under the date of July 1, 1874,
Mrs. Hunt thus writes, evidently having before invited
Miss Field to visit Denver: —

July 1, 1874.

Dear Kate, — I'm sorry; I think it would have done
you good. But there is no doubt that it is frightfully dear.
A summer in England would cost less.

Your letter troubled me, Dear. I never dreamed that
you were going on the stage for such reasons. I did not
know that you had a living soul in any way dependent on
you, and you have seemed of late so prosperous and at ease
that I was totally unprepared for what you tell me. I am
very, very sorry. I most earnestly trust you may succeed,
dear girl. The activity of the life may be a great gain. It
is that which has kept dear Charlotte Cushman alive these
late years. To me, who am ill directly unless I am asleep
by ten o'clock every night, the very thought of such a life
is terrible. But you have youth on your side; that wins
always. Don't stay in New York through August. No

water cure in creation can make that tolerable. Go to Provincetown, Mass., — where I wish I was this minute, — only three hours from Boston, twelve hundred feet above the sea, never a hot minute. I shall go there every summer as long as I live, if I can. A shady field and grove just behind the house to sit in all day long, and absolute quiet and stillness. It will rest you and strengthen you, if you can do without people. The house is small, and there might be only Philistines in it. The summer Miss —— and I were there, two years ago, it was delightful, — a dozen really nice and clever people. Last summer there was the other sort. It is so near Boston that there are all kinds of chances. I don't know when I shall come home. I say next fall, but a prophetic sense warns me that it may not be till next spring. While I have touches of sore throat I will not venture. I am very well, but over-fatigue or exposure to damp even here will give me a slight sore throat, so I know that the old wound is not yet fully healed.

It is n't so bad as you would think, living here, not by half. There are pleasant people, and everybody on earth turns up in the summer. I wish you would let me know how the venture goes. Write just a line now and then. God speed you.

Yours ever,

HELEN HUNT.

It was indeed dramatic study that chiefly absorbed her mind in the winter of 1873–74. For she had decided on a new venture, — that of going on the stage. She regretted that she had not been placed there at fifteen, but there were many reasons why the transition still seemed feasible to her. In appearance she was *petite*, delicate, and so vivacious and spirituelle as to appear ten years younger than her actual age. Indeed, this apparent youthfulness signally characterized her until within the last two years of her life, when ill health and anxieties produced in one year the changes that might well have been those of twenty. She lived so essentially the life of ideas and purpose that no one would have dreamed that the slight, graceful woman who looked like a girl, with her clustering auburn hair and luminous eyes, had seen even twenty-five summers. Her inheritance of temperament was dramatic and she had been, as we have seen, almost cradled on the stage. It was only strange that this turning to dramatic art had not appealed to her as a settled purpose years before. Her life presents as many states as that of a painter, and the manner in which they succeeded each other was sometimes rather bewildering to the on-looker. Miss Field had many undoubted gifts for the stage. Her beautiful voice, her flawless and exquisite enunciation, her keen perception of the canons of art, her experience as a dramatic critic, — all these were in the direction that attracted her. But as Shakespeare wisely says, " It is easier to teach twenty what were good to be done than be one of the twenty to follow mine own teaching," and Kate was destined to prove the truth of this bit of epigrammatic wisdom. Her purpose, however, did not fail to win the ardent interest, if not the entire confidence, of her friends ; and no less an authority than the New York " Herald " gave the importance of a leading editorial to the announcement that Miss Field would make her *début* as Peg Woffington at Booth's Theatre on Nov. 14, 1874. The " Herald " said : —

" We should be glad, indeed, if, as Miss Cushman retires from the stage she has so long adorned, another American artist should emulate her success, in the person of Miss

Kate Field, who is to make her first appearance at Booth's Theatre on Saturday night. If intelligence alone could make an actress, there would not be the slightest question of Miss Field's complete success, and certainly intellect is always wanted on the stage. In literature she has shown rare powers, — knowledge of the world, fine descriptive ability, a delicate and far-reaching humor, appreciation of the characteristic, and more than usual versatility."

Mrs. Louise Chandler Moulton wrote to Miss Field this graceful word : —

DEAR KATE, — I see your *début* advertised for next Saturday night, and I cannot let you go to the theatre without a God-speed from me. I want to come on and see you. I can't go to New York just now, so I must send you my written good wishes instead of speaking them, as I should like best.

I have faith in your ability to succeed, because I have heard such good things of you in private theatricals, and of course this is the same thing, only more so ; and then I think a woman of your intellectual force can reasonably expect success in whatever she undertakes.

So go in and win, my dear. I shall await news eagerly.

Affectionately,

LOUISE CHANDLER MOULTON.

Miss Field made her *début* in Peg Woffington on the evening of Nov. 14, 1874, in Booth's Theatre, New York. This dramatic venture, which was written down as a failure, was perhaps the severest trial in Kate's experiences, and the more so that her own impressions of that evening quite entitled her to believe it a success. Booth's Theatre was crowded from orchestra to the gods' gallery with one of the most distinguished audiences ever gathered in New

York. To a large degree it was one made up of her personal friends, who were ardent in their applause, and the *débutante* was smothered in flowers and the usual incense of partial friends. The next morning brought her a friendly note from Mr. Whitelaw Reid, which ran as follows: —

23 PARK AVENUE, Nov. 15, 1874, 9 A. M.

DEAR K. F., — I congratulate you with all my heart. You can never appear before a more severe audience than that of last night, for it was made up of your personal friends, who expected you to fail. And you did not fail.

I broke an engagement in the country last night to witness the *début*, and so am writing in hot haste now, before starting to meet the wagon to be sent in for me to Weehawken, this morning, to meet the early boat.

But I renew my very sincere congratulations, and am always,

Very truly your friend,

WHITELAW REID.

This note Kate read before seeing the criticism in "The Tribune," and regarded as a proof of successful estimate. The criticism in the paper effectually negatived this, and a letter that she wrote to Mr. Reid can almost be read in the light of his reply, which is as follows: —

23 PARK AVENUE, Dec. 4, 1874.

DEAR MISS FIELD, — I received yesterday your note of the second, in which you say that I have stabbed you to the heart by writing you an opinion about your appearance on the stage and allowing the publication of another; that, in my place, you would have been burnt alive before printing "The Tribune's" notice; that your fair words, in case of need, would not be confined to private notes;

that, thank God, you are incapable of meanness, and that your ideas of friendship are Quixotic.

You will do me the justice to remember that, in common with most of your friends, I did what I could to dissuade you from your late venture; and that after your appearance at Thomas's Garden, in answer to your frank question, I said with the equal frankness that true friendship required, that you had not shown a spark of dramatic power. You knew, therefore, that I went to the theatre, as most of your friends did, expecting you to fail, to break down. Not doubting early the next morning that you must be in need of the kindest words friends could honestly utter, I hastened, before leaving town for a couple of days, to say my utmost. I congratulated you with all my heart on not having failed, — not having broken down. It never occurred to me that you could, by any possibility, misunderstand the significant omission to say that you had succeeded.

" The Tribune's " criticism was to the precise effect of my note. It said, with an effort to spare your feelings which I fear you have not valued, that you had not failed, and then with all possible kindliness of course pointed out wherein you had not attained success.

I am deeply grieved at your note. But even if I had done you the injustice to expect it, I should not have changed the tone of Mr. Winter's criticism. I should be as despicable as you describe me if I forced a most capable, friendly, and conscientious critic to say, in a great journal, what neither he nor I believed, to sustain a private friend in a course he and I thought unwise and hopeless.

It would be idle to attempt to misunderstand the purpose of your note. I shall not offend you by attempting to keep up the old friendly relations. But I shall never forget your generous and helpful friendship in the past. I hope never to miss an honorable opportunity of doing you service, and I shall always be,

Your sincere well-wisher,

WHITELAW REID.

MISS KATE FIELD, 145 East Twenty-First Street.

Yet Kate's own sweetness of spirit that never bore malice, never held resentment, is indicated by the following letter from Mr. Reid, which readily suggests to the reader the kind of response made by Miss Field to which it is the answer: —

23 PARK AVENUE, Dec. 29, 1874.

MY DEAR MISS KATE, — I was interrupted in the midst of proof-reading, late Sunday night, by the arrival of the little box, containing the charming souvenirs you were so good as to send. Believe me, I shall prize all very highly, for the reason that, as you say, they are not so much mere gifts as "bits of yourself." The rare old Dutch spoon is an especial treasure, which will be most jealously saved and used. My younger niece does not come on, for her school, until next week; so that you have provided a renewal of the Christmas pleasures, to make bright her coming.

I wish that the New Year, so nearly upon us, may bring you rest, health, all the success your heart can wish, and happiness. And I am always,

Very truly yours,

WHITELAW REID.

There were two causes which contributed to Miss Field's failure as an actress, — one of which was in herself and the other in the circumstances of the time. That inherent in herself was a too pronounced individuality, — the inability to make herself a flexible mould in which the character of another might be poured, so to speak, and impersonated. It is not —

as has been said — that she was "too intellectual" for an actress; no one is too intellectual for the art which, in its ideal perfection, includes all arts; but the drama requires a complete abandonment of temperament in a way foreign, if not impossible, to the very nature of Kate Field. The other cause which must have contributed to the disastrous result lay in the fact that Miss Field had become entirely familiar with the more natural art of the French stage, which differs essentially from the more theatrical art then prevalent and held as a standard on the stage in America. The reader will recall that Kate had her first visit to Paris and her first enchanted sight of the Comédie Française in the winter of 1859 when she was just past her eighteenth birthday; and at this impressible age the traditions of the house of Molière sank deep in her mind. From that time she had been, in her residence abroad, familiar with that natural school of acting which is now seen on the American stage. Twenty-five years ago, and, in fact, until the visits of Madame Bernhardt, of Mounet-Sully, Coquelin, and others and the change in our own stage traditions had familiarized the public with the new school, — the standard held by theatre audiences, however cultivated and critical, demanded more of the artificially theatrical than that with which Kate invested the character of Peg Woffington. The public inclined to believe that the actor should act, and even so notable a critic as Mr. Winter may have somewhat shared the traditions of his time, although his criticism has always been a progressive art, and he has led, rather than followed, the dramatic progress of the times.

Mr. Stedman — always the ideal of the loyal

friend — wrote a letter to " The Tribune " regarding
Miss Field's appearance which is so ideally fair in its
attitude toward the stage and toward dramatic criticism, so finely appreciative without partiality, and
which, withal, relates itself in so universal a manner
to dramatic art at all times, that no apology is needed
for introducing this interesting document in full.   It
is a criticism that deserves more of literary immortality than is possible to the daily press.   Mr. Stedman wrote : —

To the Editor of the Tribune.

SIR, — Permit an old contributor to write you with respect
to an event which has excited unusual interest and discussion.

My subject relates to the theatre, but I do not wish to
venture upon dramatic criticism.   I am too much of a
stickler for the precedence due to trained service in any
department of criticism to set up my chance views against
the opinions of the sincere and practised writers who discuss theatrical matters for our leading journals.   What I ask
leave to do is to state how a layman was impressed by the
event in question, and to refer, with honest deference, to a
few points which have escaped general mention.

I was present last Saturday evening at the " first appearance on any stage " of Miss Kate Field.   To begin with,
let me say that I seriously inferred, from Miss Field's acting
and the manner in which the play went off, that the *début*
was, upon the whole, an unusual success.   The very large
audience — and I am not only speaking of the lady's friends,
who mustered in such numbers, but to the three galleries as
well — seemed, if one might judge by its close attention
and intelligent applause, to be under the same pleasant belief ; so that I had nothing to disturb my illusion until I
read some of the morning newspapers.

New York is a city of theatre-goers, many of whom have observed the rise and decline of theatres and actors, and their judgment, though not literary, is shrewd and valuable. It is upon the verdict of such people that a player's success or failure somewhat depends. For example, go upon the Stock Exchange, where a thousand men meet together, representing every type of character and opinion. Talking with various members of that body, who also witnessed Miss Field's performance, I find that their notion of its success was similar to my own, and that they were no less surprised than myself at the severe sentence pronounced in a few of the newspapers, and the friendly but desponding tone of criticism in certain others.

I have a most hearty respect for the judgment of the distinguished critic of " The Tribune," and for that of the acute and sparkling writer who holds the post of dramatic editor upon " The World." The articles of both these gentlemen were careful, scholarly, and written with the utmost taste, delicacy, and good feeling. Indeed, as to the latter point, — when a brave and refined woman, one of our own guild, dependent wholly upon her talents for a career, returns to her father's profession from sheer love of it, — how any writer could go outside of the record to inflict an unnecessary wound is beyond my understanding. But I wish to refer to certain points which even the admirable critics I have cited have, it seems to me, not fully borne in view.

These writers have paid Miss Field a very high honor, but an honor scarcely to be desired by the most brilliant aspirant at such a crisis. They discuss her representation of Peg Woffington as if they were criticising an actress of long standing, not a *débutante*, appearing under trying conditions. She is not a star who comes to us from another region, where she has gained experience and reputation, but in one sense a novice, making her entry upon the most difficult of professions.

Neither an actor nor an artist of any kind can be " written up " or down. I have no desire to attempt the former process in Miss Field's case ; my interest is solely that which every author has in the drama, and in the lives of those who have won an honorable standing in his own craft. In the long run, talent vouches for itself. But a novice's career may be seriously retarded, especially in practical and business matters, unless the facts that tell in his behalf are fairly understood.

The house on Saturday night embraced a numerous cohort, not only of the actress's friends, but of authors, journalists, men and women of culture, attracted by the unusual nature of the occasion. How many of these would, under any circumstances, have advised in favor of her appearance ? How many were there who anticipated that, whatever her talent might be, she would make anything else than a failure ?

I have seen a *débutante*, who afterwards became a finished and popular actress, fall into a distressing series of blunders on her first night, even when in an inferior part and assisted throughout by comrades no less thoughtful than Miss Field's associates upon the stage. I have seen her awkward in her movements and neglectful of the stage business ; have seen her lose her voice, forget her cues, tip over tables and screens, make wrong exits, — in short, barely struggle through the play, to her own mortification and the embarrassment of the audience. An actress's friends, however much they may sustain her, often, in their effort to render an impartial verdict, are her severest critics. Doubtless many of the acquaintances of Kate Field, who assisted upon this occasion with warm hearts and kindly offices, were disturbed by a suspicion that they were aiding to maintain the decencies of a funeral — or some equally mournful affair. The nearer friends came laden with flowers, it is true, but somewhat as chief mourners bring camellias and tuberoses with which to strew the remains of a loved and lost one. A select few, I am sure, were prepared to tenderly perform the last offices, at whatever cost of pain and lamentation to themselves.

These people must have been agreeably surprised. Their flowers were bestowed with sentiments precisely the reverse of that pronounced by the Queen above Ophelia's grave. From the moment when the candidate made her entrance and gained control of her voice, it was evident that they would be subjected to no distress upon her account. Among half-a-dozen " first appearances " I do not recall one wherein the novice, from first to last, showed more self-possession, acquaintance with her part, and ability to dispel the fears of a sympathetic audience, or so fair a knowledge and instinctive management of what is called the stage-business. In a very difficult rôle, she went through the play without a serious mishap of any kind. This is the more noteworthy, since it is understood that, owing to the difficulty of securing a stock engagement, she never rehearsed any stage-part with a company until within a few days of her appearance. Much of this technical success should be due to the teachings of Miss Moran, and to rehearsals with Mr. Wheatleigh, and much to remembered knowledge of details with which she was familiar in her childhood. For, in one sense, again, she is not a novice : in youth she had the atmosphere of the stage about her, which, thus inhaled, is never forgotten.

A word as to the part assumed, and the temerity of the lady in undertaking any leading part that would require the weight of the performance to fall upon herself. Was not this owing to the impossibility of making a *début* under any circumstances of her own choosing? Doubtless Miss Field, who always has shown the true professional spirit, would have preferred to begin with routine duties under a regular and quiet engagement. As it is, she has accepted the only opening which, after many efforts, she could find, — that of the off-nights at Booth's, and the assumption of a leading part with all its difficulties and dangers. However arduous the rôle of Peg Woffington, it seems to me as well fitted to her as another part would be which some other actress would find easier. We all know Miss Field's abundant brisk wit and vivacity, and many are familiar with her *esprit* and somewhat capricious raillery, both in public and private life. I should think her high spirits and thorough unconventionalism would enable her to enter with zest upon the part of Mistress Woffington. Her acting was often tame and formal, as if under instructions, in the first two acts; but in the third, where most actresses are least successful, and which requires so much movement and versatility, she acted with great spirit, and frequently received genuine applause. Her minor accomplishments — recitation, music, dancing, etc. — are not, it seems to me, to be despised; they are so much clear gain, though only accessory to her main purpose.

One other point, and I have done. The success of any *débutante* in greatly impressing or "magnetizing" her audience, even if she can under such circumstances forget herself in her part, depends greatly, in my opinion, upon certain qualities of the theatre and the stage. People remember the excitement aroused by Miss Heron's Camille, in Wallack's tasteful little down-town theatre eighteen or nineteen years ago. The actress readily established a wonderful sympathy with an audience that hung upon every accent of her thin, falsetto voice, and watched her slightest motion on the stage. Not long afterwards I saw the same actress in the same part, but in a theatre approaching the proportions of Booth's, and the charm was almost entirely gone. I scarcely believe that Matilda Heron, with her long experience and unquestionable genius, would have made an instant sensation if she had come out at Niblo's or the Win-

ter Garden.   At Booth's, last Saturday, the size, grandeur,
and all the associations of the stage and theatre told against
the effect of the play and of Miss Field's enactment.

I am sure, however, that the dramatic critics will watch
the progress of this lady — formerly one of their own number — with thoughtful and impartial interest, and if they see
her profiting by their hints, and exhibiting not only an artist's devotion, but true histrionic power, will record every
advance made upon her first experiment.   If I were one of
our actors at this juncture, when an old warfare is renewed
against their historic and beautiful profession, I should
warmly welcome the accession of a woman so enthusiastic,
cultured, and favorably known.   If I were Mr. Wallack or
Mr. Palmer, gentlemen who work so earnestly for the true
success of the drama, and for the delight of this generation
of play-goers, I should try to make a place for this aspirant
in my company, and give her a chance not only to prove
her industry and sincerity, but to develop whatever genius
she may possess.   In short,

" If I were King of France, or, what's better, Pope of Rome,"

I should try to arrange matters so that all things would find
their right places with less of jostling and confusion.   As it
is, the least and most that I can do is to relieve the editor
from any responsibility for what I now have written.

Respectfully yours,

E. C. STEDMAN.

No. 205 WEST FIFTY-SIXTH ST., Nov. 17, 1874.

Still, while Miss Field's appearance at Booth's
Theatre closed with the second evening and the
attempt must be classed as a failure, it is yet true that
for the succeeding three years of 1875–78, she was
almost constantly on the stage, appearing in a number of plays, and that the panorama of her experience

suggests the subtle triumphs of Emerson's Brahma, when he is made to say: —

> " They know not well the subtle ways
> I keep, and pass, and turn again."

Miss Field's first appearance again on the stage after her fateful *début* was on the ninth of the following June, when a complimentary benefit was extended to her at the Union Square Theatre in New York, the invitation being signed by the Mayor of the city, Bayard Taylor, Edmund C. Stedman, Whitelaw Reid, O. B. Frothingham, Vincenza Botta, and other men of note, and her performance in this was more than a *succès d'estime*. The play on this occasion was " Gabrielle; or, A Night in the Bastile," — an adaptation made by her father, Joseph M. Field, from Dumas, *père*. Miss Field appeared in the title rôle, in which she sang an Italian hymn of the fifteenth century, with such pathos and power as to bring tears to the eye. In this play Miss Ida Vernon, that incomparably fine *artiste*, appeared as the Marquise de la Prie, and Mr. Eben Plympton and other able actors of the day filled the cast. This play was followed by one of Miss Field's own sparkling comediettas, " The Opera Box," — a clever adaptation from the French, in which Kate impersonated Mademoiselle de Liria, a singing rôle. Of this a New York critic said: —

" Miss Field quite surprised the audience with the vivacity of her singing of a French *chanson*, and, upon an *encore*, with the brilliancy of her vocalization of an English song of her own composition."

In the following autumn Miss Field played in a number of cities the programme including " The

Opera Box" as a curtain-raiser, followed by " Peg Woffington," in which her dancing and singing, especially, caught the eye; and the press notices given her in Providence, Springfield, Buffalo, Cleveland, and various other points on this tour are not only favorable, but are often enthusiastic. So apparent was her success that John T. Raymond, then starring in Mark Twain's play, " The Gilded Age," engaged Miss Field for the season as his leading lady, playing Laura Hawkins to his Colonel Sellers. When they appeared in New York no less an authority than Mr. William Winter of " The Tribune " said: —

" The entrance of Miss Kate Field upon the American stage seems to us entirely justified by her acting as Laura Hawkins. It was full of refinement and intelligence, earnest enough, not affected or stagy, and she met the trying scene of passion and murder with a rush and force that were not melodramatic, and that gave a decided impression of strength, and the possibility of even better things."

There can be little question that if Kate Field could have entered on the stage at a later period of the development of dramatic art in America, the result might have been far more favorable to her. She had the natural method of the Comédie Française; but it was not until the first appearance of Sarah Bernhardt in this country (in 1880) that the natural school of acting was fully inaugurated here. The barrier to Kate's complete success lay, of course, partly in her vehement individuality, and also partly in the conditions of the time.

One of Mr. Stedman's charming letters to her, under date of Nov. 22, 1875, begins, " Dear Woffington," and in it he writes: —

" Last Saturday night I was a guest at the big Lotos dinner to Lord Houghton. (*Toujours perdrix.*) Occupied the second place of honor, on the right of the President, Reid. Was delighted to hear him speak more warmly of you than he often does of any one. It seemed like old times. He praised your Jefferson-Vezin letter; said it was just what he wanted, and would always be glad of that kind of letters from you. Bayard Taylor and Chandos Fulton joined in, and spoke in admiration of your pluck and talent. I asked the latter personage, who introduced himself to me, to tell me frankly what he thought of you and your prospects. He said you did Laura Hawkins splendidly the first night; afterwards, through some cause he did n't understand, not so well; but that you were a genuine actress. I told him you were succeeding abroad. He had heard of it. I think it is about time to let the newspapers hear of it; as everybody in our group, and of course everybody's friends, knows you are acting, and I fear some wrong statement will appear. . . . Lord Houghton returns to England this week. We all like him. If you ever see Swinburne, tell him that Lord H. has backed him everywhere, and read his poem ' From Spring to Fall ' at a dinner. It is now going the press rounds. Tell him also that a revulsion in his favor has set in, owing to the eleventh chapter in my book, which surprised everybody. Bradlaugh is here, and goes out often with Mrs. Wallace, and frequently to Frothingham's church. Bradlaugh has become more *refined* and quiet since his stay in America; has recently been quite ill. Taylor is interesting himself greatly in literary and public matters here, and is a good fellow. I hope to see him the ' figure-head ' here in our best projects : he is old enough, and loyal to the core, and will do anything I ask him to. He ought to succeed Bryant as Poet of the Century. Mrs. Bullard is having a visit from Mrs. Moulton, and they both are matronizing Joaquin Miller, who knows how ' to take captive ' generous women. We elected Hazzard to the Century. Did I tell you?"

In January of 1876 the American minister writes: —

January 31, 1876.

Dear Miss Field, — Categorically —

1. I thank God you were not involved in the dreadful crash in which poor young Boucicault perished so sadly.

2. We shall be glad to see you as soon as you are done hunting "a local habitation." "A name" you have made already. Some of us are always here, if friends drop in to tea, at 5 to 6. My daughters are going to have Friday again for their regular "at home" day.

3. Thanks for your sympathy with me under the infamous . . . falsehood with which I have been assailed. . . . I have something to tell you, and something to ask you, about certain of your friends.

4. Touching the opening of Parliament, I 'll do what I can for you, but can't encourage you to expect anything. You had better consult with a Peer. The Master of Ceremonies has written to me that seats can only be given to a "very few ladies of the highest position," and refers me to the Lord *Great* Chamberlain (did you know there are a "Lord *High* Chamberlain" and a "Lord *Great* Chamberlain," the latter office hereditary?), and I am now in correspondence with that sublime functionary (spell that with a *big* S and F) to ascertain if any of my daughters can have places.

Yours sincerely,

Robert C. Schenck.

Among several pleasant letters from Mr. Moncure D. Conway is this: —

May 29, 1876.

Dear Miss Kate, — I send you a letter of mine to the Cincinnati "Commercial" which may interest you.

I ought to have written to you before to say that I liked your singing of the Spanish ballad very much. I don't know whether any one told you of a bit of drollery which occurred just after you left the stage. There was applause which would have continued had not one of the gods of the gallery caused a laugh by crying out, " I don't understand it." To which another boy on the other side of the gallery cried, " You don't understand it; I 'll report you to the School Board."

I shall be glad to hear of any further engagements you get. We have received a private letter from Halstead, alluding with pleasure to you and your prospects, which wife wrote him were very good.

Faithfully yours, M. D. Conway.

On the death of Mrs. Reid, the mother of Mr. Whitelaw Reid, this reply comes to Miss Field's message of sympathy : —

New York, 23 Park Avenue,
July 26, 1876.

Dear Miss Kate, — Many thanks for your words of sympathy. The whole case was, as you truly say, a most pathetic one ; and even yet I have scarcely recovered from the stunning effect of it sufficiently to realize the extent of the bereavement.

Very truly yours, Whitelaw Reid.

Miss Kate Field,
 15 New Cavendish St.,
  Portland Square, W. London.

The following letter from Wilkie Collins relating to the dramatization of his novel, " The New Magdalen " is of interest: —

90 Gloucester Place, Portman Square, W.
9 February, 1877.

Dear Miss Field, — Three times I have tried to get to New Cavendish Street, and three times some atrocious obstacle has started up and stopped me. To-day I go to Paris for a week or ten days, and when I come back " I 'm darned if I don't try again."

In the mean time, I have read three acts of the piece, — with all the more interest, seeing that I know it thoroughly well. I saw it (superbly acted by the principal woman) in Paris about seventy or eighty years ago. I have also got it among my volumes of . . . There is no doubt about the " situation," but they won't do for the English stage in their French form. As to Miss Ada Cavendish, I have spoken to her about it. At present she is so ill that she can barely get on to the stage, and she is too young and slim to " make up " for a woman with a big son who fights duels in the " sacred cause of virtue." It is a part for an older actress, — supposing it has not already been tried on the English stage. I must inquire and tell you what I can find out when I return.

I send back . . . with this note. It would be easy to change the scene of the piece to our war in the Peninsula against Napoleon — and to make the soldiers Englishmen. But we must first be sure that this has not already been done . . . be essential to the success of the play in England. In great haste,

Yours truly,   WILKIE COLLINS.

There is no opportunity left.

Very truly yours,   WILKIE COLLINS.

The year of 1877 found Kate again in London, and during the succeeding two years she played frequently in her brilliant little comedy, " Extremes Meet," and under the name of Mary Keemle (which, as the reader will recall, was a part of her own name) she played all through the larger towns in England. A well-known press correspondent thus wrote of her : —

"The London managers and critics are attracted by Kate Field's peculiar capacity, and are watching her progress with interest. I am touched and impressed by the pluck and cleverness of this little American woman, so frankly and thoroughly American, wherever she goes and whatever she does. Think of her fighting her own way in England, travelling through the North country for the practice in her art denied her at home, and at the same time finding strength to write her letters, alike brilliant and solid, to the 'Courier-Journal' and the 'Tribune,' besides contributing to the leading London reviews, and figuring in the most intellectual and famous circles of London !

"After playing at Newcastle, where she is also engaged to lecture, she will probably appear at Dundee and Aberdeen in Scotland."

In the rôle of Violante in "The Honeymoon," she indeed won praise from the leading London critics. The "Athenæum" noted that she had "a genuine feeling for comedy," and that she was "an actress of great intelligence and vivacity;" another critic spoke of her beautiful singing, both in English and in French, and added: "She produces her voice in a pure, lark-like, and thrilling manner, and excels particularly in expression; and by *nuances* of phrasing adds to, or illustrates, the beauty of really fine passages. She is a pupil of Manuel Garcia, Malibran's brother, who predicts for her a brilliant future on the stage."

Congratulations from New York came in the following letter : —

NEW YORK, 47 EAST 25TH ST., May 6, 1876.

DEAR MISS FIELD, — I was very much rejoiced at the telegraphic announcements in last Monday's "Herald" of your success as Violante in "The Honeymoon." That is a brilliant comedy, by the way, more so in my estimation, even, than the "School for Scandal." The part you took I should think to be an admirable one for you. Please bear in mind that I do not congratulate you *now*, simply at the moment of your dawning success, as I suppose many will who have heretofore withheld their praise, but that I have always, always entertained the strongest belief in your genius for the stage, or in anything almost that you might devote yourself to, which belief I shall still hold, whatever befall.

Your description of the House of Lords in the "Graphic" pleased me greatly. Good-by.

Very sincerely yours,

Henry B. Millard.

It was, perhaps, in this summer that, in company with Mrs. Louise Chandler Moulton, Kate made a visit to Edinburgh as the guest of her valued friend, Mr. Laurence Hutton, and his mother. Writing in a press letter from Edinburgh of its unfortunate classes, she said: —

"If I show the dark side of a beautiful town, it is because I love humanity better than places, and believe that mankind is best helped by telling the truth.

"Is there no silver lining to this cloud? Yes. Glasgow, recently the wickedest of all towns, has waked up to a sense of its own degradation, and now owns its water, rapid transit, gas, and street railroads. Within a few years what have been the worst parts of the city will be owned and administered by the municipality itself. This healthy movement is spreading, and Edinburgh cannot escape the blessed infection."

The curiously prophetic cast of Kate's mind is again revealed by her questioning in this letter: —

" Why will not some of our kindly disposed millionaires who are anxious to help their less fortunate brothers and sisters study the new dispensation that has dawned upon Scotland, and see whether it cannot be applied to the slums of American cities? Should not Good Government clubs find ample food for thought and action in such investigation? "

And within the year 1899 the Twentieth Century Club of Boston, under the able leadership of its president, Mr. Edwin D. Mead, called an eminent Scotchman to its lecture-desk to describe the municipal methods of Glasgow, with a view to their introduction in this country with whatever modifications our conditions required.

Desiring at one time to take a house in London, her genial friend, Mr. Frank Millet, was assisting her, and in regard to some details he wrote: —

" My pencil, Kathleen Mavourneen, is not the pencil of a ready draughtsman, but I send you herewith such a plan of your future residence as I have been able to construct, with all the measures duly detailed. At least, this is the upper portion of the dwelling. I think and most sincerely hope that you may be comfortable there. I will do and am doing my utmost to urge on the workmen. I have told them that it is let for November, and that I shall be prosecuted according to law with most awful consequences if I do not perform my contract."

The letter was signed " Your affectionate landlord " with the added question in parenthesis, " Was there ever such a thing? "

The following letter reveals some of the perturbations that beset Wilkie Collins: —

90 GLOUCESTER PLACE, *Portman Square*, W.
LONDON, Sept. 25, 1875.

DEAR MISS FIELD, — I have just got back, and have held a court of justice on my servants. They all declared that no such lady as Miss Kate Field ever appeared at this house, or did me the honor of leaving her card ; and they all remember perfectly that I expressly instructed them to show Miss Field upstairs into my study on the day when I expected to have the pleasure of receiving her. The only explanations of this *contretemps* are two in number. 1, That the servants have all three lied. 2, That you called at the *wrong* Gloucester Place. There are *two* Gloucester Places in London ; the oldest and first named I live in. It is close to *Portman Square* (underlined on this address). The other Gloucester Place lies out Bayswater way, close to Westbourne Terrace ; and is known as Gloucester Place, Hyde Park. The Editor of the Louisville " Courier Journal," when he was last in England, went to the wrong Gloucester Place (being invited to lunch with me). I asked a " party " to meet him, and while we were waiting vainly for him here, he was waiting vainly at the other Gloucester Place for *us*. I am so sorry and so ashamed at what has happened that I take kindly in the theory that *you* have followed the lead of the editor. In any case, pray accept my excuses, and pray give me another chance when we are next in London together.

You deserve to succeed in these days of mean intriguing and puffery. Your resolutions and self-respect are doubly admirable. Whatever I can do to help you shall be gladly done. If you go to Edinburgh, I know the Manager of the new theatre and winter garden there, — Mr. Wybert Reeve (my Count Fosco in America), — and a letter to him is heartily at your service. As for me, I am better, but not yet well. In a week or so, I think of going to

Germany for a month. Letters will be forwarded from this address.

Yours truly,

WILKIE COLLINS.

Another letter from Mr. Collins is as follows: —

90 GLOUCESTER PLACE, Portman Square, W.
April 22, 1876.

DEAR MISS FIELD, — I was very sorry to miss you, but I sleep badly since my illness, and cannot get up in the morning. The doctor allows me to get out for a walk (with a patch over my eye), but he has not yet allowed me to see my own play, and he forbids me to see your "matinée." The lights and the atmosphere are the things he objects to, and I am afraid he is right. The pain I have suffered has seriously weakened me. I can only wish you success most sincerely, and hope for another chance of making one of your audience.

I am glad you liked the piece and the acting. You must have been looking at the wrong "compartment" when Cecil drew the curtains and opened the windows. It is (of course) the first thing he does on entering the "drawing-room." The play cannot end unless he does it, for the matron and the policeman in plain clothes (who bring the curtain down) enter by the window. The rest of your questions I hope to answer *viva voce*, but I *am* surprised at your never having met in real life with a woman who fell in love with a man utterly unworthy of her. Oh, Miss Keemle, Miss Keemle, have you still to discover one of the brightest virtues of the sex?

Yours always truly,

WILKIE COLLINS.

A pleasant little group of friends gathered at the Boucicaults to watch the old year out and the new year in, when 1877 merged itself in 1878, and Kate records meeting then Clement Scott, the well-known critic, the Wyndhams, and Mr. Farquhar, the novelist. It is difficult to realize that at a time little more than twenty years past the telephone was a new invention that was inspiring transcendent scientific interest. The idea of the telephone dates back to 1844, when Alexander Melville Bell of Edinburgh first published a system of symbols by which the sounds of all language could be defined and compared by scientists. Many interesting experiments were made by several persons, all tending toward the final invention; and Prof. Charles Page of Salem, Mass., who in 1837 published an article on " Galvanic Music; " and Dr. Clarence J. Blake, the distinguished aurist of Boston, who suggested to Alexander Graham Bell the human ear itself as a model of mechanism in constructing a phonautograph, — were among the early researchers who contributed to the results afterwards achieved. It was, however, in 1876, at the Centennial in Philadelphia, that the first definite recognition was made in an official report, signed by Sir William Thompson and others, stating that " Mr. Alexander Graham Bell exhibits apparatus by which he has achieved a result of transcendent scientific interest, — the transmission of spoken words by electric currents." The invention was spoken of as " the greatest marvel hitherto achieved by the electric telegraph," and when the first public exhibition of the new invention was made in Salem, Mass., on Feb. 12, 1877, connecting the Essex Institute with a house in Boston, and music and conversation were transmitted, the public amazement and excitement was great. All this range of achievement deeply interested Kate Field. As the mysterious writing of " Planchette " had appealed to her when she had sought to analyze and discover the agency, she was again and always keenly alive to intimations from the realm of unseen realities; so that plunging headlong, so to speak, with all her ardor and enthusiasm into the possibilities of the new invention, was a predestined thing. In February of 1878 Miss Field thus racily describes her first experience with the new invention: —

"I sat at a desk, at the top of which was an electric bell. On both sides of the desk, depending from iron arms, was a small pear-shaped wooden instrument, bearing a strong family resemblance to the stethoscope. The small end of each instrument was connected with a telegraphic wire. I was in the presence of the Telephone. 'Is this all?' I asked. 'All!' exclaimed the superintendent. 'Is n't it enough, provided the object be attained? Is n't simplicity a charm in inventions as well as in people? Would you feel happier if the Telephone were the size of a steam-engine? Before you say another word, touch that electric bell, put one telephone to your ear and the other to your mouth.' Feeling quite crushed at being so sat upon, I obeyed orders, and straightway I heard an unknown voice exclaim, —

"'All right; what do you want?'

"'Who are you?'" I asked.

"'I'm every inch a man, and by your voice I know that my questioner is a lady.'"

"'How far away are you?'

"'Half a mile.'

"'Will you whistle?'

"'Certainly.'

"Sure enough, I heard with the utmost distinctness, 'Whistle, and I'll come to thee, my lad.'

"'Capital,' I said. 'Now a song, if you please.'

" Did n't I laugh when my unknown acquaintance sang, ' Thou art so near and yet so far ' ?

" ' Why did you laugh?' asked the Invisible, at the conclusion of his song.

" ' Did you hear me? My mouth was some distance from the Telephone."

" ' I heard you perfectly. Now hear me breathe.'

" When that breath came to my ear I was startled. Then we whispered to each other, and finally the Invisible exclaimed, ' Just one more experiment,' and he kissed me ! I heard him. I can't say honestly that this final experiment was as satisfactory in its results as the ordinary way of performing the operation. It is not likely to supersede old-fashioned osculation, but, *faute de mieux*, it will serve. I am quite sure the young King of Spain resorted to it recently when, forced to leave Aranjuez and return to Madrid, he communicated telephonically with his *fiancée*.

" Three weeks later, when I next interviewed the Telephone, the Invisible, who had never seen me, and had only heard my voice during the short conversation I have repeated, began to laugh, and said, ' I had the honor of kissing my fair questioner three weeks ago.' This proves the wonderful delicacy of the instrument, and how impossible it will be to practise deception through it. Since then I have heard four-part singing, ' sounding like distant music on the water,' to borrow the happy expression of the Duke of Connaught, who was delighted with the effect. It 's a singular fact that part singing, which is by no means true, comes out beautifully at the distant end of the Telephone. Electricity has so exquisite an ear that it seems to harmonize all differences. It will be a good idea for impresarios to pass all their doubtful singers through the Telephone. They will never be out of tune, no matter how flat or sharp they start. Then, I 've heard a solo and pianoforte accompaniment, with every note and word as audible as possible ;

I 've heard bugle-playing fifty miles distant that was charming, and I 've heard an organ 130 miles away. Now I 'm prepared for the deluge, or whatever Nature pleases. It 's impossible to be surprised any more. Before long we shall fold our arms, and let electricity do everything for us. We 'll go to bed and get up by electricity; we 'll eat by electricity, and be saved the bore of knives and forks. We 'll write by electricity, and see by the same means. Yes, you need n't open your eyes. I 've just read of the electroscope, the province of which is to transmit waves of light by electricity. Combine it with the Telephone, and while two persons, hundreds of miles apart, are talking together, they will actually *see* each other. Won't this be fun? If your lover happens to be an amateur photographer, he 'll take your picture, my dear, across the ocean. Only let electricity circumvent the Atlantic, and I 'm its slave for life."

Kate Field had a strong scientific vein in her nature. Anything in the line of unknown forces held her with the most absorbing interest, and in her later years, when Edison and Tesla were astonishing the world, she made visits to their laboratories and studied and wrote of their work. With characteristic enthusiasm, then, she gave herself to the work of making known the telephone to both the English and American public. Her diary for 1878 tells a characteristic story. On January 2 she records that she has written two articles on the telephone for Leicester and Ireland. On January 4 she writes: —

Telephone article in "Welshman." Letter from Ristori, who will get my article printed in Rome, and says she will do all in her power for the Telephone if I 'll come to Italy to advance it.

January 7th, Monday. I have already written twenty-one

articles on the Telephone and inspired others. My idea is now to invite the Press to a Matinée Téléphonique and get one general chorus of gratuitous advertising before the opening of Parliament, when everything will go to the wall.

8th, Tuesday. Labouchère told Nash, the solicitor, that the Telephone was splendidly managed, — that he watched the way the subject was kept before the public without in any way having the suspicion of advertising. He little thinks that "Puss" of his "Truth" has had the management of it all. In my opinion, women of discernment manage the diplomacy of business infinitely better than men.

9th, Wednesday. The Queen has invited Bell to exhibit the Telephone at Osborne House on the 14th. Consequently I'll delay the press meeting until two days after, which will be the day before Parliament meets. Am writing all the invitations myself, which is no joke. Shall be particular to include all the leading provincial papers. They make opinion.

10th, Thursday. Dr. Marston and Hermann Vezin met at my rooms to discuss with me the Spanish play the former has written on my adaptation. Neither Vezin nor I like the second act, and, after much discussion, Marston has promised to make the changes we think necessary. I believe in the play. When shall I be able to produce it? Ah, when? All comes to those who can wait.

11th, Friday. The Telephone needs managing, and —— and I are going to Osborne with "the show." Miss Herring will accompany me. Went to Professor Bell's to-night and heard a quartette of tonic sol-fa singers. They sang execrably, but the effect through the Telephone was excellent. All the discords were set right by electricity apparently, and all shrillness taken out of the soprano. I sang through it to my own accompaniment, and they say both voice and piano came out splendidly.

12*th, Saturday*. Took an electric bath. Believe this form of electricity will do me good. Writing my Telephone invitations for dear life and packing for to-morrow. Will take my new gown of blue silk embroidered with rosebuds, so that I may be prepared to go to court if asked. I must be where I can report matters.

13*th, Sunday*. At 9.30 A. M. Miss Herring and I drove to Long's Hotel, where we took up ——· *en route* to Waterloo Station. Took train for Southampton, arriving at half-past one. Going on board "Prince Leopold," steamed to Cowes. Weather fair. Not ill. Reaching Isle of Wight at 4 P. M., went direct to Marine Hotel, where we found rooms and succeeded in being comfortable.

14*th, Monday*. Drove early to Osborne Cottage, where Sir Thomas Biddulph invited me to come in the evening. Arrived there all fine in my new gown at 8.30 P. M. Met Lady Biddulph, Sir Thomas General Ponsonby, Mrs. Ponsonby, and others. Very polite, and very courteous about Telephone. I sang "Kathleen Mavourneen" to the Queen, who was delighted and thanked me telephonically. Sang "Cuckoo Song," "Comin' thro' the Rye," and recited Rosalind's epilogue. All delighted. Then I went to Osborne House and met the Duke of Connaught. Experiments a great success.

15*th, Tuesday*. Did n't get to bed until 3 A. M. Up at 5. Took boat at 7 and reached London at 11.30. Drove to "Associated Press," and sent off telegrams to America. Went home and prepared telegrams for New York "Herald," Newcastle "Chronicle," Liverpool "Post," Manchester "Guardian." After dinner wrote notices for "Times," "Telegraph," and "Daily News." Then with Mr. Munger drove in hansom to the several offices and delivered copy.

16*th, Wednesday*. To-day town all alive with the Telephone news furnished by me. Our Matinée Téléphonique a great success. Quite two hundred persons were present, including the American Minister, Sir Julius Benedict, Hermann Vezin, Genevieve Ward, Colonel Forney, Du Maurier, and William Black. All delighted with Telephone. The lunch was good, and nobody wanted to leave. I was on my feet from 11 until 5.30, and when I got home I was deathly ill.

17*th*, *Thursday*. Tired fearfully. Took an electric bath to revive me. Colonel —— came in during the evening and said both he and Bell were delighted with my matinée. Bell says my "Times" article on Telephone is the best that ever was written. Now I want to give some Telephone concerts, and Colonel —— has promised to cable for Gower's Telephone harp.

18*th*, *Friday*. All the weekly papers full of the Osborne House experiments, and I'm considered a great creature because I've sung to the Queen. Miss Ward, Colonel ——, and I went to hear "L'Ombra." A poorer opera and a worse performance I never listened to. Only the tenor deserved applause.

19*th*, *Saturday*. Took electric bath and wrote a column on Telephone for the New York "Herald." Sir Charles Dilke came in, looking very well. He does not believe there will be war, but thinks the peace being patched up cannot last more than a year or two. He promised to interest House of Commons in Telephone.

This episode of the telephone had an unforeseen and an important result for Miss Field, in a way quite undreamed of by her. From her childhood she had never known what it was to be free from financial anxieties. Curiously, her life had been attended almost constantly by the results, or some of the results of wealth, without the wealth itself. She had enjoyed such advantages, indeed, as money alone could not insure; as the beautiful friendship of Mrs.

23

Browning, for instance, and other social privileges that brought her in close and intimate association with noble and lofty people. " Philosophy can bake no bread; but she can procure for us God, Freedom, and Immortality," said Novalis. Money, likewise, can procure a vast amount of commodities which serve in convenience or comfort; it can even open the doors of a great range of privileges in art and study and travel; yet, with all that may be claimed for wealth, it has absolutely no power over the best and the highest things in life. The portals leading to the great do not open to the golden key.

> " For a cap and bells our lives we pay;
>   Bubbles we earn with a whole soul's tasking.
> 'T is heaven alone that is given away;
>   'T is only God may be had for the asking.
> No price is set on the lavish summer;
> June may be had by the poorest comer."

Kate Field had freely enjoyed much of the best of earth in her friendships with noble and gifted people and in her own life of ceaseless aspiration and struggle. Yet that the struggle was hard for a delicate girl, whose energy always far transcended her strength, no one could deny. To her uncle, who had frequently been very generous and kind, she yet sensitively preferred repaying, so far as was possible, whatever money he had given to her. It is possible that the entire amount was not refunded, but it was at least approximately and perhaps wholly repaid. Nor was this done with any sense of bitterness or hardship. Apparently she had never uttered a word of complaint or disappointment when, after her vehement young assertion of her right to express her own opinions regarding the issues of the Civil War, however they differed from his, — when after this, he reversed the intention he had expressed for making her his heiress, she simply took the ground that he had a right to do as he pleased with his own money; and that, as she could not place herself in mental obedience and subjection to his views, — as she would, with all her ardor, espouse the cause of the Union, — then having thus disappointed and in a way defied him, it was not right, she reasoned, that she should avail herself of his generosity. That she longed for his friendly regard and protection always was true. Equally true it proved that Kate was as high-spirited as she was sensitive, and that she would never bear any infringement of her own sense of justice. There should be no implication here on the character of Mr. Sanford. He was a man of generous impulses and of many admirable deeds. If he had his defects, he simply shared the common lot of all humanity. He was a keen, shrewd business man, very proud of his beautiful and gifted wife, Kate's idolized "Aunt Corda," and exceedingly generous and good to her relatives; but Kate's nature was an enigma to him, and to its labyrinth he held no clue. In her first year in Italy as a girl of eighteen she once wrote to her aunt: —

"I feel more and more that Uncle Milt is disappointed in me, and I grieve at it, but regrets are useless. He ought to understand my real feelings, and he knows that were he in my position he would be actuated by the same desires. I feel that with my ideas of right and wrong, with my convictions, he would ever be incensed with me for almost everything I might do. He thinks my effect upon his wife is injurious, for he has often said so; certainly his letters to me bear every evidence of an entire misunderstanding of my motives and character. Then it is better for all that I do my duty. My first thought is my mother."

It is quite probable that Kate might have been more tactful with advantage to herself; but she always had the defects of her qualities. If she felt that she was misunderstood, she scorned to explain herself to the person in question when sometimes explanation might have been better. Yet with all her heart she longed for harmony and good will, and in a letter to her Aunt Corda in regard to an expression from her Uncle Milton which she felt to be unjust, she said : —

" Let me say, too, in my heart I bear no malice toward Mr. Sanford ; he knows not what he does, and fails to see me in my real character. Should misfortune or sorrow ever remove the scales from his eyes, and his opinion of me change, I shall be only too happy to bury the past. For me life is too short to be devoted to hatred and bickering. Until that time comes my proper womanly pride will make me look upon him as a stranger. . . . Family dissensions are terrible ; but in all this matter, from beginning to end, my conscience does not reproach me. If it did, I should not hesitate to plead for pardon wherever I had unwittingly done wrong."

There is no earnest life in which the temptation to command the stones to become bread, and to enjoy all the kingdoms of the world, does not present itself. To Kate it came in the guise of her uncle's and aunt's desire that she should accept their home and protection and resign her ambitions, which, to her, would have been simply to stifle her energies. In reply to one letter from her uncle, she wrote : —

"To solemnly declare that I will never appear in public is beyond my power. I would make no such promise to any human being, not even to my dear father and mother, were they alive, — but they would not ask it. If I have the gift of speaking ; if I can move people by so doing, and if in addition I can make money, — I think it my duty to use all the faculties given me.

"You offer to put aside for my use the interest on $10,000, provided I will give up at least $10,000 a year ! Don't you see how impossible this is ? I want money for others as well as for myself. I want to help the Wilcoxes ; I want if I live to do a thousand things. It is useless to cramp me. If I am deprived by health of an active life, then I must be resigned to fate, and accept poverty if necessary, but until then I want freedom to work in whatever direction I feel called.

"I don't want your money, Uncle Milt, — I want health and independence ; but to prove I am not mercenary, I will compromise. Withdraw your offer of $600 a year, — for I suppose that is the amount, — and I will consider Aunt Corda's health in all that I may do publicly, lecturing comparatively little and making every effort not to go great distances. Next winter (D. V.) I have no desire to lecture extensively ; but I shall have something to say, if I live, about the low-down people of England, and I want to say it in New York, Boston, and other cities."

A biography must be a record of facts ; and Kate Field's life was so largely determined in all her early womanhood by the influence and attitude of her uncle and aunt that its story could not be adequately presented without these references. But all this must not be taken too seriously. Kate was a very sensitive, high-strung girl, independent to a fault, and yet more dependent on understanding and sympathy than any one, except her gentle mother, could realize; and such a nature inevitably encounters discords in its ardor and uncompromising demands. A more mercurial nature than that of Kate Field never lived. She had a quick temper, but its flash was as brief as it was swift, and she never held ill-feeling. She was always more than ready to forgive, or to ask to be forgiven if she felt she had been in the wrong. Her life, as we have seen, was a most arduous struggle. It was, to the eye of the world, a very brilliant one. She was sunny, joyous, witty; she was always a charming presence, with an air of elegance about her that was due both to her personal distinction of manner and her Parisian completeness of costume; but at what cost of energy all this outer life was achieved no one could have dreamed.

Singularly, and in the most unforeseen way, the tide of financial fortune was now to set toward Kate Field. For her services in the unique way in which she had been instrumental in thus introducing the telephone to the public, the Bell Telephone Company gave her a number of shares. At the time they had no great value, nor, perhaps, was it definitely foreseen that they would have; but this stock became, as the world knows, a very lucrative investment, and Miss Field soon found herself the possessor of a moderate little fortune verging toward some two hundred thousand dollars.

This little fortune was not realized, however, immediately, nor would any degree even of fabulous wealth have ever lessened Kate's active efforts in one direction or another. Work was to her expression, and financial ease would simply have enabled her to insure for it better conditions.

A great number of very interesting letters from the most prominent people of the day were showered upon Miss Field in connection with the interest that she aroused in the new invention which was the initiative of the modern advance in physical science that is destined to change all the relations of men. An autograph letter from Lord Beaconsfield to her under date of Jan. 19, 1878, is as follows: —

MADAME, — Her Majesty the Queen expresses so much interest in the telephone that His Noble Lordship, the Minister of Foreign Affairs, suggests that a trial of this invention be made in the private parlors of the home office on Friday morning at eleven o'clock. The Earl of Beaconsfield concurs. You are hereby invited to be present and, if you are disposed, to sing some selections to be transmitted from the Library over the wire. His Lordship would be obliged with the favor. With respect, madame, I am,

Yours, etc.,   BEACONSFIELD.

TO MISS KATE FIELD.

Another interesting letter of this time was the following from Mr. Alexander Graham Bell: —

LONDON, 115 CANNON ST., Jan. 18, 1878.

MISS KATE FIELD.

DEAR MADAM, — I am requested by Sir Thomas Biddulph to convey to you Her Majesty's thanks for your assistance at the telephone experiment at Osborne.

In his letter to me Sir Thomas says: I hope you are aware how much gratified and surprised the Queen was at the exhibition of the Telephone here on Monday evening. Her Majesty desires me to express her thanks to you and the ladies and gentlemen who were associated with you on that occasion. I am,

Yours truly,
ALEXANDER GRAHAM BELL.

Another from a member of the peerage in attendance at court wrote: —

DEAR MISS FIELD, — The Prince Imperial is very anxious to test the Telephone as Macduff and I did the other day. I promised to write to him after hearing from you, if it would be convenient for *him* to fix his own day and time. He is very much engaged just now, and it would be a great chance if he could come on your appointment. Please let me have a line by bearer or as soon as you can.

Absorbing as was the fascinating interest in the telephone, it by no means exclusively occupied Miss Field's time and thought. She was writing brilliant letters to the New York " Herald; " constantly sending news by cable; she was an editorial writer on the " London Times "; she was contributing to " Truth " a series of humorous letters on the various kaleidoscopic aspects of London life; she was appearing at the Princess Theatre nightly for a part of this time, in her own comedy " Extremes Meet," which, as a " curtain-raiser," preceded the play of the evening, and she was then, as always, a brilliant figure in the social life of the day. In a press letter describing London in the season, she gives a vivid page out of her own experiences when she writes: —

" While nothing in the world can compensate me for the absence of a bright sun and dry atmosphere, I yet like London, in spite of its climate. I like it best in the winter months, when the weather is worst. I like it because of the people.

" ' What ! out of the season? ' Yes, precisely for this reason. During May, June, and July, which are called the season because extreme fashion comes up from the country to go to the opera, inspect the Royal Academy, and visit one another, — everything is topsy-turvy. Life is a succession of balls and receptions, four and five deep nightly. You see nobody except for five minutes in the glare of gaslight, for you no sooner arrive at one party than it is time to go to another. As the majority of London houses are very small, and the success of a party depends upon its size, as the rule is to invite three times as many people as can be accommodated, there is a possibility of not being able to get up stairs, in which dilemma you hail your host and hostess, as ships hail one another at sea, by means of signals. Under these circumstances, I do not call society satisfactory. It is a delusion, a snare, a madness, an idiotic invention of a barbaric civilization, an unmitigated bore.

"This is London during the season. London out of season tells a different tale ; and, mark the insolence of Fashion ! three and a half millions of people reside in London from January until December, only taking vacations during August and September ; but because a few thousand butterflies appear with the early summer, this big, bustling Babel is out of season so long as the butterflies do not flutter in Hyde Park ! London out of season, I repeat, is most interesting. How can it be otherwise when it is not only the centre of Great Britain and Ireland, attracting to it the brains and energy of the United Kingdom, but the centre of the world, luring, if only for a moment, everybody from everywhere? If, therefore, as I sincerely believe, the proper study of mankind is man, where else can the observer so readily whet his curiosity, and revel in variety of culture and intelligence? The cream of external life is there, writes Hawthorne ; and whatever merely intellectual or natural good we fail to find perfect in London, we may as well content ourselves to seek the unattainable thing no farther on this earth.

"Almost all the clever literary, artistic, scientific, and critical English men and women reside permanently in

London or its vicinity. They must of necessity be near the great market which demands what they can supply. These in themselves are one of the most magnetic features of society; for what can be more attractive to a cultivated person than a dinner with Robert Browning, whose conversation is as entertaining and varied as the museum at South Kensington; a visit to George Eliot and George Lewes, — she, perhaps, the cleverest woman living, and he a really brilliant man; a walk along the Thames with that great, contradictory, inconceivable, intellectual despot, Thomas Carlyle; a matinée musicale at a charming house, with Prince Poniatowski and Miss Virginia Gabriel at the piano, and perhaps Joachim at the violin; and receptions where you are sure to meet Tyndall, Huxley, Herbert Spencer, Miss Thackeray, and others equally interesting though unknown to fame? All this one may obtain before the Christmas holidays. In February the assembling of Parliament brings together whatever there is of political eminence; and, to my way of thinking, — although I cordially detest the form of government, which is that of a pure aristocracy; although the House of Commons more or less muddles every reform it attempts, — many of its members are the most delightful companions. The very men whose public careers are utterly opposed — from my point of view, be it understood — to every principle of justice are charming socially; and while we fight the moment politics becomes the subject of conversation, we never cease to be good-natured. We find so many topics upon which to sympathize as to tolerate each other's failings (for of course I am thought as mad as I consider them wrong-headed and obstinate), and the acquaintances of an hour become the stanch friends of a lifetime. Then, when I meet an advanced English liberal, I embrace him (metaphorically) on the spot, seeing no difference between him and a fine American, saving that often he is more cultivated, and therefore more after my own heart. Of course these specimens are rare, but when found they should be treasured ; for I really know nothing nobler in humanity than an unprejudiced, radical, first-class English gentleman. His respect for women is not outdone by the most chivalrous American, although he may be less demonstrative in those little attentions to which we are accustomed ; his belief in women's capacity is not exceeded by that of George William Curtis ; and his friendly feeling toward America is so frank and so optimistic as to make you tremble lest he may decide to cross the Atlantic and discover that we, too, have our plague-spots. The world does not often hear of this type of Englishman, but he exists ; otherwise, how could I know him ? "

A Shakespeare Memorial Association had been formed in London in 1874 whose object was to build at Stratford-on-Avon a theatre worthy of the memory of the poet, and to further the interests of dramatic art and culture. Mr. Charles E. Flower gave strength and reality to the scheme by endowing it with a site on the banks of the river within view of the church where Shakespeare is buried. It was resolved to build a theatre, a library for Shakespearian books and a gallery for Shakespearian paintings and sculpture. The land to spare after it was thus occupied was laid out in gardens sloping down to the river, that mirrors them in its calm bosom.

In this work Miss Field was deeply interested, and when in the spring of 1878 it was resolved to hold a week's festival in the new theatre, she was one of the accomplished group of actors and musicians who gave their services. For the opening Dr. Westland Marston had written a poem which Miss Field was asked to recite. The evening came, and before a house crowded with the intellect and fashion of London that came down on a special train, Miss Field was led on the stage by Mr. Chatterton, to recite the opening address, written by Dr. Westland Marston. She was received with a hearty round of applause, and she declaimed the poem with admirable effect. The epilogue was in complete harmony with the time and object of the hour: —

" To-day — the day that marks our Shakespeare's birth —
In this new fane raised on his native earth,
We greet you, friends.   Here, trust we, with each aid
Our later arts afford, shall be displayed
The events and beings that his fancy drew,
Amid the scenes which met his actual view ;
And where of yore his mortal voice was heard,
A thousand hearts be by his spirit stirred —
That spirit, clear, profound, which ne'er mistook
One line, one phrase of Nature's varied book,
Solved all its meanings, secret or perplexed,
And found the cipher easy as the text."

" Much Ado About Nothing" was the comedy selected to open this first season of playing in the Memorial Theatre, and it was received with every manifestation of satisfaction. Miss Helen Faucit, looking like a picture out of some old-world theatrical album, showed how genius may overcome age, even in acting. She was a graceful Beatrice: her business was full of interest to those who would contrast so-called modern naturalness with studied art, and her voice was as soft and musical as it had been thirty years before, when the art world of London was at her feet.

The most fashionable evening of the week's festival was the musical night, when the stage of the new theatre was occupied by a concert party, including

Mrs. Osgood, Kate Field, Mme. Antoinette Sterling, Mr. W. H. Cummings, Mr. W. Shakespeare, and Mr. Santley, The London Concert and Glee Union, Mme. Arabella Goddard and Sir Julius Benedict. Mr. William Shakespeare, who did not claim to be a descendant of the bard, was not unlike the most popular and best-authenticated portraits of his name-sake. Mrs. Osgood was in excellent voice, and the purity of her style and her exquisite dramatic skill lent a fresh charm to " Orpheus with his Lute," very tenderly set by Arthur Sullivan. She also sang " Blow, blow, thou Winter Wind," and on her lips the " As You Like It " words had a new and touching significance. Miss Field had an enthusiastic reception. She sang, " I Know a Bank," "Where the Bee Sucks," and "Should he Upbraid " in a manner in which there was no trace of the amateur. She sang the difficult music with precision and her enunciation was especially admirable.

During this week, while in Stratford-on-Avon, Miss Field was the guest of the manager of this Shake-spearian Festival. To her Aunt Corda Kate wrote:

" Dr. Westland Marston said he 'd write the address if I 'd deliver it, so I promised, and I had a nice lot of verse to get into my head for one night, but having recited it in town to Dr. Marston, Hermann Vezin, and Mrs. Sterling — the best judges in the world — and having had their appro-bation, I went before the audience here with less trepida-tion than I otherwise should have felt, and made what all the papers call a 'great success.' I am very glad, being an American. Two nights later, I sang 'I Know a Bank,' 'Where the Bee Sucks,' and 'Should he Upbraid ' at the concert, and was complimented by Sir Julius Benedict, Madame Arabella Goddard and others."

Very lovely Kate looked on these appearances. On the first night she was in a Paris costume of a silvery blue with water-lilies drooping from the corsage; and on the musical night, in full evening dress of creamy white with the glimmer of pearls around her throat and wearing, as her only ornament, the little chain and locket given to her by Robert Browning, she was exquisite in her simplicity and elegance.

So interested did Miss Field become in the completion of this theatre that on the twenty-second of May following, she gave for it a benefit performance in London which was a memorable occasion. With her indefatigable zeal she had undertaken to secure subscriptions from American friends for the final decoration of the interior of the theatre, and a large blank book filled with the names and amounts sent testify to her success. The list includes the names of Longfellow, Mr. and Mrs. Fields, Mr. Stedman, Mrs. Anne Lynch Botta, Henry James, and a great number of the most distinguished people in this country. The entertainment that she organized and carried through with her unfailing energy was a notable success. An American in London wrote to her, saying: —

" I am proud of you as an American. No one but an *American* could have achieved such a splendid success as you have done. In your entertainment yesterday afternoon I was present and was delighted with all the arrangements."

Miss Field conceived the idea of introducing the wonder of the day — the telephone — at this matinée for the benefit of the Shakespeare Memorial fund, and thus wrote to the manager: —

15 New Cavendish Street, Portland Place,
April 17, 1878.

Dear Mr. McCure, — On May 22nd, an afternoon performance will be given at the Gaiety Theatre for the benefit of the Shakespeare Memorial at Stratford-on-Avon which needs but a few thousand pounds to make it complete. Mr. Henry Irving has sent a subscription of £25, not being able to act, while Mr. and Mrs. Kendal, Mr. Hermann Vezin, Miss Genevieve Ward, Miss Ellen Terry, Mr. Arthur Cecil, and the best artists in London have volunteered their services. With the exception of a comedietta the programme will be entirely Shakespearian, and I have thought that the introduction of the Telephone harp in one or more entr'actes, especially if the harp were played in Shakespeare's house at Stratford, would add greatly to the interest of the occasion. Hoping this suggestion may be approved by the Telephone Company, Limited, and that I may hear from you at an early date, I am

Yours truly,

Kate Field.

One of Kate Field's most important and agreeable press associations was that with the "New York Herald," beginning under the elder Bennett. The cosmopolitan scope and splendid enterprise of that journal captivated her imagination, and found response in her own indomitable energy. Her connection with the "Herald" had been initiated some two years before this time by the following letter:

New York, Feb. 16, 1874.

My dear Miss Field, — Mr. Bennett would like to make an arrangement with you to write an editorial on social and other topics of a kindred nature for publication every Sunday. He would like to have you write articles also on the theatres, charities, and other subjects interesting to women.

Can you do it, and on what terms? Please answer at your earliest convenience, and oblige

Your friend truly,

THOMAS B. CONNERY.

Miss Field had accepted this flattering offer, which came to her at a time of peculiar need, — a fact that may not have been entirely unknown to the great founder and editor of the " Herald." At all events, Kate accepted the offer gratefully and filled it brilliantly. Mr. Bennett sometimes related with amusement that an editorial written by Kate Field would be ascribed to a great financier or some keen-witted lawyer. Her adaptability gave her that infinite variety traditionally ascribed to Cleopatra.

In view of all this pleasant relation to the " Herald," it was with special gratification that Kate received the following note of congratulation on her Shakespeare-Memorial benefit: —

THE NEW YORK HERALD OFFICE, London Office,
46 Fleet Street, May 22, 1878.

MY DEAR MISS FIELD, — I must thank you for the great intellectual treat of this afternoon. Your comedietta is charming and all the Shakespearian part of the performance was immense. To Miss Ward undoubtedly belongs the honors. She is, indeed, a great artist. Croisette's death scenes are no stronger. There is no actress on the English stage who can compare with Miss Ward in these great parts. Altogether the whole entertainment was highly interesting, and I trust your energy may be rewarded by a good round sum which will at once put the roof on the Memorial.

Yours thankfully,

WENTWORTH HUGHES.

Sir Morell Mackenzie writes: —

36 BEDFORD PLACE, May 22, 1878.

DEAR MISS FIELD, — Permit me to congratulate you on your very brilliant success, in all respects, in your very brilliant Shakespeare Memorial benefit to-day. As we look to results in this short life, I suppose you are to be most congratulated on your great managerial talent, of which to-day you gave substantial proof. I cannot, however, refrain from saying that you looked lovely, sang superbly, and acted naturally. I hear you warmly praised on all sides. I trust that hearty public appreciation of your well-directed successful effort will be considered by you as compensation for your arduous and fatiguing labors. With great respect I am,

Faithfully yours,

MORELL MACKENZIE.

From the Shakespeare Memorial Association came this tribute : —

SHAKESPEARE MEMORIAL, STRATFORD-ON-AVON,
June 3, 1878.

DEAR MADAME, — At a meeting of the Council of the above Association held at the Town Hall on Friday, May 31st, it was resolved : —

That the special thanks of the Council are due and are hereby tendered to Miss Kate Field for her valuable assistance on the occasion of the performance at the Gaiety Theatre on May 22, in aid of the Shakespeare Memorial Fund.

I am also directed to inform you that the Council have the pleasure of presenting you with a proof Impression on India paper of David Garrick by Gainsborough, which is sent by mail to-day. Kindly acknowledge the same and return the case at your earliest convenience. I am, dear Madam,

Yours obediently,

CHARLES LOUNDES, *Secretary*.

MISS KATE FIELD.

24

In the early summer of 1878 Madame Ristori wrote to Kate: —

" If you want an entire change of air come with me and my daughter to St. Moritz." Miss Field responded to the bidding, and from this place — six thousand feet above the sea — she wrote: —

"Among other things, it rains principessas, duchessas, countessas, and marchesas. Man in Switzerland begins with Baron. Republican as I am, I saw myself in the Fremdenblatt (which is German for Visitor's List) as a Countessa until I expostulated and declared that America soared above titles. Women abound, apparently having packed up their husbands and male kind for the summer, and one soon learns on the promenade who is who. Madame Ristori, Marchesa del Grillo, is always the centre of a gay circle at the wells. Beauty, wit, intelligence gather around the tragic queen as naturally as though she were the Elizabeth, the Mary Stuart, the Marie Antoinette she so marvellously represents. Her passion for the stage is undiminished, and in October she will begin a three months' professional tour in Spain and Portugal. In addition to her old repertoire she will produce a new one-act tragedy translated by herself from the Spanish and entitled ' The Gladiator of Ravenna.' The scene is laid in Rome in the time of Caligula. A tragedy in one act is a novelty, and certainly the story of ' The Gladiator of Ravenna ' is powerful and dramatic. Perhaps in September Ristori may appear for a few nights at the Italiens, in Paris, acting Lady Macbeth to Salvini's Macbeth. Such a conjunction would be most interesting. I am afraid, however, that it is too good to be true. Both actor and actress wish it, but ' there 's many a slip 'twixt the cup and the lip.' Madame Ristori's daughter is as charming as ever, and her brother George has lately developed a talent for figure painting. He has a studio in Paris and studies with Bonnat."

Those summer days in the Alps with the great Ristori were always treasured by Kate as among her richest experiences. They discussed art, poetry, the drama. The intensity of temperament which characterized Madame Ristori satisfied the somewhat exacting, not to say imperious demands of Miss Field's own nature. The swift impulses that so pre-eminently dominated Kate were equally marked in Madame Ristori, and constituted, indeed, a signal part of her greatness. Sensitive to atmosphere and environment as they both were, there was in each the capacity for that sudden inspiration which has its spring in enthusiasm and imaginative power. They were akin, too, in earnestness of purpose. Madame Ristori was not alone the great artist, but a great woman. She conceived nobly of life as well as of art, and her serious and conscientious purpose appealed to Kate with a force not overbalanced by the brilliancy and grace of her gifts. In the comparisons of Rachel and Ristori which Kate delighted to make, drawing finely critical parallels between the two, she always found in Rachel the greater artist; in Ristori the greater genius. The former was educated in the purest school of dramatic art; the latter was far less indebted to any outer influence or suggestions. " Rachel fascinated and held one spellbound; Ristori inspired love," Kate would say in after days, recalling this summer's intimate study of the great Italian tragedienne. " Rachel freezes; Ristori brings tears." Kate was fond of quoting Jules Janin's words of Ristori, — that she was tragedy itself, comedy itself. " She is the drama," he exclaimed. Kate recognized her genius as universal, and often remarked that what Shakespeare was among dramatists, Ristori was among actors.

There can be no question that Kate's friendship with the great artist was the most sympathetic one of her entire life, and the exquisite experiences of that summer lingered with her when its days had vanished from all save memory. Any reference to that time always touched her visibly, and recalled the subtile truth in the poet's lines, —

> " But the rose's scent is bitterness
> To him that loved the rose."

In September Kate proceeded to Paris, which she found in the usual gleam and glow.

" Miss Field is at home in Paris," wrote a press correspondent, " as she herself has all the sparkle of a born Parisienne. She is a rare union of qualities, combining an almost masculine strength of intellect with all that is sweetest in feminine nature."

The Paris Exposition of 1878 interested Miss Field, and she sent from there a number of press articles whose effect was almost electrical in their vividness and power. Among these is an interview with Prof. John D. Philbrick, superintendent of the educational department of the United States exhibit, which filled four columns of " The Tribune." Writing from Paris under date of Sept. 16, 1878, Miss Field says : —

" The Champ de Mars is a misnomer. Peace has silenced the clashing of arms, and on a mimic battlefield the French Republic has welcomed the genius, industry and energy of the civilized world. One would have thought that the United States, eager to support the great nation which is so bravely sowing the seeds of Democracy in Europe, would have been first to claim space in the Exposition so recently past ; but Congress, purblind to our commercial interests (for the reason that there are too many lawyers and too few merchants among its members), ignored France's invitation until the eleventh hour, and then, appropriating the miserable sum of $150,000, sent the New World half-dressed into the presence of the Old. Wise men predicted failure. If they proved false prophets, it is because the American people are far more clever than their representatives; because, too, the President and Secretary of State appreciated the situation and appointed a commissioner whose executive ability is only second to his patriotism. Consequently the United States — though the last to enter the lists, though restricted in time, space, expenditure, and exhibits — has taken proportionately more awards than any other nation, and has opened up markets heretofore closed to us."

After this general introduction she gives an interview with Mr. Philbrick, which is fairly an educational document in its exhaustive scope, and the letter closes with this paragraph: —

"'And now, Mr. Philbrick,' I said, as he paused for breath, 'though you have well-nigh exhausted the universe, is there nothing to deprecate in the attitude of those Americans who maintain that an elementary education alone is needed for the welfare of the Republic?' 'Yes,' he replied earnestly; 'that is a vital point. I am more than ever convinced that no nation can be upheld by elementary education alone. Renan has well said that the United States will long have to expiate the want of higher education. Massachusetts leads the Republic. Why? Because she began her history with Harvard University and very soon provided for high schools. There is no use to deny facts. We must borrow many ideas from France as she will borrow from us. We must educate or die, and we must raise our educational standard. In the lower grades of schools we are in advance of France and Germany. In the higher grades they are superior to us.'

"Are not these words of wisdom, and should they not be

taken to heart? 'The substance of culture is knowing the best things,' declares Matthew Arnold. The Paris Exposition brought together the best things, and the representatives of the United States Public Schools need only turn to Mr. Philbrick to reap its harvest of culture."

The late winter of 1878–79 found Miss Field again in London — one of the busiest of women. She was writing plays; furnishing correspondence and editorials for the London "Times" and "Truth," and articles for the magazines, and, as if this were not enough, she was acting, and delivering frequent lectures.

A letter that she received from Dr. Schliemann is as follows: —

ATHENS, Feb. 8, 1879.

DEAR MISS FIELD, — Please accept my warmest thanks for your very kind letter of the 28th ult. as well as for your continued endeavors to procure me the U. S. consulate. On the 1st March I have to continue the excavations at Troy and anticipate very hard times there, particularly for the first month, because I have to live in a miserable wooden house, which affords but little protection against the inclemencies of the weather. Nevertheless this year's excavations will probably be very interesting, for, through Sir A. Layard, the British Ambassador at Constantinople, I have at last obtained permission to excavate the conical tombs, and, if not more, I promise to find in each of them *at least* the key to its chronology. I am always overwhelmed with work at Troy; but I shall always be charmed to hear from you; nay, your letters will be a great stimulus to me in my hard work. Mrs. Schliemann joins me in kindest regards.

Yours very truly,

HENRY SCHLIEMANN.

My address is Troy near the Dardanelles.

In October of 1879 Kate again returned to her own country, with a new comedietta " Caught Napping," which she had written while in London, founding it on a French play; and with two new and widely diverse schemes in her head: one to write a " Musical Monologue " and the other to found an establishment which subsequently materialized under the name of the Co-operative Dress Association.

A SIGNIFICANT PERIOD

Thou, born for noblest life,
For action's field, for victory's car,
Thou living champion of the right.
                                        EMERSON.

" Disturber " and " Dreamer," Philistines cried, when he
    preached an ideal creed,
Till they learned that the men who have changed the world with
    the world have disagreed.
                                        BOYLE O'REILLY.

I walked on, musing with myself
On life and art, and whether, after all,
A larger metaphysics might not help our physics; a completer
    poetry
Adjust our daily life and vulgar wants. . . .
                                        ELIZABETH BARRETT BROWNING.

CHAPTER VI

What being here below would not desire to render himself worthy of entrance into the sphere of those who live in secret by Love and Wisdom?

SWEDENBORG.

Thy truth, then, be thy dower. — *King Lear*.

Never to tire; never to grow cold; to be patient, sympathetic, tender; to
look for the budding flower and the opening heart; to hope always like God;
to love always, — this is duty. — AMIEL.

RETURN TO AMERICA. NEW YORK LIFE. THE LANDOR ALBUM.
SOCIAL INTERESTS. THE CO-OPERATIVE DRESS ASSOCIATION.
AN UNSUSPECTED ROMANCE.

THE year of 1880 found Miss Field in an interlude
of prosperous conditions. She had returned to New
York with the freedom from material anxieties insured
by the possession of a comfortable bank account; she
was still in the youthful maturity of her life; her
health was better, — health with her being always
more the result of mental than physical conditions, —
and she returned to a wide and warm circle of friends,
to find that her journalistic and magazine work had
already achieved for her a brilliant reputation. She
located herself in a pleasant suite of rooms in the
Victoria Hotel on Fifth Avenue which became a
centre of charming and hospitable life. Her apartment was attractive with the choice pictures on the
walls, several of them gifts from the artists themselves, — Vedder, Hennessy, Coleman, Frank Millet,
and Oliver Lay; the fine portraits of her father and

mother; a drawing of Gainsborough that was very rare and valuable; her grand piano and a well-stocked music stand, and books, and her souvenirs of travel that gave individuality to the rooms. A rosewood writing-desk that had been her mother's was laden with a scattered mass of letters and papers, and sofa, table, and chairs were not unlikely to be strewn with the latest books and magazines and the morning newspapers. Her favorite working-place was in her old steamer chair, a wonderful, storm-beaten bamboo construction which a friend once brought her from Japan, and which ever after followed her in all her vicissitudes of travel until, on her last journey — when she set forth for the islands in the Pacific from which she never returned — it was mysteriously lost. This chair was as adjustable as its occupant, being arranged to run the whole scale of ups and downs, and the right arm was capable of being transformed into a shelf on which her writing-pad and papers rested. Here in luxurious ease, with her favorite fountain pen, she would lie and write by the **hour** together.

Among her treasured souvenirs were the study of Landor's head, painted by Charles Caryll Coleman, and an immense album that Mr. Landor had given to her. "To express a liking for any of Landor's pictures — provided you were a friend — was almost sufficient to cause them to be taken down and presented to you; hence to praise anything in his presence was exceedingly unsafe," remarked Kate one day when some conversational reference had turned on this album. "I remember looking over his large collection that once belonged to Barker, the English artist, which Landor had purchased to relieve him

of certain debts, and particularly admiring four original sketches by Turner — two in oil and two in india
ink — that had been given to Barker by his brother
painter," she continued: " No sooner had I spoken
than Landor went in search of the scissors and, had
I not earnestly protested, would have cut out the
Turners and given them to me. I would not permit
him to do this, but the last day I was at his house
just before leaving Florence, as the hour for my
departure came, Mr. Landor appeared from an inner
room dragging this immense album after him. 'You
are not to get rid of me yet,' he exclaimed. 'I
shall see you home and bid you good-by at your
own door.' 'But dear Mr. Landor,' I exclaimed,
'what *are* you doing with that big book?' 'This
album is for you,' he replied, 'and you shall take it
with you.' I endeavored to dissuade him; it seemed
to me impossible to accept so munificent a gift; and
yet I knew not how to refuse it without offending
him. So I begged him to compromise by leaving
it to me in his will. 'No, my dear,' he replied; 'I
have lived long enough to know that a bird in the
hand is worth two in the bush;' and so, deaf to all
my entreaties, he carried it down stairs, and deposited
it in the carriage. 'A will is an uncanny thing, and
I'd rather remember my friends out of it than in it.
I shall never see you again,' he added, 'and I want
you to think of the foolish old creature sometimes.'
We drove to my abiding place and the good-by
came. 'May God bless you!' the lonely old man
exclaimed, and in another moment the carriage was
out of sight, — and it was, indeed, the last time I was
to see him, although I continued to hear from him
while he lived."

This album contained somewhere about a hundred and forty sketches and paintings, among which are very rare gems, — as heads by Raphael, flowers from Leonardo da Vinci; a landscape in oils by Salvator Rosa, sixteen sketches by Turner, a number by Gainsborough, and others by Claude Lorraine, Poussin, Allston, and several artists of the early Italian school. After Miss Field's death this album was submitted to General Charles A. Loring, Director of the Boston Museum of Fine Arts, who had a catalogue of it made which is an authoritative document in art, coming from so able a connoisseur as General Loring. Another interesting souvenir in Miss Field's rooms was a fine portrait of Charles Dickens accompanied by the following autograph letter: —

WESTMINSTER HOTEL, NEW YORK, Jan. 3, 1868.

MY DEAR MISS KATE FIELD, — I entreat you to accept my most cordial thanks for your charming New Year's present. If you could know what pleasure it yielded me you would be almost repaid even for your delicate and sympathetic kindness.

But I must avow that nothing in the pretty basket of flowers was *quite* so interesting to me as a certain bright, fresh face I had seen at my readings which I am told you may see when you look in the glass.

With all good wishes believe me,

Always faithfully yours,

CHARLES DICKENS.

At the Victoria Miss Field made a genuine home for herself. She gave delightful little dinners and had friends and guests constantly around her. So wonderfully had she retained the grace and vivacity of early youth, in her slender, girlish figure, her dainty loveliness of dress, and the enchantment that was always about her as an atmosphere, that her personality and her years of life had nothing in common. Practically, both in appearance and in her glow and enthusiasm she was still a young woman, and she became a brilliant figure in New York life as she had been in London and in Paris. For the first January days of 1880 Miss Field seems to have made some attempt of diary record, and this was the last of her journal-keeping. From this time until in the spring of 1896 when she went on to the unseen world, life was so relentless and swift-rushing as, apparently, to make diary-keeping impossible. The only perfect condition for a full diary is an empty life, — periods in which nothing happens, for when one has nothing to record, then there is plenty of time in which to record it.

On New Year's Day of 1880, Miss Field was invited to receive with Mrs. Stone, this custom having lingered in New York till well into that decade. She confides to her diary that she had made about sixty presents during the holidays "to those who most needed them, and who can make no return, which seems to me is sensible. Going to a Christmas tree and seeing how pampered are the children of the rich, I determined that when *I* had a Christmas tree, it should be planted in Five Points." She continues : —

"Santa Claus was good to me. In addition to Aunt Corda's gift I received a portemonnaie containing $100, a very pretty purse with nothing in it, — but as it has a silver horseshoe at one end and a pig at the other, it ought to bring good luck, — two volumes of poems, some charming

Xmas cards (what a capital one you sent !) a lovely fichu of Duchesse lace, a gold button-hook made into a charm, a very artistic calendar for 1881, and a Greek necklace, which I 've long been wanting."

Miss Field became much engrossed in discussing the co-operative idea, which had impressed her mind from its workings in England. She had just completed her monologue called, " Eyes and Ears in London," a very clever, witty skit on current phases of London life, and she began to study and practise it in preparation for her appearance in public. Engaged in this on a morning in early January, there came up to her the card of Mr. Albert Ives, who had come over in the " Scythia " with Parnell. " At once I interviewed him for 'The Herald,' " Kate records; " a good stroke of journalism." Again the next morning she began studying her Monologue, and cards came up so thick and fast that she had to have herself denied to every one; but the evening, which she always held as a gala time, was made pleasant by a little supper with Mrs. Laura Curtis Bullard, at which there was a pleasant group of intimate friends, including Mrs. Louise Chandler Moulton and Mr. Hatton. On January 5 of that month Miss Field records : —

" To-day Dr. Holland gave me a reception to which two hundred and fifty persons were invited. I stood up and shook hands with them all, and now I know how the President of the United States feels. It was a very agreeable evening. Every one seemed glad to see me, and I realized that I had the respect of my countrymen and countrywomen, at least of those whose good opinion is worth having. It was very kind of Dr. Holland to think of giving me this reception. I presented Mrs. Holland with a panel photograph of myself with back and profile, whereupon Dr. Holland exclaimed, 'Why, that's Kate Field's back.' At this Mr. —— wrote on a card which he placed before the photograph, 'Welcome Back.' This was very neat. I met Helen Hunt's husband for the first time. He seems to be a good fellow, but in no way brilliant. Brilliancy, however, is not necessary to happiness, whereas heart is. I said to him that I'd never be able to call his wife anything but ' H. H.' '*She* can never drop her H.'s,' I added. Jackson smiled. H. H. has grown very stout. *C'est égal,* she is clever. —— brought me a lovely basket of flowers home. I wore my cardinal brocade, which, as gowns go, was a success."

The journal runs on: —

January 12. To-day my contract with my agent Lombard begins. Heaven only knows whether I'll be successful. No telling what the public will like.

January 13. Ralph Mecher has given me a wonderful self-feeding pen, from which I shall derive great comfort. Martena Gilder has painted a scented bag for me. Very sweet of both.

January 14. To-day is the anniversary of our Telephonic séance at Osborne House, Isle of Wight. What a change since then ! Within a week I've sold seventy-five shares for nearly $8000. A few months ago I'd have sold them for $800. Dined at Delmonico's with —— and then saw " French Flats " at the Union Square, — a play that needs all *finesse* of the Palais Royal to make it go. The men offended me by keeping on their hats in drawing-rooms, and the women by their manner of speaking. . . . Through my suggestion Aunt Corda has bought a landscape from Coleman for $800. It is possible to help out even when one has no money. Last night I sent Mrs. Dusenbury to ———. She found him in a bad way, but helped him greatly. She said he cried, declaring Kate Field was almost the only friend he had in the world. I pity the poor man.

January 9. Rehearsed music of Monologue with Casa at Chickering Hall. It went very well. I'm nervous about the talking part. . . .

In the early spring Miss Field gave her Musical Monologue, which ran for several consecutive performances in New York, opening with "one of the most brilliant audiences ever assembled in this city," said "The Tribune." The music, written by George Grossmith of London, was sparkling and piquant, and Miss Field's singing of a Spanish song, accompanying herself with castanets, was warmly applauded. "The Tribune's" criticism further said : —

"Every movement was one of grace, and a firm, intellectual character shaped and controlled her satire and drollery, from entrance to exit. The presence of a bright mind, honest convictions, sensibility, and sweetness — combined with decided ability in character-acting — was felt all through the performance, and these redeemed the comparative thinness of the talk and justified the wholly unambitious quality of the entertainment."

Bringing this entertainment to Boston, so critical an observer as Mr. James T. Fields thus wrote to Kate in a private letter : —

BOSTON, March 28, 1880.

DEAR K. F., — No end of thanks should follow your kind letter so full of good will. First, your delightful evening I shall not soon forget, and how sorry I am that I did not go in front to see Part I. as I did for Part II. I laugh now this very morning as I think of the "Cheap Jack."

O, how good that is. And the unheard young woman at
the party, and lots of other capital things. Well, well, it
is all admirable, and much good will come of your successful endeavor to win smiles from an (heretofore) smileless
people. With Annie's and my best regards, .

Yours, JAMES T. FIELDS.

Miss Field's dancing and singing in this Monologue
were beautiful, and her perfect grace and poetry of
motion, as well as her exquisitely trained voice, delighted a critical audience. And in the Monologue
there were irresistible descriptions, as this of a London dinner party : —

" You won't believe it, but often I 've gone in to dinner with
men whom I 've never seen, and who have not been introduced to me. They 've bowed and offered me an arm,
and we 've sat down in complete ignorance of each other's
identity. Conversation under these circumstances is about
as cheerful as tooth-extracting. If the man be English and
untravelled, he is profoundly ceremonious, with a tendency
to depressing monosyllables. My first aim is to get a
glimpse of my companion's dinner-card, so that I may know
his name. If this be attained, and he be a public man, I
have an idea of his politics at least, and do not ruffle his
feathers by abusing his party ; but if he be Mr. Smith, I am
plunged in perplexity. Is it the Lord of the Admiralty,
and shall I congratulate him upon the prowess of the navy?
or is it the Mr. Smith who loathes the Lord of the Admiralty, and thinks the country is going to perdition? In
this state of uncertainty, it is safe to introduce the weather
as a topic of conversation ; but though there is a great deal
of it, it is neither inspiring nor original. You ask why
does n't the man entertain *me* ? You 're American, and
don't understand English society. Our men try to please
women. Here women try to please men, and men let them.

A cosmopolitan Englishman is a delightful companion. He has all the virtues of his own country, and all the ease and accomplishments of sunnier climes. He begins to talk with or without introduction. The next day, I learn that Smith is the greatest authority in the world on conchology. Why did n't the host tell me so? How was I to evolve shells out of my inner consciousness? Had I known Smith's specialty, I 'd have started him on snails, and gradually crawled through the entire kingdom of crustacea."

To those familiar with foreign life this appealed as a delightful bit of Comedy; but a parody is only appreciated by those who know the original. A musical recital which she occasionally gave was more calculated to win general favor, and in the summer following, she gave this one evening at Clifton Springs, New York, for the benefit of the women employees of the Sanitarium, that they might be able to employ a writing teacher during the winter. The recital was a delightful one, including the scene and aria " Numi che intesi mai " from Mercadante; a Spanish mule-teer song, " Como me gusta," from Leon Vasseur; and the song of the Spanish Orange girl, " La Naran-jera," from Scochdopole; Sullivan's " Little Maid of Arcadie," the " Salve Maria," from Mercadante, the " Brindisi " from Victor Massé's opera of " Galathée," and other numbers from the Italian, Spanish, and English. Miss Field's Spanish songs called forth especial enthusiasm. She was a most accomplished performer of Spanish music, rendering it with excep-tional spirit, and her selections all called forth re-peated encores and floral demonstrations.

No interpretation of Kate Field's character would approach to any semblance of the original that did

not emphasize her never-failing purpose to help people. Whether it were the maids of a summer hotel
where she sojourned or an official in high life, made
little difference, and in contrast to her recital for the
purpose of furthering the education of hotel employees, is the following letter, which quite explains
itself, written to Colonel Hay, now the American
Ambassador to the Court of St. James : —

HOTEL VICTORIA, NEW YORK, May 9, 1880.

(Which the same I am in Albany, but the above is my
address.)

DEAR COLONEL HAY, — Mr. Francis (" Troy Times ") and
I have just been talking over Dr. Schliemann and the propriety of making him our Consul at Athens. Two years ago I
did what I could to stir up the powers but produced no effect,
and now Mr. Francis says he has been pouring Schliemann
into your not unwilling ear. Having mentioned that I had
the pleasure of knowing you, Mr. Francis urged me to write
a good word for the learned champion. Will it do one particle of good?

Why should Schliemann be Consul at Athens? Because
he is so proud of being an American citizen that on the
frontispiece of his books is printed " Citizen of the United
States." Because, in his way, he is a great man and would
reflect honor on the country. Because he would, in gratitude
for the compliment, bequeath America many of his treasures,
and would assist in stocking our Museums.

Because he would give his services gratuitously. Because
he has a beautiful palace in Athens and would entertain
finely. Because having made a large fortune as a merchant,
he possesses an order of intelligence that would benefit
American commerce. Because he has a knowledge of the
East, and speaks Greek. Because his wife is extremely
nice and is Greek. Finally, because he longs to be Consul.

Are these reasons enough? It seems to me that our Consular service needs a good deal of overhauling, and to ignore a man like Schliemann is throwing away an excellent opportunity of getting a good deal for nothing. Am I right or wrong? Now don't make a pretty speech, but say exactly what you mean and oblige,

Yours faithfully,

KATE FIELD.

Miss Field had known the celebrated archæologist well, meeting him in London, and many letters of his remain among her papers. Her first meeting with him in London came about from the desire of their mutual friend, General di Cesnola, who said to Miss Field, " You ought to know this German lion." The occasion came and the " German lion " and the American woman discovered a mutual interest in each other, and the London magazine " Belgravia " accepted Miss Field's proposition to contribute to its pages a biographical sketch of Dr. Schliemann and his work. He was gratified by this project. " But how," he remarked to Miss Field, " can I tell you the story of my work ? I'm engaged every hour of the day and night. It's breakfast here, and dine there, and I've no time even to sleep."

" I did arrange it," Miss Field gleefully related afterwards. " When he came to tell his story he was in evening dress and I received him in a ball costume. It was six o'clock in the morning, and we each came from one of those London entertainments which no one goes to till after midnight, nor leaves till after the sun ought to be shining — but is n't. Then and there I took down the notes for his biography."

On this return from London, Miss Field had

brought with her one thing on which, however valuable she may have conceived it to be, the custom house levied no duty, — the idea of founding in New York a Co-operative Dress Association on the London plan of co-operative stores. Again her irresistible energy overbore all obstacles and difficulties, and secured for her a list of subscribers that included, among its trustees, Hon. R. A. McCormick, who had served as the U. S. Commissioner to the Paris Exposition of 1878 and who was then President of the Mining Exchange in New York, Richard Mears, and Mrs. Julia Ward Howe.

Miss Field always had magnificent ideas in carrying out any plan and the Co-operative Dress Association was no exception. An imposing store on West Twenty-third street was taken, and there were a small army of employees and vast mechanism of merchandise, not to speak of a library, parlors, dining-room and various conveniences. Although it was, perhaps, predestined to fail, it may be said here that Miss Field's own purpose in organizing it comprised the twofold motive of attempting to provide better shopping facilities at more moderate rates, and giving employment to American women. For Kate Field was never so absorbed in art or literature that she had not time and thought for very generous and noble purposes toward humanity.

Miss Field set about creating interest in this venture with all her usual energy. The following note from Gail Hamilton (Miss Dodge) sufficiently indicates the proposition to which it was a reply. Writing from Washington in the autumn of 1880, Miss Dodge said: —

My dear Miss Field, — I don't believe you will need do anything but announce your presence, place and hour, and you will have a room full. The afternoon I received your letter was Mrs. Blaine's reception day, and I talked to all the ladies about it, and they were every one interested. Mrs. Hayes is *terra incognita* to all. I shall be happy to see you on every account. The Riggs House is all right. I think what you should do is to put in the Washington papers the hour and day when you will meet ladies in the Riggs House and explain your errand. That is what I should do though I am not a famous business manager among those who know me. Mr. Blaine may be out of town on Friday, but Mrs. Blaine and myself you may depend on for audience. I hear your musical monologue very highly spoken of.

I wish you all sorts of success, though I never expect to have a well fitting dress again in this life. I never had but one, but that gives me the right to the hope again.

Very truly yours,

Mary Abby Dodge.

In the autumn of 1880 Miss Field passed some little time in Boston as the guest of her old friends, Mr. and Mrs. A. V. S. Anthony, in their Beacon Street home. Although she reached her forty-second birthday on the first of this October, her appearance was that of a woman much younger. The abundant and beautiful auburn hair had deepened to a rich, soft brown; the refined, spirited face, very delicate in contour, was full of animation and purpose, and a Paris gown whose soft tint harmonized with her hair, and whose mode suggested the *élégante*, contributed to the impression one received of an artistic personality. Miss Field was warmly greeted by her old friends in Boston and as usual, was sought by many representatives of the press. Among these was Mrs. Sallie Joy White, who for a quarter of a century held a distinctive and most honorable place in Boston journalism and whose ability was equalled by her sweetness of spirit and a charmingly vivid and agreeable literary style. Another friend of Miss Field's, also connected with the press as a special writer of humorous prose, was Miss Josephine Jenkins, a niece of N. P. Willis. Miss Field was deeply occupied during this visit in completing the organization of the Co-operative Dress Association, whose tenure of life was comprised within two years, and in the spring of 1882 its failure came, involving her in serious financial loss. Her establishment of this organization was deeply deplored by her friends. Looking backward now one sees that on her return from Europe and the establishment of her pleasant home in New York, in 1880, she was, however unconsciously, at a parting of the ways. With her little fortune in Bell telephone stocks and the very considerable income she could have derived from her pen — to say nothing of her appearances in lectures or entertainments — she might, apparently, have lived a life of ease in the midst of a congenial and stimulating social atmosphere, with the gratification of her tastes in art, music or literature. She might have done this, it seems, as one now reviews the conjunction of circumstances; but what she *did* do was to found a mercantile establishment, involve herself in perpetual worry and strain and annoyance; to find her motives misunderstood and maligned, and her life in general invaded by an atmosphere foreign to her true nature. Referring to all this at the time in a private letter to a friend she said: " I want the

C. D. A. to be impersonal. I do not want women writing to me about the fit of their gowns. I believe in beautiful adornment, but I do not want to talk or think about it. The birds don't — even the finest of them."

The failure of this establishment was the occasion of a considerable financial loss to Miss Field, but it proved to be a factor in her life whose result was the opening of a new door leading her on to undreamed-of experiences. The idea in forming this undertaking was one that social economists recognize as the true ideal in business enterprises. The failure was a mere matter of detail; but to have so early grasped the equity of the co-operative idea and to have endeavored to aid in its introduction in American commerce was a purpose wholly worthy of Kate Field.

This work brought Miss Field into an atmosphere of annoyance and discord; still it was the path that was destined to lead her on to the one most important and most memorable work of her life, — that which had its national value in affecting Mormon legislation.

Mrs. Browning has a passage in "Aurora Leigh" that runs : —

> "Whate'er our state, we must have made it first;
> And though the thing displease us, ay, perhaps
> Displease us warrantably, never doubt
> That other states, thought possible once, and then
> Rejected by the instinct of our lives, —
> If then adopted, had displeased us more
> Than this, in which the choice, the will, the love,
> Has stamped the honour of a patent act
> From henceforth. What we choose, may not be good;
> But, that we choose it, proves it good for *us*."

Undoubtedly these lines embody a true philosophy. At all events, it is not the easiest life that is best, nor the life most full of personal enjoyment or privilege. The best life is that which contributes most to social welfare and vital progress; which pours itself through the channels of influence and gives of its noblest powers in the time allotted to its earthly pilgrimage.

" Get work;
Be sure 't is better than what you work to get."

This predestined endeavor was still in the unseen future, and Kate little dreamed of the new departure that she was so soon to enter upon.

On Dec. 22, 1880, the world was startled by the death of Marian Evans Cross, she who was best known by her pen name of George Eliot. Hon. Whitelaw Reid immediately asked Miss Field to write some Recollections of the great author for " The Tribune," and the following beautiful paper, dated " The Victoria, 9 P. M. Dec. 22," was written with the swift spontaneity that characterized her electric pen. As it offers a more intimate portrait of the great novelist than has ever elsewhere been presented it is here given in full. Miss Field wrote: —

To the Editor of the Tribune: —

Sir, — George Eliot dead ! and you ask for my recollections of her? Memory is almost lost in regret, for she was great, and good, and kind to me, but I will try to recall the past. Come with me to Florence, " Flower of all cities, and city of all flowers."

Here, when left as a school-girl to study singing and Italian, I first met George Eliot. Being in charge of an accomplished Englishwoman, who numbered among her friends all that were best in literature, art and diplomacy, I enjoyed advantages far beyond my years, and found a second home at Villino Trollope, the residence of Thomas Adolphus Trollope. Will you come with me there and meet George Eliot? It is a Sunday evening, and she is expected with her husband.

Ah, this Villino Trollope is quaintly fascinating with its marble pillars, its grim men in armor, starting like sentinels from the walls, and its curiosities greeting you at every step. The antiquary revels in its majolica, its old bridal chests and carved furniture, its beautiful terra-cotta of the Virgin and Child by Orgagna, its hundred *oggetti* of the Cinque Cento. The bibliopole grows silently ecstatic as he sinks quietly into a mediæval chair and feasts his eyes on a model library, bubbling over with five thousand rare books, many wonderfully illuminated and enriched by costly engravings. To those who prefer an earnest talk with the host and hostess on politics, art, religion, or the last new book, there is the cozy study where Puss and Bran, the honest dog, lie side by side on Christian terms, and where the daughter of the house will sing you the Tuscan *canti popolari* like a young nightingale in voice, but with more than youthful expression.

Here is Anthony Trollope, and it is no ordinary pleasure to enjoy simultaneously the philosophic reasoning of Thomas Trollope — looking half Socrates and half Galileo — whom Mrs. Browning called "Aristides the Just," and the almost boyish enthusiasm and impulsive argumentation of Anthony Trollope, who is an admirable specimen of a frank and loyal Englishman.

It is late in spring. Soft winds kiss the budding foliage and warm it into bloom; the beautiful terrace of Villino Trollope is transformed into a reception-room. Opening upon a garden, with its lofty pillars, its tessellated marble floor, its walls inlaid with terra-cotta, bas-reliefs, inscriptions, and coats of arms, with here and there a niche devoted to some antique Madonna, the terrace has all the charm of a *campo santo* without the chill of the grave upon it ; or were a few cowled monks to walk with folded arms along its space, one might fancy it the cloister of a monastery. On this warm spring night there is laughter and the buzz of many tongues. No lights but the stars are burning, and men and women, talking in almost every civilized tongue, are sipping iced lemonade, — one of the specialties of Villino Trollope.

Dall' Ongaro, the poet, is reciting verses to my chaperone, and I sit beside her wondering whether George Eliot will deign to notice me. There she stands quietly in the moonlight, speaking earnestly to Adolphus Trollope, while Lewes hovers near, calling her attention to the exquisite beauty of the lights and shades made by the moon. One by one the guests are presented to the author of " Adam Bede," who receives all with shrinking diffidence ; more and more I wonder whether Mr. Trollope will remember the American girl in the corner, — a nobody. There I sit growing very dejected, when the host offers his arm to George Eliot, and they walk toward a Madonna which is above my head. They stop to admire the work ; the host discovers me, I am introduced, and my heart beats quickly as George Eliot takes my hand and seats herself beside me, expressing great interest in all young girls who aspire to lead broader lives than those carved out by society. I gaze at her with delight and see a woman of medium stature, of large frame and fair Saxon coloring. In heaviness of jaw and height of cheek-bone she greatly resembles a German, nor are her features unlike those of Wordsworth, whom Hazlitt swore looked just like a horse. We are all said to resemble some animal, and George Eliot's animal, like Wordsworth's, is the horse. Her eyes are pale blue, her mouth large and sensitive, her teeth large and white. The expression of her face is gentle, while her manner is singularly timid ; yet, as if by force of will, as if she had been told something about me by good Mr. Trollope, she puts this timidity aside, relates her own literary experience, and suggests advice.

True genius is ever allied to humility, and in seeing George Eliot do the work of a good Samaritan so unobtrusively I learn to respect the woman as much as I had before admired the writer. " For years," she says, " I wrote reviews because I knew too little of humanity, and I doubt whether I should ever have ventured upon a novel had not Mr. Lewes urged me to it. To him I submitted my ' Scenes of Clerical Life,' short stories of the worth of which I was in doubt. Mr. Lewes insisted upon their publication, and their success put an end to my reviews. All my manuscripts pass through his hands before they are submitted to the public. He is my critic and my inspiration."

To think that George Eliot should be telling all this to a school-girl ! Why, I can scarcely believe my own ears ; yet I venture to ask whether she enjoys writing ; whether it is easy work ? " No," she replies ; " I am miserable when writing, but I am still more miserable when not writing." After more kindly words, George Eliot rises ; her husband comes forward and claims acquaintance with " the little republican." I find myself absolutely laughing and talking with these two wonderful creatures, and then they bid me good-night. That is all I see of them, their fortnight's stay in Florence being over.

In the maturity of her wisdom this gifted woman startled the world with " Scenes of Clerical Life," " Adam Bede," " Mill on the Floss," and " Silas Marner," making an era in English fiction, and raising herself above rivalry. Experience was much to her. Her men are men, her women are women, and long did English readers rack their brains to discover the sex of ' George Eliot.' Mrs. Lewes need not necessarily have encountered the characters she so vividly portrayed. Genius looks upon Nature, and then creates. The pot-house scene in "Silas Marner" is as perfect as a Dutch painting, yet the author never entered a pot-house. Her strong physique enabled her in earlier days to brush against the world, and in thus brushing she gathered up the dust, fine and coarse, out of which humanity is made. It is a powerful argument in the "Woman Question," that — without going to France for George Sand — "Adam Bede" and the wonderfully unique conception of "Paul Ferroll" should be women's work; and real men cannot know women by knowing men, and a discriminating public will soon admit, if it has not done so already, that women are quite as capable of drawing male portraits as men are of drawing female. Half a century ago a woman maintained that genius has no sex; a truth just dawning on the world.

I know not whether George Eliot visited Florence *con intenzione*, yet it almost seems as though "Romola" were the product of that fortnight's sojourn. It could scarcely have been written by one whose eyes were unfamiliar with the tone of Florentine localities. As a novel, "Romola" is never likely to be popular, however extensively read; but, viewed as a sketch of Savonarola and his times, it is most interesting and valuable. The deep research and knowledge of mediæval life and manners displayed are cause of wonderment to erudite Florentines who have lived to learn from a foreigner. The *couleur locale* is marvellous. Nothing can be more delightfully real, for example, than the scenes which transpire in Nello's barber-shop. The *dramatis personæ* are not English men and women in fancy dress, but true Tuscans, who express themselves after the manner of natives. It would be difficult to find a greater contrast than exists between "Romola" and George Eliot's previous novels. They have little in common but genius; and genius, I begin to think, not only has no sex, but no nationality. " Romola " has peopled the streets of Florence still more densely to memory.

The next time I saw George Eliot was in her own house, the Priory, 21 North Bank, Regent's Park; much as I wanted to renew the acquaintance, I stayed away from the Priory until invited, as I knew George Eliot shrank from strangers, and I had no reason to suppose that she would remember an American girl in Florence. Fortunately for me I was not forgotten ; and when one foggy Sunday I entered her pleasant London drawing-room, both she and Mr. Lewes warmly welcomed me.

Sunday was their reception day. From 3 to 7 the cleverest men and women in London felt honored in being received by the quiet woman who sat by the fire with her back to the window and talked earnestly in almost a whisper, while Lewes pervaded the atmosphere, speaking first with one and then with another, always interesting and frequently brilliant, the ugliest of men, who made you forget his pocked face and shaggy red hair in about fifteen minutes. Often he came to my rooms and delighted me with his conversation and advice, but she never came. She visited no one ; all visited her, — all save music and art. At every " private view," at every fine classical concert, George Eliot was sure to be present, dressed unobtrusively and seemingly oblivious of every one about her. She loved music ardently, and was herself a pianist of no mean order. Only once did I succeed in luring her away from the Priory, and that was to see the Telephone, about which she was very curious. Yes, she would come with Mr. Lewes, provided no one else was present. So one afternoon George Eliot visited the office of Bell's Telephone in the city and for an hour tested its capacity. " It is very wonderful, very useful," she said. " What marvellous inventions you Americans have ! " It was the last time I ever saw her or him. Lewes died suddenly not long after ; and now she has passed away, too soon for her friends, but not too soon for her fame.

I have several letters from her, many more from him. His are more brilliant, her temperament not so quickly lending itself to the epistolary touch and go. Unfortunately these letters are packed away.

A noble intellect, a big heart, — this was the real George Eliot. Let those who never knew the woman pause before they cast a stone. KATE FIELD.

Among the many tributes of admiration which this paper called forth is the following letter from the poet and the well-known educator, Miss Anna C. Brackett: —

DEAR MISS FIELD, — "The Tribune" brings me to-day your letter about Mrs. Lewes, for which will you let me thank you, though I am a stranger to you.

You speak brave, true words of her, as any true woman knows. I never knew her except through her books, but how any woman who had known her in her writings even could dare to say one word against her, I can never understand. As to her marriage with Mr. Cross, I had faith enough in her to say, "I do not understand it, but if George Eliot did it, it is right." If the world were only big enough to judge circumstances by people, and not people by circumstances! If they only were! She had "a noble intellect and a big heart," as you say. And she could well afford to have smaller and narrower natures criticise and carp at her life, — which they judge by their own petty standards.

If she had not been so much of a woman, those criticisms would not have touched her. Thank you again.

Truly, ANNA C. BRACKETT.

I have met you at Dr. Holland's, but you will not remember me. A. C. B.

26

In the latter assertion Miss Brackett was quite mistaken, for Miss Field not only remembered her then, but always, with an ardent appreciation of her lofty personality.

Not long after this, Miss Field had the pleasure of writing to her old friend, Hon. Whitelaw Reid, personally, on a subject to which his reply offers the clue.

271 LEXINGTON AVE., S. E. Corner 36th St.,
April 11, 1881.

DEAR MISS KATE, — I thank you very heartily for your congratulations. If you knew Miss Mills you could then begin to form some adequate idea of how fortunate I am, and how appropriate therefore the congratulations are.

I'm sorry to hear of your illness, but trust the ocean may prove this time, as it has for you so often before, a kindly and successful nurse. With best wishes I am,

Very truly yours,

WHITELAW REID.

To MISS KATE FIELD, Hotel Victoria.

In the Academy exhibition in New York in the spring of 1881, there was a portrait of Miss Field painted by Mr. Frank D. Millet. The picture in full length represents her seated on a sofa, piled with yellow cushions, in a black evening gown *décolleté* and sleeveless, the grace and style revealing that it was a Worth creation. The picture was conspicuously hung and at the time attracted much attention, the pose being a beautiful one, and the painting of the hands and the arms especially revealed their classic beauty.

A letter from Wilkie Collins during this year is as follows: —

90 GLOUCESTER PLACE, Portman Square, W.
January, 1881.

DEAR MISS FIELD, — If you are in the U. S. A. and if
you ever see Frank Leslie's " Illustrated Newspaper," you
will find a serial story in it which may suggest indulgence
to an overworked man.   If you know nothing of " Heart
and Science," I go down on both my knees and beg your
pardon.   I am in sober earnest, so weary after finishing
my story that a sinking of the soul (and body) comes over
me at the sight of a pen.   As to writing letters while I am
at work, " that way madness lies."   Is there any fatigue
in this weary world which is equal to the fatigue that comes
of daily working of the brains for hours together ?   George
Sand thought all other fatigues unimportant by comparison — and I agree with George S.

Let me thank you for " Fechter."   The illustrations
(excepting the photographed head of him in " Hamlet ")
are so utterly unlike, that *I* should not have known what
man they were meant for ; and his old doctor here (Carr
Beard), to whom I showed the book, agreed with me.
This is my only objection.   I think your part of the volume
eminently readable — and done in an excellent spirit.   Here
and there, poor dear F., or somebody else, has misled you
about his importance in Paris, but that is no fault of
yours.   And I repeat my congratulations and my thanks.

" Boz " rhymes (in sound) to " was."

Oh, good land ! referring to your letter I find *no address.*
" Hotel Victoria," — that, I swear, is all.   Oh, woman,
lovely woman !   What is a man to do, who remembers
Victoria Hotels in his own country, in your country, at
Naples, at Rome, and on the continent generally ?   Will
Osgood forward ?   Here goes at Osgood.   Farewell.

Yours ever,

WILKIE COLLINS.

A series of dramatic biographies under the title of the " American Actor Series," edited by Mr. Laurence Hutton, was in process of publication by the Osgood House at this time, and Miss Field was asked to write for it the volume on Fechter. Her criticism of his playing, ten years before, made the same deep impression as had her criticism on Ristori, and that she was the predestined biographer of Fechter was a foregone conclusion. At the time that Kate had been writing in the daily press of his stage appearances, her criticism charmed Mrs. Anne Lynch Botta, one of the finest of literary judges, and she wrote to Miss Field the following note under date of November 27 : —

DEAR K. F., — Thanks for the paper containing your admirable critique on Fechter's " Claude." The concluding paragraph I have read the day before in the " Evening Mail," read it through and went in ecstasy over it before I discovered the initials at the end. Every woman ought to love you for it. I am glad you are coming. Do stay with us. Believe me always,

Yours affectionately,

ANNE C. L. BOTTA.

In the preparation of Fechter's Life, Kate wrote to her old friend, Wilkie Collins, asking if he had any interesting letters from the French actor, to which Mr. Collins replied : —

90 GLOUCESTER PLACE, Portman Square, W.
LONDON, Dec. 14, 1880.

DEAR MISS FIELD, — I am suffering from my native winter climate, and I am writing a serial story (with printers and publishers waiting here, there, and everywhere, New York included, for their weekly instalments). Add to this, correspondence and " taking care of one's health," and you will, I hope, excuse me for not having more speedily answered your letter.

If you are not in a hurry — a very serious " if," in these days — I will gladly search my archives for such few letters of poor dear Fechter as autograph-collectors have left to me. And if there is anything I can tell you besides, you shall be welcome to some of the least melancholy recollections associated with my old friend. But if the book must be published immediately, I fear I must wait for a new edition. The strain of this last story is heavy on me. But I hope to be free from my " Black Robe " in six weeks' time.

Very truly yours,

WILKIE COLLINS.

I have received a letter from Mr. Osgood on the same subject. I write to acknowledge it, and I venture to refer them to you for the things called " particulars."

W. C.

A later letter from Mr. Collins is as follows : —

90 GLOUCESTER PLACE, Portman Square, W.
July 26, 1882.

DEAR MISS FIELD, — Miss Hogarth took me to see the pictures to which you refer, some months since. They were then in Bond Street. The proprietor referred to an old friend of Dickens, who declared it to be a portrait of him. But Miss Hogarth's opinion was unreservedly adverse. She positively refused to recognize the likeness. As for me, I had never even seen Dickens at the time when the picture was painted ; and I represented the ignorant public. This is all I know of the matter ; and it is, of course, for your personal information only.

Is your " Fechter " published ? And how can I get the book ? Shall I write to Mr. Osgood ? I ought to have

asked these questions when you kindly called here.   But I
never do what I ought.

Very truly yours,

WILKIE COLLINS.

Still again Mr. Collins writes : —

90 GLOUCESTER PLACE, Portman Square, W..
LONDON, Jan. 18, 1882.

DEAR Mr. OSGOOD, — By mail of Saturday next — the
21st — I shall at last send you my " Recollections of Fechter."   My health is mainly to blame for this long delay.
But besides this, the subject is beset with difficulties and
requires careful handling with a margin of time to do it in.

If I am too late, I can only say I am sorry, and ask
you to let me have the manuscripts back again.

If the book is still to be written, then my recollections
are at Miss Kate Field's service — *on one condition :* viz.
that they are printed and published without alteration of
any sort, *exactly* as I have written them.   My motive for
making this stipulation, which I am sure I may trust to
your care to see strictly carried out, is expressed in the
manuscript I may add, remembering what has been fool-
ishly and falsely said of Fechter in the United States (and
repeated, I am sorry to find, by Miss Field in one of her
letters to me), that I will not appear before my American
readers, unless I tell the truth honestly, on my own
responsibility, as one of the very few Englishmen now living, who knew Fechter intimately in every aspect of his
character.

Therefore, please accept this letter as authority for at
once returning my manuscript to me, if you have any reason to suppose that the stipulation which I attach to it is
not likely to be literally observed.

Please tell Miss Kate Field, with my kind remembrances,
that the questions about Fechter which she puts to me in
her letters — in so far as they are not treated of in the

" Recollections " — are questions which I am quite un-able to answer. His two children's names are " Marie " and " Paul," — " Marie " being the eldest. Beyond this, I know nothing of his domestic affairs. I am not even acquainted with the address of his widow. As for his book of " Othello," I do not possess it — and I could not lend it for public quotations if I did. His " Othello " and his " book " were among the mistakes of his career, poor dear fellow. For the sake of his memory, I ask Miss Field to pass over them.

Nothing more occurs to me just now, and my letter is too long already.

I contend with this dreadful damp winter (in England) more successfully than I had hoped. If I could only breathe your dry air in Boston (dry by comparison with our island air on the worst day you have), I should do very well. Believe me, dear Mr. Osgood,

Very truly yours,

WILKIE COLLINS.

Please let me hear if the manuscript is safely received. If it is set up in type, proof in duplicate might perhaps help me to make some additions.   W. C.

Miss Field has left to literature an admirable bi-ography in this book, made especially valuable by her critical consideration of Fechter's Hamlet, which she described as " not the introspective student of tradition, but a man of the world in the noblest sense." She asserts that Fechter's Hamlet was never at any time really mad, and she supported this conception of the character with Lowell's criticism: " If you deprive Hamlet of reason, there is no truly tragic motive left. He would be a fit subject for Bedlam, but not for the stage. We might have pathology enough, but no pathos." Miss Field thoroughly

sympathized in Fechter's conception of Hamlet, and
she approved of certain scenic innovations, as that of
picturing the time of the churchyard scene as a brilliant sunset, " making a fine contrast between the joy
of nature and the grief of humanity." A great number of the most cultivated people in London accepted
Fechter's innovation in the time-honored methods of
presenting the melancholy Dane, with no slight enthusiasm; but in America there were many of the
most critical judges who were ready to exclaim, *C'est
magnifique, mais ce n'est pas la guerre.*

Miss Field relates that on one occasion when
Fechter was playing in London Louis Napoleon was
present, and after the performance sought the actor,
and this conversation ensued : —

" Upon bidding Fechter good-by, Napoleon seemed much
touched at the thought of his own continued exile from
France, and said, ' The next time we meet will be in the
Tuileries.'

" ' That is somewhat doubtful,' answered Fechter, ' for
I really do not intend to be king.'

" ' *No,*' replied the man of destiny, ' *but I intend to be
Emperor !* '

" To smile was impossible. Napoleon's tone and manner
were such as to convince Fechter that an oracle had spoken,
and when the prince became President of the Republic,
Fechter knew how the drama would end. Napoleon was
right. The next time they met was in the Tuileries, and
when Fechter acted for him at Fontainebleau the Emperor
took off his watch and chain and begged his acceptance
of them."

On receiving from Miss Field a copy of her
" Fechter," Mr. Lawrence Barrett wrote under date
of Sept. 3, 1883 : —

My dear Miss Field, — It is a feast for the eyes to gaze upon your zigzag chirography and read this valuable book, and to know that you are enjoying a good share of happiness. . . . My season opens with a gold mine. Mary Anderson has made a hit in London, and you will rejoice thereby. It was genuine, and she sends a long cablegram full of glee. God bless her, and you, and every good soul alive !

Faithfully yours,
Lawrence Barrett.

Completing this book, Miss Field turned again to her Co-operative Dress Association enterprise, and in the providing of seats for women employees she was ahead of the time, as the following letter which she wrote to " The Tribune " under date of Feb. 16, 1882, attests: —

Editor of "The Tribune," — Sir, it required no law or knowledge of the existence of legislation in behalf of shop-girls to inspire a feeling of humanity in the directors of the Co-operative Dress Association Limited. As soon as their building was secured, a resolution was passed making seats for female employees obligatory. To-day there is a patent self-acting seat for every other girl on the street floor, and on the other floors the women can sit whenever unemployed. You are cordially invited to inspect the Association from top to bottom. The legislator at Albany who declared that no store in New York had complied with the law was indebted to his imagination for his facts, so far as concerns an Association that aims at co-operation in its best sense.

Yours truly,
Kate Field, *President C. D. A.*

There were not wanting those who commented adversely upon Miss Field's unwisdom — as they termed it — of founding this establishment, when its failure proved it to have been a disastrous venture, in which she herself was the most unfortunate loser. But seeing it all in its larger relation to the entire purpose through her life, it is more than an open question as to whether there is anything to regret. Our failures are· not unfrequently quite as important as are our successes.

> " Measure not the work
> Until the day's out and the labor done ;
> Then bring your gauges."

Miss Field had given somewhat of a social flavor to the C. D. A., in frequently entertaining her friends there and using its large parlors for evening receptions. One pleasant lunch that she gave is still remembered, the guests being Mrs. Edwin P. Whipple; Miss Maud Howe, a beauty and a belle, as well as a charming woman of letters, who is now Mrs. John Elliott of Rome; Mr. Frank D. Millet, the clever artist; and Mr. Samuel Ward, the wit and *bon vivant ;* and the hour was sparkling in the wit and repartee of the brilliant hostess and distinguished guests. Miss Field was the President of this Association, and passed a part of every day in the establishment. The " President's room " was fitted up in great beauty, and Kate was not without an enjoyment and pride in the establishment.

In May of 1882 Miss Field sailed again for London, where she remained until the end of July, when she went to Mont Doré in France, returning in the autumn to Paris. From London she wrote to a friend : —

" I 've dived into art. My soul hungers and thirsts for music — for pictures — for all the things I 've had no taste

of since I 've *been in trade!* Music I had in the form of
Wagner's 'Meistersingers,' and of Patti. The 'Meistersingers' I heard twice, and the more I heard the more I
liked it. It is Wagner's sole attempt at comic opera, and
certainly it is strange comic opera, but there are splendid
things in it. Wagner is all wrong in writing for the voice,
but admitting this fact, which will prevent any singer like
Patti from touching his music, there is that within which
commands admiration. I don't believe I shall ever go mad
over Wagner, but I can't call him a humbug. He is a
great intellect.

"I heard Patti in a new French opera, 'La Velleda,'
and in 'Traviata.' She worked like a Trojan to make
'Velleda' go, but with all the flowers and applause, it was
but a *succès d'estime*. Lenepreu, the composer, proved
cleverness, but no originality or inspiration. He had
worked tremendously, but he had nothing new to tell the
world. After a second night 'La Velleda' disappeared.
After hearing and seeing Patti in her pet rôle of 'Traviata'
I return to my original conclusion that she is a delightful
singer, without any real dramatic ability. She does not
once touch. And she leaves out 'Gran Dio morir si
giovane.' No dramatic artist would throw away the passionate gem of the opera. Albani sings beautifully, and is
an acknowledged favorite with the Queen. Her high notes
are singularly pure, while Lucca has a fine middle register,
but no high notes. There's a new tenor, a Pole, Mier-
winsky, who pleases me greatly.

"In acting I 've seen Irving's production of 'Romeo and
Juliet' sumptuously put upon the stage, and as Juliet Ellen
Terry is very picturesque. To-night I 'm to see Modjeska
in Odette. The Kendals in 'The Squire' are very good,
but the play will not bear transplanting. Edwin Booth has
appeared as Richelieu, and has had good notices.

. . . "I 'm quite miserable over the paintings I can't

buy.   There's a fine portrait of Dickens in 1842 for sale for
$750.   It would fetch double that in America.   There's a
charming Gainsborough for $150, and another for $125, —
a Sir Peter Lely for $300.   I go and look at these things,
and ache at not being able to buy them.

.   .   .   .

"Mont Doré is a charming place when the sun shines.
When it rains, as it has been doing for four days, it is horrid.   There is no perfect climate this side of heaven,
I fancy.   The views and excursions are lovely.   We have
rooms on the third story opening upon a balcony, from
which we command the Valley of the Dordogne and the
splendid amphitheatre of mountains to the south of it.
The sun, when it shines at all, beats upon us all day, and
physical existence becomes a pleasure.

.   .   .   .

"Paris is always interesting, until one has heard all the
music, and seen all the plays and pictures, and bought all
the new books.   Then I want to cross over to England,
where people think in an Anglo-Saxon way. . . .

"I saw Bernhardt in 'Camille' last Wednesday night.
She is an admirable artist, who acts from the head down.
Still, I prefer Modjeska's conception and rendering of the
part, as truer to Dumas's novel."

Returning to New York in October, Miss Field
passed the winter in that city.   She was in a tide of
social life; she was writing various magazine papers,
and bearing, through all, a burden of anxiety which
had culminated just before Christmas in the failure
of the Co-operative Dress Association.

The reader may recall the very striking and unique
letter written by Miss Field to one who must be
nameless in these pages, under the date of May 31,
1868, which appears in a preceding chapter.   It is

curious to see how, in any moment of need, the friend to whom this letter was addressed seemed destined to reappear in her life and, as has before been noted, his death occurred within the same year as that of her own. As the years had vanished between 1868 and 1880, he seemed to have come to feel something of that intensity expressed in the poet's lines, —

> " There will no man do for your sake, I think,
>   What I would have done for the least word said :
> I had wrung life dry for your lips to drink ;
>   Broken it up for your daily bread."

His was a nature that failed in power of self-expression, but something of this sentiment was apparent in him, and the experiences between Kate and himself had left their impress on both lives since that far-away May-day when she had written him the letter included in this volume; still something in time, place, or circumstance prevented the feeling between them from ever finding its inflorescence in the love that alone would have satisfied Kate Field.

She seemed to distrust the possibilities of married happiness, although on two occasions he had sought to win her to be his wife. Her letter of that May-day had aroused in him his better self. Never had he been so worthy of her as on her final refusal. The silent tragedy in life that may result from the lack of correspondence in date of a strong feeling between two persons has never found more keen expression than in the lines : —

> "A year divides us, love, from love :
>   Though you love now, though I loved then,
> The gulf is straight but deep enough.
>   Who shall recross ? who among men
>   Shall cross again ?

" Do the stars answer ? in the night
Have ye found comfort ? or by day
Have ye seen gods ?   What hope, what light,
Falls from the farthest starriest way
On you that pray ? "

As has previously been remarked, it was often a
subject of wonder that a woman so attractive as Kate
Field, and one who always frankly preferred the
companionship of men to women, did not marry;
but there seemed to be some instinct warning her
back from the final step.   Opportunities for marriage,
brilliant in every worldly sense, came to her, but she
refused to consider them.   Twice in her life came
love, and why, in both these instances, she shrank
from marriage, even she herself could not have told.
" I am a strange being," she once said in a moment
of intimate confidence with her present biographer:
"I am a mystery to myself, doing things that the
conventional world would perhaps call unwomanly,
and yet so very a woman that I ought never to have
been born.   You little dreamed that I cared more
for —— than for any one in the world. . . . I need
a clear head to accomplish the work I must do in this
world, and nothing so unfits a sensitive nature for
mental exertion as emotional intensities."

Perhaps these self-revealing words from a woman
usually so reticent that even her nearest friends
gained little clue from herself to her inner thought,
may offer a clue to the labyrinthine mazes of her
life.   It was in Florence, in the early summer of
1861, that she first met and loved this man, whose
death occurred, like her own, in 1896, and looking
backward to that May among the Florentine lilies
they both might have said : —

> " The year 's a little older grown :
>   And fair white boughs by green ways blown
>   In these new days no more are known.
>   (Oh, who can bring the May again ?)
>
> " And we are wiser grown, we two ;
>   Our story 's told ; each word was true.
>   (Oh, who can bring the May again ?)
>   Was it not sweeter e'er we knew ?
>   Yet who can bring the May again ? "

That long-lost Maytime may have awaited them in some fairer clime.

Emerson tells us : —

> " The world rolls round ; mistrust it not.
>   Befalls again what once befell ;
>   All things return."

Surely we must believe that these rudimentary experiences find their full fruition in the rich and infinite future.

Aside, however, from all this undercurrent of the romance in her life which was unsuspected by her friends; into the actual day and daylight world came the lover again in the guise of the following letter at the time when her business enterprise, the Co-operative Dress Association, failed and she stood alone in loss and perplexity. Under the date of Dec. 27, 1882, he wrote : —

> " I forbear to call upon you at a time when you are, per-haps, over-burdened by well-meaning, but inconsiderate friends.   But I write to remind you that I claim to be your *friend*. . . .
>
> " Should the closing of C. D. A. embarrass you financially, I beg that you will allow me to do all that a sincere and devoted friend ought to.   If you will permit me to be of

service to you, as occasion demands, I shall take it as a great favor. . . .

" I hope you will not think me officious and presumptuous, but believe me to be earnestly and loyally,

—————."

A greater energy of nature on the part of the writer of this letter would have swept her distrust away; as it was, that which she most asked of him was precisely that which he did not possess.

The larger interests and the higher individual development that are the gifts of modern life to women have effaced the type described in the lines, —

"Love is of man's life a thing apart;
'T is woman's whole existence."

Still, by a paradox, it is only the woman who can live her life bravely, even happily, without love, who most appreciates and reverences its holiness and its power for bestowing every gift and grace. Miss Field held this faith in all its purity and perfection. She insisted always on marriage and motherhood as the only complete fulfilment of the ideal of womanly life. Yet, for herself, the path of destiny led otherwhere than to " the sweet, safe corner by the household fire." Kate Field was born under a star that danced.

INTO UNKNOWN WAYS

> The Summers of Hesperides
> Are long.   ·
> EMILY DICKINSON.

I doubt whether a mortal can arrive at a greater degree of perfection than steadily to do good, and, for that very reason, patiently and meekly to suffer evil. — *A Letter to John Wesley from His Father.*

There is no end to the great ends of life. If one is living in the resolute pursuit of them, he may first welcome, and then rejoice to leave behind, the several means which in succession come to offer him their help toward the attainment of those ends, as the traveller whose heart is set upon some distant city rejoices when he comes to, and then rejoices when he gets beyond, each field and river which must be crossed before he enters the far-off city gates. — PHILLIPS BROOKS.

> Ah, happy if a sun or star
> Could chain the wheel of Fortune's car,
> And give to hold an even state,
> Neither dejected nor elate.
> In vain : the stars are glowing wheels,
> Giddy with motion Nature reels,
> Sun, moon, man, undulate and stream,
> The mountains flow, the solids seem,
> Change acts, reacts ; back, forward hurled,
> And pause were palsy to the world.
> EMERSON.

CHAPTER VII

Great is he,
Who uses his greatness for all.
His name shall stand perpetually
As a name to applaud and cherish.

MRS. BROWNING.

Nor stony tower, nor walls of beaten brass,
Nor airless dungeon, nor strong links of iron
Can be retentive to the strength of spirit.

Julius Cæsar.

SUMMER DAYS IN COLORADO. THE MORMON PROBLEM. ALASKA
AND THE GOLDEN GATE. PICTURESQUE JOURNEYS. COMMENTS
ON AFFAIRS. IMPORTANT LECTURES. FAME AND FRIENDS.

THE late summer of 1883 found Miss Field preparing for a journey to the far West. She
passed a few days with her uncle and aunt, the Sanfords, in Newport, at their beautiful villa on the old
Point, where her own room — a blue room, with a
Venetian window looking out on the water, beyond
which the sunsets shone gloriously— again made her
happy to be in it and sad to leave. In the early
summer of 1883, however, she fared forth on a
journey westward toward issues of which she little
dreamed. With Ulysses she might have said: —

" It may be that the gulfs will wash us down;
It may be we shall touch the Happy Isles."

It will be remembered that, amid all the varied
charms and interests of her foreign life, passed in the
most cultivated and refined social circles of Europe,
Kate Field never forgot that she was an American,

and patriotism grew to be a passion with her. She had been a student of English and American politics, and her revelations of the ponderous machinery of the British Parliament, in that series of strong and brilliant press letters, collected into the little volume called " Hap-Hazard," was as fine and impressive in its way as was her dramatic criticism or literary papers. All this, perhaps, had paved the way for her to enter into a close and comprehensive study of the social and the political crimes of Utah. The serious attention which she gave to this problem stamps her lectures on this theme as among the most potent political influences of that time. Miss Field's discussion of Mormonism was one of those events which seem predetermined by the law of the unconscious, and which seem to choose the individual rather than to be chosen by him. In this summer of 1883, as we have seen, Miss Field determined to hitch her wagon to a star and journey westward. She lingered for a month in Denver, where she received distinguished social attention, and where, by special request, she gave her lecture on an " Evening with Dickens " and her " Musical Monologue." Of this Dickens lecture a Denver journal said : —

" Charles Dickens was the novelist of humanity, and Kate Field is, to-day, his most sympathetic and intelligent interpreter. Those who were so fortunate as to attend her reading last evening enjoyed an intellectual pleasure not soon forgotten. They saw a slender, graceful woman, dressed in creamy white, with soft laces falling about her ; with low, broad brow, and earnest, sympathetic eyes, under a cloud of soft brown hair. With a rich and finely modulated voice of remarkable power of expression, she held her audience for two hours spellbound by the magic of her genius."

In Colorado Miss Field enjoyed an unique and picturesque holiday. Picnics and excursions were gotten up in her honor; special trains were run; she rode on horseback with gay parties of friends twenty-five miles a day; she joined friends from New York who were camping out on "The Needles," and she made a visit to the San Juan silver-mining district. Among other diversions she had the honor of naming a new watering-place, located on "The Divide," an hour by rail from Denver, to which, in honor of General Palmer, who had practically "made" that region, she gave the name of Palmero, the Spanish for Palmer.

On first reaching Denver, under date of July 22, 1883, Kate thus writes to a friend to whom for fifteen years — from 1880 until the lack of mail facilities from Honolulu, the year before her death, interrupted the correspondence — she wrote almost daily. This friend was then living quietly in one place; Kate was continually flying about; but her address for every day, as approximately as it was possible to calculate, was always with the friend whose devotion to the brilliant and noble woman was fairly in the nature of an occupation. All Kate's letters that are quoted in this Record are from this correspondence exclusively unless otherwise specified. From Denver Miss Field wrote : —

" Here I am, my dear, feeling very like the traditional cat in a strange garret, yet very much interested, and new things turn up so fast that my head feels as though it would burst. A sister of Julia Dean, the famous actress, has just left me, having called on the strength of knowing my dear mother, and the result is that I 'm going to visit her ranch.

" People appear here in the most amazing manner, and one makes friends inside of five minutes. My journey west was uneventful and perfectly comfortable, thanks to Pullman cars. I stopped over night at Chicago and went with Mr. Pullman to his town, which is unique and wonderful and such a monument as does honor to its founder. It is worth a journey west to see ' Pullman ' alone. . . . I had not been two hours in town before a committee of ladies engaged me to give my monologue on the 31st. Eugene Field called at once and has been as kind and attentive as though he were a real cousin — kinder. He is very clever. Senator and Mrs. Hill came to see me last evening. . . . Denver is wonderful for so young a town, and the distant mountains are fine." . . .

Of the grave of Helen Hunt Jackson she wrote:

. . . " I 've been to Colorado Springs, lectured there and visited H. H.'s grave. It is on Cheyenne Mountain, 2,500 feet above the town, reached by a mountain road good enough for carriage and two horses. The situation of the grave is beautiful, romantic, and appropriate. I walked several rods in a foot of snow to get to the grave, but only a few steps beyond I found bare rock, where I sat in the sun for an hour, and thinking of the unique woman and generous heart that had passed many a day in the same place, I gazed upon the beautiful plain that stretches to the Missouri River. No monument at present marks H.H.'s grave, and it would require a sympathetic genius to create a fitting design. The usual white marble atrocity would desecrate nature and insult the dead. . . . I liked her very much for her great cleverness and vivacity. It is impossible for me to give an analysis of her character as she appeared to me. . . . As I care for Shakespeare and a few old fellows supremely, perhaps you can understand why the poetry of H. H. does not appeal to me. . . . You will, of course, use your judgment in publishing scraps that I send. . . . But for yourself, pray don't think it womanly to be too easily disgusted. Whatever a man can read, a woman can read. Whatever a man can write about, a woman can write about."

Again she says : —

" The farther West I go, the more interested I become in the people."

The death of Miss Field's uncle, Mr. Sanford, occurred suddenly about this time, and to her Aunt Corda she wrote : —

" God bless you and make you brave ! I wish I were with you. It seems such an awful distance away when sorrow comes.

" Poor Uncle Milton ! Yet why should I write ' poor ' ? No. He leaves his tired body, and begins life over again with truer insight and higher aspirations, as we all must. You think of this, I know, dearest aunt, and you accept temporary separation with resignation to a will wiser than we can conceive."

No adequate idea of the breadth and fulness of her life could be given without some representation of her relations with the daily press. They were singularly happy ones; and even when some adverse comment was made on her, she took the matter with good grace and evidently believed, with the Rev. Dr. Crothers, that "When a man comes to appreciate his own blunders, he has found an unexhaustible supply of innocent enjoyment." There was no feature of her own life which she held as more responsible than her journalistic work, and she once remarked to a friend : " I honor the journalist because he does work that is needed from day to day. He is the contemporary historian, and quietly submits to oblivion; in fact, takes it for granted and puts on no airs."

She was herself always a close student of the daily press; and if one stops to think of it, there is a distinctive difference between the woman who reads the newspapers and the woman who does not. In Miss Field's apartments neither belles-lettres nor bric-à-brac ever crowded out the semi-daily papers. They had place in her rooms and space in her life; and as a natural consequence, she brought to bear on the current questions of the hour a just and thorough acquaintance with them. A vigorous daily journal crowds out an immense amount of nonsense and frippery in a woman's life, if once one happens to reflect upon it.

During 1883–84 Miss Field wrote a series of letters on the political situation in Utah to the Boston "Herald," which dealt in a masterly way with the problems of the hour. In one of these under date of Feb. 4, 1884, she writes this pungent sketch of her view of Utah: —

"When I arrived here, Mormons told me that Governor Murray was a fool, a rascal, and a dude. What an extraordinary combination! Murray had only one thing to recommend him, and that was good looks; his vanity, however, was so great on account of his beauty as to render him insufferable. I had never met the Governor, and marvelled exceedingly that the President should have sent a trinity of folly, rascality, and dudeism to so critical a community as the Latter Day Saints. To be sure, the Gentiles told me a diametrically opposite story. They said Murray was every inch a gentleman; that he was sound in head and heart, and that he was as true to his trust as the needle to the pole. 'He has been here four years,' said one clever man, 'and, hated as he is by the Mormons, anxious as they have been to pick holes in his record, they have not succeeded in finding a flaw.' Where lay the truth?

" ' Externally,' said a high priest, ' Governor Murray is an accomplished, agreeable, amiable gentleman, but internally he is a black-hearted scoundrel.'

" ' Why is he a scoundrel?' I asked, expecting at last to place my finger on something tangible.

" ' Well, Governor Murray would head a mob against our people.'

" ' How do you know he would head a mob against your people or any other? Soldiers have special detestation of mobs. I don't believe any officer of the United States army, volunteer or regular, would head a mob against anybody.'

" ' I believe Murray would,' replied the high priest.

" ' If you want me to share your detestation of Governor Murray, you must produce stronger evidence than supposition,' I continued. ' What else have you against him?'

" ' At a Fourth of July celebration here, Governor Murray declared that there was wood enough in the mountains to make coffins for all traitors, and he meant us!'

" ' How do you know he meant you? Are you traitors?'

" Here the conversation ceased, for I did not want to tell my friend that he had put the cap upon his own head, and, if it fitted, so much the worse for him. I repeat this dialogue because it is a fair illustration of the reason brought to bear by Mormon judgment on Governor Murray or any other faithful official.

.   .   .   .

" Governor Murray is neither a fool nor a rascal. Moreover, he is not a dude. It is my good fortune to know him, and I have rarely met a man with a more generous heart. I do not think he could betray a trust if he tried. It is not in his nature. His head has been wise enough to grasp the situation here, and to advocate the only policy compatible with common sense. He cannot be bought by flattery or gold. Thanks to his parents, he has a fine, manly physique, which fact seems to be a crime in Mormon eyes. This is something Governor Murray cannot help. Therefore he should be forgiven. But he can help being well dressed; hence he is a dude. I don't wonder that the 'saints' are shocked at good tailoring. Utah has made its own clothes by divine revelation for so many years as to look upon uninspired broadcloth as the work of the evil one.

"If Eli H. Murray is not reappointed Governor of Utah Territory, a great injustice will be done to a faithful servant, as well as to the cause of liberty."

That we are led by a way we know not, is a truth that was emphasized by the unconscious way in which Miss Field came to be interested in the Mormon problem. In a letter to the Boston "Herald," under date of January, 1884, she tells the story: —

"I know of nothing that would do Bostonians so much good as a prolonged trip across this continent, giving themselves sufficient time to tarry at different points and study the people. For myself — about half a Bostonian — I became so ashamed of sailing east year after year, that last summer I made up my mind to hitch my wagon to the star of empire and learn as much of my own country as I knew of Europe. I started from New York in July, expecting to be absent three months, and in that period obtain an intelligent idea of the far West. After passing two months and a half in wonderful Colorado, and only seeing a fraction of the Centennial State, I began to realize that in two years I might, with diligence, get a tolerable idea of this republic west of the Mississippi. Cold weather setting in, and the fall of snow rendering mountain travelling in Colorado neither safe nor agreeable, I came to Utah over the wonderful Denver and Rio Grande Railroad, intending to pass a week prior to visiting New Mexico and Arizona. My week expired on the 22d day of October, and still I linger among the ' saints.' I am regarded as more or less demented by Eastern friends. If becoming interested in a most extraordinary anomaly to such an extent as to desire to study it and to be able to form an intelligent opinion therein is being demented, then I am mad indeed, for I 've not yet got to the bottom of the Utah problem, and if I lived here years, there would still be much to learn. Despite this last discouraging fact, I have improved my opportunities and am able to paragraph what has come under my own observation or been acquired by absorption of Mormon and Gentile literature. If the commissioners sent here by Congress to investigate the Mormon question, at an annual expense of forty thousand dollars per annum, had studied this question as earnestly as I have, they never would have told the country that polygamy is dying out. One or two members of that commission know better, and sooner or later they must tell the truth or stultify their own souls."

This extract reveals how deeply the anomaly of Mormon life had at once impressed her. Miss Field was too keen and cultivated an observer not to see beneath the surface of this phase of living a problem whose roots struck deep into national prosperity and safety. The distinguished essayist and critic, Mr. Edwin P. Whipple, said of her study of Mormonism : —

" She undertook a perfectly original method of arriving at the truth, by intimate conversations with Mormon husbands and wives, as well as with the most intelligent of the ' Gentiles.' She discarded from her mind pre-conceptions and all prejudices which discolor and distort objects which should be rigidly investigated, and looked at the mass of facts before her in what Bacon calls ' dry light.' Cornelius Vanderbilt, the elder, was accustomed to account for the failures and ruin of the brilliant young brokers who tried to corner the stocks in which he had an interest, by declaring that ' these dashing young fellars did n't see things as they be.' Miss Field saw things in Utah ' as they be.' She collected facts of personal observation, analyzed and generalized them, and, by degrees, her sight became insight and the passage from insight to foresight is rapid. After thorough investigation, her insight enabled her to penetrate into the secret of that ' mystery of iniquity ' which Mormonism really is ; while her foresight showed her what would be the inevitable result of the growth and diffusion of such a horrible creed."

The winter lapsed into spring, and still she lingered in Salt Lake City. She relinquished all pleasure for the real work of studying deeply the anomaly of a polygamous hierarchy thriving in the heart of the republic. Every facility was accorded to her by United States officials, military officers, leading Gentiles and apostates. Prominent " Latter Day Saints" offered her marked courtesy. She pursued this research unremittingly for eight months and when, at last, she left Salt Lake City, the leading Gentile paper, " The Tribune," devoted a leading editorial to Miss Field's marvellously thorough study of Mormon conditions, and, on her departure, said : —

" Miss Field is probably the best posted person, outside the high Mormon church officials and others who have been in the church, on this institution, in the world, and its effects upon men, women, and governments. With a fixedness of purpose which nothing could swerve, and with an energy which neither storm, mud, snow, cold looks, the persuasions or even the loss of friends, could for a moment dampen, she has held on her course. In the tabernacle, in the ward meeting-house, in the homes of high Mormons, and, when these were closed to her, in the homes of the poor, she has worked upon the theme, while every scrap of history which offered to give any light upon the Mormon organization she has devoured. Mormonism has been to her like a fever. It has run its course, and now she is going away. If she proposes to lecture, she ought to be able to prepare a better lecture on Mormonism than she has ever yet delivered; if a book is in process of incubation, it ought to be of more value than any former book on this subject. Lecture or book will be intense enough to satisfy all demands. 'The Tribune' gives the world notice in advance that Miss Field has a most intimate knowledge of the Mormon kingdom.''

Returning to the East, she stopped on the way in Missouri and at Nauvoo, Illinois, looking up all the old camping-grounds of Mormonism, and meeting and interviewing people who had been connected with it, including two sons of Joseph Smith. Miss Field opened her course of lectures on Mormonism in Boston before a brilliant and distinguished audience, including the Governor and other officials of state, Harvard University professors, and men and women eminent in art, literature, and society. She dealt with the political crimes of the Mormons, arguing that the great wrong was not, as many had believed, polygamy, but treason!

There is no exaggeration in saying that Miss Field aroused the entire country with these lectures. Her statements offered a revelation of conditions little known. Rarely has such fire and eloquence and

splendor of oratory, combined with the mental discipline of trained thought, scholarly acquirements, and
finished elegance, been known in the annals of the
lyceum. These lectures yielded her returns in fame
and friends which were of a priceless nature. The
importance of her theme, the wide and accurate
knowledge, and the dignity with which she invested
it impressed the statesmen and the leading thinkers
of the day. The celebrated Boston divine, Rev. Dr.
S. K. Lothrop, said: " I am very glad Kate Field has
taken up a theme so worthy of the vituperative indignation of every intelligent and patriotic and Christian woman and man in this enlightened American
Republic."

Miss Field received, indeed, many letters of compliment after her initial lecture of the course, and
among them was this from the Rev. Dr. Phillips
Brooks, afterward the Bishop of Massachusetts:

BOSTON, 232 CLARENDON STREET, Nov. 24, 1884.

MY DEAR MISS FIELD, — I listened with interest to your
lecture last evening, and I thank you for giving me the
privilege of hearing it. As to the possibility of interesting
the people of Boston in any active measures with reference
to the matter in which you are so deeply interested, I can
form no judgment. I have had no means of testing public
sentiment upon the subject, and your own judgment would
be worth more than mine.

I need not say that I should be heartily rejoiced if the true
method of dealing with the problem could be discovered
and vigorously pursued. I am,

Yours most sincerely,

PHILLIPS BROOKS.

Rev. Dr. Bartol wrote: —

DEAR MISS FIELD, — I appreciate and bless you for your enthusiasm. Do not think people indifferent or thoughtless on the matter that so stirs you, because they are too much preoccupied to attend to lectures or unable for any reason to go to them. I judge your discourses made their mark on the mountain of wrong and prejudice to be removed thereby, as the work must go on. I have no new expedient to suggest, but am cordially yours, also very busy.

C. A. BARTOL.

Mr. T. B. Aldrich also wrote to Miss Field : —

"THE ATLANTIC MONTHLY,"
BOSTON, Nov. 22, 1884.

DEAR MISS KATE FIELD, — My wife bids me send you her thanks for those passes, which she has used with the unalloyed joy that attaches itself to free tickets in a world where one does n't usually get anything for nothing. I suppose that my humble applause did n't reach you the other evening so as to be distinguishable, though I made quite a spectacle of myself two or three times.

Yours very sincerely,

T. B. ALDRICH.

Miss Field's methods of investigation while in Salt Lake City had been those of the closest personal observation and conversational intercourse with all classes of people. The method itself is something of a commentary on her original genius. Her press letters on political topics at this time were not invariably diplomatic in the policy they advocated, but they were penetrating and fearless.

In the summer of 1885 she filled many lecture engagements before assemblies and institutes in the East, and a picture of her during a little interlude, when she was the guest of Mrs. Émile Marquéze, in

her seaside cottage on the North shore of Massachusetts, recurs to memory. At the corner of the piazza
a hammock was swung, and in it, reclining against
cushions, was the pretty figure of Kate Field, while
all the blue Atlantic rolling in formed the background. It was out on the extreme point of Marblehead Neck, — the very jumping-off place of the North
Shore, — and the white wings of yachts and sail-boats
flitted over the blue waters, lying sparkling and shim-
mering under a golden flood of sunshine. The
" Point " here curves about far out at sea, making a
small bay, on which the quaint old town of Marblehead fronts, and across which the dwellers on the
" Point " can row to the mainland, or instead they
may drive over the long neck of land that connects
Marblehead Point with the main shore. Here on this
extreme end of land out at sea are dozens of cottages,
where Bostonians install themselves, and here, too,
is the Eastern Yacht Club House, gay with banners
and pennons streaming to the wind. At the outer-
most edge of this point, with piazzas and balconies
overhanging the sea, which breaks against great
ledges of rocks, Mrs. Marquéze had a summer cottage, in which the law of hospitality was that each
guest should enjoy himself after the devices of his
own heart. The hostess flitted about her pretty
rooms here and there; Miss Field swung idly in the
hammock, and threw in conversational interludes of
glancing wit and brilliancy, altogether Kate Fieldian,
and therefore indescribable. "The idea," said some
one at last, " of a newspaper correspondent who is
tolerated by the press of the country being up here
with the great authority on Mormonism, and not interviewing her. Tell me, O my lady of the ham-

mock," continued the youth, "whether there is any danger of a Mormon uprising on their anniversary (July 24), their Pioneer Day."

Miss Field gazed serenely out at sea. Her thoughts were far away, sailing the Vesuvian Bay or some other locality. But she was recalled to *terra firma :* "About the Mormons?" "The Mormons are serfs," she replied with her characteristic incisive energy. "They have been taught from the beginning to obey counsel. I cannot believe that they would act individually on their own responsibility. Whatever is done will be by order of the Church. Unless the Presidency have gone mad, there will be no demonstration against the Gentiles. John Taylor and George Q. Cannon are not fools; they know perfectly well that in any physical contest they must eventually be worsted, and I cannot think they wish to bring about a collision. There may be a Guiteau among the saints, but I very much doubt it. They are under too good Church discipline to think for themselves."

Miss Field ardently enjoyed the North Shore, where long drives through piny woods with sudden glimpses of the sea, — where the waves breaking against rocky cliffs and a sea of silver lying at night beneath a moonlit sky, all charmed her anew. One day her hostess drove her to Manchester-by-the-Sea, where James T. Fields had his country seat, still occupied by Mrs. Fields, and of which the story is told that Mr. Fields, writing a letter to Dr. Holmes, dated his note Manchester-by-the-Sea: to which the witty Autocrat, determined not to be outdone, replied, dating "Beverly-farms-near-the-depot."

"I almost fancy I hear the Beverly Bells, — Lucy Larcom's bells," remarked Kate, as she swung idly in

28

the hammock one summer day; and half dreamily,
in her vibrant, musical voice, she repeated : —

> " Beverly Bells !
> Ring to the tide as it ebbs and swells.
> This was the anguish a moment tells,
> The passionate sorrow death quickly knells ;
> But the pain that is caused by a lifelong woe
> Is left for the desolate heart to know,
> Whose tides with the dull years come and go."

During the later years of this decade (1880–90)
Miss Field visited the Yellowstone Park and the
Yosemite; passed one winter at Coronado Beach,
which she pronounced the most enchanting of places ;
passed some time at San Rafael and in San Francisco,
and made two trips to Alaska, on one of which she
gave the first lecture ever delivered in that country.

Miss Field's pungent humor was always appreciated by the press of her country, and she was the
heroine of an alarming number of racy paragraphs.
Eugene Field, the poet and wit, who, though they
were not related, always called her " Cousin Katherine " set afloat one of his characteristic paragraphs
as follows, during one of Miss Field's California
sojourns : —

" Miss Kate Field is so delighted with California that
she has decided to spend the evening of her life there.
Accordingly she has purchased an orange grove near Los
Angeles and is erecting a splendid villa overlooking the
sea. This beautiful estate she calls Castellata in honor of
her friend, the Duque de la Castellata, of Madrid. It was
the duke's eldest son who was killed at a bull-fight some
years ago, and it has been hinted that Miss Field had more
than a passing regard for the unhappy lad."

Pasting this on the top of a letter to Kate, he wrote as follows : —

DEAR COUSIN KATHERINE, — It is not probable that Mr. Stone's retirement from the " Daily News " will interfere with my arrangements here ; at the same time, however, I am mighty sorry to be deprived of the companionship of so good a man and so true a friend.   Your manuscript is in the hands of the new editor and proprietor, Mr. Victor F. Lawson, and it will have prompt attention.   I see by " Yenowine's Milwaukee News " that you are to remain in California ; is this true?   It would be indelicate, perhaps, to ask if the story about the unhappy young heir of de la Castellata be equally true.   I have heard a good deal about that bull-fight, but you never spoke of it to me.   My folks are all well, and they wish to be remembered cordially to you.   God bless you, dear cousin, and fill you with pleasant thoughts of him who now and hereunto subscribes himself yours affectionately,

EUGENE FIELD.

CHICAGO, May 27, 1888.

On one of Miss Field's departures from the West to the Atlantic seacoast again, Mr. Stedman rivalled Thomas Hood's celebration of his " fair Inez " by writing to Kate on a post-card : —

> O, saw ye not fair Katie ?
>   She 's going to the East,
> To take from out our loaf of cake,
>   Its most ethereal yeast !

E. C. S.

All this infinite jest followed her as a part of her own atmosphere, and made itself a recognized element of her genial, brilliant life.   At one time she heard a lecture from a state official in the West who argued for phonetic spelling.   Miss Field replied, as Max

Muller or Archbishop Trench might have done, in defence of language. " Why," she said, as her face glowed with enthusiasm, " pure language is the one imperishable bequest of the centuries. It is the crystallization of all human thought and emotion. It is history, poetry, art, and science, all rolled into one, and if you hack and mutilate it as you suggest, you leave us only parrot calls."

A Christmas brought her this note from her old friend Laurence Hutton.

CHRISTMAS MORNING.

Perhaps Miss Field will care to possess this bit of English Mistletoe, the real thing, cut in Warwickshire not more than two weeks ago. " A rare old plant " and seasonable, suggestive of " God bless us every one ; " and it may help to " keep *his* memory green."

Respectfully,   LAURENCE HUTTON.

Mrs. Laurence Hutton, in playful allusion to some splendid elk-heads which Miss Field had sent to Mr. Hutton from Colorado, and which he had attached to the wall of his house, thus wrote to Kate in assumed formality : —

MISS KATE FIELD.

DEAR MADAM, — Mr. Laurence Hutton requests me to inform you that he regrets to state that the firm of Elk-Head hangers, whom he has employed for the last twenty years to hang his Elk-Heads, have attached yours so firmly to the wall that it cannot be taken down without removing the side of the house. Mr. Hutton has made provision in his will that you and your heirs shall be permitted every Sunday afternoon, forever, between the hours of three and five, to look at the head, on the payment of a small fee to the servant who opens the door.

I remain, dear madam, yours with consideration,

BETTA.

In reply to a question regarding the Yosemite she said : —

"What do I think of the Yosemite Valley? I want to quote Emerson and then stop : 'It is the only scenery that comes up to its brag.' To attempt to describe it is absurd — as attempting to describe the Niagara Falls. There are persons who undertake this big contract, just as there are artists who paint the falls. With what results? They only display their own littleness. Fanny Kemble had more sense. When she was a girl and visited Niagara for the first time, she kept a diary which was afterward published. Instead of indulging in bathos, as the average young person would have done, she exclaims, 'O God !' That tells the story. In the presence of Yosemite Valley I feel like making the same brief and eloquent criticism."

Of a summer she passed some weeks lecturing in Michigan she said : —

"I started for Alaska, and at the rate of speed with which I was approaching it, I probably would have reached it near the close of the twentieth century. I have been figuring on the subject somewhat, and the seeming fly-tracks you see here represent the tangents I pursued while traversing that State. I have delivered my Mormon lecture at Paw Paw, Weeping Water, Lone Mound, — in short, I have elucidated the problem of polygamy at every little cross-roads in Michigan and in Iowa. Last week I began to realize that if I had kept on fly-tracking the intervening territory, I would have reached Alaska in 1970 — that is to say, eighty-four years hence. Much as I wish to see Alaska, I really have not the time to devote to this method of accomplishing a realization of that wish ; so I have abandoned the Slayton lecture route to our iceberg possessions."

This lecture tour had involved the utmost hardships in night travel, — in being called at two or three o'clock in the morning to take some local train which was perhaps two hours late, and would have left her stranded in some rural station with a long delay for another train; but she bore it with seeming good humor and always extracted what Mr. Stedman well called the Kate Fieldian view. Her intense earnestness, her impassioned power, were relieved by this humorous vein in her character.

Notwithstanding the fact that every Boston woman who respects herself regards her genius as the guiding star foreordained of heaven in all emergencies, there is still one forum in the modern Athens on which the foot of woman has never stood, — that of the Lowell Institute. It was reserved for Kate Field to initiate the storming of this impregnable fort of exclusive masculine wisdom, — an attack of which the following correspondence suggests the rise, decline, and fall.

March 19, 1885.

To Augustus Lowell, Esq.

Dear Sir, — Going West for pleasure I was arrested against my will by the presence in Utah of a hierarchy in the heart of a republic. After months of study I have returned and am doing all in my power to enlighten public opinion in order that Congress may be forced to consider it and take speedy action. The lecture which I am giving to the general public in no way covers the whole ground of Mormonism. I am preparing half a dozen lectures with a view to delivering them to thinking associations, etc., early next autumn. As Lowell Institute is in the habit of giving courses of lectures, I now write to inquire whether such a subject as mine — of vital national importance — commends itself to your consideration. It would be easy for me to obtain letters of introduction to you from Mr. James Russell Lowell and other prominent Americans, but I prefer to let this matter rest entirely upon its merits. Whether I know what I talk about can be told you by Judge Field of the Supreme Court, Washington, D. C., Judge Arthur McArthur of the District Court, Washington, D. C., Senator Dawes of Massachusetts, Governor Murray of Utah, and many another, if you care for references. As I leave town in a few days, an early answer will oblige,

Yours truly,   KATE FIELD.

171 COMMONWEALTH AVE., 19 March, 1885.

To MISS KATE FIELD.

MY DEAR MADAM, — I sympathize very cordially in the work you have undertaken against Mormonism, and should be very glad to do anything in my power to advance it. I hesitate, however, to break through a rule of more than forty years' standing, which has confined the platform of the Lowell Institute to men as lecturers, foreseeing the very serious embarrassment which such a break may bring upon me, and feel compelled, though with more reluctance than ever before, to decline the suggestion. I remain,

Yours very truly,   AUGUSTUS LOWELL.

March 21, 1885.

To AUGUSTUS LOWELL, ESQ.

DEAR SIR, — Many thanks for your prompt reply to my letter of inquiry. Will you kindly answer three questions?

Did the generous donor of the Lowell Institute Fund specify the sex of the lecturer, or does he leave this matter to the discretion of his executors?

Were I a man, would you entertain the idea of lectures on Mormon Treason before the Institute?

Were a man delegated to deliver my lecture, would this arrangement be acceptable?

Yours truly,   KATE FIELD.

To Miss Kate Field.   March 21, 1885.

My dear Madam, — Upon my return I find your note of this morning, and reply to your questions. . . .

A literal interpretation of the language of the testator would certainly confine the lectureships of the Lowell Institute to men, and such has been the practice from the beginning.

While, as I wrote you, I feel personally great sympathy with any attempt to put down Mormonism, I am not clear that an institution devoted to instruction is a fitting place to use it, or that I should be doing my duty to permit it to be so used.

The suggestion that some man should be permitted to read your lectures would be introducing an entirely new feature, for which I am not prepared. I remain,

Yours truly,

Augustus Lowell.

In the winters of 1885 and 1886, Miss Field gave three lectures on the Mormon question in Washington, and in reply to her desire to meet the President was this autograph note from Mr. Cleveland: —

Executive Mansion, Washington,
Feb. 22, 1886.

My dear Miss Field, — I have received your note, and in reply have to say that I shall be pleased to see you to-morrow afternoon (Tuesday) at half-past three o'clock.

Yours sincerely,

Grover Cleveland.

"So you have been interviewing Presidents?" remarked a friend to Miss Field at the breakfast-table, in the Brunswick Hotel, a day or two later, as she came on to Boston.

"Yes," she replied, smiling; "President Cleveland was good enough to waste some time upon me; and while it could have been of no particular advantage to him, it was a very great pleasure and satisfaction to me. Only a few days since in Buffalo I made it my business to interview every prominent man and woman with whom I came in contact, on Grover Cleveland, as they say that you never know anything about a man until you get the opinion of his lifelong neighbors. Inasmuch as I am no partisan, and don't care who is President of the United States, provided he is honest, intelligent, and a patriot, it was a great comfort to be assured by Mr. Cleveland's political opponents as well as by his warm friends, that he was as honest as the sun, true to his convictions, entirely incorruptible, and while he was an ardent Democrat, he was first a patriot."

"Well, Kathleen," chimed in another familiar spirit, "do illuminate our understandings with some gleam of light as to what Mr. Cleveland is about? I'm a sceptic, ready to be fairly won over if you'll turn on all your dazzling brilliancy."

"It's too early in the day to be resplendent," flashed back Miss Field; "but I do believe that Mr. Cleveland wants to make a good President, first and foremost; that he wants to help this country in preference to helping himself, and if he does he is the right man in the right place. We are approaching a very serious epoch in our history. The genius of good luck seems to have presided at our birth. She gave us George Washington for our first revolution; that great man Abraham Lincoln for the second, and in the social revolution that is to come who knows but Grover Cleveland may be the saviour of his country?"

" Who, indeed?" exclaimed another friend, toying with his coffee. " For my part, I have learned to believe in miracles, and I am only surprised when they do *not* happen."

Kate's merry laugh replied. She looked very lovely that morning in her dark-blue costume, wearing a picture hat with long plumes; her blue eyes sparkled and her face was aglow with animation.

After this conversation she wrote as follows to the President: —

DEAR MR. CLEVELAND, — As you say that friends are always sending you unkind remarks about yourself, I venture to enclose an interview extorted from me during my recent visit to Boston. The reporter was very anxious to know what you said. I think I know one woman who can hold her tongue. What I told the reporter I believe.

Apropos of the Utah U. S. Marshal, if you meet John W. Mackay of Nevada, ask him what he thinks of P. H. . . . There never lived a truer man, a sounder Democrat, a pluckier soul or one who understood so well the requirements of Utah. Several things have occurred recently to prove the weakness of the present incumbent, who is, however, an honest, well-meaning man. Natural limitations are a misfortune, not a fault.

I also enclose some Mormon scraps to be read by you at your leisure. It is said that a good way to influence men is through their wives. If Mormon agitation can be made fashionable, matters can be expedited. . . .

That brilliant editor, Charles A. Dana, who made " The Sun " to shine for all, liked nothing better as a *jeu d'esprit* than to flash his trenchant pen against Kate Field's steel; and on her appearance in New York with her Mormon lectures he gave this living picture of the occasion.

Under the heading, " Miss Kate Field as a Model of Self-Possession and Enduring Interest," Mr. Dana wrote : —

" Kate Field is a remarkable type of the self-possessed woman. She has wit, and a purpose in what she does gives expression to her bright eyes. Newspaper correspondent, European tourist, monologue performer, lecturer, and woman of business, Kate Field has been before the public ; and it is to her credit that in her various rôles she has had always something to offer which the public has found it worth while to listen to.

" Her present hobby is Mormonism, and yesterday she delivered her eighth lecture on the subject in this city. The topic might properly be regarded as a delicate one for a woman to discuss. Miss Field apparently has no scruples upon that point. She deals frankly, even boldly, with the vices and evils as she has found them to exist in Utah. Her argument in a word is this : Mormonism has never been painted black enough, and the Government of the United States, and the people who make public opinion, have never really appreciated the enormity of its sinfulness. Polygamy and Mormonism she treats as practically synonymous, and, therefore, Mormons are criminals and traitors, and should be dealt with by force of arms if necessary.

" The methods by which Kate Field holds the interest of her audiences are simple and straightforward. She is direct and earnest in her appeal, and seems to fully feel the force of her own arguments.

" When the lights were turned on brightly in Chickering Hall the other evening, Kate Field came unannounced upon the stage, and with a quiet, gliding step swept gracefully to a place before the footlights. The red portfolio of notes which she carried she opened upon a small table at her side, and turning her face to the audience she began to speak in a clear, musical voice. Her tone was distinctly colloquial, and she became more familiar in addressing her audience in the second person as she warmed to her subject. Her enunciation was conspicuously and consciously distinct and clear cut.

"Miss Field has the reputation of dressing. Her gown was of black silk, trailing far astern. The front breadth of the skirt was of cherry silk, and the same rich hue swept the length of the train. Rows of sparkling jet beads glistened from the folds of the drapery. The bodice was sleeveless and V-shaped at the throat. The edges of the opening were softened with black lace, and a fringe of the same flimsy fabric took the place of sleeves. A large bunch of pink roses, held together with a light blue ribbon, adorned the front of the bodice. The arms, otherwise bare, were encased to the elbows in buff gloves so light as not to be easily distinguishable from the white flesh.

"So much for the attire. The face is less easily described. The brow is broad and low, and fringed by dark hair matted in ringlets. A coil of indistinguishable style holds together the back hair. The eyes are bright and direct in their gaze, the complexion a triple 'peach-blow,' and the lips are full and make no show of pretty puckering. Kate Field's mouth, to tell the truth, is large. Around her white neck she wore a band of black velvet to emphasize the whiteness, and a buckle set with brilliants adorned the velvet.

"As Miss Field stepped to the footlights she appeared to discredit the record of her birth which is preserved in the old family Bible. She looked young. Her graceful figure was lithe, and she was wholly at her ease under the critical stare of her audience. Having taken her stand she did not move her feet for two hours. Her hands were lightly clasped at her waist and held a dainty lace kerchief. She was admirably at ease. As she spoke every one settled comfortably in his seat, prepared to listen attentively, and a certain musical modulation of her voice made listening easy and pleasant. There was nothing of the recitation in her manner of speaking. She was in earnest. She appeared to believe in the importance of her subject and to feel that she had to overcome the indifference of her audience. Utah and Mormonism are so far away from the East that it is difficult to wake people up to a realization of the true state of affairs. As the feebleness of her single-handed combat with the hydra-headed monster seemed at moments to strike her, she would raise her voice and her daintily gloved hand, and her eyes would flash sparks of indignant fire. Dropping from the height of an impassioned climax, she would wipe the floor with the United States Congress in a whirl of sarcasm and bitter invective. But she never smiled, even at her own most audacious bursts of irony.

" ' Think of it ! ' she exclaimed, her eyes very wide open and very eloquent in expression ; ' think of it ! New York and Utah under the same flag ! We ought to be ashamed of ourselves,' she said fiercely, and then, dropping her voice and speaking with great deliberation, she added, ' That is, those of us who vote.'

" Brigham Young she spoke of as ' that vulgar, illogical wonderful old man.' She paid her respects to Uncle Sam with pointed anger. ' John T. Kane, Mormon, upholder of polygamy, traitor,' she said savagely, received $2,400 a year more for upholding polygamy in Congress than Governor Murray of Utah, a patriot, received for enforcing the laws. ' We have,' she added, ' an abominably magnanimous Government ! ' Speaking of the removal of Governor Murray, she said in her most impressive manner : ' It is the greatest blunder of President Cleveland's Administration. I say it with all good wishes for the President and with grief in my heart.' And, it might be added, with grief in her voice as well.

" After describing the evils of polygamy as she saw them during a long residence in Utah, Miss Field appealed to the people to do something. 'The United States Government,' she said with passion, 'is responsible for thirty years' growth of polygamy, with its degradation of woman and brutalization of man, and it is time that you who hold the ballot should cry, halt!' She spoke with a fervor that could not be without effect, and the applause which followed would have elected Miss Field to a place in Congress if such an expression of public approval could be thus counted in her favor. 'The sooner the East gets it out of its head that there is nothing the matter with Mormonism except polygamy, the better,' she went on. 'The great crime of Utah is treason!'

"Miss Field sang a Mormon hymn. She did not change the attitude which she had maintained throughout her lecture, and there was no straining after operatic effect. The air was not strikingly unlike a Methodist hymn tune, but the sentiment of the song was profane and treasonable. 'That is a hymn,' she remarked. 'I was afraid you would not know it.'

"In reviewing the acts of Congress respecting the practice of polygamy in Utah she dismissed them scornfully in two words, thus: 'All farces.' The cure for the disease, she said, was in a universal marriage law. 'It is a disgrace that there is no United States marriage law.'

"Throughout her address there had been no ranting. Her zeal had never exceeded the bounds of convincing earnestness. In concluding, Miss Field dropped her voice and spoke to her hearers as to an individual, face to face: 'Men and women of the great Empire State, you who do so much to make public opinion, what are you going to do about it?'"

In this transcript from Mr. Dana's instantaneous mental photography there is a vital portrait of Kate Field, the lecturer, that is unsurpassed; and the keen, half caustic, teasing vein in which it is written makes

this critical description, or descriptive criticism, one
of the most typical specimens of the writing of the
most unique and brilliant American journalists.

Again in Washington Miss Field delivered her
Mormon lectures.

Letters from Hon. T. B. Reed, Senator Morrill,
Judge Field, and many others from statesmen and
officials flowed in upon her with encouragement in
her work. Judge Field thus wrote: —

WASHINGTON, D. C., Feb. 23, 1885.

MY DEAR MISS FIELD, — Thanks for the tickets received
this morning. I shall certainly attend your lecture on
Thursday evening if I can get rid of my present cold.

I think it would be a wise thing to send tickets to the
other judges. Just at this time the condition of things in
Utah excites much interest with them.

Very sincerely yours, STEPHEN FIELD.

After one of these lectures the following acknowledgment came to her: —

A. M. Soteldo, Minister of Venezuela, sends compliments
to Miss Kate Field and his cordial congratulations for the
success of her very interesting, admirable lecture of last
night, on Utah, the Mormons, and Mormonism.

The Hon. George Bancroft wrote: —

1623 H. STREET, N. W.,
WASHINGTON, D. C., Feb. 25, 1886.

DEAR MISS KATE FIELD, — I was not aware that you
had been so good as to call at my house yesterday. I very
greatly regret having missed your visit. On inquiry I find
that the servant who went to the door misunderstood your
question and made no report of it to me. It would have
given me particular pleasure to have met you.

If among your other great qualities you have that of

being able to lift twenty years from the back of a man of more than fourscore and will exercise it upon me, I shall be one of the most attentive, pleased, and instructed of your listeners to-morrow evening. Otherwise I dare not depart from my habit. I have not been this winter to lecture, opera, or play.

Yours very truly,
GEORGE BANCROFT.

It is hardly an exaggeration to say that the press comments on Kate Field's Mormon lectures could only be estimated by volumes, so numerous they are. Individual expressions abound, and one of these — made by Mrs. May Wright Sewall of Indianapolis, the foremost leader of the day among the younger women, and the successor of Lady Aberdeen as President of the International Council — is as follows : —

" Kate Field, — when did I first see her? As she came out upon the platform at Plymouth Church in Indianapolis to speak on ' The Mormon Monster.' No one who heard it will ever forget that lucid exposure and relentless denunciation of the subtle private deterioration and subtle public dangers that lurk in polygamy. That night I got the impression of versatility and freedom which in my mind are always associated with the name of Kate Field. She looked as unlike the lyceum lecturer as possible : in manner and in dress she seemed the woman of fashion ; in thought and in speech, the statesman."

A letter to Miss Field from Mr. S. L. Clemens, (Mark Twain) is as follows : —

HARTFORD, March 8, 1886.

DEAR MISS FIELD, — Oh, dear me, *no*. That would be the same as saying that because you differ from me upon the rights and equities of a subject, I am at liberty to hold a "poor opinion" of you for voicing your sentiments in the matter.

Your notion and mine about polygamy is without doubt exactly the same; but you probably think we have some cause of quarrel with those people for putting it into their religion, whereas I think the opposite. Considering our complacent cant about this country of ours being the home of liberty of conscience, it seems to me that the attitude of our Congress and people toward the Mormon Church is matter for limitless laughter and derision. The Mormon religion *is* a religion : the negative vote of all of the rest of the globe could not break down that fact ; and so I shall probably always go on thinking that the attitude of our Congress and nation toward it is merely good trivial stuff to make fun of.

Am I a friend to the Mormon religion? No. I would like to see it extirpated, but always by fair means, not these Congressional rascalities. If you can destroy it with a book, — by arguments and facts, not brute force, — you will do a good and wholesome work. And I should be very far from unwilling to publish such a book in case my business decks were clear. They are not clear now, however, and it is hard to tell when they will be. They are piled up with contracts which two or three years — and possibly four — will be required to fulfil. I have even had to rule myself out, and am now an author without a publisher. My book is finished and ready, and I have spent nearly ten thousand dollars in its preparation ; but it is pigeon-holed indefinitely, to make room for other people's more important books. (In this line of business we generally publish only one — and never more than two — books in a year.) I think I could write a very good moral fable about an author who turned publisher in order to get a better show, and got shut up entirely.

Truly yours,   S. L. CLEMENS.

The subject of cremation occupied Miss Field very much during this decade, and she was a pioneer in the movement. She wrote a paper advocating it which she read before the Nineteenth Century Club in New York City and before drawing-room audiences in Boston, Philadelphia, and Washington. She argued for it on the grounds that are now so increasingly securing its adoption, — those of the health and safety of the living, the insurance from the terrible fate of burial before life is extinct, and of the economic interests. That cremation is making great advances among the most enlightened communities is largely due to the efforts of Miss Field, who argued its claims by press work as well as lectures, and who was one of the first members of the cremation society in New York. Miss Field's efforts contributed greatly to influencing public sentiment toward this form of disposing of the dead, and among other able advocates of cremation are Rev. R. Heber Newton, D.D., of New York, Prof. Charles Eliot Norton, and Hon. Charles Francis Adams. In her incisive way Miss Field said : —

" I am a cremationist, because I believe cremation is not only the healthiest and cleanest, but the most poetical way of disposing of the dead. Whoever prefers loathsome worms to ashes, possesses a strange imagination."

Another measure which she championed by voice and pen during this period was the advocacy of a national marriage law. In her public speaking on this question she frankly ignored divorce as of secondary importance to the far more vital subject of marriage. "In this free and easy country men and women marry early and often, for the reason that they

can be very much married in some States and not at
all in others, while few precautions are taken against
fraud," said Miss Field, and added: "Were marriage made more difficult, there would be fewer
unhappy households. Then divorces would be less
frequent, and special legislation, which is always
dangerous, would be unnecessary. What this Republic needs is a national marriage law."

Writing to the New York "Tribune" on "Utah
Politics and Morals," written during this period,
Miss Field opens her letter with this vigorous
paragraph: —

To the Editor of "The Tribune."

Sir, — The Mormons have a very great advantage over
any other class of people. Nobody out of Utah can contradict them for the excellent reason that nobody knows
enough. When Matthew Arnold comes from England and
gives this Republic the benefit of his opinions concerning
Emerson, Boston arises as one man and with a howl of indignation denies the hard impeachment. When Monsignor
Capel tells Americans that in those Catholic countries where
marriage is a sacrament and divorce impossible there is
infinitely more social morality than elsewhere, the charming
Jesuit is torn to pieces, metaphorically, in scores of journals,
East and West. But when a Mormon elder rises to explain
on being interviewed by ubiquitous reporters, he carries
everything before him. There is no critic sufficiently conversant with the subject under discussion to say him nay.
What a commentary on our boasted intelligence ! When a
nation is so big that portions of it become a *terra incognita*
to those who make public opinion and the laws, " there 's
something rotten " this side of Denmark. . . .

In 1887, Miss Field again fared forth to the West on
a long lecture tour, and of a public reception given to

her in Salt Lake City by the Loyal Legion, she thus writes in a private letter: —

. . . " Never was a woman more taken by surprise than was I on being presented with a beautiful gold badge set with diamonds. I had been entirely thrown off my guard by being called upon to pay for the regulation badge prior to my initiation. Governor Murray is commander of the corps here and expressed great delight at my becoming a member of his flock."

The long series of private letters from which these extracts are made concerned themselves largely with the topics of the day. There was in them curiously little of the usual feminine personalities and chatter. Always she took the large and objective view of life. Regarding the discussion over the political course of James Russell Lowell, in 1887, Kate writes: —

. . . " I think the ' North American ' is too severe on Lowell. He may deserve all that criticism, but I doubt it. The great crime seems to be that he is a *Mugwump*. As I am a Mugwump, I feel differently. Lowell's great trouble is that he has always been self-indulgent, and has never liked the people. The people are *not* agreeable at dinner parties, and Lowell likes clean clothes and wit."

Meeting the "bonanza king," John Mackay, she thus writes of him: —

" John W. Mackay has been to see me, and I think I shall like him very much. He is not at all the type of man I imagined he would be. He is five feet ten inches, very erect, iron gray hair and mustache, heavy eyebrows, keen gray eyes, a strong jaw and mouth, and aquiline nose. He looks like the president of a big bank and a United States Senator. The many generous things I have heard about him from those who know him best make me ready to like

him, and I don't often care for rich men. The poor ones
are generally far more interesting.

. . . .

" Think of my being more impressed by a wreck of humanity in ragged clothes who trims gardens, and whose
only friend is Nature, than by all the well-to-do inhabitants
of this sleepy valley ! I believe I was intended to consort
with outcasts and sinners. I 'm at home with them."

Extending her tour to Alaska, Miss Field gave the
first lecture ever delivered in that country. Her
steamer, "The Ancon," reached Juneau, a mining
town, at 7 A. M. The passengers went on shore; and
Miss Field delivered her lecture on Charles Dickens
in a dance-house, to an audience of miners, who were
one of the most appreciative audiences that she ever
had. They gave her a vote of thanks, presented her
with a bottle of virgin gold and a jelly cake, and she
was then taken three miles in a tug to join the steamer
at Douglas Island.

To her most constant correspondent Kate wrote of
this Alaskan experience : —

" It rained twelve days out of seventeen ; and we had fog
two more ! I wore out a pair of arctics on shore and went
about in a riding-habit and a seal-skin. The habit did
away with petticoats, and in it I defied mud and ascended
the Muir glacier. Alaska is very interesting to me, and I
shall probably go to work on a lecture at once. I remain
here to consult Judge Swan, an Indian authority, and then
go over to the Britishers in Victoria. Here I am the guest
of Beecher's son. He has a charming little boy named
after his grandfather." . . .

Captain Beecher, to whom Miss Field referred, is
a son of Henry Ward Beecher, and his little son,

named for his illustrious grandfather, greatly interested Kate by his childish precocity.

Referring to a question of her correspondent's, she said : —

" If I did not write about the Yosemite, it was not from lack of appreciation. It is great, and I want to go back there. The big trees, too, impressed me tremendously."

Fortunately there has been preserved a pictorial reminiscence of that wonderful tour. A friend who was one of the party with Miss Field in the Yosemite thus describes the experience : —

. . . "As Kate Field and I rode side by side on our horses through the hushed silence of that awful grandeur, her soul seemed to commune with God."

This friend relates that after this trip was over and Miss Field had gone on to Victoria on her way to Alaska, she wrote to Kate, speaking earnestly of the unusual influence toward all that was noble and divine which she had received from this companionship in the Yosemite, to which Miss Field replied : —

" Thank you very much for your extremely kind words, which, I confess, surprised me, as I do not understand why I should produce such an influence upon any one. Nevertheless, I am glad I do you good, unworthy as I may be."

On her homeward journey from Alaska Miss Field stopped at Vancouver's Island, where she gave her monologue, " Eyes and Ears in London," to a British audience, who laughed heartily at the inimitable hits on London life, and she began to study the literature giving accounts of the coast Indians. She met and interviewed Judge Swan of Port Townsend, formerly of Boston, and a regular correspondent of the Smithsonian Institute. The monographs of Judge Swan which the Institute publishes are considered very valuable. From Victoria, under date of July 29, 1887, Miss Field writes to a friend: —

. . . "I lectured in Tacoma before a very cordial audience. Yesterday I came here, and give 'Dickens' tonight and Monologue to-morrow night. As the town, though twelve thousand souled, is only one-tenth Caucasian, the rest being natives, half-breeds, and Chinese, the outlook is a problem; but as I am here for investigation, it is not of vital importance. The theatre is the nicest I've seen since I left Salt Lake, and my pianist is a very clever young man who is English and studied in London with Shakespeare. Last night I visited Chinatown, and had an interesting experience. These Pig Tails are wonderful in many respects, and are a great study. They mean more in the civilization of the new world than we dream at present. Thousands are now going East, and the Chinese question will come before you as it never has before."

This prophetic forecast of Miss Field's has come true. Her insight into political conditions was singularly unerring. Again she writes: —

. . . "The smugglers of Port Townsend, enraged that Special Agent Beecher, who is in the Custom House, should be an honest man, have attacked him in the most shameful manner."

Later, from San Francisco, under date of Oct. 19, 1887, Kate writes: —

. . . "I've met a lovely woman here, — Mrs. Sarah B. Cooper, who is the President of the Kindergartens. She makes one believe in goodness and everything beautiful. She is a cousin of Robert G. Ingersoll."

Miss Field passed the winter of 1887–88 at that wonderfully beautiful resort, Coronado Beach, and in one letter she says: —

. . . "Coronado Beach is across the bay from San Diego and is well situated for view of ocean and mountain. The day is lovely, and as I look out upon mountain, sunshine, and the glitter of a placid sea, I wish you were here to enjoy its loveliness. An Eastern woman is playing Mendelssohn extremely well in the adjoining parlor. *Les extrèmes se touchent.* I know *you* would exclaim at the fine scenery, the delightful air, the glorious sun, delicious fruit, and the general *dolce far niente.* . . .

. . . .

"Mrs. Oliphant's ' Old Lady Mary ' has arrived, and what a pretty story it is ! Far ahead of 'Vestigia' in interest. Then the other two books have come, also 'Life,' also that sweet poem of yours, for which accept my grateful thanks. You 've lots of fancy and emotion. What you need to cultivate is your reason. When you can, read logic and study Geometry. Your life all runs one way. Go in for Montaigne and Bacon and hard-headed old brains like theirs.

. . . .

"Over and over again I wish you were here. It *is* so lovely and so lazy. I can't do anything — not even write a letter without an effort. The work I came here to do remains undone, and I am desperate in one sense while utterly indifferent in another. But it will soon come to an end, and I shall have my nose to a very sharp grindstone. Miss Willard's note has just arrived. . . .

. . . .

"Do you know where Alice and Phœbe Cary were born? Are they of Irish origin? I ask to oblige a *waiter* here, who is very fond of Alice's poetry and who would dearly like to know. You, who are up in all such things, can probably enlighten me."

. . . .

Xmas. 1886.

Dear ——;—

Why did you?
The pretty present with
its tender inscription,
has just come and my
eyes have filled with
tears in reading the
engraved lines— Ah,
my dear friend, the
Love that is true, for
which we all aspire
in some form or other
comes, perhaps, here-
after— But there can

be honest, helpful
friendship, genuine
affection in which is
no time-serving—and
let us thank God for
it, "hitching our wagon
to a star" meanwhile,
and hoping for every-
thing. You remember
Lowell's lines:

"Perhaps the longing
            to be so
Helps make the Soul
            immortal."

Regarding the reports of a lecture by Henry Irving, the actor (now Sir Henry), Miss Field commented: —

.   .   .   .

"The matter of his lecture is not new, always excepting the anecdote of Charlotte Cushman, which *is* new and good of its kind.   Mr. Irving has genius, — the genius of stage decoration and much beside.   He understands his age.   I saw him and Ellen Terry in ' Much Ado ' lately."

.   .   .   .

And again from Coronado on March 1, 1888, she writes: —

. . . " I 've been trying to catch up with the news in intervals of writing letters and being interviewed.   I 'm told that the *ideal* climate is found on the Sandwich Islands.

"Here 's something funny.   A journalist attached to your ' Inter-Ocean ' has just called for my autograph.   Looking over his book I found

'George Q. Cannon,
Salt Lake City,'
at the top of a page, written just ten years ago.   Opposite his name I 've written, 'Where is he now?'   You know he is hiding from justice.   Below I wrote 'Extremes meet,' and signed my name with date."

In reference to some remark of her correspondent's regarding Edgar Fawcett, the poet and novelist, Miss Field replied: —

"Edgar Fawcett is an unusual man, and I 'd like to know him.   How clever his letters are !   Where does he get the time to write them?   My scrawls are the veriest shreds and patches.

.   .   .   .

"I do not think of birthdays myself.   They mean nothing

if people don't grow, and if people grow they mean less. It's experience and discipline and illumination that count — not years or the lack of them.

. . . .

" I wish the word *unwomanly* meant as much the lack of moral courage as does the word *unmanly*. It ought.

. . . .

" Do see ' Held By The Enemy.' That is an *acting play*, hailed with delight in London as I knew it would be."

. . . .

In the summer of 1888 the State Viticultural Committee of California asked Miss Field to present, in lectures in Eastern cities, the claim of pure California wine as a table beverage, and to recommend its universal use as the only means of settling the much-mooted question of temperance reform in a satisfactory way. To President Wetmore of the State Board, Miss Field replied, acceding to the proposition. The undertaking was a mistake on her part. Her attitude and ideas were grossly maligned and misrepresented ; and the question as to whether light wines for table use would replace the present excess of tea and coffee ; and whether, if they did, their use would restrict rather than increase any desire for more harmful beverages, — is still an open question with perhaps no probabilities in its favor. The New York " Tribune " of July 17, 1889, said editorially :

" Miss Field believes with many thousands of sincere persons that the general introduction of pure native wines would promote practical temperance. She and those who agree with her may be utterly mistaken. A zealous effort to prove them in the wrong would be entirely commendable, whereas a campaign of personal defamation, though it may have driven her temporarily from the field, is not only a despicable, but in the long run an exceedingly disastrous, mode of warfare."

The Rev. Dr. Phillips Brooks in his "Fast-Day" sermon of that year expressed his serious doubts regarding the efficacy of prohibition. Miss Field's own view was thus given by herself: —

"No, I am not blind to the evil of drunkenness. It is terrible, both in itself and in the results. But my remedy is not that of the Prohibitionist. I believe that is only going to make matters worse. I do believe in temperance, not merely in drinking, but in eating and general living; and I tell you drunkenness is almost entirely unknown in the vineyard countries of the world where the wines are made. The poorest person has his bottle of wine with his frugal meal; it is harmless, it is inexpensive, it is pure."

Miss Field's attitude toward the entire matter was not unlike that of Phillips Brooks, who maintained that every individual soul must be educated to recognize its individual responsibilities and "be subject unto the higher powers."

Yet while it was a mistake for Miss Field to lend her influence even briefly — for she entirely withdrew from this within one year — to any such theory, still, misrepresentation, personal malignment, a distortion of facts, due either to mental failure to perceive intelligently, or to wilful blindness, are not calculated to impress the world as methods of either temperance or of Christianity. There is one great law of prohibition on which humanity will agree, and that is the divine prohibition which says, "Thou shalt not bear false witness against thy neighbor."

The error had, however, no permanent consequences, and the just and sympathetic recognition of her real motives, expressed by many representative Prohibitionists, was very grateful to her. Bishop Vincent, referring to one of her lectures before the Chautauqua Assembly, wrote her, saying: —

"Your visit to Chautauqua was a source of great delight to our people. Everybody was charmed."

The falling into errors of judgment and mistaken ideas is a part of the mortal pilgrimage; but the test of the noble soul is not to remain in these errors. The life on earth is a moral school, and to acquire constantly advancing ideals and be loyal to the best that is revealed is to achieve success.

The question was asked by Miss Field as to whether Rev. Dr. Edward Everett Hale was a Prohibitionist, and a friend of hers undertook to procure his views, which the distinguished divine thus expressed: —

My DEAR MISS ——, — For many years after I began housekeeping I had not a wineglass in my house. I do not know that there is one in the house now.

This will represent my feeling in the matter. I think it is necessary to drink wine sometimes; I am ordered to myself by my medical advisers. But I do not think it necessary to present it to one's guests as an elegance with every fascination that art, poetry, and literature can give it.

I do not offer sherry or champagne to my guests any more than I offer them quinine or paregoric. If they need either, I should hope they would ask me, and I should try to provide them as well as I could, but I should not make this a matter of elegant hospitality.

You may send this note to Miss Field.

Very truly yours,

EDWARD EVERETT HALE.

All these years from 1883–90 were a ceaseless round of travelling and lecturing. She studied and read and thought; she was in social contact with representative people all over the country; and her polished and many-sided culture added its charm to a woman singularly charming by natural gifts. She had fire, and force, and fervor; sense, sweetness, and sincerity, — finely balanced and held in equipoise. Too often the fateful dower of genius is neutralized by the fatal lack of common sense. Lombroso is not alone in his theories which so many facts support. Kate Field escaped this penalty that is so frequently imposed on exceptional organizations. She had tact as well as talent; and an extraordinary versatility, a power of adaptation, a facile adjustment of forces, lent energy of achievement to every plan and endeavor.

In all her intense activity in various and varied directions, Kate Field was always to one friend a prompt and a constant correspondent. These private letters were very rich in thought and expression. When "Robert Elsmere" first appeared, she was lecturing in the Far West, and as the friend sent her, at once, a copy of the much-talked of novel, she wrote:

"'Robert Elsmere' is all you claim for it. I am deeply moved by it, and am more indebted to you than you can think. What a study it is! How great, how earnest, how artistic! Nothing slighted, and the broad mind does the suffering as usual, and finds little sympathy at home. What a tragedy!"

During this decade of 1880–90 Miss Field had passed two summers in Europe, sojourning in London, Paris, and Switzerland; she had made three journeys to the Pacific coast, extending two of these

to Alaska, and she had travelled several times over
the region covering Boston, New York, Washington,
Chicago, Minneapolis, and Denver. Always on her
arrival in any city she was in a maze of social engagements, newspaper interviews, and turmoil in general.
Her returns to the East were the signal for press interviews again, and in one of these, in the New York
" Herald," she said in reply to a question : —

" I remained in Zion one month, and having been asked
to lecture there, and having been told by the Mormons
that my lecture concerning them was a tissue of falsehoods,
I delivered the tissue of falsehoods in the city of the
enemy, and had the satisfaction of having it universally in-
dorsed by the Gentiles and apostate Mormons, and being
treated with profound silence by the Mormons themselves.
It was all the proof I wanted that I had told the truth. It
was then that I was made a member of the Women's Relief
Corps of the Grand Army of the Republic, and presented
with a very beautiful gold and diamond badge by the loyal
citizens of Utah, — a memento which I assure you I treasure
profoundly."

During the seven years when she was making these
Western trips her private letters, as has already been
noted, were intensely interesting. The friend to whom
she wrote constantly sent to her the new books, newspaper clippings, reviews, and the general movement
of the East, and Kate's comments on all the literary
and social panorama would make a lively volume,
albeit one that could more appropriately be published
a century hence, according to Mark Twain's latest
idea. When Mr. Aldrich made the literary sensation
of the hour by publishing " A Brother of Dragons "
in the " Atlantic Monthly," and when, fast following,

came that curious creation, "The Quick and the
Dead," a copy was sent to Kate, who wrote in
response : —

"I've read 'The Quick and the Dead,' and I must confess that I do not like hysterics in any form, especially in
literature. I suppose there are indications of power in the
story, but what gasping, gurgling bosh the whole thing is !
And that's what half-educated people will call 'passion.'
Oh, dear ! What's the use of art and taste, when the public
will buy this counterfeit? One bookseller in San Francisco
sold three hundred copies of ' Quick, etc.,' in one week.

"'Why do people buy it?' I asked.

"'Because they think it is improper,' replied the clerk.

"From my point of view the impropriety consists in very
bad taste, bad art, and straining after effect."

Again, of meeting Mrs. Howe in California, she
writes : —

"I've just returned from lunching with Mrs. Howe at
her sister's (Mrs. Maillard) whose husband (*what* a sentence !) has a ranch eight miles away. Mrs. Maillard is a
lady and sweet, but she is not J. W. H. Mr. Maillard is a
handsome Frenchman, who came over here with Joseph
Bonaparte and shared the fortunes of the house. There
are two daughters, unmarried ; one especially is very interesting in her appearance. The Maillards have been rich.
. . . Mrs. Howe has been lecturing successfully, and is
greatly pleased with the coast."

Meeting Mr. Cushing, the ethnologist, she says : —

"Frank Cushing, whose health is much better than it was
a year ago, is again visiting San Francisco. He lunched
with me here lately and was delighted with the scenery. If
possible, he will come over again and we'll go in search of

Indian remains. How lucky he is to be backed by a woman like Mrs. Hemenway!"

Everywhere Miss Field found or made friends. She was the guest of honor at many a festive occasion gotten up for her, and she rode, and drove, and observed, and thought.

In reply to some playful allusion to Boston's musical status at the moment, she wrote: —

" I fail to see why a season of opera in the *bel lingua del si* should retard either musical taste or the advent of national opera. On the contrary, as the study of all literature and all schools of painting are necessary to the development of authors and painters, so the study of all schools of music is advantageous to musical students. . . .

" I had a fine ride several days ago, and think I 've found a decent saddle-horse. But I sha'n't remain here longer than I can help, as I want to see Monterey, where the Hotel Del Monte is said to be wonderfully fine. Then there is the great Lick Observatory to visit and lots of things to be done. Life is too short for one to accomplish anything."

All this large knowledge of the resources and the people of the country was the inspiration out of which she evolved her next undertaking, — that of founding a journal of her own and fixing her residence in the nation's Capital. She had so come into touch with the great West during these years that she was eager to discuss conditions, social, political, and economic, in a way that demanded an individual channel. Out of this longing she evolved the idea of her national review, — with whose appearance the next decade of her life was to open, — her journal, which was named " Kate Field's Washington."

KATE FIELD'S WASHINGTON

I cannot bear to think what life would be
With high hope shrunk to endurance, stunted aims,
A self sunk down to look with level eyes
On low achievements.
I accept the peril,
I choose to walk high with sublime dread
Rather than crawl in safety.

. . . .

GEORGE ELIOT.

An old French sentence says: "God works in moments," —
"En peu d'heure Dieu labeure." We ask for long life, but 't is
deep life or grand moments that signify. Let the measure of
time be spiritual, not mechanical. Life is unnecessarily long.
Moments of insight, of fine personal relation, a smile, a glance, —
what ample borrowers of eternity they are! Life culminates
and concentrates; and Homer said: "The gods ever give to
mortals their apportioned share of reason only on one day." —
EMERSON.

For who would lose,
Though full of pain, this intellectual being,
Those thoughts that wander through eternity.

MILTON.

CHAPTER VIII

If we shall stand still,
In fear our motion will be mocked or carped at,
We should take root here where we sit, or sit
State-statues only.

King Henry the Eighth.

Genius is not, generally speaking, unconscious of what it experiences or of what it is capable. It is not the suspended harp which sounds (as the statue of Memnon in the desert sounds in the sun), at the changing, unforeseen breath of wind that sweeps across its strings ; it is the conscious power of the soul of a man, rising from amidst his fellow-men, believing and calling himself a son of God, an apostle of eternal truth and beauty upon the earth, the privileged worshipper of an ideal as yet concealed from the majority; he is almost always sufficiently tormented by his contemporaries to need the consolation of this faith in himself, and this communion in spirit with the generations to come. — MAZZINI.

"KATE FIELD'S WASHINGTON." A UNIQUE ENTERPRISE. MISS GILDER'S FRIENDSHIP. CHARMING LIFE IN THE CAPITAL. THE COLUMBIAN EXPOSITION. FRANCE CONFERS THE " PALMS OF THE ACADEMY " ON MISS FIELD.

DURING this most significant decade of 1880-90, Miss Field had laid the foundations, unconsciously to herself at the time, of an unique enterprise, — that of her weekly review, called " Kate Field's Washington," whose initial number was issued on Jan. 1, 1890. Consulting with friends from the coast of the blue Atlantic to the sunset shore of the Pacific, she met warm encouragement and sustaining sympathy. Subscriptions set in almost on the first intimation of the idea. The prospectus was richly freighted with advertising, and a writer who had gained an even larger practical experience in

the world than had Kate Field might well have believed that the conditions were most favorable for a
financial as well as for a literary success. There had
been nothing in Kate's entire life which had so concentrated her interest, and stimulated every gift and
grace of her nature, as this enterprise of founding
and conducting a national review of her own. She
thought of it by day and dreamed of it by night. One
reason lay in the fact that, to a very unusual degree, Kate Field lived and moved and had her being
in the current of events; she was intensely interested
in her own time. With Mrs. Browning she could
have said : —

> " I do distrust the poet who discerns
>   No character or glory in his times,
>   And trundles back his soul five hundred years,
>   Past moat and drawbridge, into a castle-court."

In addition to this profound sympathy with contemporary progress, Miss Field had in her nature a
dominant vein of leadership. This was instinctive;
and while it never degenerated into arrogance or mere
self-assertion; while it was of too noble and aspiring
a trend to work on the lower planes, — it was yet
so essentially an element in her temperament as to
color and control her life. Always she revealed this
strong affirmative force.

It was natural that, with her profound interest in
political matters, Miss Field should be strongly attracted to Washington as a residence. Its brilliant
and varied social life appealed to her in its cosmopolitan quality, and the absence of trade and traffic
offered an equally strong inducement to her to there
set up her household gods. Of all Miss Field's
friends the one who perhaps entered most intimately

Sincerely your friend,
Kate Field.

into her counsel at this time was Miss Jeannette L. Gilder, the accomplished editor of "The Critic," who some years before had gone through the same distinctive experience of founding a weekly journal. Miss Gilder, as is well known, is the sister of the poet-editor of the "Century Magazine," and although some years the junior of Miss Field, they had been warm friends since Miss Gilder's earliest girlhood, when Kate had been very helpful to her in securing a connection with a leading New York daily, and suggesting a certain dramatic treatment of literary criticism which Miss Gilder evolved to a high degree of brilliancy. In the latter-day life of letters in America, Jeannette Gilder has made herself a prominent and honorable figure; and on her literary judgment and warm personal friendship Miss Field greatly relied. The little scene of the first creation of " Kate Field's Washington," as a castle in the air, so to speak, was dramatized by Miss Field in an humorous paragraph, with the scene laid in the Victoria Hotel in New York, and Miss Gilder and herself discovered. As the conversation of these two leading characters progressed, Miss Gilder seems to have been responsible for the title of Miss Field's review.

" In spite of love-sick Juliet there's a deal in a good name," exclaimed Miss Gilder. " Call it ' Kate Field's Weekly.' You must use your own name," she continued ; " it is your trade-mark."

Accordingly this title was decided upon, save that the *Weekly* was changed to *Washington*. Colonel Crocker of San Francisco and the brilliant Colonel Henry Watterson came on the scene. Both approved the idea, and Miss Field became convinced *les beaux esprits se rencontrent*. The impelling force in this ven-

ture was well defined by the Springfield " Republican "
in the remark that " Kate Field's vehement individuality wants an outlet, and nothing else will serve so
well." The initial number, bearing date of Jan. 1,
1890, offered to its readers Miss Field's " Credo "
embodied as follows : —

" I believe in Washington as the hub of a great nation.

" I believe that the capital of a republic of sixty millions
of human beings is the locality for a review knowing no
sectional prejudices and loving truth better than party.

" I believe that ' men and women are eternally equal and
eternally different ; ' hence I believe there is a fair field in
Washington for a national weekly edited by a woman.

" I believe in home industries ; in a reduced tariff ; in
civil-service reform ; in extending our commerce ; in
American shipping ; in strengthening our army and navy ;
in temperance which does not mean enforcing total absti-
nence on one's neighbor ; in personal liberty.

" I believe in literature, art, science, music, and the
drama, as handmaids of civilization.

" I believe society should be the best expression of
humanity.

" I believe in a religion of deeds.

A more extraordinary way of establishing a journal could hardly be devised. It was Kate Fieldian
throughout.

This journal started on a fairly good financial basis,
a part of the stock being taken by eminent financiers.
Miss Field secured an accomplished journalist, Mr.
Francis Leupp, a correspondent of the New York
"Evening Post," as her managing editor, and two very
able and accomplished young women, graduates of
Vassar, — Miss Leonard and Miss Lingle, — made up
the staff. An office in the Corcoran Building was taken,

and Miss Field located herself in a suite in Washington's most fashionable hotel, the Shoreham, where from her windows she looked out on Washington's monument and the blue waters of the Potomac.

"Fancy the thermometer at 70°," she wrote to a friend one February day. "Who wants to go further South? How I wish you were here to see how beautiful the Washington Monument is against the blue sky!

"I shall be happy to meet Madame Helen Hope-kirk or any other friend of yours. You need never ask in advance. I'm at her service, and will do all I can for her."

This January of 1890 found President Harrison in the White House, the Fifty-First Congress assembled, Chief Justice Fuller confirmed for the Supreme Bench, and Hon. Thomas B. Reed in the Speaker's chair. "No Speaker within the memory of the oldest inhabitant has done so much work in so little time," Miss Field remarked, editorially, of Speaker Reed. Besides political affairs Miss Field was deeply interested in the site of the Columbian Exposition, which was then a question of the hour, and she warmly advocated Washington, on its claims as the Nation's Capital. Regarding one suggestion made by Miss Field, the Chicago "Inter-Ocean" commented: —

"That is a brilliant idea of Miss Kate Field, expressed in her 'Washington' this week, — of a comic opera founded on a return of Columbus to Chicago in 1893, to observe the customs and manners of the country he discovered. Miss Field is given to having brilliant ideas by nature and grace, but this is an especially felicitous one. Where is the American Gilbert and Sullivan to write the opera?"

The initial number of the " Washington " contained a Christmas comedietta called " Plato and Cupid," written by Miss Field, who had been for many years a member of the Dramatic Authors Society of England. In the literary world realism was holding its triumphant — if transient — sway; the drama was endeavoring to persuade itself and the public that Ibsen was the predestined star of the stage; the self-revelations of Marie Bashkirtseff were being discussed with a fervency worthy a more important theme, and the theosophical movement was making rapid progress as a subject of intelligent consideration by the press and the people. Always hospitable to every new illumination thrown on the problem of life, Miss Field secured from Mr. W. Q. Judge — afterward the President of the Theosophical Society in America — a series of articles entitled " Echoes from the Orient," setting forth this philosophy over the signature of " Occultus." The State of Washington — then newly admitted to the Union — engaged Miss Field's interest also; and an interview with Senator Squire, conducted, as was humorously asserted, by " grape-vine telephone," thus opened : —

" Is this Senator Squire of Washington ? "

" Yes, both Squire and *Es*quire, ready to break a lance in behalf of KATE FIELD'S WASHINGTON, first, because the new weekly deserves success ; secondly, because —

> ' Namesakes ever should be friends,
> So the Spanish proverb tends.'

Pardon me for ' dropping into poetry,' like our old friend Wegg, but even politics can't kill all sentiment burning within the Senatorial breast."

" I'm delighted at your confession. One of the most

agreeable dinners I attended last year was seasoned by
poetry falling from the lips of Senator Edmunds as gracefully as falls the Bridal Veil in Yosemite Valley. But if you
really love poetry, why in the name of all that is fitting did
you not baptize your State Tacoma? There should be one
Washington and no more, — Washington, the Capital of the
Nation. Now, *you* are Washington, and *we* are Washington,
D. C. It is too bad. The way ignorant postmasters and
incompetent clerks are doomed to ' mix those babies up '
adds a new terror to our aggravating postal service."

" My dear friend, listen to reason. Tacoma is a beautiful name, beautifully derived, supposed by some to mean
' nourishing breast,' and, by Theodore Winthrop, to be
' applied to all snow peaks,' while better authority claims
that it merely signifies ' the mountain.' However, be that
as it may, we already have a fine town named Tacoma, the
second largest in the State, Seattle being first, and Spokane
Falls third."

The new journal took great interest in the South,
also, as well as in the great West, from its earliest
number, and Miss Field's earnest aim was that of true
and devoted service to national progress. By no
means averse to fame and fortune, it may yet be
seriously stated that Kate's first thought and supreme
aim was to serve genuinely the best interests of the
time. The scope of her paper included literature
and the drama, and a column headed " The Players "
was each week filled with matter pertaining to the
stage, a good proportion of this being of permanent
nature in dramatic literature. When her " Washington " was first started, Miss Field had asked her old
friend Edwin Booth to give the name to its dramatic
column, and he wrote: —

THE PLAYERS, 16 GRAMERCY PARK,
December 4, 1889.

MY DEAR MISS FIELD, — You'll hardly credit it, but I have really made two attempts since our little chat t' other evening to do something for " WASHINGTON," but in despair I retire to my tent. I have also endeavored to find a fitting motto for you, but in vain. If the column should be entitled " The Players," how would these do for headlines, in lieu of a motto?

" Hither are they come to offer you service.
Let them be well used.
The players cannot keep counsel : they 'll tell all."

I like your prospectus very much and think the " Players " column an excellent idea. I wish I could contribute something to it. " The Players " must subscribe for it. If they do not I will do so for my personal use.

You have my sincere wishes for immediate and lasting success. Very truly yours,

EDWIN BOOTH.

The keen comedian, William Florence, characteristically wrote : " Splendid manifesto ! Go in and win. Congratulations."

Robert Underwood Johnson, that charming poet, who is associated with Mr. Gilder in the editorship of the " Century," — a magazine whose quality proves that two poets may be the most successful of editors, — joined with Miss Field in consideration of the best care of the Yosemite. Miss Field had indeed a series of " causes " that she espoused in her " Washington," among which, besides free art and the international copyright, was the preservation of the Yosemite, in which she and Mr. Johnson seem to have entered into a conspiracy together. Two letters from Mr. Johnson run : —

Dear Miss Field, — Your Yosemite letter is *admirable* and will prove effective. I am circulating it. I enclose the " Times' " comment on it. With thanks for your article and your father's clever copyright verses,

Very sincerely yours,
Robert Underwood Johnson.

I 'll keep you informed of anything important in the Yosemite matter. Will you kindly do the same for me?

And again : —

Dear Miss Field, — It may be whistling before we are out of the woods, but I wish to congratulate you on the present state of the free art question, with a Heaven forfend that there should be any accident to the cause to which you have contributed time, labor, money, and enthusiasm to such a distinguished degree. You have borne the heat and burden of the day, and yours is the chief share in the victory. This is another proof that *with a good cause* all that is needed is to keep up the fight. Sooner or later our legislators must listen, and consider, and decide.

I hope you will keep pegging away at the Yosemite question. California next winter ought to recede the old grant of 1864, to be . . . in the Yosemite National Park, and thus rid herself of the disgrace and scandal of a perpetually mismanaged trust. The money-changers are in that Temple of Nature, and nothing but the lashing of an indignant public opinion will ever drive them out.

Always faithfully yours,
Robert Underwood Johnson.

All these various and varying matters enlisted Kate's earnest attention.

And now, while only five more years remained to her in this world, could the recorder of the story of her life regard this period as the entering on the last chapter ? By no means. Miss Field's power of con-

centrating events and experiences invested this brief
time with the significance that might have diffused
itself through half a century. She entered on the
conduct of her journal with all her energy of purpose.
It became, inevitably, the personal expression of her
own many-sided individuality. It made a distinct
impression on the public, — this keen, brilliant, and
inclusive commentary on life and affairs, — distinctly
individual and unique in all journalism.

Of the many cities in which Miss Field had lived
at various times, she was the most attached to Washington. To a friend who wrote to her regarding
Europe as the more congenial atmosphere for a literary worker she replied : —

"Don't think Europe the place for an American. It is
well to visit. It is no place for work. I think there 's
more material for art in this country than in all the Old
World combined. What European novel by an American
can touch 'The Scarlet Letter'? Study in the Old World if
you like, but work at home."

Miss Field held that Washington was destined to
be the social, literary, and artistic centre of this country, as well as the political. It is the only town, she
said, which is beautifully and systematically laid out;
whose streets are properly paved; where there are
breathing places throughout the town, — lungs, as it
were; where there is no commerce; where there is
a certain repose necessary for society; and where the
climate, if not absolutely perfect, is, on the whole,
better all the year round than anywhere else in the
United States. Of social life she held always, as we
have seen, a high ideal, fully sympathizing with
Emerson when he said: "There is the promise and

the preparation of a day when the air of the world shall be purified by nobler society; when the measure of greatness shall be usefulness in the highest sense, — greatness consisting in truth, reverence, and good will." Her interest in political progress could here be satisfied at the fountain head, and in Washington Miss Field had especial social prestige because her genius and culture and intellectual vigor were more appreciated by the significant society, *par excellence*, of the Capital than the same gifts could have been in a society of wealth and fashion alone. Apparently, again life stretched fair before her; but there was in her nature an unrest — divine or otherwise — that would never permit her to repose in a haven of peace. One of her first movements after finding herself and her new Review fairly settled, was to accept the invitation of a press excursion to cross the continent again, San Francisco being the objective point, the journey being made in a special train fitted up with every conceivable luxury. Although she had a stateroom to herself, the journey fatigued her more than usual; and on her return she came for a little time to the Hotel Brunswick in Boston, on a visit to her Aunt Corda, who passed the winter of 1889–90 at this house, so delightfully located in Copley Square, with Trinity Church, the Museum of Fine Arts, and the Public Library at its very doors; and both her aunt, and a friend to whom Kate was very dear, felt that she was in great need of rest and care. But no rest ever came. She continued to lecture, to travel, to write half the matter, or more, in every issue of her paper, and she was a prominent and always charming figure in the diplomatic and social life of dinners and receptions. She was living a half-dozen lives at once,

any one of which was enough to have absorbed all
her strength. Devoting, as she did, so much space
to Congressional proceedings, " Kate Field's Washington" was the object of no little interest on the
part of the political magnates of the country. In
literature she occasionally made an impression that,
in one instance at least, very nearly approached a sensation. This was at the time that Tolstoi's " Kreutzer
Sonata" appeared, when, in her Review for June 11,
1890, she wrote of it an editorial article that fairly
electrified a great number of readers. Both praise
and blame were freely expressed all through the
country. Mr. Howells commended Miss Field's
article, and said that both he and Mrs. Howells, when
reading the book, felt that Tolstoi did not represent his own views on marriage in the character of
Posdnicheff, but used the character to point out
great evils, and that they regarded it as one of the
most valuable works Tolstoi had ever written.

There remains now among Miss Field's manuscripts
a large package of letters from strangers and friends,
written to her expressing the most fervent admiration
of her comments on this literary firebrand. A practical result to her was a host of new subscribers.
" You are everlastingly right," wrote one well-known
littérateur; " from my point of view it is the strongest, the most searching article you have ever penned."
Another author wrote, saying: —

" I have waded through pages of reviews of the ' Kreutzer
Sonata,' and, absolutely, yours is the first rational or satisfactory word I 've seen on the subject. It is incredibly
delightful to find a woman not afraid to say a word in defence of love and the senses. As one is extremely sure of

being classified either as sentimentalist or sensualist, it argues a good deal of courage or a good deal of conviction to speak freely. The conviction is still better than the courage — to my mind."

Miss Field's expressions that attracted so much attention were these : —

" If it be a crime to tell the truth, of course Tolstoi should be suppressed. But is it ?

"Tolstoi's story is no less disagreeable than strong, written evidently as a sermon, not as a work of art. As a sermon it fulfils its mission, despite ravings permissible as emanating from a conscience-stricken wife-murderer. I cannot believe that Tolstoi would personally make the statement, ' Women know very well that the noblest and most poetic love depends, not on moral qualities, but on the physical intimacy, and also on the manner of doing the hair and the color and shape of the dress.' That moral qualities alone do not inspire the ' noblest and most poetic love ' is true enough. A personality must be sympathetic to be loved, but it is paying a poor compliment to the Creator to assume that physical attraction is necessarily gross, something to be despised. . . .

" To scoff at magnetic attraction is merely to write oneself down a vulgar being to whom the laws of life are a sealed book. . . .

"When a man or a woman's highest ideal ceases to be union, — a union based on love which is the consecration of passion, — the world will be in worse condition than it is to-day. . . .

" The greatest thing in all the world is a grand passion, and the man or woman capable of it is capable of the greatest heroism."

The editorial pages of this clever Review were trenchant, broad, and very hospitable to new ideas.

Like Mazzini, Kate Field believed in God and the people.

"The people make awful mistakes," she remarked to a friend, "as they did in the French Revolution; but look at the provocation the French had. It is the business of American patriots to anticipate evils sure to accrue if the problem of capital and labor is not solved with absolute justice to both. The fact is," Kate continued, "if everybody followed the golden rule there would be no trouble in this world; but up-to-date Christianity has failed to make Christians. Perhaps there may be a new dispensation with the dawn of the Twentieth Century."

Constantly, unremittingly, Kate wrote, lectured, and pleaded in all ways and at all times, for better conditions for humanity. Her vein of sarcasm was sometimes aroused, as when a New York man who aspired to be the Beau Brummel of his time produced a book on etiquette, and Miss Field thus held it up to ridicule: —

"Do you know the latest fashion in gentlemen? Apropos of good manners, Mr. —— has written a book that will enlighten two continents next autumn. Meanwhile, society is groping about with the aid of tallow candles — this is metaphor — and occasional hints dropped by this authority as to what constitutes a gentleman. Evidently Christianity is all wrong. Its Founder would certainly be cut were he to walk up Fifth Avenue — that is, if 'a very accomplished leader of the german,' quoted by Mr. ——, represents anybody but himself. This leader, who is 'one of our most fashionable men,' is said to have declared that he would cut his own grandmother on the street if she were shabbily dressed. We must get up a new kind of New Testament. Our old one is evidently out of date. No good Samaritan must offer anybody's grandmother a cup of water or a helping hand unless that grandmother be dressed 'according to Hoyle.' We shall next be graduating our bows according to dressmakers and tailors.

"'Here comes a Worth gown!' Off with your hats, down with your heads! So much for style!

"'Here's a last year's Knox!' A frigid nod of disapproval.

"How delightful a prospect!

.   .   .   .

"When a man cannot afford to speak or be spoken to by any one, there must be something dubious about him. To fear the criticism of his own 'friends,' if caught with inferiors in dress or position, shows the quality of the birds with whom he flocks. 'What makes you wear such a shocking bad hat?' asked a friend of a rich man visiting New York. 'Why not?' replied the millionaire. 'My friends know I can afford a better, and those who don't know me don't care.' That man is most truly a gentlemen who, well dressed himself, as should be every person of taste, has too good a heart to be more afraid of the criticism of friends than of his own conscience. Such a man of fashion as Mr. —— depicts is only fit for production in a so-called American comedy, — to be laughed at one moment and forgotten the next."

Miss Field's life touched the greatest variety of interests. Societies, conventions, and military posts recognized her work. The George Maxwell Post of the G. A. R., Utah, passed this resolution : —

Resolved : That we truly appreciate the fervent patriotism of Miss Kate Field of Washington, D. C., and that a vote of thanks of this Post is hereby extended to her, for her noble efforts in behalf of the old soldiers, their widows

and orphans; that the same be published in the Sait Lake
"Tribune," and a copy sent to Miss Field.

S. EWING, *Post Commander.*

Wherever she travelled, receptions were constantly
given to her by the most prominent people, and she
was probably more in personal touch with the significant forces of the day than any other woman of the
time, not even excepting the noble Frances Willard,
whose work was concentrated more entirely in one
especial line.

The following autumn found Miss Field lecturing
again; and while visiting her friends Governor and
Mrs. Campbell in Columbus, Ohio, she expressed
a desire to attend the Chapel services on Sunday.
Accordingly the Governor and his family accompanied her, and the prisoners, on learning that the
visitor was the distinguished lecturer, petitioned that
she should address them. Not to have responded to
any appeal for the unfortunate would not have been
possible to Kate Field. She at once consented, and
out of her repertoire chose her delightful lecture on
" Charles Dickens," prefacing it with some such
remarks as these: " Our chaplain this morning bade
us stop and think. I stopped and thought that under
similar circumstances I'd be where you are. I stopped
and thought that were I in your place I should not
like to be shut up in a cell all Sunday, and so I have
come to help you pass a pleasant hour with Charles
Dickens, your old friend."

The effect of the sincere and earnest sympathy on
the prisoners was very marked, and perhaps never
did Miss Field lecture to a more responsive audience.
In the lecture she recited Dickens's " Hymn to the

Wiltshire Laborers," to which her vibrant and exquisitely modulated voice lent new beauty.

On her return to Washington Miss Field sent sixteen hundred copies of her journal to the prisoners,
which were distributed by the Governor, who gratefully thanked her on their behalf.

Kate Field's religious feeling was always revealed
in such practical forms as this. Her religion was of
deeds, and her comparison of sentiment and action is
indicated in a private letter under date of April 16,
1892, when she wrote to a friend: —

. . . "Though Easter means no more to me than any
other time of year, I appreciate true religious fervor, and
I believe in love and affection day in and day out. Thank
you for the poem so full of noblest wishes. I try to do well
what comes to me : I try to consider those in trouble and
to forget myself as much as a grim fate will permit. If
peace comes I shall be thankful. It has not perched on
my banner as a rule. May the Easter mean sunshine to
you." . . .

Out of Kate's close study of political affairs in the
heart of the nation she wrote a notable editorial
article headed "America for Americans." In it she
discussed the immigration problem, and of this able
paper Rear-Admiral Jouett wrote to her: —

PERSONAL

1349 L STREET, WASHINGTON, D. C., March 30, 1891.

DEAR MISS FIELD, — I have read with deep satisfaction
and pleasure your article "America for Americans." It's
the one bold, fearless, and just article that I have read upon
the New Orleans tragedy. That article should voice the
entire American people ; it should be read at every Ameri-

can fireside, and upon all public occasions. I am glad that you have come to the rescue of the American Flag as well as the American people.

Your article has made me a subscriber to your loyal and valuable paper. May all America read that article understandingly and act upon it, is the hope and the prayer of,

Yours most respectfully,

JAMES E. JOUETT,

Rear-Admiral U. S. Navy.

Among the innumerable expressions of interest in her new work that Miss Field received, were these words in a letter from Mrs. Mary Mapes Dodge, the brilliant editor of "St. Nicholas," under date of Feb. 25, 1890 : —

"I wish 'Kate Field's Washington' and its editor success. Every number I have taken up, so far, has interested me. I am sure to find there something that I like to know, and that I cannot find in other papers.

"It has, too, a dual quality of earnestness and brilliancy that arrests attention, in some way suggesting that queer feeling one has in noting the identity of spelling and wide divergence of effect, in the words *Man's laughter* — so cheery and inspiring — and *Manslaughter* — depressing and dire ! "

"Kate Field's Washington" gave attention to a great number of widely diverging interests all over the country, — a fact largely due to the extensive personal acquaintance that Miss Field had acquired in her lecturing tour from 1869–71, as a young girl, and her later lecturing life from 1882–90. She had come into singularly close local and personal touch with

the people. In Minneapolis she had often been the
guest of Hon. and Mrs. Thomas F. Lowry, and had
met and known a great number of the citizens, and in
behalf of the Business Union in that City the following letter reached her: —

Miss Kate Field, Editor "Kate Field's Washington,"
    Washington, D. C.

Dear Madam, — At a final meeting of the Minneapolis
Harvest Festival Committee held this a. m. in the Masonic
Temple, it was the unanimous sense of the gentlemen present that a vote of thanks be extended to you for the kindly
interest you have shown in various ways, in the city of Minneapolis and the Harvest Festival.

The many words of praise which you have given expression to have endeared yourself to our citizens, so that you
will be kindly remembered and these words of ours will but
faintly express their appreciation of the same. Wishing
you the greatest success with your valuable magazine, and
expressing a hope that you may favor this city with another visit, when convenient, we are yours with very great
respect.

                          Geo. A. Brackett, *Chairman.*
                          F. H. Forbes, *Secretary.*

Thus, in her "Washington," she discussed educational and mining interests in Alaska; internal
improvements in California; the Hawaiian problem,
which then began to appear; labor interests, art facilities for the West, the desirability of a National
Conservatory of Music, and every important matter
of the day in thought and event.

In this spring of 1892, Miss Field added to her
distinctive work of having influenced better legislation for Utah the signal work of securing the removal

of the thirty per cent tax on paintings and statuary. This tax had proved to be disastrous in its results. Duties fell from $307,000 in '83 to $191,000 in '84, a decline of forty per cent, while general trade only fell seven per cent, and jewels advanced.

The sales of American artists decreased; the demands for American art lessened. The export of paintings amounted to $387,000 in '83, and fell to $176,000 in '84. Foreign nations remonstrated, as well they might, for in Italy, France, Germany, and Russia, art is free; while in all other countries, except Servia and those speaking Spanish, it is taxed only eight per cent.

Miss Field went before the Congressional Committee on Ways and Means on March 27, 1892, to plead for the abolition of the tax. In part her argument was : —

" Keeping out foreign art decreases popular interest in art, deprives home artists of inspiration, and renders their work less valuable and less profitable. To claim that this tax falls solely on the rich is to ignore artists, who are, as a class, poor. It is to forget the people who are dependent upon public sales, exhibitions, and museums for their knowledge of the beautiful, whereby they become better educated and consequently make better citizens. Not only this, but it is to forget all artisans who are prevented from attaining a high standard of work in many industries.

" Not the least objectionable feature of this outrageous tariff is the resentment it inspires in foreign artists, and the difficult position in which our own art students abroad are thereby placed."

Twelve hours after her return from the Capitol she received this note : —

HOUSE OF REPRESENTATIVES, WASHINGTON.

DEAR MISS FIELD, — Governor Gear and myself were authorized to inform you that, after your eloquent plea, the committee unanimously voted to place art on the *free list.* The Governor wishes to join with me in congratulations.

Yours truly,

SERENO E. PAYNE.

The McKinley bill then passed the House without a moment's discussion about this art clause, although the Senate restored the entire tax, but finally compromised on fifteen per cent. This success incited Miss Field to endeavor to found a National Art Association; and in May of that spring, an Art Congress, due to her own efforts, convened in Washington, and a loan exhibition of pictures was given in the Chapel of the Smithsonian Institution from May 18 to 27 inclusive, representing such artists as John S. Sargent, Abbey, Boughton, Cecilia Beaux, George Fuller, Edward Simmons, Vedder, St. Gaudens, McMonnies, Picknell, Bierstadt, Hunt, and Inness.

Mr. Edmund Clarence Stedman wrote to Miss Field under date of May 26, 1892 : —

"If 'Kate Field's Washington' were not (as it is) the brightest weekly that comes to us, your success in reducing the art duties would have been its sufficient excuse for being.

"I say success, because such revolutions don't go backward. Your next campaign against the tariff on foreign paintings will 'reform it altogether.'

"A next winter's Art Congress seems to me one of your own specific, inventive ideas. Yes, and I should add, inclusive. Perhaps it is just as well that a Government 'Commission of Art and Architecture' should have been deferred until now. We used to deprecate the ramshackle structure of our buildings. Now we see that it was as well that they were made so that they could readily be pulled down when we should learn how to combine architectural strength and beauty. I think that a Government Commission now would include architects, sculptors, painters, etc., upon whose judgments we could rest secure.

" Our governmental theory is not paternal. But the influence of those high in its administration is unquestionable. The open support given to our copyright movement by the President and Mrs. Cleveland was the omen of its speedy triumph. The White House now can do much for American art. A National Loan Exhibition will do even more, as the conspicuous preamble to the Art Exposition of '93. Go on, and open the eyes of our people to the fidelity and beauty of our native landscape school; to the fact that such a school exists, that we have painters of our skies and woods and waters as faithful and luminous as those whose canvases reach us (and still teach us) from abroad. Do justice, too, to our brilliant rising school of portraiture. Again, what foreign artists equal ours in drawing, on the wood or otherwise, for illustration? Where are architects of town façades and of country houses more ingenious and tasteful, at this moment, than in these States both east and west?"

Rev. Dr. Phillips Brooks wrote thus : —

BOSTON, 232 CLARENDON STREET, May 17, 1892.

MY DEAR MISS FIELD, — I am in the heartiest sympathy with the purposes of your National Art Association, and I wish sincerely that it were possible for me to be present at its meeting, which occurs to-day. I am sorry that I cannot do so.

I am sorry, also, that I have not been able to send you before this the assurance of my cordial sympathy and my sincere hope for the best success of your efforts in the good work which you have in hand. Pray believe me, Yours sincerely,

PHILLIPS BROOKS.

The distinguished Catholic prelate, His Eminence, Cardinal Gibbons, wrote: —

MY DEAR MADAM, — In reply to your favor I beg to say that I am in favor of free art, which you are so earnestly espousing, or at least of a great reduction of the tariff.

It is only by bringing foreign works of art into competition with our own that we fully recognize our shortcomings and that we are aroused to emulation.

I am willing to join the association. I regret that my engagements will not permit me to attend your convention on Tuesday.

Faithfully yours,

JAMES, CARDINAL GIBBONS.

Desiring to enlist the interest of Dr. Depew, Kate wrote to him of the proposed art association, to which he replied: —

NEW YORK, Feb. 1, 1892.

DEAR MISS FIELD, — Thanks for the very unique and artistic water jar which came to me from you this morning. It has been the wonder and admiration of all the antiquaries in this neighborhood.

I shall be very happy to see you any morning you may have the leisure to call at my office between ten and eleven o'clock.   Yours very truly,

CHAUNCEY M. DEPEW.

MISS KATE FIELD.

Mr. Eastman Johnson wrote: —

DEAR MISS FIELD, — I have delayed acknowledging your note till I could see some one of the Library Committee of the Century Club, which I have been unable to do until to-night, when I straightened out the matter of having your paper on our tables.

I had the good luck to see Stedman to-night as he was going to the Committee meeting, and told him what must be done. He said, " Certainly; by all means. I take it myself and send it to others. It shall be done." I saw him after the meeting and he said it *had* been done. So we shall now sell your paper, and Stedman is your friend, and whoever is his friend is not without a blessing.

Thanks for your words about Cleveland, or the portrait. It will go to Washington in a few days.

Very truly yours,
EASTMAN JOHNSON.

I cannot lay my hands on your note, but this will reach you.   E. J.

Mrs. Harrison was "the first lady of the land" at this time, and she entered sympathetically into the interests of the Congress, and would have given a reception for artists the previous year but for the reasons explained in this note from Private Secretary Halford to Miss Field : —

EXECUTIVE MANSION, WASHINGTON, Feb. 7, 1891.

MISS KATE FIELD,
  "THE SHOREHAM."

MY DEAR MISS FIELD, — I have tried for two or three days to see you, but Providence and Kate Field have interfered. I want to talk with you about the proposed reception and the necessary effect which the death of Secretary Windom would have upon it. Of course, it would not be possible to hold it this month under the circumstances, and that would drive it altogether too late to be of any value in view of the adjournment of Congress. I have talked over the matter with Mrs. Harrison, and it seems to me, and to her as well, that the best thing to do would be to arrange that it should be the first event of next season, immediately after the assembling of Congress, when the season will be young and vigorous, and the proposed conference and reception can be made the success that I know is in your heart and mind to have it.

Very truly yours,

E. W. HALFORD, *Private Secretary*.

Numbers of letters bearing the address " Executive Mansion " from the private secretaries of both President Harrison and President Cleveland, and occasional autograph notes from some member of the President's family, are among Miss Field's voluminous correspondence.

Two letters from George William Curtis are as follows : —

WEST NEW BRIGHTON,
STATEN ISLAND, N. J., Feb. 23, 1890.

MY DEAR MISS FIELD, — I am very much obliged to you for your note and for the copies of your paper. I am too good a newspaper man, however, not to have seen them already and to have admired the energy and courage and journalistic instinct which they display, and also to wish your " Washington " and you success. But I am so constantly interviewing myself in the form of editorial articles upon the subjects that you mention and all others of current public interest, that I am very much disinclined to warm them over in formal interviews. So you will understand that while I am fully conscious of the honor that you propose to me, I must put the crown aside. With the sincerest thanks and good wishes, I am,

Very truly yours,

GEORGE WILLIAM CURTIS.

Again Mr. Curtis writes : —

WEST NEW BRIGHTON,
STATEN ISLAND, N. Y., May 13, 1892.

DEAR MISS FIELD, — He must be an eccentric American who could decline to join an association which asks no fees and requires only firm faith in free art. Upon that basis I accept gladly your invitation to become a member, feeling myself to be thoroughly qualified. Many provisions of the tariff may be wrong and unjust, but the tax on foreign works of art is chiefly grotesque. A prohibitory tariff upon the works of Raphael and Giorgione would not produce Raphaels and Giorgiones, and its effect would be not to compel us to buy American pictures, but to deprive American artists and lovers of art of the inestimable advantage of familiarity with great works. The New York " Tribune " is a protection journal, but as a protectionist it very properly opposes the duty on works of art, because the genius that can produce such work will not be fostered by such exclusion. When artists themselves, for whose benefit the duty is said to be laid, and the great body of intelligent citizens, whether advocates of protection or of revenue duties, unite to demand the free entry of works of art, the member of Congress who hesitates challenges us to take candles, with Charles Lamb, to examine his bumps.

Very truly yours,
GEORGE WILLIAM CURTIS.

Miss Sarah Freeman Clarke, a sister of James Freeman Clarke, also reveals her interest in another cause which had awakened Miss Field's energies :

MY DEAR KATE FIELD, — I rejoice in your vigorous efforts in behalf of civilization and against barbarism in trying to avert the destruction of the beautiful architecture of Jackson Park.

> " For out of thought's interior sphere
> These wonders rose to upper air."

As Emerson says of the Parthenon and Pyramids, and though we cannot hope to continue the quotation and say with him,

> " And nature kindly gave them places,
> Adopted them into her races,
> And granted them an equal date
> With Andes and with Ararat,"

yet to see them destroyed within a year of their completion is too monstrous an outrage to be silently endured. The Parks belong to the people of Chicago, will they not try to protect their own interest by ordering their commissioners, their servants, to release the other party of their share in the insane contract by which desolation will be restored and beauty and value destroyed, a contract worthy of savages? I am but one unit of the millions who have not seen these wonders of the nineteenth century's end. If you succeed in your righteous efforts, next year will see a stream of pilgrims flowing through Chicago, enriching it with money, embellishing it with praise, and this will continue as long as the buildings last; and that you may succeed is the earnest wish of your friend,

SARAH FREEMAN CLARKE.

November 25, 1893.

When Miss Field championed the cause of international copyright, her work brought her a shower of interesting letters of which the following are typical: —

DEAR MISS FIELD, — I have nothing to add to my recorded opinion of the dishonesty of stealing the products of the labor of the soft-handed sons of toil. I cannot see that a callus on the palm confers any better claim to fair treatment than a furrow in the forehead and an aching in the brain.

Very truly yours,

OLIVER WENDELL HOLMES.

BOSTON, May 15, 1890.

Mr. Lowell wrote : —

DEAR MISS FIELD, — I have had too long an experience of the providential thickness of the human skull, as well as of the eventual success of all reasonable reforms, to be discouraged by the temporary defeat of any measure which I believe to be sound. I say "providential" because the world is thereby saved many a rash experiment in specious legislation. Were it otherwise, the Huon's horn of inconsiderate enthusiasm would lead us a pretty dance among the briars. Unfortunately there is, as usual, an exception to this general rule, for the sutures of the political cranium are so loosely knit as to leave a crevice through which considerations of ephemeral expediency find too easy entrance. Such considerations, it should always be remembered, are most liable to disastrous recoil.

I grant that our hope has been long drawn out, but since material for it (as for every hope that has a moral care) has been constantly supplied, it has never become too attenuated to bear the strain put upon it.

J. R. LOWELL.

CAMBRIDGE, MASS., May 15, 1890.

When the good and great Mrs. Hemenway died, the Boston philanthropist, Mr. Frank Cushing of Zuni fame thus wrote to Miss Field in reference to her tribute to Mrs. Hemenway : —

God bless you, my dear Miss Kate Field, for saying that beautiful word about Mrs. Hemenway in connection with your "Personal" relative to myself. You deserve every good for your good, and in one way or another you will get it, as surely as you shall have my gratitude and gladness of friendship.   Ever truly,

FRANK CUSHING.

When the African explorer, Mr. Stanley, came to America with his laurels still green, Rev. Dr. Huntington of Grace Church, New York, thus referred to him in a letter to Miss Field: —

MY DEAR MISS FIELD, — I am bidden to dine with the African Lion Stanley, a professional feed which I must attend to, so shall not be able to reach Hotel Chatham so early as I was hoping for your good company to the concert — if they don't rain. I breakfasted this morning with Colonel M. C. Kaye, whereby his pretty French wife began asking me if I knew who was Miss Kate Field? She has been reading your letters from . . . diligently and admiringly. She speaks pretty English, not broken, but chopped a little, that it is a pleasure to listen. The Colonel wanted to make your acquaintance, but I told him it was too late, by reason of your immediate departure. Barker (Dr.) will be at Brunswick Hotel, Jermyn Street, London, after next Wednesday.

IS THIS PLAIN NOW?

Very truly yours,

W. H. HUNTINGTON.

And it looks like poetry for all the world.

Senator and Mrs. William Chandler of New Hampshire were among the nearer friends of Miss Field, who greatly appreciated them. Mrs. Chandler (the daughter of Senator Hale) is one of the notable women of the age, and her keen intellect and fine culture have always given to her a distinctive place in Washington's diplomatic life. Mr. and Mrs. Charles

M. Ffoulke, Senator and Mrs. Brice, Mrs. Hearst, Chief Justice and Mrs. Fuller, and Prof. Charles Warren Stoddard were also among her most prized friends in Washington. A playful note from Professor Stoddard thus runs : —

> THE CATHOLIC UNIVERSITY OF AMERICA,
> WASHINGTON, D. C., May 12, 1891.
>
> MY "BONNIE KATE," — Did you and your clever friend get home in safety? I hope to heaven you did, for I enjoyed the visit beyond expression, and I hate to think you ran a risk in making me so *Happy*.
>
> I am reading your "Ten Days in Spain." Oh, it is delicious beyond expression. Addio, in haste.
>
> Thine evermore,   C. W. S.

This intense and many-sided life wore on Miss Field to a degree that, in the spring of 1893, began to be very perceptible. Her energy was indomitable, and she cultivated cheerfulness to the degree of assuming that virtue, whether she had it or not; but there were undercurrents of depression only revealed, and even then very seldom revealed, to those nearest to her. In one letter to a friend who was watching her unceasing work with solicitude that would sometimes express itself, she wrote : —

> " If impulse could produce letters, you would have received an Easter Greeting at date ; but I'm so tired. It was sweet of you to send me that beautiful souvenir of two good men, — James Freeman Clarke and Phillips Brooks, — sweetest of all to know that you think of me, as the lines in the poem attest. I have no offering in return but the best wishes of my heart for you here and beyond. I wish I were spiritual. I wish I knew what all this struggle means. I am groping in the dark, and I often wish it were all over. . . . *Pax vobiscum.*"

The Columbian Exposition of 1893 enlisted Miss Field's enthusiasm, and gave to her a summer of special interest. While she had first hoped that Washington would be chosen for its site, she recognized the greater advantages of Chicago, with its beautiful lake and vast resources; and from its opening in May until after its close in November she remained in that city at the Lexington Hotel on Michigan Boulevard, and she made herself a factor in its progress in a valuable way that won cosmopolitan recognition. For a year before its opening she was working to forward its interests, and her journal was somewhat relied upon by the women officials, as the following note from Mrs. Potter Palmer indicates: —

OFFICE OF THE PRESIDENT,
BOARD OF LADY MANAGERS,
WORLD'S COLUMBIAN EXPOSITION,
CHICAGO, ILL., March 18, 1892.

MY DEAR MISS FIELD, — Your note of March 13 is received, and I am greatly obliged for the accompanying clipping from "Kate Field's Washington."

I have read your kind words with much interest, and feel that your efforts in our behalf will be productive of the best results.

With renewed thanks for your courtesy, and regret that I did not have the pleasure of meeting you while in Washington, I am,

Most cordially yours,
BERTHA M. H. PALMER, *Pres. B. L. M.*
MISS KATE FIELD, Washington, D. C.

Reading an open letter which Miss Field wrote to the Directors of the Columbian Exposition, an eminent member of the Board wrote to her, under date of July, 1893, "Your ideas are good and to the point,

32

and we shall profit by them." Maintaining all through the Exposition a syndicate weekly press correspondence, she also edited her own paper, wrote dozens of special articles on art, inventions, education, and affairs, and seldom missed a day or evening from the White City, in whose beauty she revelled. In her press letters she urged upon railroad officials the policy of reduced rates for the people; she urged upon the people to come to the Exposition. " It is a sin against humanity," she said, " that twenty trains a day are not carrying twenty thousand on each train to Jackson Park."

Again she wrote: —

" The more I see of the Dream City that has been wrought out of brain, and muscle, and iron, and wood; and that wonderful staff, which, so far as concerns the Exposition, may truly be called the staff of life, the more I want it made possible for every man, woman, and child in the United States to come and praise God for the divine revelations of Jackson Park.

" Never before has the divinity of man been so powerfully demonstrated, and from my point of view it is the solemn duty of every one whose eyes have seen this glory of the coming of the Lord to labor unceasingly toward bringing our people within reach of the beneficent spectacle."

Miss Field's criticism of the noble music given under the never-to-be-forgotten organization of Theodore Thomas was a notable contribution to the literature of musical art.

Everywhere was her presence welcomed. She was in demand for the Ethnological Building, in whose exhibition she took such intelligent interest; in the Electrical; in the representative buildings of the various States; and her perfect command of the French and Italian languages made her an especially sought guest among foreign visitors. The beautiful language of Spain always appealed to her, and she spoke a little Spanish and read it still better; while in Spanish music she was an accomplished performer.

One evening, whose poetic charm must always linger in the memory of all who were present, was when a group of friends met in Cairo, — not on the Nile, but in the Midway Plaisance, — where they were bestowed in a seventeenth-century house, beautiful beyond words in its antique decoration, its huge divans, latticed window coverings, and Oriental decoration in every way. Miss Field consented to read to the merry group one of her recent editorial papers in "Kate Field's Washington," called "A Door in Cairo," telling a story full of charm and interest. The scene of the reading was one to record itself in memory. The company were in an interior of old Egyptian architecture. The decorations and furnishing were all in the rich Oriental style. The subdued brilliancy of the lights shone down on the *fin du siècle* journalists sitting on divans on the floor, in window seats, or otherwise informally bestowed. In the latticed window, where a few were sitting, a panel was open, and the silver radiance of the full moon sailing through a cloudless blue sky shone in. Under the casement a group of Arabs and Egyptians were singing strange songs. A side-light fell on the graceful figure of Kate Field, revealing her pretty hands as she held her paper, and every one listened intently to the fascinating sketch that she read. From a seat in the latticed window where a troubadour might have played the lute, one or two of the group watched the romantic scene. Madame Korany of Syria — impulsive, impassioned, and fascinating, speaking English almost like a native, strong and swift in her likes and dislikes — sat near. And at midnight the party sauntered homeward through the half-deserted Plaisance, with the strange mixture of foreign races, — with its strains of music and snatches of song, — on, on, away from the enchanting White City, lying under the white radiance of a full moon, to the prosaic steam-cars, which whirled them back to Chicago in eighteen minutes, the journey being on the shore of the lake, rippling and dancing under the flood of magic moonlight. And so the days and nights ran on, — those enchanted Chicago days of the Exposition.

One special achievement of Miss Field's during this summer was the organizing of a Labor Bureau that was of some practical assistance to laboring men.

Lady Dilke of London (whom the readers of this Record will recall as one of Miss Field's early friends, under the name of Mrs. Mark Pattison) sent a paper to the Labor Congress on the working women of England, with the request that Miss Field should read it. At this assembly Kate met several of the well-known leaders of the Labor movement, and they invited her to address them at another meeting soon to be called. She did so, and, growing more intimately and intelligently in sympathy with the true interests of the working man, she originated the plan of Labor Bureaus, and editorially she said : —

"If I had a $1,000,000 to give away I would found a Labor Bureau with branches in a dozen or more populous towns. I would bid men and women in search of work to apply to the bureau. When my experiment became a solid success, I would appeal to rich men and women to spread the blessed gospel of help. This is the way to arrest congestion of labor in crowded centres. There's work enough for everybody, if properly distributed. It is a crime that a national bureau such as I suggest does not now exist. There is a Labor Commissioner at Washington who gathers statistics, but for any relief of misery and a glutted market he might as well not be born. What we need is Labor in the Cabinet and such a series of national bureaus as I have indicated. Then the brotherhood of man would cease to be a dream."

Of this scheme Dr. Chauncey Depew said, "It is feasible," although he urged the substitution of private beneficence for national legislation; and in explanation of his idea Dr. Depew said : —

"I will tell you what would be possible and a practical work of the highest beneficence. Millions are constantly being donated for hospitals and educational institutions. One takes care of the wounded and the other recruits the ranks already crowded. If some philanthropist would concentrate his capital upon a labor bureau whose purpose should be to find employment, it could perform incalculable service."

To which Miss Field replied : —

"I fail to see why a Congress that is equal to regulating the army, navy, foreign affairs, the treasury, and agriculture should not concern itself with the welfare of the masses upon whom depends the very existence of the republic. There should be no more difficulty in establishing a cordon of labor bureaus than in establishing custom-houses and post-offices, — in fact, not nearly as much. Look at the beneficence of the Signal Service Bureau ! Look at the daily reports of the markets ! Are conditions of the weather, of hog and hominy, and of wheat and whisky more important to the human race than the industrial condition of men, women, and children?"

Regarding some form of relief for labor, Kate Field was deeply concerned. "What sort of civilization have we," she exclaimed, "that so sports with flesh and blood? Where is the evidence of a practical Christianity in this wicked disregard of human necessities? Where is that love of one's neighbor which is the watchword of Christ? Can nothing be done to make such misery impossible?"

One of the many unique features of that Exposition summer was the mass meeting in three sessions, morning, afternoon, and evening, called by Mr. Stead one Sunday in Central Music Hall. Miss Field attended each meeting, responded to an invitation to speak in the evening, and of it, and the unique personality of Mr. Stead, she wrote: —

"Mr. Stead has a strong individuality. There are no two ways about that. He is every inch himself. His talk, walk, manner, actions, are *sui generis*. His voice is agreeable in tone, sufficiently powerful to be heard in large halls, his enunciation is distinct, and he gives the impression of earnestness. He is accused of aiming at sensationalism. Whether this criticism is just or false, I don't know. This I do know, — that sensation moves humanity, and until it is created there can be no progress in any direction. If sensationalism be Mr. Stead's way of attracting public attention to great evils, Mr. Stead is so far wise in his generation. I *do* know that this unique Englishman lacks tact, grace, and many qualities needed in an ideal Chairman ; but I also know that he ' got there ' last Sunday.

" Deeply interested in Mr. Stead's address in the afternoon because of its sympathy with our struggling masses, I
went again to Central Music Hall Sunday night to learn what
would be proposed to better their condition. So densely
packed was the auditorium as to force me to seek refuge
on the platform, where I otherwise should not have been.
Thus it is that accident makes us actors in many an unexpected drama. At this second meeting Mr. Stead was his
own Chairman. He was not satisfied with the Chairman
of the afternoon, knew best what he wanted, and proposed
to attain his purpose. We all like courage.

" The very audacity of Mr. Stead commanded admiration.
He did his own praying, delivered his own benediction,
did his own thinking, quickly shut off speakers who rambled,
and snubbed those who introduced dynamite, religion, and
politics. He rambled himself, was at times inconsequent
and intolerant, displayed weak spots in his armor, but he
accomplished something before the night was over. A
great audience sat eagerly from 7.30 until 11 o'clock listening, for the most part with approbation, to remarks
from the Chairman and various speakers. That audience
did not go home until it was resolved with only three dis-
senting voices that the formation of a civic federation for
public welfare was eminently feasible, and that a committee
named then and there should meet to appoint a committee
of twenty-one to begin work.

" Call Mr. Stead what you please, he has planted good
seed. Let the proposed civic federation take root in the
Western metropolis, and I prophesy that its branches will
extend throughout the republic to the glory of Christ and
the redemption of humanity. There is nothing Utopian
about it. If after professing Christianity for eighteen hundred years, earnest men and women of different trades
and professions cannot unite on the broad platform of the
golden rule and set to work cleaning out such an Augean

stable as Hercules never conceived, the ' heathen' left over from the parliament of religions can truthfully say that the pretended followers of Jesus have not yet learned the alphabet of their professed faith."

During this summer Miss Field became fully convinced of the necessity for the political enfranchisement of women, and the formal " laying on of hands," so to speak, adopting her into the woman suffrage ranks, came in this letter from Mrs. Lucy Stone: —

MY DEAR MISS FIELD, — I want to congratulate you and the suffrage cause on your frankly avowed accession to it. It is rather bold for me to do this, all the same I do it. I cannot tell you how gladly.

The movement has reached a point now where women like yourself will be wings to it, and this will make parties in power glad to make friends by being just to those who may be valuable allies. Again congratulating you, I am,

Sincerely yours,

LUCY STONE.

An undated letter from Mrs. Elizabeth Cady Stanton alludes, presumably, to this newly-proclaimed attitude of Miss Field's.

DEAR MISS FIELD, — It has given me great pleasure to see the flattering notices of you in the press.

I always feel elated with each new achievement of my sex, for whatever one does well reflects glory on all the rest.

May we not see and hear you at our coming anniversary, which promises to be all we could desire in numbers, quality, and interest?

With kind regards,

ELIZABETH CADY STANTON.

Miss Susan B. Anthony gave to Miss Field a warm personal greeting, on a public platform, one day, before one of the Congresses of the Exposition, and the always cordial relations between the elder and the younger woman were still more firmly established. Miss Field had always shared in the deep affection and respect inspired by Miss Anthony, whose name will forever lead in the galaxy of America's noble women.

An editorial article which Miss Field wrote about this time, entitled " A Vision of the Centuries," is almost a classic in its poetic beauty and merits literary immortality. It is subjoined.

" On Sunday night, I stood alone in the Court of Honor of the Columbian Exposition. Though eighty-eight thousand persons had passed the turnstiles during the day, I was sole spectator of a scene that can never be forgotten. No one who has not beheld that marvellous creation of brain and gold in the mysterious solitude of night has the faintest conception of its weird and awful beauty. Eastward shimmered Lake Michigan, beside which arose the graceful columns of the peristyle ; westward, a quarter of a mile away, loomed the Administration Building ablaze with light, its dome looking like the jewelled crown of a colossal king. Between these two architectural inspirations rippled the waters of that exquisite lagoon which makes the Exposition of 1893 unique in the world's history ; north stood the great expanse of the Manufactures Building ; beyond lay that dedicated to Electricity ; southward, Machinery Hall and the Agricultural Building filled in the long stretch and completed such a court as mortal eye never before gazed upon. Electric lights outlined all these wondrous structures and told a story in fire that never can be told in words. The great gold statue of the republic seemed to rise from the water and extend her arms in benediction, while Diana looked down from the Agricultural Building as if she would clasp hands with the Genius of the Court.

"Stars were my sole companions. Chicago that night harbored two million souls, half of whom were bent upon standing where I then stood a few hours later. Why was I alone in paying tribute to a silent beauty that a few weeks hence will live only in memory? Why was I alone thanking God for this manifestation of the divinity of humanity? The solitude was all the more unearthly for being so brilliantly illuminated. All this for the joy of one small woman! I rubbed my eyes and peered into the night. A solitary Columbian guard brought me to my senses. Aladdin had not loaned me his lamps. The mid-autumn dream which no poet dare set to verse, its own rhythm transcending language, was a great palpitating fact, a vision of all the centuries grouped on the shores of Lake Michigan to teach the New World reverence for the ideal.

"A westerly wind blew dust in my eyes and made me shiver. How miserable are the limitations of mortality! I had determined to pass the night with Diana and the Republic. I longed to see the sun rise above Lake Michigan and kiss the Genius of the Court of Honor on the morning of all mornings of The Fair. That shiver warned me of pneumonia, and, like the poor bit of humanity that I am, I clambered up the steps of the elevated railway station and went home to sleep in bed. Thus does prose kill poetry."

The social side of the Exposition was exceptionally charming to Miss Field, as her familiarity with French and Italian made her at home with foreigners who spoke those languages, and her periods of residence abroad had habituated her to foreign preferences and customs. She was constantly sought as a guest at dinners and receptions; as a speaker at clubs and meetings and informal gatherings. The demands upon her were incessant; yet she seldom or never failed to meet them, and after late hours at night she often rose at five for her unremitting press work. To a friend who sent her a little remembrance in rhyme for her birthday that year, accompanied with roses, she wrote under date of October 1, 1893 : —

. . . " That you should remember what I had forgotten ! I am very much touched by your poem and the flower of it. I cannot rhyme you in return, but I can wish that your life be a poem. May all good things come to you, and God bless all of us ! I only ask to be able to meet the duty of the hour and to be of some little use. I expect nothing. There is only one birthday worth celebrating, — that of the day when we can say, I accept the inevitable."

Looking back, it is easy to see how bravely she carried her burdens, and how she seemed to have half-conscious impressions that the end was not far distant.

The winter of 1893–94 she passed in Washington, with frequent interludes in New York, and in the spring she repeated in Washington her course of lectures on the political problems involved in Mormonism. Under date of March 15, 1894, Dr. William T. Harris, National Superintendent of Education, wrote to her : —

MY DEAR MISS FIELD, — I write to thank you for the complimentary tickets to your lecture. I am very glad that you are giving this interesting and instructive course of lectures. You have a way of putting things that brings home to the judgment the right and wrong of the matter. I have purchased a course ticket, and hope that I shall be able to attend some of them, but I am in feeble health just now, having a side hit of the grip.

Very sincerely yours,
WILLIAM T. HARRIS.

The great achievements and the singularly exalted and winning character of Dr. Harris greatly impressed Miss Field, and she held him in an almost reverent esteem.

In the summer of 1894 Miss Field's beloved aunt, Mrs. Sanford, died on August 1, and her body was brought for burial beside her husband in a country town cemetery near Boston. Kate had been remaining in Washington, deeply engaged in work all summer, and was much exhausted by the intense heat. She came to Boston to attend the burial of her aunt, and remained for a few days as the guest of a friend at the Brunswick Hotel, where she was always fond of sojourning. It was evident then that her health was seriously failing, and that she was in grave need of the rest that circumstances did not permit her to take. The evening after the funeral services she lay exhausted on the sofa, while her mind reverted to the panorama of her own life that had been so closely linked with that of her Aunt Corda.

" Sleep after toil, port after stormy seas,
Ease after war, death after life does greatly please ! "

she repeated, half dreamily, as she lay with closed eyes, with a rose half falling from one delicate little hand. The August moonlight came in at the windows; the electric lights were turned off in favor of the silver radiance without; and Kate's conversation turned on the wonder and mystery of the Unseen.

In a little memorial reminiscence of her aunt and her home in Newport which she gave in her paper, she wrote of it as " artistic in construction and adornment," and that " many a gay party of kindred souls have watched the setting sun and bade the moon welcome on the broad piazza of Edna Villa." And she added: " A magnificent grand piano made the drawing-room of the villa as attractive as the charming waterscape without, for the nimble fingers and well-trained voice of the hostess created such music as is rarely heard from amateurs. Beautiful was her speaking voice, silvery was her laugh, keen were her criticisms of men and things, passionate was her love of art. In her Elihu Vedder found his first patron, and in her William Morris Hunt had a warm friend."

So vanished from the earthly life Corda Riddle Sanford. She was a woman who inhabited a high sphere of thought, whose mind was stored with classic literature, whose presence had a suggestion of the majestic, whose conversation was exceptionally charming, and whose life contributed to the interests of art, and especially of music, for which her own talent was almost genius.

Miss Field returned to Washington, but something of the energy and exhilaration of life had left her. During this autumn of 1894 the French Government bestowed a well-merited honor upon Miss Field by decorating her with the " Palms of the Academy," with the title of " *Officier de l'Instruction publique*," — the highest distinction which the French Republic could bestow. The French Government were swift to recognize Miss Field's eminent service to art two years before, and the honor was offered her then; but she refused to accept it until the battle was entirely won, and art made free, the entire repeal being secured in 1894. Since that date, it is sad to record, the tax has again been added. There passed between the French Minister and Miss Field the following correspondence:

CORRESPONDENCE

LÉGATION DE FRANCE AUX ETATS-UNIS,
WASHINGTON, D. C., Dec. 2, 1892.

DEAR MISS FIELD, — Mr. Patenôtre this day sent a letter to you at the Shoreham, in which he informs you that the French Government has made you an officer of public instruction. This is the highest distinction the Department of Public Instruction can bestow for service rendered to literature and to art. The brevet is enclosed in the letter, but the Minister wishes to hand you the decoration in person upon your return.

Nobody takes greater delight than I in the bestowal to you of this well-deserved honor. Please accept my most heartfelt congratulations.

Sincerely and respectfully yours,
JULES BŒUFVÉ,
Chancellor of the French Legation.

LÉGATION DE LA RÉPUBLIQUE FRANÇAISE AUX ETATS-UNIS,
WASHINGTON, le 30 Novembre 1892.

MADEMOISELLE, — Le Gouvernement Français, désireux de reconnaître les services que rend à la cause de l'art le journal que vous dirigez avec tant d'intelligence et de talent a décidé, sur ma demande, de vous conférer les palmes académiques, instituées, comme vous le savez, par notre Département de l'Instruction Publique pour récompenser les artistes et les littérateurs. Je suis heureux d'être appelé à vous informer de cette décision et je m'empresse de vous envoyer le brevet qui vous est destiné. J'aurai l'honneur, lors de votre retour à Washington, de vous remettre les insignes de la décoration qui vient de vous être décernée.

Veuillez agréer, Mademoiselle, avec mes bien sincères félicitations, l'assurance de mon respectueux dévouement.

PATENÔTRE.

WASHINGTON CITY, Nov. 17, 1894.

TO HIS EXCELLENCY THE AMBASSADOR OF FRANCE.

SIR, — The honor conferred upon me as editor of a national review by the Government of France through you, who so ably represent the great republic of Europe, is the more delightful for being unexpected. I will not affect modesty, preferring to emulate the example of that eminent diplomatist and lawyer, the Hon. Edward J. Phelps, who, after listening to his own praises at a banquet in New York, replied that he "had quite made up his mind it was far pleasanter to *receive* plaudits than to have the merit to deserve them." Accept my heart's assurance that I am profoundly grateful to your Government for decorating me with the palms of the Academy, the possession of which will be a constant inspiration.

> "Perhaps the longing to be so
> Helps make the soul immortal,"

sings Lowell. Perhaps the longing to deserve this great recognition will help make me worthy of it.

That the union between your country and mine may be as close as that which unites you, dear sir, to one of America's fairest daughters, is the fond prayer of,

Yours truly and gratefully,

KATE FIELD.

The parchment read as follows : —

RÉPUBLIQUE FRANÇAISE.

MINISTÈRE DE L'INSTRUCTION PUBLIQUE ET DES BEAUX-ARTS.

Le Ministre de l'Instruction publique et des Beaux-Arts,

Vu l'article 32 du décret organique du 17 mars 1808;

Vu les ordonnances royales des 14 novembre 1844, 9 septembre 1845 et 1ᵉʳ novembre 1846;

Vu les décrets des 9 décembre 1850, 7 avril et 27 décembre 1866, et 24 décembre 1885,

Arrête:

Miss Kate Field, Conférencière à Washington est nommé Officier de l'Instruction publique.

Fait à Paris, le 24 Septembre 1892.

SEAL.   *Le Ministre de l'Instruction publique et des Beaux-Arts,*
Signé : Léon Bourgeois.

Pour ampliation :
Le Chef du Cabinet, Mehumel.

Congratulations both public and private were showered upon Miss Field. The generous world of the press echoed and re-echoed this merited honor; and never in her life, perhaps, had Miss Field been so touched by the evidence of the wide and warm friendships that environed her as at this time. Among the words of the press, those of her friend, Mr. Henry MacFarland, the able Washington representative of the Boston "Herald," were peculiarly grateful to Miss Field. Mr. MacFarland said: —

· · · "I was the more pleased because, so far as I have seen, there has been no public expression of appreciation of Miss Field's services in this behalf in our own country. I do not know, of course, what private testimonials she has received, but I had expected that when the long battle for free art, in which she took so large a part, was won, that she would be publicly honored by the artists and art lovers of America, to say nothing of other intelligent and cultivated and patriotic people, according to her rich deserts.

"I can personally testify, as one who has witnessed the whole fight for free art before Congress, that Miss Field, with voice and pen, privately and publicly, before committees and in her weekly periodical, 'Kate Field's Washington,' in season and out of season, exerted all her powers and all her influence to secure free art, and that she did it in so practical a way as to accomplish more than any of the others who worked with her.

. . . .

"Senators and representatives, members of the finance and ways and means committees, would, I doubt not, sustain me in saying that Miss Field was by far the most effective advocate of this cause.

"No woman, or man either, of less courage, patience, and persistence, would have maintained the struggle, which at times was apparently almost hopeless, and certainly most disheartening.

"But Miss Field is just the person to lead a forlorn hope, and she did it in this case nobly. She wrested from indifference and opposition, first, a reduction of fifteen per cent, and finally the removal of the entire duty in the last tariff bill.

"Our government did all it is likely to do, I suppose, in tardily and reluctantly granting Miss Field's request for free art, but it does seem to me that, even if she cannot have governmental recognition, the United States ought not to be outdone by the republic of France in publicly rewarding her self-sacrificing labors."

The New York "Evening Post" said : —

33

" In conferring upon Miss Kate Field the 'Academic Palm,' the highest distinction the Department of Public Instruction can bestow, the French republic formally recognizes, in a manner as rare as it is complimentary, one of the foremost women of America. Essentially an American woman, she has not only rendered service to literature and art, but has been a leader of public thought. To Miss Field's efforts, on the platform and with her pen, was due in no small degree the solution of the Mormon problem, which made statehood for Utah possible, and in other questions of moment her influence has been widely felt. 'The Post' extends to Miss Field its most cordial congratulations upon the great honor her talents have won."

To Miss Field, herself, however, while she gratefully appreciated this recognition, her best reward was in the results achieved for the benefit of art and artists.

" Kate Field's Washington " had a little over five years' tenure of life. During that time Miss Field rendered signal services to art, to the development and progress of the great West and Alaska, to education in the United States, to music and the drama, and to international copyright. Not the least of its interest was in her power to condense, in a phrase, a complete portrait of an individual, as when she said of Paderewski that he had " the head of a poet and the face of a spirit." She also said of him: " If there ever were a poet pianist, Paderewski is he. . . . He is Italy in the flesh. His is the sentiment and dreamy beauty of the land of Dante, of Rafael, of Cimarosa. He is first and always sympathetic. . . . When he first appears on the platform, a new kind of creature seems to have come upon the earth. It is not the being we call man; it certainly is not woman.

It is just Paderewski. The genius of his playing is its spirituality. He is fine in the Hungarian rhapsody, but he is unique in the moonlight of music, — in nocturnes, in the minuet and trio of Beethoven's sonata, Opus 31, and in Chopin."

The Columbian Exposition awarded to Miss Field's journal a medal and diploma. The official declaration pronounced "Kate Field's Washington" to be "intelligently devoted to timely discussion of the affairs of government, art, the sciences, literature, the drama, the functions of society, and the steady march of mankind toward the highest summit of human achievement," and added: —

This journal is edited and controlled by Kate Field, — a most gifted and accomplished American woman, — and "Kate Field's Washington" is the very best and highest expression of woman's capability to lead in the triumphant advance of all that is noblest and most salutary in the progress of an exalted civilization.

The literary contents of this journal are of the very highest character, bearing the stamp of originality, cultivated thought, mature judgment, poetic sentiment, sparkling wit, refreshing humor, and, above all, the sterling and unflinching spirit of patriotic adherence to American institutions.

In my judgment Miss Field is entitled not only to the most honorable mention, but to an award as well for the advanced skill and signal ability disclosed by her in producing a periodical journal at once so utilitarian and fascinating as to make it a most welcome and valuable source of education to every home and fireside, and to every library and literary circle wherever the English tongue is spoken, or the welfare of man is a motive of human thought and action.

(Signed)   Francis A. Riddle,
Judge Dep't L., Group 150.

This honor was peculiarly gratifying to Miss Field, as, out of all the projects of her life, her journal was dearest to her heart. Bayard Taylor, meeting her in Florence, had remarked: "There is a girl with the most remarkable literary promise who is yet possessed to go on the operatic stage." The "literary promise" persisted, and her mature life more than fulfilled the prophecy of her youth, although in a different trend from that of pure literature. Ideas engaged her; literary work in any form of expression was to her a vehicle for the communication of energy to a desired movement. Her journalism was her instrument by means of which she could work to certain essential ends. The stirring questions of the day enlisted her eager interest, to the exclusion, or, rather, the postponement of abstract problems of thought. For she always saw life under the conditions of eternity. She was not given to talking of this, but it was the basis, consciously and unconsciously, of all her action. As she was nearing the limits of her stay on earth, she felt the importance of time more and more profoundly; and to the friend to whom her almost daily letters, through a period of fifteen years, had revealed with exceptional clearness her lofty nature, she said in a letter of 1894, "I want to live every day as if it were my last." There was nothing morbid about this; seen now, in the light of the experiences awaiting her, it suggests that her spiritual vision discerned the brief space of time left to her here, and that it inevitably colored and predetermined her action. The relinquishment of her journal was a peculiarly hard thing for her; it meant the relinquishment of ardent hopes, of infinite aspiration, of an energy of purpose seldom known. Nor was this unappreciated by the journalistic fraternity. She issued a circular stating to her subscribers and to the press that ill health compelled the cessation of her journalistic work. The press comments from thousands of papers were most kindly and sympathetic and full of generous appreciation of her journal.

The multitude of kindly messages and expressions of sympathy flowed in upon her, publicly and privately, and gave her great comfort. A letter from Mr. Albert Shaw, the editor of the "Review of Reviews," ran: —

July 1, 1895.

DEAR MISS FIELD, — I am truly sorry that you are too ill to keep the "Washington" running steadily, but I admire and commend your good sense in valuing yourself more highly than the paper. "Kate Field's Washington" has been one of the really creditable successes of our recent American journalism; but yours is personal journalism, as you say yourself, and "Kate Field's Washington" without Kate Field would be an impossibility.

It will give me great pleasure to send the "Review of Reviews" to you, and your address will be changed, in care of the "Chicago Times-Herald." I hope that no care or worry will interfere with your getting the complete rest that you need, and I am one of the many people who will be very glad when you come back home with restored vigor.

Believe me sincerely yours,

ALBERT SHAW.

Mr. Gilder and Mr. Underwood of the "Century;" Miss Gilder of "The Critic;" the editor of the N. Y. "Evening Post," and many other of the most prominent editors in the periodical and press literature of the country expressed to her their personal sympathy.

In this apparent reversal of success she only clung more closely to all noble faiths. The merry repartee and glancing wit that all her friends had recognized as Kate Fieldian had departed, and there was about her an atmosphere that was most touching in its mingled sadness and sweetness; but the finer qualities of her character — her crystal truth, her unfaltering courage, her justice of mental attitude — only shone the more clearly. In this critical hour testing her own endurance, she received, from one of the innumerable strangers who were always writing to her, a letter expressing great dissatisfaction with life, and to this Kate replied under date of July 14, 1895, as follows:

. . . " If you knew how overburdened my life has been from childhood, you would have more charity for those who are apparently successful, and would discover that yours is not the worst fate in the world. I contend that we must all bear our burdens cheerfully without complaint and do the best we can under the circumstances. I have not one moment to spare. I must leave soon for a sea-voyage and have work still before me that would appall, did I not take it in sections. *Believe* in endless progression and you'll attain your star sooner or later. *This is not the end.*

Sincerely,

Kate Field.

This was the mental attitude in which Kate Field closed all her affairs in Washington. She left behind her five years of brilliant life in the Capital. She had been *persona grata* in the most brilliant and significant social life; she had been a factor of importance in national movements; she had known beautiful women and eminent men. More than once, indeed, wealth and station had entreated her acceptance of them and of all the ease and luxury of life they represented; but Kate Field never wavered from her fidelity to the love of romance as the only basis for marriage, and though she had long since " left the coasts of life to travel inland," her faith in love was as pure and as complete as that of an untried girl. A woman of the world, she yet never became a worldly woman. She had learned the meaning of the poet's lines: —

> " By thine own soul's law learn to live,
>   And if men thwart thee take no heed,
>   And if men hate thee have no care;
>   Sing thou thy song and do thy deed,
>   Hope thou thy hope and pray thy prayer,
>   And claim no crown they will not give,
>   Nor bays they grudge thee for thy hair."

It chanced that Kate wrote to her most constant correspondent on the date of May 19, 1895, — just one year before her death, which occurred on the May 19th of the next year: and in this letter she said: " I 'm busy day and night winding up a five years' volume of my life."

Looking backward now, the coincidence of the dates is a curious little fact. It was, indeed, the winding up of the last chapter of her life in her own country.

A new chapter, however, awaited her in the summer islands of the Pacific, and one whose importance was worthy of the closing of her life. The elasticity of her temperament led her to anticipate the new scenes and interests with a kind of sad pleasure; and in this spirit, sad, yet not undismayed, Kate packed innumerable trunks left stored in Washington; she made her will; she closed all her affairs, and turned her face toward the voyage which was, indeed, in a deeper sense than her friends could dream, to lead her to the Fortunate Isles.

CROSSING THE BAR

" Her life was earnest work, not play ;
Her tired feet climbed a weary way ;
Unguessed of her in life the love
That rained its tears her grave above."

What is your brave act without a brave nature behind it?
What is your smile unless I know that you are kind? What is
your indignant blow unless your heart is on fire? What is all
your activity without you? How instantly the impression of a
character creates itself, springs into shape behind a deed.

PHILLIPS BROOKS.

" Life made by duty epical
And rhythmic with the truth."

"That noble, loving heart, — that gift
Of a mind earnest, clear, profound, —
.Affinities which only could
Cling to the pure, the true, the good."

Love is the whole. Now love in the thought or purpose
means "look out and not in." Love in the act means "lend a
hand." . . . Faith, hope, and love make the whole of life, and
love the largest of the three. — EDWARD EVERETT HALE.

There shall never be one lost good! What was, shall live as
    before ;
The evil is null, is naught, is silence implying sound ;
What was good, shall be good, with, for evil, so much good
    more ;
On the earth the broken arcs; in the heaven, a perfect round.

ROBERT BROWNING.

CHAPTER IX

... Take along with you this holy earnestness, for earnestness alone makes life eternity. — GOETHE.

A supernatural state of society? It is a goal; otherwise, of what use is society? ... I would have every attribute of man a symbol of civilization and an attribute of progress; I would present liberty to the intellect, equality to the heart, fraternity to the soul. — VICTOR HUGO.

... A Hand
Shall throw open the gates of new life to thee !
See the Christ stand!
ROBERT BROWNING.

CROSSING THE BAR. A JOURNEY OF DESTINY. LIFE AND STUDIES IN HAWAII. NOBLE AND GENEROUS WORK. THE ANGEL OF DEATH.

THE link of destiny that was to lead Kate Field to Hawaii, and from those islands of the sea on into the unseen realm, was forged when on the death of Kalakaua she began to advocate annexation. The King of Hawaii was a personal figure that attracted her attention. In an editorial note regarding him in her own Review she had once written:

" Kalakaua, the late King of Hawaii, was a true Bohemian. In his palace at Honolulu he set apart a chamber in which it was his intention to hold high revels at intervals. There only the elect were permitted to enter; there His Majesty laid off his robes of state, hung his crown on the hat-rack, and, while never forgetting his dignity, he would

play a capital banjo accompaniment to the college songs
and native choruses rendered by his guests.

"The men who knew him best were fondest of him; so
some of these, poets and painters, conceived the happy
thought of making an offering to the royal Bohemian chamber. Artists painted pictures, poets wrote couplets which
were richly illuminated and framed and hung upon the
walls. These were all voluntary tributes of good fellowship
to a mighty good fellow who thoroughly appreciated his
friends.

"The following is one of the tributes which His Majesty
inspired. It is an acrostic on the word *Aloha* — which
means *Love*, or *Love to you*. It is the national greeting of
the Hawaiian people, and is almost constantly upon their
lips."

The acrostic to which Miss Field alluded is this
clever stanza by Prof. Charles Warren Stoddard of
the Catholic University of Washington : —

"Aloha ! Royal Health to Royal Host !
  Long live the King beneath his royal palms,
  O'er him, ye soft winds, breathe your sweetest psalms.
  Hail him, ye seas that fawn upon his coast.
  Aloha ! and Aloha ! and Aloha ! — *Pros't !*"

Frequent expressions regarding Hawaii and the
affairs of the islands appeared from the pen of Miss
Field ; and when Mr. Blount was sent to Hawaii by the
Administration, — although for years he had been a
member of Congress, and even the Chairman of the
House Committee on Foreign Affairs, — Miss Field
reiterated editorially that he was not a fitting person
to be entrusted with a diplomatic mission. Later
she regretted that Mr. Willis had not been sent first
instead of last; and she frequently noted in " Kate
Field's Washington " the advanced state of civilization

in Hawaii. She contended that those islands were important to the commerce of this country, and she so pushed her researches into the matter as to find out how many American vessels had arrived at the principal ports, with the amount of tonnage of each, for the year ending June 30, 1894. Giving these statistics, editorially, in her "Washington," Miss Field added : —

"Perhaps, after comparing these figures and discovering the value of Honolulu to American shipping, they may not be quite so anxious to give Great Britain leave to lease Neckar Island and establish cable communications with British Columbia. This Congress has wondrous facility in committing Hari-kari, but if there be an atom of sense and patriotism left, the cable to Hawaii will be controlled by the United States."

As early, indeed, as in 1891, the Hawaiian problem began to engage her attention. One of her first editorials was for cable communication, of which she wrote : —

"That there should be a cable between this country and Hawaii is as evident as that the Hawaiian Islands are ours by the trend of the land. Not to equip the harbor of Pearl River for a naval station is to fly in the face of Providence."

From time to time she recurred to the subject; and this period of unconscious preparation finally led to her undertaking the great work to which her energy was given with a devotion that cost her life.

It was on July 25, 1895, that Kate Field left Washington never to return. She stopped in Chicago, her stay there proving longer than she had expected, and it was well into September before she left that city to embark for Hawaii. Again she lingered *en route*, in Denver, in Salt Lake City, and finally in San Francisco, so that she did not sail until the middle of November, reaching Honolulu six days later. Reading her life backward through these months, it almost seems as if she had a prescience that these were her last days in her own country. Curiously, when, on November 14th, she embarked from San Francisco, she gave to a friend directions as to what should be done in case she should die in Hawaii and her body be brought back, — directions that were carried out in little more than one year. There was a pervading depth of sadness in her life at this time, although she was very brave, and she had consolation in the nature of an increasingly larger perception of the unseen forces which gave her strength. Then, too, she never lost her interest in the life of the moment. Few persons ever lived *de jour au jour* to such an extent as Kate Field. In a private letter she once said to a friend : —

" I don't know what becomes of my time. I only know that I 'm occupied every moment of the day, and accomplish nothing. And here it is the end of June, with '89 going down hill ! It always makes me sad to turn my back on the longest day of the year."

This last sentence suggests the range of her ceaseless activities.

Truth is stranger than fiction in the curious links of personality and circumstance by means of which life progresses. We all realize certain fateful crises in our own lives of which we say, had it *not* been that such a friend came forward at that moment; or, had it not been that such a thing happened, — what should I have done? But the friend who was needed appeared; the one event so essential *did* happen; for a care and a guidance that is closer and more tender than we realize is over and about us all. The Divine overruling is the one supreme reality in all the universe.

The provision for this fateful emergency in her life had already been made for Kate Field. During the Columbian Exposition she had made the acquaintance of Mr. and Mrs. H. H. Kohlsaat of Chicago, and soon after this Mr. Kohlsaat became the proprietor of a daily Chicago journal, the " Times-Herald." Appreciating very keenly Miss Field's exceptional power, he aided her in closing the business matters of her own journal; aided her with a generosity and delicate kindness which finds record more enduring than that of any printed page, and which was only made possible by his sympathy with her perplexities and her failing health, and by his own command of liberal resources. Mr. Kohlsaat was also, himself, deeply interested in the problem of the annexation of Hawaii, and so it came about that he gave Miss Field a " roving commission " as correspondent for his journal. Mr. Kohlsaat's great enterprise was supported by his great wealth; his terms to her were generously satisfactory, and his appreciation of her fitness for so important a mission in what may be called diplomatic journalism was most grateful to her. So again, in this most dramatic life of Kate Field, was a failure, or a loss, instantly transmuted into a success, or a gain. Miss Field accepted Mr. Kohlsaat's proposition that she go to Hawaii to study the conditions and to advocate annexation in case her observations confirmed her judgment in that direction. While in Chicago, another matter temporarily engaged her attention that seemed like a rhythmic sequence rounding out her purposes in life. It will be remembered that in her early youth the first public work in which she ever engaged was that of telling, on the lecture platform, the story of John Brown's neglected grave and raising funds to purchase his farm in the Adirondacks and to redeem this historic spot from vandalism. And so the last work of her life in America was to arrange for the transportation of the John Brown Fort — which had been shown in Chicago during the Columbian Exposition — to a site in Harper's Ferry. In the midsummer heat Miss Field worked, wrote, and addressed meetings in Chicago to raise the funds for this purpose, as she had already secured a site which, by her appeal, had been donated by Stowe College, an institution for colored people. This site is on the magnificent heights overlooking the Shenandoah valley, and is well calculated to make John Brown's Fort a Mecca for travellers. Miss Field ardently desired to see it placed where John Brown left it, where the story can be told on its own ground with the battle-fields of the two great armies within sight, and with Sheridan's ride ringing in the air.

This purpose was achieved, and it seems the crowning sequence of the work of Kate Field for "Old John Brown," whose heroic soul, we may well believe, is still marching on.

All this time, while reluctant to journey on, in a way that was curiously unlike her old self, she was still eager to enter on the new field of study and work in Hawaii. " If I allowed myself to waste vitality in regrets, I 'd deplore not having been in

Hawaii several months ago. But the inevitable is to be gracefully accepted," she wrote to her most constant correspondent. During this enforced pause she often dropped into reminiscence in her letters. In reference to some question of her correspondent regarding her London visit of 1882, she recalled some incidents, and among others this memory of Ristori :

" I had gone to old Drury Lane Theatre to get seats for Wagner's ' Meistersingers,' when what should my eyes fall upon but great posters announcing 'Ristori in English ! Macbeth ! ' What pluck and what perseverance? I gave Ristori her first lessons in English ' when I was a boy,' so to speak, and then found her daring enough to attempt Shakespeare in his native tongue and on his native heath.

" ' Give me Madame Ristori's address,' I said to the box-office man.

" ' Don't ! ' whispered an invisible voice, proceeding from a man who on catching sight of me rushed forth exclaiming, ' Oh, it is *you*, Miss Field? That's quite another matter. So many people ask for Madame's address, and we refuse to give it out of self-defence, but *you*, *c'est une autre affaire*.' It was Wertheimer, Ristori's agent.

" Ristori was rehearsing. Would I go in front? Of course, so we stumbled along the dark corridors into the big theatre, and I sat (an audience of one) in a stall while Wertheimer went to Ristori.

" ' Katey Field ! Katey Field ! est-ce possible? mais viens ici, tout de suite ! ' exclaimed Ristori, and in a moment more I was on the grand old stage being kissed and embraced by the greatest living actress. ' Only last night we were wondering where you were,' she said, ' and behold ! It is magnetism.' I sat out the rehearsal, meeting the manager, Augustus Harris, and several of the actors that I knew. It was very interesting, Ristori talking to me in

34

Italian, giving her instructions to Harris in French to interpret into English and then speaking Shakespeare with an
accent. Ah ! I wish you could have been present. While sitting there an idea of an article occurred to me, 'A Rehearsal
at Drury Lane,' and at once I began to take notes, much
to Harris's edification, whom I interviewed, later, as the
stage manager. This was an example of the way I 'rested'
that summer ! . . . I think I must have written you at the
time of my experience in Wagner opera that season. I heard
the ' Meistersingers ' one night when Richter, the celebrated
conductor, had an ovation. His orchestra was magnificent.
. . . I went with De Wartegg, Minnie Hauk's husband.
She was in Baden-Baden. We encountered accidentally in
the street, and as we were neighbors and liked the same
things, we went about together. He was an amiable and
clever man (journalist) of fine family and standing in
Austria."

During all this lingering Kate's letters were more
or less reminiscent, as if she were half-conscious of
standing on the verge of all her past life. To some
reference of her correspondent to Mr. Lowell she
replied : —

" Did I ever tell you that I only just missed having an
original poem from Lowell to recite on the occasion of the
Stratford-on-Avon festival for the benefit of the theatre
when I recited one written by Dr. Marston ? I had written to
Mr. Lowell begging he would do the Shakespeare Memorial
Association this great favor, and I enclose you his reply."

The letter to which Miss Field here referred is as
follows : —

MADRID, March 15, 1879.

You have been in Spain and know what *mañana* means
in its ordinary application, but you don't know what it

means to a minister without a secretary in the busiest legation we have. It means that when so long a date as 23
April is given, one stands whistling for some verses (that
won't come) to send to Miss Field, and thinks, " to-morrow
I will write and say it is hopeless." I have so many bothers
and so many occupations that all I can recollect about
Shakspeare is that his name is not spelt as I spell it, and
that he did *not* die on the same day with Cervantes.
These materials don't go far to the making of a poem, you
will allow — even if I could make one.

I am really sorry that I can't, since you ask it, and all the
more because I am going to ask a favor of you. Here it
is. Do you happen to have by you a copy of your little
book about Spain? And if you have, would you be good
enough to send it to me, not for myself, but for a very
charming Spanish friend of mine here who would be very
glad to see it again? If you have n't, I can write home for
it, but if you have, and could spare it, I should get it a
month sooner.

You see I am asking you to do something for me because
I won't do anything for you ; but to be always trying to get
something for nothing is the business which I have been
learning these two years.

Faithfully yours,

JAMES RUSSELL LOWELL.

In this way her mind seemed constantly reverting
to the past, rather than, as usual, to the future that lay
before her, and this was a new phase of her personality. " If I am anything I am a woman of To-morrow,"
she had once written in reply to a friend who had
begged to include her in a series of sketches to be
called " Women of To-day." Always before her
thoughts had been engaged pressing on to things
in advance, almost forgetting those that lay behind.

But her prophetic mind undoubtedly caught some impression that a more mysterious journey than a voyage to the Hawaiian Islands lay before her.

The summer flowers bloomed and faded, and in the early September Kate left Chicago for San Francisco, pausing at Salt Lake City. She remained there for some days, and her hotel was constantly thronged with callers. A little more than ten years had passed since her first visit to Zion, and in all the subsequent time she had taken the most active interest in the progress of the people. She had watched the breaking up of old lines, the cessation of animosity between the Gentile and the Mormon; and no one was more familiar with all the conditions than was Kate Field. She found a very curious reversal of former states. To the friend to whom her almost daily letters never failed until made impossible by the unfrequent mails from Hawaii, she wrote : —

"I did not expect to see my press letters quoted in Utah, for the reason that I was not partisan. Fancy my amazement at seeing both sides making 'elegant extracts.' They take what agrees with their complexion and leave out the rest ; and the 'Herald' had the gall to reproach the 'Tribune' for ignoring what would n't be to its advantage to print. Thereupon the 'Tribune' makes a bluff by declaring that when Miss Field writes about the glories of Salt Lake, it is its business to assist Zion by copying the same, but it does not propose to resurrect graveyard reminiscences. This is a specimen of the way the press goes on in Utah ; both sides think one thing, and write another. The atmosphere reeks with insincerity. There is more lying to the square foot in Utah than any place on the habitable globe, I verily believe. That the Republican party and the Mormon Church should now be embracing each other, is a spectacle for gods and men. The rupture begun by the Democratic re-convention cannot be snuffed out if there be one particle of manhood in young Utah. It gives me great hope, and it would not surprise me, if I live five years and come back to Utah, to be received with open arms by the very people who now think me their worst foe. Those people are Mormon Democrats. Was there ever anything stranger than this evolution?"

As will be seen, Kate's sense of humor had not deserted her. Then came San Francisco, and in a private letter she writes: —

"I arrived here last night. . . . The journey from Salt Lake City is thirty-six hours, and I spent the time in bed. . . . The Press Club gives me a reception to-morrow afternoon, and I shall be dining out a bit. . . . I have engaged passage on the 'Mariposa,' that sails on November 14 for Australia, and stops at Honolulu. I've a room on deck that the Captain takes me to look at to-morrow, and I shall get as much comfort as I can out of what I detest, — a sea voyage. Six days, however, do not last forever."

Again, on receipt of a little package, she wrote:

"The flowers have not lost their fragrance, and that you associate me with them is very sweet. May flowers come to you in all ways, and make you feel that love and friendship are more than words. . . .

"It was perfectly natural that my dear mother should have dreaded to leave me alone, but she understands it all now and knows that I am far better alone than I should be with . . . Marriage is not a panacea — very good when right — terrible when wrong — I have escaped several probabilities of misery, and am to be congratulated."

In November she sailed and the voyage proved endurable if not enjoyable, and the first view of the "paradise of the Pacific" enchanted her eye. She had a pleasant apartment at the Hawaiian hotel opening on a private "lanai" (verandah); and a piano, with some books and art draperies she carried with her, made her rooms very individual and attractive. In a private letter, in reply to solicitude about her health, she wrote: —

"Don't worry. This is the laziest climate on earth, and I'm lazier than I've ever been in my life. . . . The thermometer stands at 74°, the sun shines, the birds sing, all the doors and windows are open. The situation is extremely interesting. I find agreeable men and women, and am greatly taken with President Dole. He is a fine fellow in every way. The U. S. S. 'Bennington' is here, and at the concert two nights ago, when I sang for the benefit of the lepers, the officers loaded me down with flowers. It was a great success, my Spanish song just suiting the audience, who applauded wildly and encored me to the echo. We made several hundred dollars, to be expended in Christmas gifts to the lepers who are segregated on the island of Molokai fifty miles away.

"No mail to the U. S. for twenty days. It is awful. If Congress does not give these islands a cable, the people will eat each other up for lack of other excitement. If you can stir any papers up on this matter, please do. A cable is now being proposed and is before Congress. Were you here, you would write poems about the sea and sky and mountains, all of which are my daily food. As I'm here for politics, I'm obliged to study the history and the people before paying my compliments to Nature. Really, I wish I had nothing to do but loaf and invite my soul. It is all this climate is good for. Yet, my dear, I can't escape a 'woman's edition' of a newspaper even here. I've just sent a contribution to one gotten up for the benefit of the kindergartens. Yes, they've all the religions and all the crazes and all the fads out here in the middle of the Pacific."

In reference to a curious little psychical experience of which a friend wrote to her, she said: —

"That's a strange experience of yours concerning ——
——, but it does not seem to me at all unlikely. Of course, materialists would laugh the idea to scorn, but I'm not one of that sort, thank God. I believe in a spiritual existence, and it's most natural to suppose that a spirit will at first hardly realize the change and will linger about old haunts. I've long since put you down as very medium-istic. You are extremely susceptible to atmospheres."

Miss Field entered upon the work of studying Hawaiian conditions with that intelligent zeal and thoroughness of method which so characterized her. She ingratiated herself with the natives by her simple and genuine good-will toward them, and gained the confidence of the authorities. Her writings were very judiciously handled; and when she spoke of the government her letters were read in Cabinet meetings before they were mailed. Sometimes they were changed in part, but usually they were sent as first written. The government recognized in Miss Field a worker for the good of the country, and seldom took exception to what she had to say.

A certain graphic instinct led her to adopt the most thorough and vivid method of work, — that of personal intercourse and observation. She entered into the very heart of the interests, both local and national, of Hawaii. The cable, the navy, the Oriental immigration, engaged her vigilant pen. The sugar plantations interested her, and she investigated productions and exports with an accuracy and a zeal unprecedented in any preceding observation of the conditions there. "The future of Hawaii," she wrote, "is vastly more important to us than the extension of British possessions in South America. The Monroe doctrine, properly interpreted, means that no wrong to republican institutions can be allowed to approach our continent. The danger line is Hawaii, and we refuse to heed the signal."

Kate Field obtained the first interview with President Dole that he had ever granted. "Our sole policy is annexation to the United States," he said to her. Miss Field especially desired to present a true picture of the domestic and material conditions of these islands, as to whether better or worse than before the overthrow of the monarchy. She found day labor and profit-sharing taking the place of the contract system. While the main interest was sugar, she found ranching, wool-growing, rice, fruit and coffee production to be the advancing industries. The eight islands with their present population of 100,000 are capable of sustaining a million inhabitants. The curious mixture of races fascinated Miss Field's attention, and she graphically depicted street scenes where there met and mingled Jew, Gentile, Portuguese, Hawaiian, Chinese, Japanese, and American. She sympathized with everything that made for progress in Honolulu. Appealed to on behalf of free kindergartens, she gave for their benefit her charming lecture, "An Evening with Dickens."

For the data of her letters she always went to headquarters for information. President Dole, Minister Willis, Consul-General Mills, and ex-Minister

Thurston were her personal friends and associates. "Few are they who visit our land and find no welcome," said a Honolulu writer ; " but few came into so genuine an adoption as that we gladly accorded Kate Field. Our lives were richer for her coming among us ; our days the happier for her smile; our hopes were stronger for the clear vibrations of her voice."

Presenting largely her information in the shape of interviews, she was preparing the way to offer her own logical generalizations. She had gathered voluminous notes in her vigilant methods of going from house to house, so to speak, from island to island, and coming into personal intercourse with all classes of the people. Her letters to the " Times-Herald " were copied by the Honolulu press as soon as received, and it is recognized that they were bringing to bear the happiest and most effective influence upon the social and political conditions prevailing in the islands.

In a private letter to a friend she wrote : —

"I have now been around this island riding and driving, and enjoyed the experience immensely. On the 24th, I sail for Hawaii (another island), where I may remain a month, going around it and visiting the volcano. . . . Any one who thinks these islands can be seen quickly and intelligently reckons without a host of problems. . . . The islands are eight in number, and I must visit at least three more, Hawaii being the largest, and the home of the great volcano. I hope the goddess Pele will perform for my benefit. If she does n't, the great sensation of the islands will be lost. . . . Of one thing you may be assured, — the monarchy can never be restored."

Miss Field's first — and only — Christmas in Hono-lulu was made pleasant to her by dining as the guest of President and Mrs. Dole, whom she greatly esteemed. The interview with the President, which she had on December 10, was a marvellous political document, and one that will always have weight among the state papers of the country. Of the President personally, she said : —

"Whoever meets Mr. Dole realizes that the noblest work of God is an honest man."

On that Christmas day she wrote to the friend who was in constant solicitude about her : —

HONOLULU, Dec. 25, 1895.

DEAR ——, — Accidentally a ship goes to the coast to-day, and I send you a little Xmas greeting. I dine with President and Mrs. Dole, so you see I am not forlorn. People are very hospitable here, and the way my time is taken up is awful for work. I have gained in flesh, and am told I look much better than on arrival. It does not look now as if I'd return in February as I expected. . . . The climate is soft and the scenery beautiful. No cable and few mails, however, make me feel lost to the world. I enclose mail dates.

I've just returned from a visit to the lepers. Very pathetic and very interesting. . . . I think I'm in favor of annexation, but shall not make up my mind in a hurry. I only write now to let you know I'm alive and content enough to stay several months.

Fancy a Xmas with the thermometer at 76° ! white muslin reigns and mosquitoes make music in the air. But for these pestiferous birds this would be an ideal spot for the tropics.

I've written a dozen letters for publication, but only one of them has national importance, — an interview with President Dole. It is the first time he has allowed himself to speak.

Two of our ships of war are in port, the " Baltimore " and " Bennington." Some of the officers are a great addition to society.

The best of years for you !

Miss Field became at once a favorite in Honolulu. Personally she was always irresistibly winning and magnetic. She was sunny of temper, with an infinite good will, and a keen sense of the ludicrous which never left her. During the winter a fête was given on the warship " Bennington," lying at Honolulu, to celebrate the arrival of the " Baltimore " from Yoko- hama, a ship that had been overdue for a week. Miss Field wrote of the fête as one that transformed the ship into an Arabian Nights' scene, " translated up to date," and she said : —

" There never was such a night even in Newport harbor in the balmy month of August. Smooth as a carpet of silver tissue lay the ocean ; still as silence itself was the air that one hardly dare to breathe, lest the spell of enchantment be broken. The lady in the moon looked on with longing eyes, wishing, I fancied, for a partner. Whether in despair she took what she could get and waltzed with that round- faced man who greets us in all latitudes, no one will ever know. Stars shone out of a cloudless sky ; the outlines of verdure-clad mountains formed a wonderful background ; while the twinkling lights of Honolulu and the harbor's shipping looked like dancing fireflies."

Writing from Honolulu at another time, she said in a private letter : —

" Surrounded by such a lot of water, I have been clinging fondly to all the land in sight, including my beautiful extinct volcano 'Punch-bowl,' that looks down from the clouds; but, alas! there seems no such thing as *terra firma* in this latitude. Last night I lay in bed thinking of the mosquitoes, whose music was all the sweeter for being outside the bar, when suddenly the deep silence was broken by a strange, uncanny rumbling I had never heard before."

An incipient earthquake ensued. The hotel quivered like a ship at sea; the bed rocked like a cradle; and she wrote further: —

"Should I get up and rush into the garden? (as I am told everybody else did) or should I remain where I was and take the consequences, whatever they might be?" questioned Miss Field. "To and fro rocked the bed; to and fro rocked the hotel; creak went everything, and seconds of time became as long as hours. 'Stay where you are,' whispered my astral. Then the rumbling and rocking ceased, and I amazed myself by going to sleep."

One of Miss Field's most important Hawaiian interviews was with Dr. John S. McGrew, formerly of Cincinnati, of whom she said: —

"Aggressively American, a member of the Loyal Legion, having served through the war as surgeon of the Eighty-third Ohio Regiment, and later as medical director of the Thirteenth Army Corps, Dr. McGrew is the last man in the world to live out of his own country except for cause. When he said he 'd been here twenty-nine years, I ventured to ask why," said Miss Field, adding, with a touch of humor: "A few years ago it was not safe to inquire too closely into the wherefore, in Hawaii, of many Americans. They emigrated more for their country's good than their own."

Dr. McGrew, however, found his *raison d'être* for going to Honolulu in that a man who owed him

$14,000 was there; and while waiting for payment, with his gaze fastened on his debtor, he grew to love the climate and place, and so stayed on. It is he who is called the " Father of Annexation." To Miss Field he said: —

" One month after my arrival — twenty-nine years ago — I made up my mind that the only way out of trouble was annexation. . . . The Hawaiian rulers were unfit to cope with the problems confronting them, and were the prey of designing white men."

Miss Field's love of scenery was one of her marked characteristics. She was swiftly responsive to the beautiful in nature or art, and the elusive tricks of meteorological conditions in Hawaii captivated her fancy. One of these she noted as follows: —

. . . " On this charming island rain dropped out of a moonlit sky last night, with less provocation than I ever saw in my somewhat varied life. It did not continue, but why it should have begun will ever remain a mystery. Even as I write a steady patter plays a soothing accompaniment to the twittering of strange birds. Mountains are as invisible as if they did not exist. Half an hour ago the sun shone with the ardor of tropical growth, and fleecy clouds floated high in the heavens, with no more apparent intention of mischief than I have of getting up a revolution."

The exasperating conditions resulting from no cable or regular mail service were constantly presented by Miss Field. " No cable, no steamers, no anything ! " she exclaimed. " I am planted on the only civilized part of the globe which is cut off from the news of the world ! Why ? Because the dominant power here is American, and Congress is as blind to the future as an owl at noon."

In a press letter under date of Feb. 1, 1896, Kate wrote of the island conditions : —

"The New York 'Sun' is right in stating that, though prompted by the best intentions, Mr. Spaulding contemplates too much at a single step. Let Congress advocate annexation, leaving details to be settled hereafter, and the Hawaiian Government will be satisfied. No one that I meet wants Hawaii to be admitted as a State. With their mixed population and peculiar problems, statehood would be a misfortune for these islands. It would be a thorn to our republic. No such idea should be considered. I firmly believe that the best, if not the only way, to rob annexation of perplexity is to give Hawaii a territorial form of government. Congress can do what it pleases with a territory, granting little or no suffrage, according to the circumstances. Look at Alaska. That great country, comprising in area one-fifth of the United States, was sold to us in 1867 under the condition that its Russian population should enjoy all the rights and privileges of American citizens. It has been shamefully neglected for twenty-nine years. Whites and natives have had no rights that Congress has felt bound to respect. Thirty thousand natives, all of whom are self-supporting, and three thousand whites exist without suffrage, without decent land laws, without a delegate to Congress to make known their wants. Broken-down politicians are sent there in the capacity of federal officers, some of whom are good, but most of whom are awful examples of unfitness. The whites, too, often prey on the natives, and the moral condition of a wonderful territory that cost but a cent an acre, and long since paid for itself, smells to heaven.

"Hawaii, however, is not Alaska. Its population has had a constitutional monarchy for years. Its dominant influence is New England, and no such ignorant misrule as has cursed Alaska would be tolerated twenty-four hours.

"What, then, would be feasible? Such a form of government as makes the District of Columbia the best-regulated section of our republic. A system that is good enough for 250,000 American citizens, 80,000 of whom are negroes, is good enough for 90,000 residents of Hawaii, 40,000 of whom are Kanakas and 30,000 are non-voting Asiatics. The ruling white element would gladly give up suffrage for the sake of a system best calculated to harmonize all interests and bring about the most beneficent results. When no one has a vote, jealousy becomes impossible, and greedy, unscrupulous politicians are held at bay. To place these islands under the control of a commission appointed by the President, with the consent of Congress, said commission to be composed of five men, three of whom should be born here, would meet the exigencies of the case, I verily believe."

This extract is typical of the statistical accuracy, the wide grasp of comparative facts, the keen observation and the catholicity of spirit that characterized Kate Field's letters from Hawaii. They photograph the conditions of 1895–96; those conditions which, in less than five years, have so swiftly evolved into new phases and reached results largely due to Miss Field's power of creating public opinion. Under date of Jan. 9, 1886, the "Commercial Advertiser" of Honolulu, devoting an editorial to Kate's work, closed with the words: "Miss Field's letters will be widely read and copied, and will have a very excellent effect upon the future of the islands." Under the date of January 31, the same journal said editorially: —

"Kate Field's past record has proved beyond question that when she once grapples with a political problem she does not allow the ink to dry in her pen until she has accomplished tangible results. In her work in this country

Miss Field has certainly shown that she has lost none of the old-time ability that first brought her into prominence as a moulder of political minds through the medium of the newspapers. Although even her best friends do not always agree with her, they have found that, notwithstanding what are put down as her peculiar ideas, she works along the line of good common sense and sound principle.

" Her interview with President Dole has done more to set this Government before the American people in its true light than anything that has thus far been written."

Both officially and personally the opinions expressed by the Hawaiians of Miss Field were such as to indicate the impression that her truth and fairness, as well as her conspicuous ability, made upon them. Her letters were very racy and graphic as well as analytic. One, in particular, in which she described an auction sale of royal relics, is inimitable. She persistently advocated the cable, that is now almost a *fait accompli*.

Among the pleasant social interludes for Miss Field was when Hon. and Mrs. P. C. Jones carried her off to their country house, seventeen miles from Honolulu, in a romantically beautiful spot surrounded with mountains save on one side, where they look out on the Pacific. Here she went out among the natives, visiting the schools and talking with them, and so won their hearts that as she was leaving they gathered around her with long garlands, with which they wreathed her, and called her " Kala wahine nananao," — the Learned Woman.

In midwinter, hearing that the volcano on the island of Hawaii had become active, she was anxious to go to it, " but," she writes to a friend, —

" events occurred that prevented, and now I 've decided not to go until I 'm ready to leave this island. It looks as if I might remain several months longer. Then what will happen I don't know. Japan? I can't say. I live from day to day and think as little as possible of the future. It is my only salvation." . . .

Again, to the same friend she writes: —

" Life here is one long summer day with mosquitoes thrown in. I don't think women's clubs are worse than mosquitoes, as you believe, because you *can* ignore clubs, and mosquitoes *won't* let you alone night or day. However, there 's a deal to interest here as long as the political situation remains doubtful. . . .

. . . .

" The climate in the island of Hawaii is said to be more bracing, and I may remain there a month, writing meanwhile and reading. After those come the islands of Maui and Kauai. Then I must look into the conditions of Japanese, Chinese, Portuguese, all of whom swarm here and are crowding out natives and whites. It 's a very serious problem, this Asiatic invasion, and bodes no good to the United States."

Living always intensely in the present, *de jour au jour*, Kate entered closely into the life of the island. She dined, lunched, and drove with friends continually. She was not strong, but she was buoyant and hopeful and interested in everything. She would question the natives on their desires and feelings, and by the aid of an interpreter would talk with them to a great extent. She visited the schools and talked with the children, most of whom were being instructed in English, and with whom she could thus speak directly. Everything in customs and manners

35

caught her eager eye. One of the last things she did before leaving Honolulu was again to give her lecture on Charles Dickens for the benefit of the free kindergarten.

Driving one day in an open carriage, Kate saw a young Kanaka girl clad only in the short white gown, barely reaching the knees, that the women of that island wear. Miss Field stopped the driver and beckoned to the girl. "Will you drive with me, my dear?" she asked. The bewildered girl cast down her eyes, abashed, but after a moment stepped into the carriage. It was the first drive of her hard and meagre life; and Miss Field took her off on a glorious round to the Waikiki beach, and thence drove the girl to her own home, a hut in Iwilei, on the outskirts of Honolulu.

In the sincerity and thoroughness of her work, Kate never missed an opportunity of friendly and familiar intercourse with the natives. She knew how to ask questions, and her friendly interest in them won their hearts. She attended a memorial meeting for Hoapili, a chief, and after it was over she herself addressed the natives, Mr. Mueller interpreting. She told them first that she was an American and that she had come in the interests of her country. "Next to that," she continued, "I want what is best for you Hawaiians, natives of the soil." She advised them to hold to their homes. "In three things," she said, "no one can equal you, — as horsemen, fishermen, and freemen. You must not let any nation take these from you. I know the present government cares for you. President Dole has a great aloha for you, as I learn from many talks with him. Your 'aloha' is one of the most beautiful words I have ever heard."

The natives listened to her with the closest and with intelligent attention, and at the close pressed around her, shaking hands heartily and greeting her with a chorus of alohas.

Writing, in a press letter, of a New England man, she said: —

" Find a progressive citizen of Hawaii, and you will find a Yankee. One of these Yankees is B. F. Dillingham, who not long ago was called crazy because he actually induced local capitalists to help him build the only railroad on this island, and the third railroad on all the islands. The first originated with another Yankee, S. G. Wilder, who built what is said to be the crookedest railroad on earth. For twenty miles, this iron, narrow-gauge snake twists and turns up and down the island of Hawaii, tapping sugar plantations and cattle ranges, and bringing their products to the sea for shipping. When Mr. Wilder died, a deal of intelligent energy was lost to this country.

"Born on Cape Cod, sailing before the mast for love of the sea, captured by the ' Florida' off Brazil in 1863, and experiencing all the hardships of a prisoner of war when a mere lad, Dillingham persisted in a life on the ocean wave, until fate lured him to Honolulu, where he anchored in 1866, and has resided ever since, engaging in mercantile business. In 1885 Mr. Dillingham secured a railroad franchise, issued and sold bonds at par to build the first fifteen miles, and invested every dollar in the enterprise, the limit of the issue being $300,000. When sufficient land was acquired to exceed in value double the amount of the bonds already taken, second mortgage bonds were put on the market. This sort of financiering is not frequent, more 's the pity."

When she resolved on leaving for a tour through the other islands of Maui, Lanai, and Hawaii, all of her friends endeavored to dissuade her; it was so evident that she was in no state of health to undertake these hardships. But their counsel had no effect. To a friend in this country she wrote under date of March 18: —

"Since I wrote last I've been round this island, riding and driving, and enjoyed the experience immensely. Next Tuesday, March 24, I sail for Hawaii, where I may remain a month, going round the island on horseback and visiting the volcano. Then I go over the island of Maui (D. V.) before returning here. This done, I have Kauai to visit. Any one who thinks these islands can be done quickly and *intelligently* reckons without a host of problems."

So she sailed away, embarking on a voyage which was to end only in the unseen realm. Her faithfulness and devotion to her work prefigured themselves fairly as a tragedy to those who were about her in her last days. "Oh, the pathos of it all," wrote Miss Anna Paris, who accompanied her on her last journey of investigation, — "the lonely coast, the eager, burning desire to see everything, the struggle for strength, the final enforced giving up of her effort. . . . She gave herself no rest. There was so much of interest to be seen, and the time was short. She talked with the Hawaiians, visited the schools, and made an address in the old church. Sand, heat, and distance counted for nothing. The old relics of Kamehameha, the hijons, the native villages, all interested her deeply."

The time was so short; ah, yes, *how* short those who watched her little dreamed! A pencilled note written to a friend on March 28 said: —

"I'm at last on the road to the volcano, but as the distance by road is 30 miles, and as the journey must be made in the saddle and will take several days, you can imagine I'm as far from it as Omaha is from N. Y. I reached Hilo after the worst sea voyage I ever took, . . . but now I'm in this strange land among natives, I'm very glad I came."

Leaving Hilo, she passed a week in Puna in the hospitable house of Mr. Rufus Lyman, to whom ex-Minister Jones had given her a letter. Mrs. Lyman made opportunities for her to meet the natives, whom she found intelligent and sympathetic, and they were so appreciative of her kindness as to overwhelm her with gifts. Journeying on, and stopping at the plantations of Mr. Rycroft and Mr. C. J. Wight, where hospitality and kindness surrounded her, she fared forth again to sleep one night in a grass house, which she wrote of to a friend as an "interesting sensation." Even then her illness was alarmingly apparent, but she gave it no heed. Going on, still on horseback, she reached Kailua; but before her lay a long lonely region teeming with historic associations and an interesting native population. To see and realize all that was here was her ardent desire. Yet mysterious gleams of prescience seemed around her, and more than once she remarked to Miss Paris, "It is the unexpected that happens." While at Kawaihae her strength failed entirely. On the Sunday afternoon of May 17, she lay on a couch on a piazza, gazing silently afar on the sea. Something was said of death in a general way by one of the family, and Miss Field turned and remarked with deep seriousness, "Say what you will, it is a great change, — a great change," she added dreamily. On this day (hardly forty-eight hours before her death) she yielded to the urgency of her friends to decide to return to Honolulu instead of pursuing her way up the mountain to the Volcano House, where she had already engaged rooms. There was about her an exquisite gentleness; and a reliance on others unknown before in all her active life. The next morning she sat up on her couch writing incessantly until the horses were ready to convey herself and Miss Paris to the boat which made the tour of the islands to and from Honolulu.

Another most significant link in this chain of events is that on this local steamer which plied about the islands, there were Prof. and Mrs. David P. Todd of Amherst College, Dr. Adriance of New York, and other friends. For it chanced — does anything chance? — that Professor Todd with his wife and his party of the "Amherst Eclipse Expedition" were on their way to Japan in a yacht to observe the total solar eclipse due on August 9, 1896. Stopping at Hawaii, they were making the tour of the islands on the local steamer, leaving their yacht anchored at Honolulu; and although they and Miss Field had not met personally, the names of each were, of course, familiar to the other, and the brave, devoted woman whose hands for the first time in her life fell helpless before her work, was met by her own country people, and by those capable of giving her not only care and aid, but sympathetic companionship as well. To those who loved her and were away at this supreme hour the comfort that this tenderness and sweetest companionship were about her is ineffable. And not this alone, but that there was with her in her last hours on earth a woman whose special literary gift could record the story makes gratitude complete. It is an impressive fact that the one of Miss Field's own country-women to be with her should have been, — not only the kind and lovely friend, but the professional woman of letters whose pen could photograph and thus preserve the closing scenes of the life of Kate Field.

Miss Paris hastened to make Miss Field as comfortable as possible in her state-room, and Mrs. Todd went in to see her, receiving a warm greeting.

"Oh," exclaimed Miss Field, "it is such a comfort to be on a boat again, though I usually hate a boat; but to be going somewhere actually again and to see white people once more, and up-to-date white people at that. I am only tired all out," she continued; "yes, I am too tired to do any more just now."

"She lay back with her cheeks very pink," Mrs. Todd related afterward, "and began to ask me questions about our expedition to Japan, in which she seemed greatly interested. Her mind continually went back to her work, however, and the social and political state of Hawaii. 'They are lovely, amicable people,' she said. 'I've enjoyed Hawaii.'"

Dr. Adriance visited and prescribed for her, and at once realized how critically ill with pneumonia she was. "For the last two weeks," he said, "she has not been able to sit up, and yet she has been riding on horseback over lava-fields!"

Once she half murmured the line, "He giveth His beloved sleep." "Yes, sleep," added the exhausted voice, while the little hot hands fell helpless by her side. That poem of Mrs. Browning's had always been a favorite with her, and the line she repeated was the one she had chosen for the inscription on her mother's tomb.

Toward evening some native Hawaiians began singing on deck outside her window, accompanying themselves on the guitar and the native *ukuleli*. She was asked if it disturbed her.

"Oh, no," she replied; "music is Paradise to me."

With her in her state-room and lying by her side, was a copy of Charles Warren Stoddard's "Hawaiian Life,"— the last book her hand ever touched. Afterward Miss Paris very kindly gave the little volume to the friend who, of all on earth, held Kate in the most tender and devoted love.

The constant care and skill of Dr. Adriance was about her through the night, but the morning revealed to him that she had but a few hours more on earth. Mrs. Todd undertook the sad office of telling her this and prepared to write any messages, but the dreaminess and bewilderment of the change was already upon her. Once Kate opened her eyes suddenly as the steamer was passing Maui, where the rugged cliffs stand out, and the blue sea, covered with white-caps, dashed against the rocks. "Oh, how beautiful!" she exclaimed, and again sinking into dreamy unconsciousness she asked of Mrs. Todd: "What did you say is the name of your expedition, and what are you going for?" and as Mrs. Todd replied Kate repeated brightly, "The Amherst Eclipse Expedition!" These were her last words.

Were they not, indeed, the fitting words for one whose whole life had been a quest of knowledge? who had lived in such daily consciousness of the Un-

seen and such absolute realization of the companion-
ships of those in that realm, and of the Divine love
and care, that the passing over the faint line that
divides the two conditions of life had for her no terror, but only joy and peace. In those last hours she
had comforters whom the kind friends about her saw
not, sustaining and guiding her release. The two
worlds are so interpenetrated, and she had always
lived partly in both, and had always partaken of the
greater significance of the pure life of the spirit. All
her life had been a quest. Always had she fared
forth on new expeditions in search of light and truth.
The riddle of progress haunted her eager mind. Her
infinite energy, her exquisite taste, her noble and
generous aspirations, leave their lasting impress.

The steamer flew on over the foam-crested waves
sparkling under the golden May sunshine, and the
blue eyes were closed and the little wasted hands
lay idly by her side. Perchance to her thoughts then
came lines she had long since loved, — lines written
by the beloved poet-friend, Mrs. Browning : —

> " If God compel thee to this destiny,
>   To die alone — with none beside thy bed,
>
>   .   .   .   .
>
> Pray then alone — ' O Christ, come tenderly !
>   .   .   .   .
>
> No earthly friend being near me, interpose
> No deathly angel 'twixt my face and Thine,
> But stoop Thyself to gather my life's rose
> And smile away my mortal to Divine.' "

While the pathos of this passing touches every
heart, — yet its poetic beauty, its unique loveliness
that so repeated the unique quality of her entire life,
makes it as distinctive as it was beautiful.

Though consciousness did not return, Kate lived until after she was tenderly carried from the steamer into the house of Dr. and Mrs. McGrew in Honolulu. It was one of the homes where she had passed many a pleasant social hour, and an interview with Dr. McGrew had been among the most interesting of her press letters. About two o'clock on the afternoon of May 19, 1896, her spirit took its flight. Just before her last breath, she opened her blue eyes and looked up at Mrs. McGrew, who was bending over her, smiled, and with one fluttering sigh Kate Field had rejoined her idolized father and mother, and gone out and on to the fairer realm which, though unseen, is still so near.

No words can in any wise interpret the pathos of these last scenes, but they had the distinction and the unusual quality which made a fitting close to her remarkable life.

> " I am going home to-night,
>   Out of blindness into sight;
>   Out of weakness, war, and pain
>   Into power, peace, and gain;
>   Out of Winter gale and gloom
>   Into Summer breath and bloom;
>   From the wand'rings of the past
>   I am going home at last.

> " Kiss my lips and let me go;
>   Nearer swells the solemn flow
>   Of the wondrous stream that rolls
>   By the borderland of souls.
>   I can catch sweet strains of songs
>   Floating down from distant throngs,
>   And can feel the touch of hands
>   Reaching out from angel bands.

" Anger's frown and envy's thrust,
    Friendship chilled by cold distrust,
    Sleepless night and weary morn,
    Toil in fruitless land forlorn,
    Aching head and breaking heart,
    Love destroyed by slander's dart,
    Drifting ship and darkened sea,
    Over there will righted be."

These beautiful lines of James G. Clark recur to the memory when picturing the return of Kate Field to the fairer world beyond.

The slender form from which *she* had gone was clad in a silvery blue robe of silken tissue which the friend, to whom of all on earth she was dearest, had sent her as the last Christmas gift. Who shall say that she herself did not guide the stranger hands that opened her wardrobe? Among the rings taken from her hand was a little worn gold circlet, — the wedding ring of her mother, which Kate had withdrawn from Mrs. Field's hand when she died at sea in the May of just twenty-five years before. In her will, as before mentioned, Kate had directed that her body should be cremated and this little ring placed with the ashes in the urn, — a wish which was afterwards entirely fulfilled.

The body was placed in a casket embowered with flowers, and over it was draped the stars and stripes, — a fit emblem for one with whom patriotism was a passion. The church where the last rites were held was filled with official representatives of many nations. Hither came the most distinguished men and women of the Hawaiian capital. Though far from her native land, Miss Field passed away among fervent friends and admirers. Her genius was not for one race, nor her fame for one people, and the gathering at Honolulu was a remarkable tribute to the American woman. Representatives of the United States gave forcible expression to the admiration of the American people for the dauntless spirit that had led in so many movements for the betterment of the race. Officials of the Republic in the far Pacific islands testified their respect for the scholar, the thinker, who took truth as her only guide and beacon. More personal, perhaps, were the tributes of women of prominence and the representatives of other nations. All united to pay honor to the memory of the noble soul that had fled its slender tenement of clay. They buried the casket in fragrant blossoms. The President and Mrs. Dole sent a wreath of lilies and palm leaves; the press, a booklet of red, white, and blue flowers; and the entire altar was a bower of floral fragrance, with its myriad offerings.

The minister of the church, Rev. D. P. Birnie, read the solemn service, and a quartette rendered exquisitely " Jesus, Lover of my Soul " and Cardinal Newman's touching hymn, " Lead, Kindly Light." While the little flower-heaped casket was tenderly borne from the church, the organist played " Home, Sweet Home," and the tears came to every eye.

The pall-bearers were Ellis Mills, Chargé d'Affaires for the United States; L. A. Thurston, ex-Minister from Hawaii to the United States; William R. Castle, ex-Minister from Hawaii to the United States; W. Porter Boyd, Vice-Consul-General; Dr. J. S. McGrew and Wallace R. Farrington, Editor of the " Honolulu Advertiser." As the cortége approached the cemetery, the Hawaiian Band, stationed near the vault, expressed the common grief in a dirge.

The casket was laid in the vault of a friend at Nuuanu cemetery. It had been decorated with flowers, and across the wall at the head of the casket was draped the American flag. To these decorations were added the flowers sent to the church, making a veritable bed of blossoms for the casket. The choir sang the last hymn, Dr. Birnie said the last prayer, and the door of the tomb was closed, awaiting the sending of the casket to America. Among those present at these ceremonies were President Dole of the Hawaiian Republic, Minister of Foreign Affairs Henry E. Cooper, Chief Justice A. F. Judd, Associate Justice Frear, Vice-President W. C. Wilder, Colonel R. H. McLain, Commander Watson of the U. S. S. "Adams;" Judge Hartwell, A. de Souza, Canavarro, Chargé d'Affaires, Portugal; Major George C. Potter, A. St. M. Mackintosh, Monsieur Vizzevona, Chargé d'Affaires France; Senator McCandless, officials of the various departments of the Hawaiian Government, members of the consular corps, members of the legislature, and representatives of the press.

The beauty equals the pathos of the closing chapter of Kate Field's life on earth. " This is not the end ; the end is never," one could almost hear her say. She was spared old age; she was withdrawn from experiences of ceaseless struggle, because of ceaseless aspiration; and though the great work of her life seemed unfinished, she passed on to complete it in a different way and from a higher plane of energy. Could she have chosen, it would have been to go in this swift, simple, and poetic way to the new life whose reality she well knew. There was no illness, so to speak; no period of inactivity. All the morning of May 18 she was writing, until at twelve she

went on board the steamer; about five in the afternoon she appeared on deck, but obeyed immediately
the gentle and wise counsel of Dr. Adriance to
return to her room; and at two o'clock on the next
afternoon she had entered on the life more abundant. It was more like translation than death, and
she would herself have only urged courage and good
cheer on all who follow her with tender devotion
to the Unseen. She would have only inspired new
endeavor, and invoked that noble spirit which breathes
through these lines of Theocritus; —

> " A shipwrecked sailor buried on this coast
> Bids you set sail ;
> Full many a gallant ship when we were lost
> Weathered the gale."

IN RETROSPECT

PARADISI GLORIA

"O frate mio! ciascuna è cittadina
D'una vera città" . . . .

THERE is a city, builded by no hand,
   And unapproachable by sea or shore,
And unassailable by any band
   Of storming soldiery for evermore.

There we no longer shall divide our time
   By acts or pleasures, — doing petty things
Of work or warfare, merchandise or rhyme;
   But we shall sit beside the silver springs

That flow from God's own footstool, and behold
   Sages and martyrs, and those blessed few
Who loved us once and were beloved of old,
   To dwell with them and walk with them anew.

In alternations of sublime repose,
   Musical motion, the perpetual play
Of every faculty that Heaven bestows
   Through the bright, busy, and eternal day.

                    THOMAS WILLIAM PARSONS.

CHAPTER X

What matters how or from what ground
The freed soul its Creator found?
Alike thy memory embalms
That orange-grove, that isle of palms.

EMERSON.

" Glory to God — to God," he saith;
" Knowledge by suffering entereth,
And Life is perfected by Death. "

ELIZABETH BARRETT BROWNING.

Still veiled in flesh, her soul shone through that veil, which grew more and more transparent day by day. The progress of the spirit piercing the last obstacle between itself and the Infinite was called an illness; the hour of life was called death.   BALZAC.

One who never turned his back, but marched breast forward;
Never doubted clouds would break;
Never dreamed, though right were worsted, wrong would triumph:
Held, we fall to rise again; are baffled, to fight better;
Sleep, to wake!

ROBERT BROWNING.

IN RETROSPECT. UNIVERSAL APPRECIATION AND LOVE. THE STRANGE ORDERING OF CIRCUMSTANCE. A SCULPTURED CROSS IN MOUNT AUBURN. DEATH ONLY AN EVENT IN LIFE.

AMONG those wonderful, glowing translations from Oriental poetry made by Emerson is the "Song of Seyd Nimetallah of Kuhistan." It is an intense bewildering measure, and in it are these lines which contain, in essence, a complete interpretation of the life of Kate Field.

" From the shore of souls arrived,
  In the sea of sense I dived ;
  But what is land or what is wave,
  To me, who only jewels crave?
  Love is the air-fed fire intense
  And my heart the frankincense :
  As the rich aloes flames, I glow,
  Yet the censer cannot know.
  I 'm all-knowing, yet unknowing :
  Stand not, pause not, in my going."

" From the shore of souls arrived " Kate Field dived with a swift intensity into the " sea of sense," seeking ever the soul of things, caring little for processes, caring everything for results. She had that endurance which is the assertion of the spirit over the flesh; she had the crystal clearness of absolute truth, of flawless integrity; she had such persistence of energy that even after death had set his seal upon her, she wrote for hours, and rode on horseback to the steamer on which her last earthly voyage was made. She was indomitable in energy. Flame might freeze, or ice might boil, before she would have relinquished a purpose. Yet when this flying aim was once caught she bade it go, and turned to another. Margaret Sullivan said of her : —

" A virtuoso in music ; at one time on the stage ; an authentic and charming interpreter of literature, — her very versatility, like an excess of riches, lured her from one domain into another ; so that, leaving proof in many of individual genius, she may have done herself injustice by not adopting a single profession and dedicating her life to it."

More than once during her life here this problem of Kate's versatility of nature was discussed and sometimes pressed upon her; and on one occasion she thus replied in a private letter to some question regarding it : —

"If anybody is clever enough to tell me what is *surely lasting* I'd like to know out of curiosity. A few beings in this world have written what all the centuries desire to read : Homer, Virgil, Goethe, Montaigne, Cervantes, Shakespeare, Dante, Tasso, and half a dozen other geniuses constitute what to my mind is 'lasting' in literature. What difference does it make whether we are remembered or not? The ambition that thirsts for praise is, in my opinion, beneath contempt. Shakespeare wrote plays for his theatre because he was impelled to write them, and not because of posterity, — an animal I'll wager he never dreamed of. The only noble ambition is the desire to be fully one's self, to act out one's whole nature ; and if that nature leads one into more than one path, I see no reason to wail. If by walking a tow-path a man or woman does one thing that is remembered twenty years longer than the varied work of a human being who has had the pleasure of many experiences and the expansion and friendships and loves that come with these experiences, I personally see no gain to the individual, — *au contraire*. But I deny that versatility must necessarily be shallow. The trouble is not on account of superficiality, but because of the want of time to carry out many ideas. But what of that? Have we not all eternity before us? — if there be another life, as I believe. We learn our lessons here to begin a broad career hereafter, and the one idea'd person may find himself obliged to go to school again in another world before taking his degree. My dear friend, Americans are the least tolerant of 'versatility' of any people on earth, and it is probably due to the hardness of life in a new world. It requires so much exhausting work to make a living at one thing that half-educated souls can't believe in the soundness of those who turn from one art or profession to another in sympathy with it. And yet Americans contradict themselves by being a doctor one year and a merchant the next; a banker one day and a diplomatist the day after; a soldier for five years and a lawyer forever after, until the speculator supplants both. The trouble with most critics is that they are led by early prejudices and not by reason."

Nothing could have been less possible — given the peculiar combination of qualities that made up the unique personality called Kate Field — than that she should devote herself to any one aim alone. She had, pre-eminently, the inspirational temperament. She was subject to a thousand heats and chills; and the victim or victor, as might be, of a thousand subtle influences and *nuances* of impression which no psychologist has yet classified in his human laboratory. In a private letter to a friend in June of 1888, she said: —

As to being helped in writing, I'm almost sure of it. I never know in advance what I'm going to say. In fact, I approach every subject with fear and trembling, and am always astounded when anything comes. Inspiration means something or nothing. If it means something, it means that a spiritual influence obsesses the mortal intellect. It always seems to me idiotic for people to be conceited about their own achievements, when so much is due to unknown influences.

Miss Field had indeed, as has before been noted, the most abiding and profound realization of what Emerson so well calls "the flowing conditions of life." In the series of private letters to the friend which has given the most intimate revelations of her daily life she was constantly making such expressions as these : —

" Life is too short to accomplish anything ; " " I am convinced that we shall enjoy ourselves hereafter by having what we call happiness repeated in a finer tone."

And again : —

" You must let me care for you in my way, which, had I the power, would be very tangible. Unfortunately I 'm not able to carry out my desires. When we meet where gold is not the current coin, you 'll know my real self better."

When Mr. Edwin P. Whipple died she wrote to this friend : —

" I know that Mrs. Whipple will show her love for her husband by loving humanity. I have no patience with those who nurse their grief and prove their faith in Christianity by acting as though there were no life or hope beyond mortality."

On the death of the poet, Mr. Boyle O'Reilly, she wrote : —

" Boyle O'Reilly is to be envied his sudden taking off, it seems to me. It is hard to live, — harder than to die, I think."

In a memorial tribute to her old and near friend Mrs. Anne Lynch Botta, Kate said editorially, in her journal : —

" I want many who never knew her, or knew her superficially, to realize the sweetness of her character ; for, after all, it is character, not reputation, that makes the real human being.

" ' Did you ever notice how much of Christ's life was spent simply in doing kind things ? ' asks Drummond.

Therein lay the greatness of Mrs. Botta's life. She was perpetually doing kind things for everybody, regardless of thanks or gratitude, beaming like the sun upon the just and unjust, conscious of her own good-will, unconscious, if possible, of slight or malice. I have never known man or woman so eager for the truth, whatever it might be; so ready to receive the light, no matter whence it came; so humble in her own esteem; so ready to praise friend and foe when praise was due. The latch-string of her heart and head, as of her hospitable door, was always out. . . . I hear a gentle, kind voice whisper to those who mourn her sudden taking off: 'Courage; the end is not yet. The end is never!'"

Numberless pages could be filled with transcriptions of Kate Field's expressions of the vitality of her faith in God and Immortality. When Wendell Phillips died she wrote in a private letter: —

"It is no matter now that Wendell Phillips has passed away. He had done his great work and needed a radical change of atmosphere to begin anew. *He has now got it!* He did me worlds of good when I was a young girl, and helped to make me a radical. My uncle was the worst sort of Democrat."

A number of years ago there was a literary project, more or less pleasantly fulfilled, of publishing a book containing the biographies of prominent women still living. When Kate was asked to permit her own to be included, she wrote to a friend: —

"The difference between a life in a book and a newspaper sketch is very great. When I die — if between now and then I do anything worthy of record — my life can be taken. While alive, I contend that lives in books are absurd."

The time now seems to have come in which even her own faultless taste would perhaps concede that her biography might be written.

It is interesting also, in this retrospective view of her life on earth, to read an analysis of her character made, when she was about thirty, by the well-known phrenologists, Messrs. Fowler and Wells, who thus defined her nature : —

"You possess a remarkable organization, and are evidently your father's child, inheriting many of his peculiarities, — his love of liberty, sense of independence, his desire for knowledge, his ambition, resolution, and executiveness. You probably have the mother's sensitiveness, sympathy, and affection, combining therefore the qualities of both parents in yourself, but the spirit of the father predominates.

"You should be known, first, for your imagination; you live much in the spheres above; are not as much wedded to the world as many, and it gives you more pleasure to live in the ethereal realms than here.

"You have a psychological nature, and foresee what is about to transpire; something of a second sight, and are prophetic. You have visions even when wide awake, and can hear the angels whisper.

"You may not compose music, you may not write poetry, but your soul is full of them. You revel in art and have abilities in this direction.

"You are original rather than imitative, though you can readily take on the ways and manners of others, and adapt yourself to almost any condition, but you are original in striking out a course for yourself, and can never be swallowed up or absorbed by others. You are creative, full of schemes, plans, projects, and full of mental resources. You may not be able to put all your purposes into execution, but you are most prolific of ideas.

" Intellectually you have always been a good observer, but a better thinker, quick to see, quick to look into new things, fond of travelling, easily informed, but more inclined to meditate, to inquire into the why, wherefore, and cause of things. The fact is not enough for you, but you must know the principles, and from a child up you have been full of questions, many of which were unanswered, and never can be in this world.

" You are also very spirited, resolute, and executive ; and if the bodily powers were equal to the mental desires, you would perform great things, but the mental machinery is far greater than the framework, and you become exhausted before you finish what you undertake." . . .

The entire analysis, which is very long, is curiously accurate. Alluding to her individuality, the writer said, " You will be misunderstood by many, misinterpreted by some, and will be a puzzle to all." These words were fulfilled. Sensitive to a fault, Kate's life was something of that spiritual tragedy which results when such a spirit beats against the adverse conditions of this world. She was the artist born, and both by gifts and grace this temperament dominated her. Yet another phase of her nature, equally strong and from force of circumstances more largely in evidence, was her intense interest in affairs and her objective life. Sometimes she expressed her weariness of practical affairs and her longing for art and thought. Her culture was as exquisite as it was extended, and her conversation was of the choicest quality. She never judged either persons or events by petty standards. A woman of marvellous gifts, of the most generous and noble nature, intense in energy, she lived and died the life of a heroine.

It was typical of that curious fate that ran through

all Kate Field's life that there should be held two funeral ceremonies, each legitimate, from force of circumstances. After the beautiful rites in Honolulu the casket was temporarily placed in the vault of a friend. As there was no cable from Hawaii, the tidings of her death did not reach the United States until May 31, having gone by mail steamer to Japan and from there cabled to this country. The wave of sorrow that ran over the entire land, finding copious expression in probably every newspaper in the United States and in nearly or quite all of the periodicals, could only suggest the lines, —

> " Unguessed of her in life, the love
> That rained its tears her grave above."

At first it was thought that her body should rest in the land with which her fame is forever linked, and where she had inspired the fervent friendship and profound admiration of the people, both natives and colonizers. Mr. Kohlsaat, in his journal, the " Times-Herald," said editorially : —

" A monument to Kate Field should rise in Hawaii, and it should proclaim to all future ages the name of one who, more than all others, contributed to the union of the islands with the United States. There Kate Field's fame would be most secure. There every traveller would find imperishable witness to her genius and her patriotism. Rarely, indeed, would letter go forth or visitor return to any part of the world without bearing testimony to the life and the death of a noble spirit."

Later, however, her will was found, directing that her body should be cremated, and that in the urn of ashes her mother's wedding ring, which she had worn, should be placed and the urn deposited in her lot in Mount Auburn Cemetery, near Boston, by the graves of her parents and brother. The delay in finding her will and the long process of communication with Hawaii deferred the final decision into the late autumn; and it was not until the following December after her death that the casket containing her body was removed from the vault in the Honolulu cemetery and brought to San Francisco, where on Dec. 27, 1896, a most impressive and beautiful service was held over the little casket in Trinity (Episcopal) Church, after which the body was cremated. Of these last rites a San Francisco journal said : —

" The services in Trinity Church and at the crematorium were solemnly impressive. They had all the pomp and circumstance of a splendid ritual and the silent tribute of a listening throng. There was no spoken eulogy to tell of the worth of a brilliant woman, and none was needed. There was the silent offering of countless fragrant flowers, the respectful, mournful presence of thousands of men and women, and the simple dignity of a general memorial to the honored dead. Kate Field's ashes will rest, as she wished them, in her own land and under the flag of her own country."

Mr. and Mrs. Henry Highton of San Francisco took the entire direction of the impressive ceremonials. Their generous friendship made the occasion beautiful with every grace that could minister to honor and to love.

The chancel was embowered in flowers, with noble palms in the background and the silken banners of various societies, while above all gleamed the ivy-bound outlines of a great cross of white lilies. On the casket rested clusters of white bride roses, sent

by the President of the United States, — Hon. Grover Cleveland, — with flowers from the Governor
of California, the Mayor of San Francisco, from the
" Times-Herald " of Chicago, lawyers, statesmen, soldiers, the press of San Francisco and other cities, and
a multitude of personal friends.   Violets, lilies of the
valley, roses, and orchids were about in profusion, and
among several inscriptions was one that ran :   " Kate
Field represented the best sentiment of the press and
the country."   A touching offering was a bunch of
edelweiss from " a workman of the docks."   It was
fitting that these mingled tributes from the loftiest to
the lowliest should be offered to Kate Field.   " High
and low, rich and poor, private citizens and public
officers, of city, State, and nation, had gathered to
honor the memory of a woman whose abilities had
won her a world-wide distinction and whose character
had earned her a place in the hearts of loving
friends," said a local paper.   The white-robed rector,
repeating the solemn words, " I am the Resurrection
and the Life," preceded the flower-laden casket, and
when that exquisite aria, " Angels Ever Bright and
Fair," was heard, when the haunting musical cadence
rose in the lines, —

> " Angels ever bright and fair,
> Take me, take me, to your care," —

there was not a dry eye in all the vast assemblage.
At the crematory, with music from an unseen organ
filling the air ; with the cross of lilies held above
while the rector pronounced the ritual of the church,
— a pall of violets was placed on the casket, and it
descended noiselessly and swiftly to the final disposition below.   The ashes were reverently placed in an
urn and conveyed by General Taylor of Boston to

her friend and one of the two executors of her will, Mr. Kohlsaat, in Chicago. On New Year's morning of 1897 to the friend who had always held her dearest, between whom and Miss Field a special New Year's letter, aside from the constant correspondence, had passed for fifteen years, — to this friend the urn containing the ashes was given on this New Year's morning, and, resting in a box filled with Annunciation lilies, it was conveyed to Boston. The committal of the urn to Mount Auburn was private. On Sunday, January 10, in the presence only of her cousin, Mr. George Riddle, and his friend, Rev. Francis G. Peabody, D.D., preacher to Harvard University, the urn, embowered in roses and lilies, was placed in the Field family lot in beautiful Mount Auburn. Over the spot were masses of roses and violets and lilies, and from Mrs. George Andrews Moriarty of Boston a pair of Crossed Palms, in memory of the French decoration bestowed upon Miss Field. Thus closed a series of international ceremonies which, while they stand alone in history, were simply the inevitable result of a peculiar combination of circumstances. Marking the committal of the urn of ashes in Mount Auburn is a sculptured cross of white Italian marble placed there in loving memory by the friend to whom of all on earth she was dearest. On the short arm of the cross there is simply the name, in raised letters, Kate Field. On the pediment are the lines from the Shakespeare whom she loved, —

> " Spirits are not finely touched
> But to fine issues."

While on the reverse of the pediment are words that were dear to her and which she often quoted in closing a letter, — PAX VOBISCUM. No other inscription is added; none is needed.

Upon a nature that was in any degree responsive to her own, Kate Field left always the sense of being a friend to be held sacredly apart from all the rest of the world; as one for whose friendship one might pray to grow less unworthy; to leave behind everything that was trivial and to aspire to somewhat of the breadth and the exaltation of that plane on which alone free and perfect communion with her could be held. This greatness of nature, this exquisite charm of temperament, will never fade from the memory of those who truly knew Kate Field.

Anthony Trollope, in his Autobiography, alludes in these words to Miss Field: —

"There is a woman of whom not to speak in a work purporting to be a memoir of my own life would be to omit an allusion to one of the chief pleasures which has graced my later years. In the last fifteen years she has been, out of my family, my most chosen friend. She is a ray of light to me from which I can always strike a spark by thinking of her. I do not know that I should please her or do any good by naming her. But not to allude to her in these pages would amount almost to a falsehood. I could not write truly of myself without saying that such a friend had been vouchsafed to me."

Of all the expressions ever made regarding Kate Field, in life or in death, this sentence of Mr. Trollope, " She is a ray of light to me from which I can always strike a spark by thinking of her," most perfectly suggests her brilliant, vivid, yet delicate personality.

> " The good stars met in her horoscope ;
>   Made her of spirit and fire and dew."

Her truth was crystal clear, and hypocrisy and in-sincerity shrank abashed before her presence. Not unfrequently she proclaimed some unpalatable fact with less tact than frankness, from which a more politic person would have refrained. Her friendships were somewhat of the heroic fibre, and those who require the ministry of flattery did not receive from her any incense to their self-love. Friendship represented to her a noble sincerity and unfaltering faith which held nothing in common with vain phrasings. She had the unconscious exactingness of a lofty nature; where she gave faith she gave largely, and she expected the same generous and genuine comprehension in return. When this failed, she scorned to explain herself, and thus she was liable to misconstruction. Her loyalty to truth and to friendship was flawless; her tender-ness, never demonstrative, was as profound and un-changing as it was reserved and delicate in outward expression.

Her life was a ceaseless conflict with unrelenting circumstances, and while the pathos of her death, alone in a foreign land, is something that "lies too deep for tears," yet not for her are lament and sorrow.

"And tears are never for those who die with their face to the
                duty done;
But we mourn for the fledglings left on the waste, and the
        fields where the wild waves run."

She had learned, with Emerson, that

"The hero is not fed on sweets;"

and the unfaltering courage of her struggle during the last five years of her life; the ceaseless and splendid energy which she opposed to a series of disasters, translates personal regard to that enthusiasm which greatness of character must compel from all. Kate Field was one, indeed,

> " Who walked too straight for fortune's end,
>   Who loved too true to keep a friend ; "

and she had the defects of her gifts, which thus sometimes led to her being misunderstood.

The drama of her life sprang from her qualities. She found in it pain, trials, loves, and friendships; artistic enjoyments; a series of worthy achievements; mystic communion; and, withal, that unfailing spring of pure joy which is always given to him who keeps faith with his ideals. Kate Field kept faith with hers. To some degree she, too, was one who, " in spirit-worlds, trod alone," and whose work has left those " air-sown words " that

> " In the next age are flaming swords."

Our real life is with most of us the life we do not live, and this was peculiarly true with Kate Field. She had a life — which was the inner and the real because the permanent one — that the casual observer or the ordinary acquaintance did not discern, but which manifested itself in her visible achievements in a loftiness of aim, a persistence of purpose, and a splendor of energy, that ranks her among the greater spirits whose lives have blessed the age in which they lived.

She believed in God and immortality. She was deeply interested in psychical science. " I am one of those who believe in the communion of the Unseen," she wrote in a private letter within a few weeks of her death. Some years before she remarked during a conversation regarding the future life, " I look to see science prove Immortality." The expression was fraught with something of that prophetic power with which a certain temperamental force of insight always invested her. That science must and will prove immortality is the message of to-day, for there is a distinct and recognizable approach of the two worlds, the seen and the unseen, each of which is flashing its signals to the other. In the higher spirit-ualization of our life here will be found the true con-ditions for communion with the life beyond.

On that life have the eager mind, the generous heart, the noble purposes, that informed the spirit of Kate Field entered; and the interest she felt in this next stage of existence is its own consolation to those to whom her companionship was so dear and her personal presence one of perpetual charm.

That she did not completely succeed in all her efforts proves only that these were great in their nature. For three distinct achievements her life stands, — the securing of better legislation for Utah; for distinguished services to art; for the potent contribution to the forming of public opinion which led to the annexation of Hawaii.

This stage of life is experimental. We are here largely to *learn how* to live; to develop the spiritual qualities which are those demanded by the succeed-ing higher conditions.

> " So much for attempt — anon
> Performance! Taught to mould the living vase,
> What matter the cracked pitchers dead and gone!"

To Kate Field herself all this earthly pilgrimage seemed prefigured as the prelude to the more real and significant life entered through the portals of death. Her religious life was that of lofty and all-embracing spirituality. It was a religion of deeds and of the quality of daily living rather than of ritual or ceremony. There are persons so constituted as to receive the direct aid of the Holy Spirit through rite and sacred ceremonial. There are others who seem to ask nothing of outward or visible form. To the latter belonged Kate Field.

The enthusiasm of patriotic feeling that invested Kate was a part of this spirituality of nature. The institutions of her country were to her mind sacred. In the republican idea she saw the Divine purpose to lead humanity to a freer, more enlightened, more earnest and noble attainment. To this end she devoted her energy through all the various forms of expression that marked her life.

" Whenever a gifted spirit passes from one world to the other," said Dean Stanley, " it brings both worlds within a nearer view : the world of this mortal life and the world of an ideal vision, of our inexhaustible longings, of our inextinguishable hopes, of our everlasting reunions, — the Eternal Love in which dwells the spirit ; the beautiful Jerusalem of which God is the Light."

Into that Light has entered Mary Katherine Keemle Field. The imperishable legacy of her life is its lesson of courage under trial, of sympathy with humanity, of swift response to all that is beautiful in nature and art, of persistence in noble purposes, of unfaltering devotion to Ideals. In the immortal words of Dante : —

> " Tanto gentile e tanto onesta pare
> La donna mia ! "

KATE FIELD

SPIRITS ARE NOT FINELY TOUCHED
BUT TO FINE ISSUES.

INDEX

ble," 202; speaks in Radical Club discussion, 203; reads Plato and Rousseau, 205; meets Wendell Phillips at lunch, 207; her opinion of him, 207; reads "Corinne," 208; writes on her initial lecture, 209; sings "The Danube River," 210; call from Henry James, *fils,* 211; makes *début* as lecturer, 211; reports Peace Jubilee for "Tribune," 212; leaves for Adirondacks, 213; loyalty to John Brown, 213; moral heroism of, 214; appears in lecture, "Woman in the Lyceum," 216; congratulations to, from eminent persons, 216-221; lectures on "The Adirondacks," 222, 223; tells story of John Brown, 224, 225; raises fund, 225; dines with Robert Collyer, 226; described by Anna Dickinson, 226; business integrity of, 228; lectures on Dickens, 228; described by Mrs. Moulton, 229; her estimate of Dickens, 230, 231; rush of life of, 232, 233; unique individuality of, 235; life of, in Boston, 243, 244, 245; poem to, by Stedman, 246, 247; "Atlantic Monthly" work, 248; impressible nature of, 249; great sorrow of, 250, 251; arranges for her mother's burial, 251, 252, 253; arrives in England, 253; common sense of, 257; clairvoyant's prophecy for, 258, 259; reaches London, 262; Browning, Miss Cobbe, and other friends sympathize with, 262, 263; convictions against mourning apparel, 263; many expressions of sympathy for, 264-266; Garcia's opinion of her voice, 267; intense life of, 269; George Eliot writes to, 270, 271; invited by Lord and Lady Houghton, 223; friendship with Browning renewed; leaves for the Continent, 275; in Germany, 277; in Geneva, 278; returns to London, 278; independence in finance, 279; interest in the Unseen, 281; attraction to political affairs, 282;

press letters of, 283; alleged message from the Unseen, 284; lectures on Dickens, 285; leaves England, 286; post-prandial speech, 287; social interests of, 288-293; Mr. Stedman's counsel to, 294; comediettas by Kate Field, 293; Memorial Collection for, 295, 296; estimate of Bradlaugh, 297; interviews Bradlaugh, 299; poem by, 301, 304; Rubinstein's compliment to, 306; enthusiasm of for direct expression, 307; dramatic sequence of her life, 309; meets Ristori again, 310; "Tribune" letters of, 312; on the Thames with Herbert Spencer, 313; is seen off for Continent by Browning, 315; visits Spain, 317; estimate of Castelar, 318; returns to New York, 319; her convictions on friendship, 329; hears "Lohengrin," 321; dramatic study, 323; decides to appear on the stage, 323; *début* in Peg Woffington, 324, 325; results, 329; Stedman's description of Kate Field's *début,* 330-335; brilliant success in "Gabrielle," 336; plays successfully in "The Gilded Age," 337, 338; return to London, 341; plays in her own comedy, "Extremes Meet," 341; success as Violante, 342; visits Edinburgh, 343; describes initial experience with telephone, 348-350; scientific vein in, 350; work for telephone, 351; sings through telephone to the Queen, 352; gives matinée téléphonique, 352; personal independence of, 356, 357; finances of, 358; describes London life, 360-363; interest in Shakespeare Memorial, 363; sings in theatre; 365; organizes matinée for Shakespeare Memorial benefit, 366-369; letters of congratulation to, 369, 370; joins Ristori in Switzerland, 371; contrast of, with Ristori, 371; compares Rachel and Ristori, 371; Ristori's friendship for, 371; described by Paris correspondent,